JAPANESE PHOENIX

JAPANESE PHOENIX
THE LONG ROAD TO ECONOMIC REVIVAL

RICHARD KATZ

AN EAST GATE BOOK

M.E. Sharpe
Armonk, New York
London, England

An East Gate Book

Library of Congress Cataloging-in-Publication Data

Katz, Richard, 1951–
    Japanese Phoenix: the long road to economic revival / Richard Katz.
        p. cm.
    Includes bibliographical references and index.
    ISBN 0-7656-1073-6 (alk. paper) — ISBN 0-7656-1074-4 (pbk.: alk. paper)
      1. Structural adjustment (Economic policy)—Japan. 2. Japan—Economic policy—
    1989–3. Economic stabilization—Japan. 4. Globalization. I. Title.

HC462.95 .K39 2002
338.952—dc21

                                                                2002029408

Printed in the United States of America

The paper used in this publication meets the minimum requirements of
American National Standard for Information Sciences
Permanence of Paper for Printed Library Materials,
ANSI Z 39.48-1984.

∞

BM (c)   10   9   8   7   6   5   4   3   2   1
BM (p)   10   9   8   7   6   5   4   3   2   1

To my parents

The late Reuben and Beatrice Katz

who would have been proud

Contents

Part Four
Structural Reform: A Progress Report

Part Five
U.S.–Japan Relations in This Crisis

Epilogue

List of Tables and Figures

Tables

Figures

Technical Notes

Throughout the book, unless otherwise stated, yen amounts are translated into dollars at constant rate of ¥124/$ regardless of the year.

In 2000, Japan changed its Gross Domestic Product measures, also known as the System of National Accounts (SNA) from a system of classifications designed in 1968 to one designed in 1993. Hence, they are commonly known as SNA 68 and SNA 93. While the SNA 68 data go back to 1955, the GDP figures based on SNA 93 go back only to 1980, and in some cases only to 1990. Hence, in some charts covering several decades, we have had to combine SNA 68 and SNA 93 numbers. In most cases, only a small adjustment is needed to make the numbers commensurate. In other cases, an adjustment is impossible. When the discrepancy raises an issue, it is noted in the chart caption, e.g., Figure 4.2.

In 2001, some Ministries were combined, leading to new names, and some existing industries even changed their names. The famous Ministry of International Trade and Industry (MITI) became the Ministry for Economy, Trade and Industry (METI). The old Economic Planning Agency was incorporated in the Cabinet Office. In the text, the current name is used throughout, even in discussing events taking place decades ago.

Acknowledgments

In looking over *Japan: The System That Soured* in order to prepare this book, two big changes struck me. Firstly, so much of that book, published as late as 1998, was obliged to prove that Japan was indeed in trouble, let alone explain why or offer solutions. Secondly, in the entire bibliography, there is only one reference to a website.

What a contrast to this book, where the Internet was not only a source of information, but of dialogue and community. Discussion groups such as the now-defunct Dead Fukuzawa Society, Social Sciences Japan Forum, and the U.S.-Japan Discussion Forum brought me into contact with experts whom I could call upon for advice and comment, some of whom I got to meet in person.

There are so many individuals who graciously helped me in thinking through the ideas that eventually became embodied in this book.

First and foremost is Peter Ennis, my editor-in-chief at *The Oriental Economist Report* (TOE), and, more importantly, my friend for the past three decades. There is hardly any idea in this book that did not benefit from innumerable conversations with him over the years—not to mention his fine editorial hand when some of this material appeared in TOE. My other colleagues at TOE took time out of their own busy schedules to help out. Julie Norwell made many good suggestions for tightening and sharpening the material. Kazuko Takizawa provided some translations of Japanese source material.

I also gained invaluable insight, not to mention good times, from years of conversations with my colleagues at *Toyo Keizai*, particularly Yoshisuke Iinuma, Yuichiro Yamagata, Fusakazu Izumura, Mitsu Kawashima, and Jun Fukui.

My decades-long guide through the labyrinth of Japanese politics is Takao Toshikawa, editor of *Japan Insideline* and *TOE's* chief correspondent in Tokyo.

Over the years, Ken Okamura, Peter Tasker, Paul Scalise, and Alexander Kinmont generously plied me with food, drink, and ideas. Paul and Peter offered valuable comments on the manuscript.

A host of individuals offered advice and/or comments on various chapters. Others participated with me in on-line discussions that helped shaped my thinking. Several Japanese officials graciously provided me with data and insight, even in some cases where I was critical of their Ministry. In addition to those noted above, my thanks go to: Akira Ariyoshi, Andrew DeWit, Robert Fauver, Robert Feldman, Yusaku Horiuchi, Ken Katayama, Edward Lincoln, Arthur Mitchell, Douglas Ostrom, Hugh Patrick, Ulrike Schaede, Len Schoppa, Michael Smitka, Takuji Tanaka, Tatsuya Terazawa, Gillian Tett, and Kozo Yamamura. Naturally, none of this help should be taken as agreement with my views.

I'd also like to thank a few reformist-minded Japanese officials who were compelled to offer their help anonymously.

At M.E. Sharpe, I was blessed with the invaluable aid of editor Doug Merwin, production editor Angela Piliouras, and marketing manager Diana McDermott. Special thanks and good wishes go to Rina Maiorano, the contracts administrator for marketing and sales.

The chief victims of bookwriting are the writer's family. My wife Linda and eight-year-old daughter Laura are no exception. I could not have written the book had not Linda graciously taken on more than her share of parental and household responsibilities. I owe my career to her unstinting help and her sage advice. Laura showed immense patience when I had to work instead of spending time with her. Despite their occasional frustration, both cheerfully and proudly gave me indispensable support and encouragement. I'm very grateful to both of them. Laura took my last effort to "show and tell" at school. Hopefully, she will consider this effort just as worthy.

Introduction

1

The Long and Bumpy Road to Revival

A half century ago Japan picked itself up from the ashes of war and, within a few short years, stunned the world with its economic achievements. It will do so again. Japan will reform and revive. When it does, its economic achievements will once again earn the world's admiration. Once again its per capita GDP will grow faster than that of the United States. Its information technology revolution will prove even greater than America's—precisely because all the waste and inefficiencies eliminated by IT are greater in Japan. As Japan brings its inefficient industries up to world benchmarks, sustained growth of 3 percent, perhaps more, is within reach.[1]

That's the good news.

The bad news is that it will take ten more years to reach this promised land. And the road will be very bumpy. The renewed recession and banking troubles that began in 2001 are some of those bumps. So was the grassroots revolt that led to the ascension of reformist Prime Minister Junichiro Koizumi in 2001.

Why ten years?

So deep-seated are Japan's dysfunctions that even if it did everything right today, it would take five years for this to show up in truly vibrant growth.

But Japan will not do everything right today. Opposition to reform is equally deep-seated. A myriad of vested interests and millions of jobs are at stake. Nor is Japan divided clearly between the parties of reform and resistance. Rather, each party and ministry and firm is divided between reformers and resisters.

Japan's dilemma is that the obstacles to growth are woven into the very fabric of its political economy. Years of corporate collusion and protective regulations have steadily eaten away at productivity growth, making it impossible for an unreformed Japan to grow faster than 1.25 to 1.5 percent

3

a year even at full capacity. High prices and negligible interest rates suppress real household income and thus purchasing power. It has become impossible for Japan to attain full capacity despite years of enormous budget deficits and zero interest rates.

Up until the 1990s, "peaceful coexistence" between economic growth and Japan's structural flaws was possible. Not any longer. GDP growth has ground to a virtual halt (Figure 1.1). Manufacturing in early 2002 was 15 percent below the 1991 peak. Japan's Cabinet Office says that, without reform, GDP growth will average only 0.5 percent through 2010—half the dismal rate of the last "lost decade."[2] When Prime Minister Koizumi says there will be no economic revival without structural reform, he's right.

The catch-22 is that the obstacles to growth are also pillars of the political system. Collusion, regulation, and high prices serve as covert social safety nets in a nation where only half the workforce is covered by unemployment insurance. They shore up moribund firms and industries, thereby sustaining millions of make-work jobs. The high prices of everything from cement to food provide covert income redistribution from Japan's efficient sectors to the inefficient ones. Much of the support base of the ruling Liberal Democratic Party (LDP)—as well as the opposition parties—relies on such practices. Each party's base is divided between those who would benefit from reform and those who would be hurt by it. Hence the very things that make structural reform economically necessary also make it politically difficult.

Japan's economic crisis is basically a crisis of governance—in both government and corporations. And so revival requires a fundamental overhaul. But even reformers disagree among themselves as to what constitutes reform. One of the tasks of this book is to offer some criteria—as well as specific proposals—for reform (see Parts Three and Four). The upshot is that, for both political and intellectual reasons, defining the programs, reaching the intellectual consensus, and forming the necessary institutional coalition will take several more years.

Why Reform Will Succeed

Still, there is little doubt that reform will succeed. While reform is destabilizing, failure to reform is, in the long run, even more destabilizing.

There are, perhaps, some rich societies that could chug along at a dismal per capita growth of 0.5 percent per year, as Japan did during 1992–2001, and still remain politically stable. Japan is not one of them.

Everything that makes Japan's political economic system work depends on a certain minimum level of nominal and real growth. Take away that

Figure 1.1 **Where Did the Growth Go?**

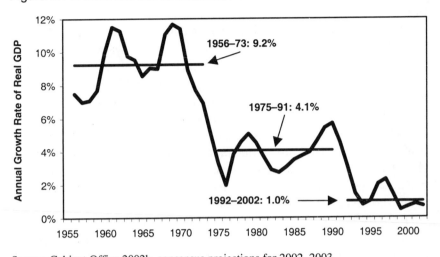

Source: Cabinet Office 2002b, consensus projections for 2002, 2003.
Note: The figures for 1955–80 are based on the SNA 68 system, since the newer SNA 93
data are not available prior to 1980.

growth, and unbridgeable strains and conflicts of interests arise. The relief
given to one interest group inevitably hurts another.

Some analysts suggest that "the vested interests" will block reform. But
these vested interests are no more unified than the Marxists' capitalist class.
Every passing day brings increasing conflicts among the LDP's assorted
constituencies: farmers versus urbanites, banks versus insurance companies, young versus retirees, efficient versus inefficient. The conflicts keep
growing even as the resources to address them keep shrinking. "Things fall
apart. The center cannot hold."[3]

When sales stagnate, Japan's characteristic high corporate debt levels
become unsustainable—hence the country's intractable banking crisis.
"Lifetime employment" and seniority wages—boons during a boom—turn
into unbearable burdens during a bust.

Impelled to cut labor costs, but constrained by law and social custom
from outright layoffs, firms have slowly used attrition to eliminate 2.6 million jobs since 1997. Another 1.5 million "discouraged workers" are missing from the labor force. Firms replace full-timers, who get large twice-yearly
bonuses, pension plans and other benefits, with part-timers who do not. The
full-timers who remain are told the only way to protect their current jobs is

to accept wage cuts. Hence, with an interruption in 2000, real wages have been falling since 1997.

But falling wages translate into anemic consumer spending. As I cut my costs, I cut your sales. Profits slump even more than wages.

To keep money-losing borrowers and their banks afloat, Tokyo has kept overnight interest rates close to zero since 1995 and 10-year government bonds at 1 to 2 percent since 1998. But how can life insurers and pension funds afford to pay old annuities with guaranteed returns of 5 or 6 percent when bonds they buy yield so much less? By late 2001, a half dozen big insurers had gone bankrupt, while more than a hundred pension funds had closed up shop. The insurers who remain have reduced their payout on new policies to as low as 0.75 percent, and some are seeking permission from the government to break their contract on old policies.

In the meantime, the zero interest rate policy (ZIRP) has decimated the income of retirees who rely on interest from savings accounts to pay their daily bills. Back in the early 1990s net interest income among household savers amounted to 9 percent of national income; by 1999 this had fallen to 4 percent. No wonder consumer spending is so flat.

In the name of supporting these retirees, the government imposed a consumption tax in 1989 and then raised it in 1997. The first time, the action cost the LDP its majority in the Upper House of the Diet, a majority it has never regained. The second hike triggered the recession of 1997–98 and led to another big defeat in the 1998 Upper House election.

Without better growth, the strains of aging can only get worse. Today there are five workers for every retiree. In twenty-five years there will be only two. To cope, the government is already imposing premium hikes and benefit cuts on everything from social security to health care, not to mention talk of further hikes in the consumption tax.

City dwellers strapped for cash rush to buy the newly available cheap imports of food and clothing from China and the rest of Asia. But this leads farmers and inefficient manufacturers to demand protection. How can the LDP appease the farmers, an indispensable support base, without further alienating city dwellers? Or vice versa?

Then there is the deflation resulting from weak demand. The high prices used as disguised income redistribution to the inefficient start to tumble when demand is stagnant. Unable to pay their debts, the weaker firms seek loan rollovers from the banks and loan guarantees from the government. They get them. And the financial crisis continues.

Even the decades-old political system is becoming a victim of the malaise that results from its own actions. What used to be disguised bailouts have now become undisguised bailouts via loan guarantees, bank bailouts, hikes in medical fees, and open import protection. As soon as the invisible handout becomes visible, it loses its political palatability.

Some who believe Japan can muddle through indefinitely point to pre-Thatcher England. But in the two decades prior to Thatcher's ascension, real per capita GDP growth averaged 2.3 percent a year, enough to increase real living standards 60 percent in that period. That kind of growth can smooth over conflicts of interests. The United Kingdom looked bad only because countries such as Italy and France were growing at per capita rates closer to 4 percent.[4]

LDP R.I.P.?

Once a regime, no matter how seemingly strong, loses its raison d'être, it sooner or later loses its être. So it was with the Communist Party of the Soviet Union, the Christian Democratic Party of Italy, dictatorships in Taiwan and South Korea, and single-party rule by the Labor Party of Sweden. So it will be with Japan's single-party democracy.

There is little wrong with Japan that couldn't be helped by some good old-fashioned competitive politics. Japan needs a modern political system where the concerns of the broad middle class rather than narrow interest groups can dominate. It cannot achieve this without competitive elections where it is normal for parties (or coalitions) to alternate in power, where policy is the outcome of genuine contention in the Diet, rather than decisions made behind the closed doors of the ministries or by a few geriatric politicians gathered in the back rooms of expensive restaurants.

Japan is the only industrial democracy that is still a one-party state. Except for two one-year interruptions, the LDP and its predecessor parties have ruled Japan from 1945 to the present. And that is why it has been so hard for Japan to address its problems. It is what lies behind the bureaucracy's inordinate power and the weakness of the Diet. Strengthening the Diet could only help the opposition parties, so the LDP and bureaucracy collaborated to keep the formal Diet weak while the LDP caucus, its Policy Affairs Research Council, served as a rump parliament. It is true that there's a lot of "structural corruption" in Japan. Yet there are few one-party states or one-party cities without pervasive corruption, arrogance, and stultifying rigidity.

During the high-growth era, the LDP genuinely represented Japan's national interest, from its alliance with the West in the cold war to the political-economic system underlining high growth. But no longer. The LDP cannot be the vehicle for reform, because it is one of the main obstacles. If the LDP genuinely tried, as Koizumi is attempting, it would tear itself apart. Yet failure to reform is already slowly tearing the LDP apart.

For decades the LDP has ruled as a catchall coalition. The result was a system that allows all the special interest Lilliputians—from gas station owners and construction firms to small retailers and even veterinarians—to hog-tie the national interest in millions of tiny threads. The nation is left unable to shift gears in accordance with changes in the national interest. One instance, laughable on its own, illustrates the syndrome. A couple of years back, as part of the effort to find regulations to terminate, a Health and Welfare Ministry official proposed ending the mandatory annual distemper shots for dogs. After all, no case had been seen for decades. When veterinarians pleaded to higher-ups that this would hurt their income, the regulation was retained.

A party whose individual Diet members require the electoral support of local organizations of such special interests (called *koenkai*) cannot suddenly choose one part of its base at the expense of the others. And yet it cannot stand still either. Paralyzed by this dilemma, the LDP wavers and waffles, pushing mild reforms one day, pulling back the next. Mostly it tries—and fails—to muddle through.

Unable to deliver the goods that keep it in power, the LDP has already split once, back in 1993, causing it to temporarily lose power. It will sooner or later split again, perhaps as a consequence of the rise of Koizumi. There is now an unprecedented gap between the interests of the party and of the nation. In a democracy, that gap cannot be sustained indefinitely.

For years this basic conflict has steadily eroded the LDP's power. Since the 1993 split, it has never again been able to win enough votes to rule on its own. On the contrary, it consistently earns only about 40 percent of the votes cast. In the year 2000 elections for the Lower House—the house that chooses the prime minister—the LDP garnered a dismal 28 percent of the vote in the proportional representation portion of the election (where 180 out of a total of 480 Lower House seats are chosen). While a jury-rigged electoral system, complete with over-representation for farm districts, gives the LDP extra seats, that is not enough. It has been able to rule only through unstable coalitions with an ever-changing set of former opposition parties (Figure 1.2).

In all likelihood, the death throes of LDP rule will continue for several more years, passing through several episodes of political realignment, with a series of new parties and new personalities rising and falling.

Figure 1.2 **LDP Stays in Power with 40 Percent of the Vote**

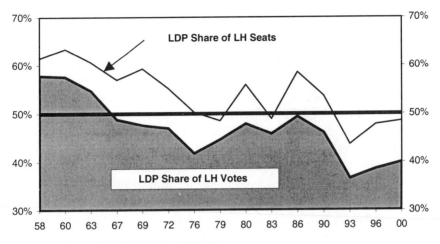

Source: Professor Gerald Curtis for 1958–96.

Note: The gray area shows the LDP's share of total votes cast in the Lower House elections during 1958 through 1993, and of the single-member-district portion of the election in 1996 and 2000. It does not include the proportional representation share of the vote, where the LDP obtained only 33 percent in 1996 and 29 percent in 2000.

There is not yet a group of opposition parties capable of displacing the LDP in an election. The largest opposition party, Minshuto, has a hapless "me-too" strategy. Believing that the Japanese people are cautious, it is afraid of scaring them with a bold program. Thus, when asked how Japan would differ under the Minshuto, its leaders hem and haw, preferring instead to speak about their lack of corruption, their environmentalism, and their youth.

Thus, for now, the real action is the centrifugal forces inside the LDP.

Koizumi: The System Tries to Reform Itself

As with Mikhail Gorbachev, the rise of Koizumi represents the inevitable attempt of the current political-economic system to reform itself. Koizumi may yet succeed, though it is increasingly doubtful. But he certainly cannot succeed as head of the LDP. His only possibility is to split the party, a course he has so far rejected.

This is not the LDP's first attempt at reform. In the last effort, the standard-bearer was Ryutaro Hashimoto, a scion of the Tanaka faction and spokesman for the vested interests who presented himself as the champion of change. Pushing for the "Big Bang" reform in finance, restructuring of the bureaucracy, and trimming of wasteful public works, he strove to reach out to the growing urban middle class voters without alienating the LDP's old base among the rural and urban special interests. The very fact that Hashimoto's faction is now seen as the headquarters of the antireform "resistance" shows how far things have come since the mid-1990s.

The process by which Koizumi came to power represents an irreversible change in Japan, regardless of what he can or cannot accomplish. He came to power when the LDP's grassroots urban machine, terrified of getting smashed in the Upper House election of 2001, staged a revolt. Acting against party orders, local urban leaders conducted plebiscites among the rank and file to choose the LDP president (and hence prime minister). Koizumi, an isolated maverick who never expected to succeed, swept the field. His campaign slogan, "Change the LDP, change Japan," saved the party from humiliating defeat, yet increased the Diet strength of the very factions that oppose his reforms. Still, the immense popular enthusiasm that greeted his arrival, a popularity rating of 90 percent, means no one can any longer say that the Japanese people are satisfied with muddling through. Their anxiety and yearning for relief are palpable. The proof of that came when Koizumi yielded to party barons and sacked his inept but popular foreign minister, Makiko Tanaka, another maverick who symbolized reform. Koizumi's own popularity abruptly halved.

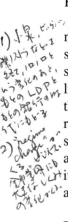

Some see the rise of Koizumi, the "Big Bang" financial reforms, announcements of corporate restructuring, and similar developments as milestones in a slow, steady, incremental process at the end of which we will see a revitalized Japan led by the same LDP and corporate-banking establishment in power today. But this is not the way reform will happen. Rather, the coming decade will see a very tumultuous battle between the forces of reform and resistance. This will be, in the words of T.J. Pempel, a "regime shift,"[5] complete with institutional upheaval in business and finance as well as politics. Single-party LDP rule will not survive the process. The LDP itself, like the Italian Christian Democrats, may dissolve once it loses power and access to the public trough for any length of time.

Koizumi's Self-Defeating Priorities

Like his Soviet counterpart, Koizumi is a sincere reformer who faces two very large obstacles: his own political party and a tragically self-defeating economic strategy.

Like Gorbachev before him, Koizumi is committing the tragic error of doing the right things in the wrong order. Proper sequencing is the *sine qua non* of successful reform. Deng Xiaoping was a genius at it. Gorbachev was not, and so far neither is Koizumi.

Koizumi's fatal error is that he prioritized budget cuts instead of eliminating the bad bank debt. With Japan falling back into recession, Koizumi chose the worst possible time for fiscal austerity. His fiscal tourniquet repeated the horrendous blunder of 1997, when Hashimoto raised taxes and sent the economy plunging. Once again, it associated reform with recession in the public mind.

Why did Koizumi reprise known errors? Some of the motivation was economic: the sincere belief that a bloated state sector is Japan's chief economic defect. Moreover, Koizumi correctly recognizes that his predecessors abused government spending as a substitute for reform and that this failed because fiscal stimulus alone cannot cure what ails Japan.

However, much of the motivation has to do with politics, a subject that captivates him far more than economics. For all Koizumi's talk of economic reform, and despite his college-age sojourn at the London School of Economics, the nitty-gritty of economics and banking seems to bore him. In private talks, he speaks passionately and tirelessly about LDP corruption or the pernicious relationship between the politicians and the state enterprises. Yet, when visitors raise the issue of nonperforming loans, the animation vanishes, his eyes seem to glaze over, and he retreats to the dry recitation of rote replies.

It would be wrong, however, to dismiss Koizumi's strategic priorities as simply a matter of personal taste. He sincerely believes that few reforms can be implemented without first decimating the political power of the iron quadrangle of LDP politicians, public enterprises, bureaucrats, and construction firms who parasitize the economy. Reducing public works, farm subsidies, and quasi-state enterprises all serve to cut the funding of vested interests and their LDP protectors. Much of what passes for fiscal reform is, in fact, an attack on the power structure of the old regime.

While Koizumi's strategy is understandable, it is neither good economics nor good politics. If public works are a problem, cut them, but cut taxes even more. Why deepen the recession and give the LDP conservatives more ammunition? Koizumi backed himself into an unnecessary corner. As of this writing, Koizumi had only partially reversed himself. For example, his original plans called for a reduction of the fiscal 2002 deficit by an amount equal to 1 percent of GDP. As of this writing, those cutbacks had already been reduced by half and further retreat is only a matter of time.

Repeatedly, on the budget deficit front, and even more so in his attacks on state enterprises and construction spending, Koizumi has started out with bold promises to fight to the death, and then made compromises in which he got little of substance. "We're willing to give him the show as long as we get the substance," said one leading pro-resistance Diet member. As of mid-2002, the "resistance" felt no need to oust Koizumi, since they were able to neuter him. As the public saw this, Koizumi kept losing his main asset: his former popularity. Each bit of temporizing left him with even less leverage for the next battle.

To make matters worse, Koizumi's actions on banking fall short of the bold campaign rhetoric that originally led to his election. He stuck with his predecessor's plan for a limited write-off of bad debt: only 18 trillion yen ($145 billion) over three years. This is a small fraction of a problem now grown to around 100 trillion yen—almost 20 percent of GDP. In a key litmus test in January 2002, Koizumi intervened to stop the bankruptcy of Daiei—a retailing empire with $17 billion in debt and 100,000 employees, by pressing the banks to keep Daiei afloat. The retailer gained 400 billion yen ($3.2 billion) in debt forgiveness in exchange for unreliable promises that, this time, its restructuring would be real.

The dilemma for Koizumi is that he cannot cut the budget and solve the bad loan problem at the same time. Dealing with bad debt will cost lots of money. The banks need a new capital injection, this time with more stringent conditions than the failed effort of 1999. Unemployment compensation expenses will soar as foreclosures eliminate at least three million to four million jobs (see Chapter 5, p. 90). Finally, there must be a tax cut for individuals—not companies—to offset the depressive effects of rising bankruptcies and unemployment.

Forced to pick his priorities, Koizumi has chosen the budget. That is the wrong choice. The private economy cannot achieve self-sustaining recovery while it remains tied down by bad debt and bad debtors. Other reforms will be much harder to achieve without the foundation of private growth. Nor can the budget deficit itself be cured without reviving private growth. Two-thirds of the growth in the deficit from 2 percent of GDP in 1990 to almost 8 percent of GDP in 2001 resulted from a drop in tax revenue; only one-third came from increased spending. The deficit is a symptom, not the underlying malady. Without a revival of the tax base, deficits will continue to expand (see Chapter 6).

The reason solving the debt problem is a prerequisite for private sector recovery is this: Behind the bad debt stand the bad debtors, the majority in sectors suffering from immense excess capacity and inefficiency. This excess capacity is an anchor on new investment and growth. Moreover, just to survive, the bad debtors are slashing prices, forcing healthier companies to match them. This adds to downward pressure on wages and consumer spending. Keeping bad debtors alive turns marginal companies into losers and good companies into marginal ones. New bad debt keeps rising faster than old debt is written off.

Like his predecessors, Koizumi feared foreclosing on the bad debtors would cost too many jobs in a nation without a good safety net. But the longer Tokyo waits, the higher the ultimate job losses.

Koizumi is like a doctor arriving at a car accident where the victim has stopped breathing and is bleeding from the arteries. What to do first? Restore the breathing. Otherwise the victim will be brain-dead within a few minutes. In Japan the banking system is the breathing and the public debt is the bleeding. Koizumi, with the best of intentions, is working very hard to staunch the hemorrhaging even as the brain cells die one by one.

Koizumi's retort is that Japan's mushrooming government debt and repeated downgrades of Japan's credit standing leave him no choice. But, as we'll discuss in Chapter 6, this is not so. Koizumi's choices were not forced on him by circumstances but were a result of his own political preferences.

Japan Is Not Argentina

In January 2002 a new joke started making the rounds of Tokyo: What is the difference between Japan and Argentina? Answer: two years. The same month, John Makin, a well-connected economist at the American Enterprise Institute, in an essay entitled "Japan in Depression," predicted an imminent "failure of the banking system . . . [and a] a full-scale 'run' on the banks." *Forbes* magazine, whose cover only a few years earlier had exhorted its readers to buy Japanese stocks "before it's too late," now warned that "Japan's economic crisis . . . might drag the world into Depression." In May 2002, Adam Posen, of the Institute for International Economics, raised the alarm that, "the Japanese economy is likely to tumble into crisis sometime before the Diet's supplemental budget process begins in September 2002." This follows Posen's failed March 2001 forecast that financial breakdown, complete with capital flight and possible bank runs, were "almost inevitable in Japan this year [2001]." Many forecasters warned, despite all the evidence to the contrary, that bank runs would ensue in the spring of 2002 when the government lifted full guarantees on all time deposits at the banks. It never happened.[6]

All this alarmism is not only wrong; it's dangerous. Fear of meltdown paralyzes the hand of reform. Even reformers fear that pulling on a few threads risks causing the entire tapestry to unravel. Daiei was bailed out in part because officials and newspapers warned that its failure could cause the entire banking system to collapse. Yet its debt to the big banks amounted to just 0.8 percent of their total loans.

More fundamentally, there is a huge difference between Japan, on the one hand, and countries such as South Korea and Argentina, which suffered genuine implosion. These countries all ran big trade deficits. When the foreigners pulled their money out, the oil and spare parts stopped coming in. Factories shut down. People were thrown on the street. None of that will happen in Japan because it is a net creditor. Tokyo has the capacity to suppress crisis by throwing a lot of money at the problem. And that is exactly what Tokyo has done: always just enough to stave off disaster, but never enough to solve the underlying malady.

In the end, Japan will act—once the pain of inaction surpasses the pain of action. Until then, the real danger in Japan is not cataclysm but relentless corrosion. Not meltdown, but the paralyzing fear of meltdown.

So Far: One Step Forward, Two Steps Back

Whatever happens under Koizumi, the coming turbulent decade will be marked by many instances of one step forward, two steps backward. As of early 2002, in the battle between reform and resistance, resistance is winning.

Take the financial "Big Bang," often hailed as a fundamental turning point. Whatever benefits the "Big Bang" might have brought in allocating capital more efficiently have been more than offset by other developments. Zero interest rates and blatant political pressure are used to keep banks rolling over loans to those who cannot pay. "Financial socialism"—that is, the share of deposits and loans mediated by government banks—has soared to 45 percent and 35 percent, respectively (see Chapter 14).

While there is much talk of corporate restructuring, the vast majority of the mergers and acquisitions have been used to combine weak firms in troubled industries into even more powerful oligopolies. Price control, not efficiency, is the name of their game. While there has been some genuine restructuring, it is mostly in industries that were already very efficient by world standards, such as autos and electronics. Japan is witnessing the most reform where it is least urgent and the least reform where it is most urgent (see Chapter 15).

There are exceptions to this pattern, to be sure. The wholesale sector has actually been slimmed down quite a bit in the past decade, while the textile/apparel sector has enjoyed the benefits of downsizing and outsourcing. Rates for long-distance phone calls have fallen dramatically due to regulatory reforms that allowed new entrants. But so far, such exceptional good news remains just that: exceptional.

Analysts looking at all these developments offer diametrically opposed visions. Japanese political and business leaders claim to be rapidly implementing reform, and quite a few observers believe them. Others counter that these formal reforms have led to little real change on the ground so far and they don't expect much more in the future. Neither of these two poles captures the dynamic: a long period of trench warfare. Neither reform nor resistance alone is the reality; it's the tension between them.

The battle for Japan is just beginning and the forces of reform are still embryonic. But time is on their side.

How the System Soured

To offer a prescription, we must first make a diagnosis. How did a nation widely predicted in 1990 to become the leading economic power of the century stumble so badly?

Answering this question was the subject of my 1998 book, *Japan: The System That Soured—The Rise and Fall of the Japanese Economic Miracle.* Let me summarize the argument.

The root of the problem is that Japan is still mired in many of the structures, policies, and mental habits that prevailed in the 1950s and 1960s. The "Japanese economic system" was a marvelous device to help a backward Japan catch up to the West. But the catch-up system turned obsolete and counterproductive once Japan had in fact caught up. South Korea's current travails reflect its attempt to deal with the same critical fork in the road.

The Japan of 1950 was a poor nation, one with more farmers than factory workers. Yet just two decades later it had raised itself from the income level of 1990 India to nearly that of 1990 South Korea. It quadrupled its living standard in only two decades while becoming an industrial superpower. No other major country, before or since, has matched this rapid takeoff.

What made the system work was that Japan's "developmental state" took the natural organic process of development and accelerated it tremendously.

In the 1950s and 1960s the economic horizon was filled with a host of infant industries, from autos to electronics. Though they had the potential to become world-class competitors, they needed a jump-start. They had not yet acquired either the economies of scale or the learning-by-doing efficiencies to be competitive. Without protection and promotion, they might have been strangled in their cradles. The auto industry, for example, was almost wiped out by a flood of European imports during a brief interlude of free trade in 1953.

Admittedly, even in the catch-up era, Tokyo also aided many industries with no potential to become exporters, from aviation to chemicals. And when it did, the measures flopped. Yet the very nature of an economy in catch-up phase is that it contains a plethora of true infant industries. Even without its developmental policies, Japan would have industrialized—but not at miracle rates.

Unfortunately, when Japan reached maturity in the mid-1970s, the very point when "developmentalist" policies should have been loosened, they were reinforced. In reaction to the oil crises of 1973 and 1979, protection of basic industries was intensified.

Japan gradually shifted from promoting winners to protecting losers. The same tools once used to turn infant industries into export stars now shielded inefficient—but politically connected—industries from competition, domestic as well as foreign.

Unlike in the 1950s–60s, the protection from foreigners was covert. Cheaper Korean steel was blocked, not by formal import quotas but by cozy deals among steelmakers and their customers, aided by collaborating shippers and longshoremen.[7] Old wine in murkier bottles.

On the domestic side, some protection was overt, in the form of regulations aimed at protecting the inefficient (see Chapter 18). But much of the protection was just as covert as the import shields: mainly a blind eye at the Japan Fair Trade Commission to anti-competitive actions by industry associations and entrenched firms (see Chapter 19).

Even in the high-growth era, there was always a duality to Japan's economic policy, a combination that political scientist Kent Calder termed "strategy" versus "compensation."[8] Strategy refers to policies aimed at promoting growth. Compensation means paying off the victims of rapid development—for example, coal miners as the economy shifts to oil. Both sides of the equation were necessary in the catch-up era. Strategy produced the growth necessary to fund compensation. Compensation paid off enough "losers" to keep the party of growth in power.

As long as strategy and compensation were in balance, the system worked. However, in the early 1970s—fueled by the rise of Prime Minister Kakuei Tanaka and the 1973 oil shock—compensation seized the throne.

As this happened, Japan turned into a deformed dual economy—a dysfunctional hybrid of superstrong exporting industries and superweak domestic sectors. Under the pressure of stiff competition overseas, exporters such as the auto and machinery industries had learned to offer some of the best technology and highest productivity in the world. Within Japan, however, the picture was quite different. Coddled domestic manufacturing sectors from food processing to textiles became woefully backward by international standards. In food processing, for example, Japan's productivity is one-third of U.S. levels and falling further behind. Yet more people work in food processing than in autos and steel combined. By the beginning of the 1990s, a mere 10–15 percent of Japan's entire workforce was employed in the efficient exporting industries.

Gradually, over the course of the 1970s and 1980s, the country's economic arteries became increasingly clogged and rigid. Even worse, the dual economy was gradually sowing the seeds of its own destruction.

For one thing, the dual economy was sustainable only so long as efficient exporters earned enough to prop up weak domestic sectors. The high prices Toyota paid for glass, rubber, basic steel, and so forth were, in effect, subsidies to these suppliers. By the late 1980s, however, the exporters found it harder to bear the burden. They fled offshore in a process commonly termed "hollowing out." In essence, Japan was being run on the principle of comparative *dis*advantage. Because it protected glass and rice and cement and steel, it drove away autos and electronics. As Japan slowly lost its most efficient sectors, the productivity of the entire economy started being dragged down to the level of the stagnant sectors (see Chapter 3).

Because the process was so gradual, no alarm bells went off. Besides, an extraordinarily high level of investment hid the problem for a while. But this could not be sustained indefinitely. Eventually those misguided investments, combined with loans to the dark side of the dual economy, would become the heart of Japan's bad debt problem.

In late 1980s, when Japan grew faster than the United States, Germany, or any other industrial country, some analysts thought the country had discovered a unique elixir for growth. In reality, Japan grew faster because countries still in the catch-up phase typically grow faster than rich ones. In fact, once one takes into account all the factors that account for growth, Japan was an overachiever in the 1950s and 1960s but a marked *under*performer in the 1970s and 1980s—the very time when it was still mistakenly considered a growth star.[9]

At the end of 1989, when Japan's "bubble economy" was at its height, Japan felt stronger than ever. But the crippling heart attack was but a few months away.

Today, with the patient still unable to get out of bed, there are those who say the problem is simply that 1990 "heart attack"—the popping of the late 1980s financial and investment bubble, and misguided policy responses. The real cause is the two decades of arteriosclerosis that preceded 1990.

Two Obstacles to Growth

Japan has two problems hindering growth: a supply-side problem and a demand-side problem.

The supply-side problem is low productivity growth caused by the "dual economy." As a result, as noted above, even if Japan were operating at full capacity, it could not grow faster than 1.25 or 1.5 percent on a sustained basis. By 2010, if Japan does not reform, full-capacity growth could fall as low as 0.5 percent, warns the Organization for Economic Cooperation and Development (OECD).[10] This aspect of the problem is now increasingly understood in Japan.

Rarely understood is the demand-side of the problem: why Japan finds it so hard to run at full capacity. The same cartelization of the private sector that saps productivity also produces notoriously high consumer prices that suppress real household income and thus consumer demand. Once Japan reached economic maturity in the early 1970s, its investment needs slowed down. In a typical economy, household income and thus consumer spending rise to take up the slack. That keeps supply and demand in balance. Not in Japan. Once Japan's high prices are factored in, total household income in the private economy (primarily wages, interest, and dividends) is actually a smaller share of national income today than it was in 1980. Consequently, consumption as a share of GDP is lower than in other advanced economies. Consumption is too low not because households save too much but because they earn too little. The consequence is a kind of economic anorexia—Japan's inability to consume all that it produces. In more technical economic terms, this is a chronic deficiency of aggregate demand, also known as a chronic investment-savings gap. Reforms that introduce more competition will not only improve supply-side efficiency but, by lowering monopolistic prices, increase real purchasing power.

How, then, did Japan manage to grow 4 percent a year during the period 1975–90? It did so, as we'll detail in Chapter 4, by artificially stimulating demand through huge trade surpluses, mammoth budget deficits, and, during the late 1980s, cheap interest rates that acted as monetary steroids

The 1980s "bubble" was a false solution to the problem of anorexia. The 1985 Plaza Accords, which sent the yen soaring, cut off the trade surplus route to growth, and the economy began to slow. Tokyo responded by artificially pumping up real estate, stocks, and capital investment via monetary ease and low interest rates. As it turned out, much of this investment had no more economic value than the fabled pyramids of Egypt. At least the latter brings in tourist dollars. But in Japan it was a pyramid of bad debt that was being constructed. Only a few years later the Japanese landscape would be dotted with empty office buildings, unused factory space, and unprecedented levels of nonperforming loans (NPLs) at the banks.

Once the bubble collapsed and investment fell, anorexia returned—worse than ever before. By the 1990s Japan found itself at the same turning point as other industrial economies before it. No industrial economy can progress beyond a certain point without becoming a mass-consumption economy. The famous Maekawa Commission Report pointed out the need for the same transformation in Japan back in 1986. Japan's leaders ignored the warning.

Today the need is greater than ever. While anorexia—the gap between demand and supply—has gotten worse, the ability of the old recipes to fix the problem has steadily eroded. Japan is like a patient who has abused antibiotics so much that the drugs no longer pack their previous punch. In the late 1990s Tokyo applied more macroeconomic stimulus than ever before yet got less results than ever before. The stimulus has been enough to prevent malaise from turning into depression. But it has not been enough to stimulate self-sustaining private growth—and never will be.

Reform and Stimulus Are Partners, Not Alternatives

For years Japan has been trapped in a false debate between structural reform and macroeconomic stimulus. The reality is that neither works without the other.

Macroeconomic stimulus has been tried—on a massive scale—and, in the absence of reform, it has failed. On the contrary, structural reform is needed just to make macroeconomic stimulus more potent. For example, according to the International Monetary Fund, fixing the banking system is a precondition for restoring the efficacy of monetary stimulus.[11]

On the other hand, the initial depressive effects of structural reform are so severe that it cannot be implemented without a macroeconomic safety net. The trick of reform is to prevent a massive microeconomic shift involving tens of thousands of firms and millions of people from turning into a macroeconomic implosion.

The question, says Ministry of Economy, Trade, and Industry (METI) official Tatsuya Terazawa, is how that macroeconomic stimulus is used—as anesthesia or morphine. In an essay written when he was a special researcher at a METI-affiliated research institute, RIETI, Terazawa declared:

> Monetary policy . . . can be seen as morphine. It can ease the pain but cannot cure the illness of the Japanese economy by itself. It can delay the necessary restructuring of the economy. This risk is especially serious when the politicians, policy makers and the media are led to believe that the so-called "quantitative" expansion of monetary policy can be a kind of magic cure. . . . On the other hand, monetary policy can have a meaningful role. That is, when monetary policy is used as anesthesia to ease the pain during "surgery" to resolve the problems of our economy. The surgery would be associated with increased bankruptcies and unemployment. . . . [It] must be used wisely to solve the problems of the Japanese economy, such as the bad loans of the banks and the companies with excessive debt.[12]

The conservatives in the LDP argue for morphine but no surgery. Seeking to cut off the morphine, Koizumi also withheld the anesthesia.

Gains from Reform: 3–4 Percent Growth

While Japan has so much to lose from the wrong policies, it has so much to gain from the right ones. In a report entitled *Why the Japanese Economy Is Not Growing*—developed with the aid of famed growth economist Paul Romer—the McKinsey Research Institute argued:

> If the impediments to competition are removed, our analyses suggest that productivity in Japan as a whole can grow by as much as 4.7 percent a year for the next ten years. . . . GDP per capita will then increase by a robust 4 percent a year.[13]

Economist David Weinstein argues that, assuming it takes twenty years for Japanese reform to bring Japan to U.S. levels of productivity, then reform could add 1.5 percent a year to Japanese growth during those two decades.[14]

How are such huge gains possible? Because so many sectors lag so far behind that bringing them up to world benchmarks would yield huge results. In food processing, for example, McKinsey estimates that Japan could bring its productivity from 35 percent of U.S. levels to 64 percent within ten years. That would amount to a 6.3 percent annual rise in productivity.[15]

Such efficiency gains would also bring huge benefits on the demand side as well. Currently Japanese spend 23 percent of their household budget on food, compared to about 10 percent for Americans. Suppose, due to reduced subsidies, cheaper imports, and more competition, food prices could be lowered. Think of all the money liberated to buy other items.

While any such estimates are educated guesses, we believe that a reformed Japan could grow at least 3 percent a year, with perhaps a fairly lengthy interlude of 3.5 or 4 percent as it moves back to full-capacity operation.

The difference in the lives of ordinary people is immense. At 3 percent annual per capita growth—the rate Japan enjoyed between 1975 and 1990— living standards double every twenty-three years. Children live twice as well as their parents. The aging can be supported without a crushing burden on the young. At the 0.5 percent rate seen in the past decade, it takes 140 years for living standards to double. Improvement is barely perceptible. Worse yet, when the average is so low, large sections of the population see their living standards decline.

Conservative Revolutionaries

There are those who say Japan will never reform because it will never accept an "American model" unsuited to Japanese values. This identification of reform with "Americanization" is fanned by the opponents of reform. Yet it reflects some real fears in the population.

Yet this fear is not insurmountable because it is not soundly based. So many of the institutions and practices that are normally regarded as the embodiment of ancient Japanese culture and values are, in fact, political constructs of rather recent vintage. From "lifetime employment" to bank-centered finance to the cartels run by industry associations, many of Japan's institutions are products of the fight against the Depression, then mobilization for war, and finally post–World War II mobilization for revival. Time and again new wine was put in bottles with very old labels to give them authenticity. This is documented in a very good volume called *Mirror of Modernity*.[16] We'll run across this phenomenon again and again in Part Four of this book. Reform does not mean becoming more "American." It means becoming a different kind of Japan, one that, in certain ways, resembles an earlier Japan.

Perhaps reformers need to learn the same trick as the resistance: to link needed changes to preservation of what is valuable in traditional values. Japan's communitarian values are admirable. The only problem is the way that these values are implemented. Japan can provide for all its citizens and still have growth. Security can be achieved with a social safety net and fluid labor markets rather than the preservation of unproductive jobs. Egalitarianism can be pursued with redistributive taxes rather than distorted prices.

Yes, Japan's people have been acculturated to be more risk-averse than Americans. And for three decades Japan sacrificed efficiency in the name of security. But the result is that they have ended up with neither. Today efficiency is not the alternative to security but its indispensable prerequisite.

Often, very revolutionary changes occur for very conservative motivations. Japan will reform not because people want change—though some, such as young, educated women, do—but because people want to hold on to what they now feel entitled to. Consider a baby boomer born in 1945 or so. Having seen real hunger as a child, and now grown accustomed to affluence, he or she finds it being snatched away. Baby boomers who never expected to be the main support for their parents now must do so because of the pension crisis. They never expected their grown children would be jobless and living at home—not after the time and money invested in "cram schools" to get them into the best colleges. But with youth unemployment at 10 percent, that is the case for millions of families. Those seeking rather modest ends will find that far-reaching changes are required to achieve them. Were Japan's political-economic system capable of incremental adaptation and reform, this would not be so. Since it isn't, thorough political-economic overhaul is needed just to regain what used to be the status quo.

Skeptics retort: Japan has already frittered away a whole decade. Why should the future be any different? But no society puts itself through wrenching transformation until it has exhausted all other alternatives. And for years many of "the best and brightest" macroeconomists claimed that such alternatives existed: just spend enough money and/or print enough money. As recently as 1999–2000, during a temporary upturn, many claimed these nostrums were working. Naturally, Japan's politicians and people preferred these consoling illusions.

Finally, events have persuaded the majority of the Japanese people and elite that without reform the situation can only get worse. But there is not yet consensus among reformers on the content of reform. The task now is to reach that consensus and to create the institutional vehicles to bring it about.

Part One

A Tale of Two Problems: Supply and Demand

2

The Incredible Shrinking Japan

So accustomed are we to Japan's malaise that we forget how stunning and recent is its descent. In looking over my 1998 book *Japan: The System That Soured* to prepare for this one, I was struck by how much time the book spent just trying to demonstrate that Japan was in serious trouble, let alone explain why. A full chapter had to be devoted to debunking the so-called revisionists, some of whom claimed Japan's travails were a hoax. As recently as 1995, journals such as *Foreign Affairs* and *Business Week* lionized a book whose subtitle was *Why Japan Is Still on Track to Overtake the U.S. by the Year 2000.*[1]

In March 1997, when many economists were trumpeting Japan's alleged comeback, this author wrote, "Unless the country undertakes a sweeping reform of institutions and policies, it will be lucky to get back to 2 percent annual growth over the next five years."[2] At the time this seemed unduly pessimistic. In retrospect it turned out to be wildly overoptimistic. If current estimates prove correct, Japan will have suffered virtually zero growth during the five years from 1998 to 2002 (Figure 2.1a).

Back in the mid-1990s, 2 percent growth was the level that reformers warned that the country might *descend* to. How things had changed by 2000, when the prime minister, Keizo Obuchi, held up 2 percent growth as the goal to strive for, and by 2002, when Koizumi held up 1.5 percent growth as the measure of victory.[3] What was once considered the worst that might happen is now, we are told, the most that Japan can achieve.

Japan's performance over the past decade has been worse than almost any other rich country in the postwar era. The nation once forecast to own the twenty-first century has seen its economic ranking fall drastically. In a number of key indicators, from share of rich-country GDP to share of world exports, Japan hit its peak in the late 1980s and has since fallen substantially. Given current trajectories, its weight in the world economy will continue to plummet.

Figure 2.1a **Five-Year GDP Growth Moving Toward Zero**

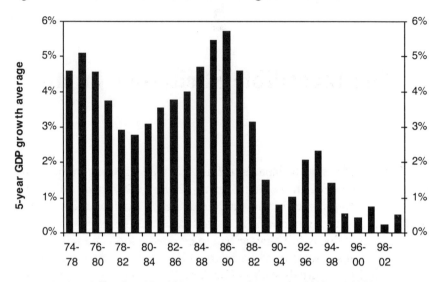

Source: Cabinet Office for 1974–2001, consensus forecast for 2002 and 2003.
Note: Each column gives the average real GDP growth for the five-year period named, e.g., 0.3 percent for 1998–2002.

Figure 2.1b **Japan's Worst Dozen Years Is Worse Than Others'**

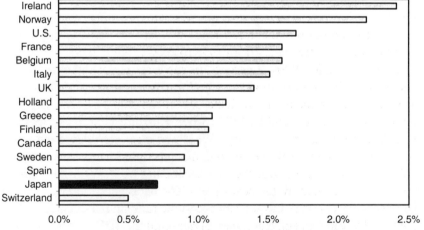

Average Per Capita Growth During Worst 12-year Period

Source: World Bank for 1960–2001, consensus GDP forecast for Japan of –0.8 percent for 2002 and 0.8 percent for 2003.
Note: Each bar shows the average annual per capita GDP growth during each nation's *worst* 12-year period since 1960, e.g., the United States grew 1.7 percent per capita during 1971–82.

A few other industrialized countries have suffered similar problems. But almost no other has suffered so severely for so long, because the other nations solved their problems. So can Japan.

During the past five decades only three other industrialized countries have averaged zero or negative growth over a five-year period: Sweden, Finland, and Switzerland, all in the early 1990s (Switzerland also suffered a five-year slump after the 1973 oil shock). Like Japan, all three countries suffered banking crises in the early 1990s, as did the United States. None grew until it solved its crisis. Almost all grew again once they solved it, Finland at rates around 5 percent. The important exception was Switzerland, which, like Japan, had deeper problems. A banking crisis alone would not have sent Japan into such intractable malaise.

Taking the longer view, Japan's average GDP growth per capita during the dozen years from 1992 to 2003 is on track to descend to a dismal 0.7 percent. Among rich countries, only Switzerland did worse. In most cases, the worst period spanned the oil shocks of 1973 and 1980 (Figure 2.1b).

The comparison with Switzerland is telling, since it was afflicted by the same witch's brew that laid low Japan: a worsening dual economy of efficient sectors and inefficient sheltered sectors, leading to steady deceleration in productivity growth and eventual banking crisis, all made worse by counterproductive fiscal policies. The encouraging news is that, after Switzerland tackled its banking crisis and began other structural reforms, its growth improved to 2 percent during the period 1997–2000.

Japan's Shrinking Weight in the World

A century from now, economic historians may well look back at 1985–91 as Japan's high-water mark in the world economy—the reversal of more than a century of history. After rising from the 1870s onward, Japan's share of world GDP peaked in 1991 at 9 percent. Even with an optimistic forecast of 2 percent growth, by 2010 Japan's share of world GDP will drop back to only 6 percent.

This alone is not necessarily a sign of weakness. As countries mature, they grow more slowly than emerging countries such as China or South Korea. More remarkable is that Japan's growth is lagging behind its fellow rich countries. Even with 2 percent growth in Japan, Japan's share of rich-country GDP will fall from 15.6 percent in 2000 to 12 percent by 2010 (Figure 2.2). More likely its share will fall even faster.

A shrinking share of the world output is, by itself, no disaster. Many fairly small countries live quite prosperously and happily. However, to the

Figure 2.2 **Japan's Share of Rich-Nation GDP Plunging**

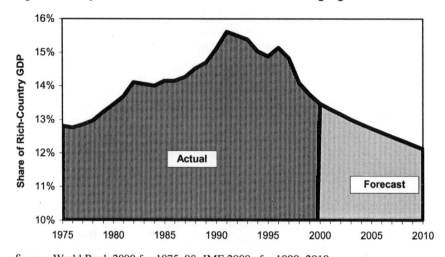

Source: World Bank 2000 for 1975–98, IMF 2000a for 1999–2010.

Note: For 1975–99, GDP is measured on the purchasing power parity (PPP) basis that is usually used for international comparisons. For 2000–10, the projection relies on IMF forecasts that advanced countries will grow 3 percent and Japan will grow at about 2 percent a year.

extent that political leverage stems from economic prowess, Japan's shrinkage has important geopolitical ramifications. Integrating a rising China into the world community of nations would be a lot easier with a vibrant Japan.

Not only is Japan's weight in the world dropping, but so is its relative living standard. After more than a century of struggle, Japan's real per capita GDP had reached almost 90 percent of U.S. levels by 1991. A decade later Japan had retreated to 76 percent of U.S. levels. In 1991 Japan's per capita GDP was 5 percent higher than the average among fifteen high-income countries. By 2000 it was 6 percent lower. A decade hence, it will be lower still.[4]

Contrary to popular impression, Japan has also fared poorly on the export front. From 1960 to 1986 Japan's vaunted export machine tripled its share of world goods and services exports from 3 percent to nearly 9 percent. Now it's down to 6.7 percent and, given current trajectories, will fall to 5.4 percent by decade's end (Figure 2.3).

Figure 2.3 **Japan's Share of World Exports Drops After 1986**

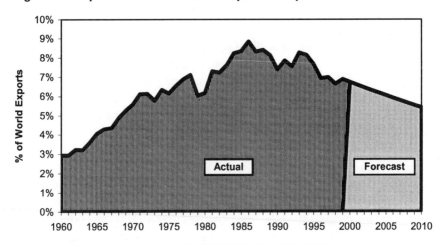

Source: World Bank 2000 for 1960–98, IMF 2000a for 1999–2010.

Note: Goods and services exports in current dollars. The projection for 1999–2010 assumes that global exports will continue to expand at the same 6.7 percent rate that the IMF forecasts through 2005. It also assumes that Japanese exports continue at the same rate as in the IMF estimate for 1992–2001, which was 4.4 percent.

What Went Wrong? Structural Versus Macroeconomic Schools

Prescribing the right medicine requires that we first make the right diagnosis. Unfortunately, economists disagree.

Some analysts, including myself, stress structural (i.e., institutional) factors that afflict both productivity growth and aggregate demand. In this view, Japan will never enjoy sustained revival without thorough overhaul.

"Nonsense," say many academic macroeconomists, who claim that easily correctable policy mistakes are the real problem. In this view, Japan followed the same path as other countries where financial bubbles popped. However, Japan's fiscal and monetary policies were too tight. If Tokyo simply applied enough stimulus, along with a cleanup of the nonperforming loan crisis, Japan would do quite nicely.

Stimulus is certainly necessary. But it is not sufficient. The macroeconomic explanation cannot be the whole story because insufficient demand is only one-quarter of Japan's problem. No matter how much demand stimulus is applied, it cannot help the supply-side factors, which make up three-quarters of the problem (Figure 2.4).

This calculation is based on data from a recent International Monetary Fund (IMF) study.[5] During 1987–90, according to the IMF, Japan's *potential* growth was 3.7 percent a year. Potential growth is the rate an economy can sustain over the long haul when operating at full capacity. The 3.7 percent estimate is not an artifact of the bubble, when actual growth averaged 5 percent. In fact, it's a bit lower than the 4.1 percent growth Japan averaged during the whole period of 1975–90.

As of 2002, Japan's GDP was 24 percent below where it would have been if Japan had continued at that 3.7 percent pace. To put it the other way, had Japan kept growing 3.7 percent a year, its 2002 GDP would have been a third larger than it actually turned out to be. Even if we factor in the demographic factor—the slowing growth of the working-age population—GDP was still 20 percent smaller than it would have been. Yet, the economy was operating "only" 5 percent below full capacity in 2002. At best, demand stimulus could have solved the 5 percent problem. What about the other 15 percent? Worse yet, for reasons we'll discuss in Part Three, stimulus has not even been able to solve the demand problem.[6]

What accounts for the other 15 percent? According to the IMF, by 2001 the growth rate of potential GDP at full capacity had fallen to 1.1 percent. That enormous drop in potential growth—from 3.7 percent to 1.1 percent—is the lion's share of Japan's problem.

Explaining the Abrupt Slowdown in Potential Growth

Japan's structural flaws have existed since the mid-1970s. Nonetheless, Japan grew 4 percent a year during 1975–90. If structural flaws caused the "lost decade," some macroeconomists ask rhetorically, why did Japan grow so fast before the bubble popped and so badly after it popped?

Our answer is this: The methods that Japan used to cover up, and offset, its structural flaws ran out of steam in the 1990s.

The critical factor was that Japan was no longer able to offset—and cover up—its structural slowdown in productivity growth by pouring on more and more investment. Business investment in plant and equipment abruptly fell from a peak of 20 percent of real GDP in early 1991 to only 14 percent in 1994. In absolute numbers, the amount of investment in 2002 is still below the peak reached in 1991.

Investment is pivotal to both supply and demand in Japan's economic growth.

Figure 2.4 **Lost GDP: Supply Factors Overwhelm Demand Factors**

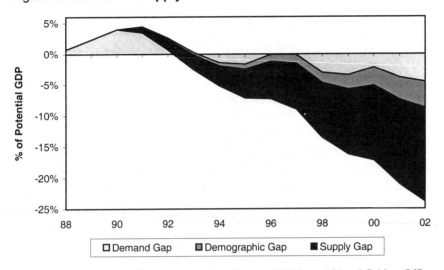

Source: Calculations by author using data from Bayoumi 2000a, p. 104 and Cabinet Office 2002a.

Note: The 0 percent axis measures Japan's potential GDP had it sustained the 3.74 percent growth rate in potential GDP that it enjoyed in 1987–90. The gray area, the demand gap, shows how far above or below potential GDP is actual GDP. At the end of the bubble, Japan was operating 4 percent above capacity; in 2002, a projected 6 percent below capacity. In 1996–97, despite the years of stagnation, Japan was actually operating above capacity. That is because its potential growth had slowed so much. The area with the diagonal lines shows the drop in capacity due to the slowdown in labor force growth. The black area shows the difference between the potential GDP at the 0 percent axis and the full-capacity GDP due to the slowdown in potential growth (excluding the demographic factor). This is caused by slowdowns in investment and productivity growth.

On the demand side, each dollar of investment has a multiplier effect. When Toyota builds a new car factory, not only does it spend money on machinery, construction, and so on, but Toyota's contractors hire new workers, who spend money on consumer goods and services, and so on. The process works just as powerfully in the opposite direction when investment plunges. Detailed studies show that, on the demand side, decreased business investment was the single biggest factor in the 1990s slowdown.[7]

At the same time, from the supply side, plunging investment is also the culprit. From 1973 to 1990, Japan increasingly relied on investment-driven growth instead of productivity-driven growth. By productivity-driven growth, we mean increases in technology and efficiency, such as using the Internet to automate routine banking transactions. This is also known as total factor productivity (TFP). Whereas labor productivity refers to the amount of GDP produced by each worker, TFP refers to the amount of GDP produced by each unit of capital as well as labor. Over the long haul, the law of diminishing returns dictates that if TFP growth slows to zero, GDP growth will eventually end as well.

That is Japan's fundamental trap. Its economic rigidities caused TFP growth to tumble from 2.5 percent in the 1970s to 1.4 percent in the 1980s and to 0.6 percent in the 1990s (Table 2.1 and Figure 2.5).

Rather than fix the TFP problem, Japan poured on tons of unproductive investment. It worked harder rather than smarter. This works—for a while. Giving each worker more tools—for example, giving a pool of ten secretaries ten PCs instead of five—allows each worker to produce more. Thus the share of GDP growth arising from investment (i.e., from growth in the capital stock) rose from a third in the 1960s and 1970s to half in the 1980s and to more than 80 percent in the 1990s. In the U.S. boom of the 1990s, by contrast, TFP outweighed investment as a source of growth.[8]

Investment-led growth meant Japan had to run faster on the treadmill just to stay in place. The tenth PC doesn't boost secretarial output as much as the first one. In 1970, every time Japan increased its capital stock by 100 yen, it gained 18 yen in GDP; by 1990, the gain had fallen to only 4 yen.[9] During 1973–90 Japan needed to invest 35 percent of its GDP (business, government, and housing investment) just to get the same growth that other countries could get with 25 percent of GDP.[10]

For example, even though Japan is smaller than the United States, it has a bigger truck fleet. Why? Because, as economist Ed Lincoln points out, the average commercial truck in Japan hauls only 10 percent as many ton-kilometers of freight each year as the average American one. Some of this difference is due to geography, but much is due to poorly designed roads, congestion, and regulations on entry, exit, routes, and rates that stifle competition. Strangely, the average truck in Japan is used for only eight years, compared to fifteen in the United States, even though Japanese automakers clearly have no problem making durable vehicles. The bottom line is that Japan has to invest more money in trucks than the United States to produce every dollar's worth of GDP. Another example of gross wastage on a Soviet scale is the inexplicably huge amount of iron and steel used in construction. In the United States iron and steel in construction amount to 8 percent of construction inputs and 1 percent of total U.S. GDP, but in Japan they add up to 34 percent of construction inputs and 2.8 of total GDP. Amazing. The entire capital investment of Japan in 1997—business, government, and housing—was 30 percent of GDP. A full one-tenth of that

Table 2.1

TFP Declines as Source of Growth

	1960–70		1970–80		1980–90		1991–97	
	Contribution to Growth	Share	Contribution to Growth	Share	Contribution to Growth	Share	Contribution to Growth	Share
GDP GROWTH	10.6%	100%	4.8%	100%	3.9%	100%	1.7%	100%
Labor	1.6%	15%	1.0%	21%	0.6%	15%	–0.3%	–17%
Capital	3.4%	32%	1.3%	27%	1.9%	49%	1.4%	82%
TFP	5.5%	53%	2.5%	53%	1.4%	36%	0.6%	35%

Source: Denison and Chung 1976, p. 94, for the 1960s and 1970s; IMF 1998 for the 1980s and 1990s.

Note: TFP means "total factor productivity," as explained in the text.

Figure 2.5 **Investment Increasingly Used to Offset TFP Slowdown**

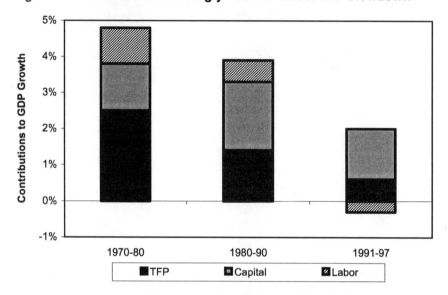

Source: Denison and Chung 1976, p. 94, for the 1960s and 1970s; IMF 1998 for the 1980s and 1990s.

Note: TFP means "total factor productivity," as explained in the text.

was simply the steel used in construction. Does that make any sense? One suspects steel was used not because it was needed but to support the steelmakers via taxpayer and consumer dollars.[11]

The result of all this waste was that it took more and more capital—factories, machines, stores, office buildings, telephone lines, and so forth—to produce each yen's worth of GDP. In 1975 it took 1.5 yen worth of capital stock to produce a yen's worth of output. By 1990 getting the same output now took 2.4 yen worth of capital. The rising capital-output ratio, in turn, meant that Japan needed to devote more and more of its GDP to investment just to prevent GDP growth from dropping. In 1981, real investment was 13 percent of GDP. By 1990, it was up to 19 percent.

Sooner or later investment-led growth was doomed to collapse of its own weight. The investment share of GDP cannot keep growing indefinitely. If investment rates merely plateaued rather than kept on rising, growth would slowly decelerate. But should investment plunge for some reason, then potential GDP growth would also plunge—even more sharply. That's exactly what happened with the collapse of the "bubble" in 1990.

Over time, Japan's excess and unproductive investment boom sowed the seeds of its own destruction. It became impossible even to sustain investment at 19–20 percent of GDP, let alone raise it further. One reason was that the decline in the productivity of investment was reflected in declining profitability (i.e., return on assets) on corporate income sheets. Second, it created a mountain of excess capacity. Japan's auto firms built up the capacity to produce fourteen million to fifteen million cars when only ten million to eleven million, including exports, could be sold. Finally, it created mountains of bad debt at the banks, since many of the investments did not earn enough to pay for themselves.

With the collapse of the bubble and the ensuing banking crisis, the government was no longer able to create the conditions that gave bad investments the illusion of profitability. At the very moment when the accelerating treadmill required even more investment, it got less. Investment abruptly plunged, and so did both demand and potential growth. A full two-thirds of the entire drop in potential growth from 3.7 percent to 1.1 percent, according to the IMF, stemmed from the collapse of investment (Figure 2.6b).[12]

That's why Japan's structural flaws led to an abrupt ratcheting down rather than a slow deceleration. Japan's demand-side and supply-side shortfalls are two sides of the same coin.

The irony is that Japan has simultaneously too much and too little investment. Too much investment for that investment to be productive, profitable, and sustainable. Too little investment to surmount declining TFP.

To really raise growth on an ongoing basis, the need is not for more investment driven by zero interest rates, but for improved TFP growth. That, in turn, requires productivity-enhancing structural reforms. The days of using investment to make up for sagging productivity are gone. Even interest rates at zero cannot bring them back.

How Fast Can Japan Grow Without Reform?

How bad will it get if Japan does not reform?

Given the poor forecasting record over the past decade, we must admit that no one really knows. However, standard estimates of Japan's long-term potential growth now range from 1 percent to 2 percent. Since Japan is now so far below full capacity, during the process of getting back to full capacity it could grow faster than its long-term potential for a while.[13]

As time goes on, estimates of long-term potential growth keep dropping. In 1994 the IMF estimated that Japan's potential growth in the late

Figure 2.6a **Full-Capacity Growth Plunges in the 1990s**

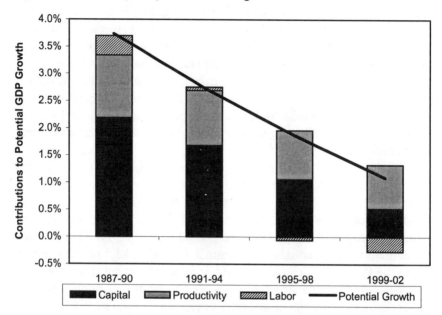

Figure 2.6b **Falling Investment Is the Biggest Cause of Falling Growth**

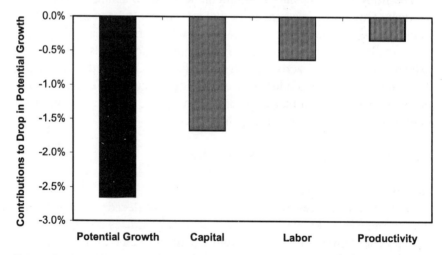

Source: Bayoumi 2000a, p. 104.

Note: Figure 2.6a shows how fast Japan could grow if it were operating at full capacity. Productivity equals total factor productivity (TFP), as explained in the text; capital equals the growth of capital stock, and labor is change in the number of workers as well as hours per worker. Figure 2.6b shows the change in potential growth and its components from 1987–90 to 1999–2002.

1990s would be about 2.5 percent. That estimate has now dropped to 1.5 percent. The Bank of Japan (BOJ) puts potential growth at 1 percent.[14]

The RAND Corporation suggests that Japan's potential growth during 2000–15 will be limited to about 1.2 percent to 1.6 percent per year.[15]

The OECD pegged Japan's potential growth during 2000–05 at about 1.25 percent. Once Japan reached full capacity, it said potential growth would rise to 1.4 percent.[16] However, the OECD went on to warn:

> If TFP does not benefit significantly from structural reform, potential growth would fall to 1 percent per year on average during the next decade or so [2000–10] and then further to around 0.25 percent to 0.75 percent thereafter. . . . Japan's per capita GDP, currently 21 percent higher than the EU average, would be 21 percent lower in 25 years.[17]

Some Japanese authorities have even more dismal forecasts, particularly over the very long haul. The Economic Planning Agency (EPA), which is now enfolded into the new Cabinet Office for Fiscal and Economic Policy, suggested that without reform, both total GDP and per capita GDP could actually *shrink* during 2005–20.[18] The Japan Center for Economic Research (JCER) warned in its 2001 forecast that without reform, GDP might grow only 0.3 percent a year during 2000–05 and then suffer essentially zero growth through 2025. However, since the JCER expects some reform and some adoption of the information technology (IT) revolution, recent long-term forecasts through 2025 have ranged anywhere from 1.0 percent a year to 2.8 percent a year—depending on the amount of reform.[19]

We do *not* expect an absolute decline in GDP, since we, too, expect Japan to adopt fundamental reforms over the coming decade. Nonetheless, the very fact that authoritative Japanese sources now seriously warn of such a possibility is an astonishing development.

The starting point for any long-term outlook is Japan's demographic crunch. During the 1980s the labor force was growing at 1 percent a year. During 2000–10 the working-age population will be *dropping* 0.5 percent a year. Thus, even if nothing else changed, an economy capable of growing at 4 percent a year during the 1980s could grow only 2.5 percent in the coming decade. But, of course, much has changed—for the worse. The capital-to-ouptut ratio is higher (which lowers growth); investment rates are lower, and TFP growth is falling.

As time goes on, the shrinking of the labor force will accelerate. Unless more women enter the workforce or retirement age is delayed, the labor force will shrink 10 percent from 2005 to 2020. By 2020 the working-age population, now at eighty-seven million, is expected to drop to seventy-four million. If current trends continue, by 2050, the working-age population will halve to fifty-four million!

What makes the demographic crunch a threat to living standards is that the labor force is falling even faster than total population. While the number of workers is plunging, the number of retirees is soaring. By 2025 the number of retirees will have doubled from fifteen million in 1990 to thirty-three million. With every passing year there will be fewer and fewer workers to support more and more retirees (Figure 2.7).

Given this demographic crunch, the only way living standards can be maintained is by a huge rise in productivity. Simple arithmetic shows why. During the next twenty years the labor force will shrink each year about 0.7 percent faster than the entire population shrinks. In that case, even if labor productivity rose 0.7 percent a year, there would still be zero growth in per capita income. Given that health care makes it more expensive to support an elderly person than a working-age person, zero growth in per capita GDP is a recipe for a substantial decline in living standards. It's also a recipe for intergenerational political conflict over shares of a dwindling pie.

Unfortunately, at the very time that Japan needs a tremendous boost in labor productivity, it instead is suffering a productivity slowdown: from 3 percent a year during the 1980s to only 0.9 percent a year in the decade ending in 2000. Only some of that decline was a statistical artifact of the long slump.

Precisely because of that productivity slowdown, the "graying" of Japan is already putting a tremendous strain on the tax and pension system. Over time the strain can only get worse.

Worse yet, a vicious cycle has set in. The demographic crunch and slowing productivity growth lowers per capita GDP growth. That low growth leads families to have even fewer children. Consequently, every time Japan does a population projection survey, the results get worse. The 1986 survey suggested that the working-age population would slowly decline to about seventy-five million people by 2050. By the 1997 survey, that projection was lowered by twenty million people. The next survey, to be completed in 2002, is expected to show even worse prospects.

Figure 2.7 **Demographic Crunch: Working-Age Cohort Plummets . . .**

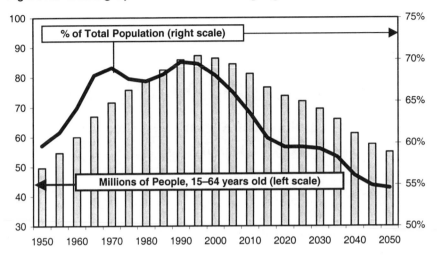

. . . While Number of Retirees Soars

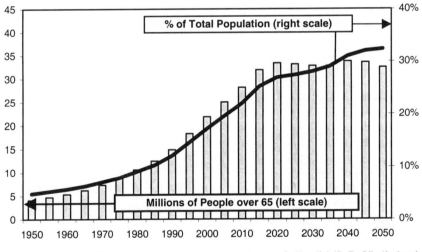

Source: Ministry of Health and Welfare, http://www.ipss.go.jp/English/S_D_I/Indip.html.

3

Overcoming the Dual Economy

Backward Sectors Are the
Key to Japan's Revival

People sometimes ask which sectors will lead Japan's revival, expecting the answer to be some high-tech area. The opposite is true. Japanese revival depends on transforming its backward sectors.

That has to be the case because the backward sectors are where most of the workers are located. A mere 20 percent of the entire Japanese labor force works in the portions of the economy that approach world standards of efficiency.[1] Large swaths of manufacturing, from food processing to materials industries such as glass and cement, lag far behind world standards. Construction and the service sector together employ twice as many workers as manufacturing (twenty-five million workers) yet offer only half the output per worker. The distribution sector employs just as many people as manufacturing, yet its productivity is one-third lower. Japan cannot improve its overall efficiency without tackling the problems of its worst-off sectors.

That's also the lesson from America's recent boom. Two-thirds of America's productivity leap came not from the "new economy" sectors, but from "old economy" sectors such as retail, banking, and "smokestack industry" as they used information technology and better organization to revolutionize themselves.[2]

The good news is that Japan's laggard sectors are so inefficient that they enjoy one of the famous "advantages of backwardness." They could improve by leaps and bounds simply by adopting world benchmark practices.

Most of Japan's food processing plants—only one-tenth the size of comparable U.S. facilities—are too small to take advantage of mass automation and other economies of scale. Japan's three biggest milk producers achieve the same level of productivity as their American counterparts, but the other milk producers, with their small-scale operations, have only half of U.S. productivity. They get away with this because milk producers find little pressure to compete. One reason is that the food processors are often linked to the politically powerful farmer cooperatives. Some fear being cut off from supplies should they undercut Japan's high farm prices.

Similar problems—seemingly amenable to easy remedies—pervade single-family home construction. Productivity is only 33 percent of U.S. levels, largely due to lack of standardization. Seventy percent of single-family houses are still built using the traditional post-and-beam method, where there can be up to 150 different dimensions instead of standard lumber sizes, such as the "2x4." In addition, poor scheduling means crews must often be tripled in the last two weeks of a job.[3]

Instead of Restructuring, Dualism Gets Worse

If serious restructuring were already occurring, then Japan's most backward sectors should have shown the most improvement. Instead the opposite occurred. Japan's dual economy has become even more dualistic.

Sectors such as machinery, already ahead of the United States in the late 1980s, showed the biggest gains in efficiency in the last decades (Figure 3.1). During 1991 through 1999, electrical machinery firms learned to produce 60 percent more output with 17 percent *fewer* workers. Conversely, the laggard sectors fell even further behind. Food industry output per man-hour actually *dropped* by 15 percent during that same period, while output per worker increased at just a snail's pace. Consequently, the food industry fell even further behind U.S. levels.[4]

If we look not just at labor productivity but at total factor productivity (TFP), the results are even more disheartening. The level of TFP in the regulated petroleum refining/coal product segment of manufacturing hit a peak in 1967 and then fell by half as of 1985. Food processing and paper production, each with low imports, hit their peak in 1973 and then fell back 25 percent and 20 percent, respectively, by 1995.[5] (The exception that proves the rule was textiles, one of the few laggards to undergo real reform, a story we'll detail below.) The overall result was a big decline in manufacturing labor productivity growth, from 4.7 percent a year in the 1980s to only 1 percent during 1991–99.[6]

Moreover, downsizing seems to have provided much of that meager productivity growth. As seen in Figure 3.2, the industries shedding workers the fastest showed the biggest hikes in labor productivity. Sheer arithmetic will show an apparent hike in average productivity if a firm merely sheds

Figure 3.1 **1980s Laggards Fall Further Behind in 1990s**

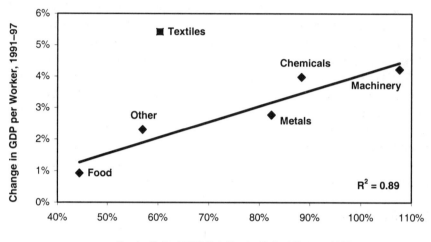

Productivity (TFP) Relative to United States, 1987

Source: Figure 3.2 for the baseline relative productivity; Cabinet Office 2001a for the growth in GDP per worker.

Note: Textiles is not included in the trend line for reasons discussed in the text. R-squared equals 0.89 means that 89 percent of the variation in productivity growth among these sectors in the 1990s can be explained by where they stood compared to the United States in 1987. Productivity growth here is measured by output per worker, whereas in Figure 3.2 the measure is output per man-hour. This sometimes gives different results for reasons discussed in the text.

its most inefficient facilities without improving the remainder. Much of the downsizing is, of course, necessary. But if downsizing is all there is, neither improvement nor growth will continue for very long.

Look who did the downsizing. It was the sectors that traditionally had shown the best productivity performance, such as machinery. In 1990, 10.3 percent of all Japanese workers labored in machinery; by 1999, that share had fallen to 8.3 percent. By contrast, the worst performers, the ones in most need of change, have done the least. Food processing actually added workers. The net result was a relative shift of workers from the most efficient sectors to the least efficient.[7]

A similar shift occurred within the economy as a whole. While four million manufacturing jobs disappeared between 1992 and 2001, public works caused the ranks of construction workers to swell by a million during 1990–98. However, as with other subsidized sectors, this level of artifi-

Figure 3.2 **Workers Shift from Efficient to Inefficient Sectors**

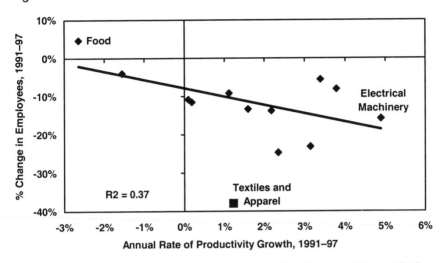

Source: Japan Productivity Center for Socio-Economic Development 2002 and Cabinet Office 2001a.

Note: The chart is based on old SNA 68 series data. We chose that because the textiles category includes apparel as well, whereas apparel is dropped out of the newer SNA 93 series. The more inclusive series is consistent with other data we use. For further explanation, see endnote 6 for Chapter 3. Textiles are not included in the trend line for reasons discussed in the text. R-squared equals 0.37 means that 37 percent of the variation in employee downsizing among these sectors in the 1990s can be explained by their relative productivity. In the United States, a similar chart would be horizontal.

cial employment became harder to maintain after the 1997–98 recession and once the mantra "No more bridges to nowhere" took hold. Half of construction's entire employment gain of 1990–98 was lost between 1998 and the end of 2001.[8]

Textiles and Trade: The Exception That Proves the Rule

The good news is that history is not destiny. Industries willing to expose themselves to the crucible of international competition can improve their performance dramatically.

During the 1990s those industries with the biggest increases in import competition also showed the most productivity improvement. In fact, among six major manufacturing sectors, there was a nearly 50 percent correlation between increased import penetration and improved output per worker. Looking at total trade, not just imports, the linkage is even stronger (Figure 3.3). The lesson is clear: If Japan wants to revive, more competing imports are

Figure 3.3 **More Trade Means More Productivity Growth . . .**

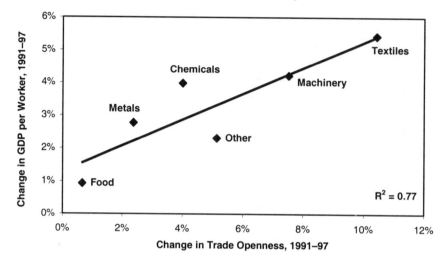

. . . And So Do More Imports

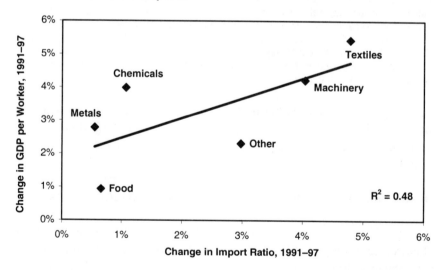

Source: Cabinet Office 2001a.

Note: In the top panel, total trade equals that industry's exports plus imports divided by its total output. The latter includes final demand plus intermediate goods. In the bottom panel, import share equals imports divided by output minus exports. In the top panel, R-squared equals 0.77 means that 77 percent of the variation in productivity growth among the sectors can be explained by the change in the ratio of trade to output. In the bottom panel, R-squared equals 0.48 has an analogous meaning.

going to have to be part of the recipe. Japan is famous for export-led growth. Now it's time for import-led growth.

This all brings us to textiles and apparel—the poster child for restructuring. In 1987 total factor productivity in textiles/apparel was only some 60 percent of U.S. levels. And yet in the 1990s the industry made huge strides, mostly by downsizing. It shed nearly half its labor force (going from 1.1 million employees to 600,000). The industry also eliminated 30 percent of its capacity between 1995 and 2001.[9]

As the industry got rid of redundant workers, output per textile employee grew 40 percent, or 5.5 percent a year. Textiles marked the single biggest improvement of any major industry in Figure 3.3.

Why did this industry do so much better than other backward sectors? At least part of the answer is the competition forced by trade.

When the yen soared following the 1985 Plaza Accords, import prices fell. As a result, in a number of industries, retailers not controlled by manufacturers began to outsource from cheaper supply bases abroad. This was particularly true in apparel. In order not to lose their markets, Japan's textile *makers* also went abroad.

In 1998 Uniqlo made headlines by importing fleece jackets from China and offering them for 1,900 yen (about $15)—half the going rate. Within two years it had sold eight million jackets. Its profits soared while those of more traditional stores suffered. It is notable that Uniqlo's owner, Fast Retailing, is an outsider. Having gotten its start in Yamaguchi prefecture years ago, it was not part of the cozy club. Since its initial success, however, Uniqlo let success go to its head, expanded too fast, and suffered drops in sales and profits starting in later 2001.[10]

As a result, there is now developing an open division on the issue of imports, with some of the smaller textile/apparel producers demanding protection but multinational producers and retailers insisting on open trade (see Chapter 10).

From 1986 through 1998 imports of textiles and apparel almost doubled as a share of household final consumption, from 19 percent to 37 percent (all in current yen).[11] As imports rose, domestic production fell. During 1986–98 textile output fell 37 percent, while the number of textile firms fell by more than half in the 1990s, from 30,000 to 14,000.[12]

Meanwhile, during the 1990s, textile prices fell 17 percent (as measured by the GDP deflator). When consumers can get cheaper fleece jackets, instead of being fleeced by monopolistic prices, both purchasing power and living standards rise.[13]

Getting Rid of Window-Sitters

One final note about textiles shows the amazing amount of disguised un-employment in Japan's backward sectors. During the 1990s, textile/apparel output per *worker* grew almost 40 percent. But, during the same period, output per worker-*hour* grew only 8 percent.[14]

Why the discrepancy? The answer is that, for a long time before the 1990s, firms had been cutting back the hours of work of each worker, but they kept redundant workers on the payroll. Finally, in the 1990s, they let the redundant workers go.

In many lagging sectors, redundant workers are kept on because Japan's rigid labor system and lack of a strong social safety net makes it harder for workers to get new jobs. Such excess workers are called window-sitters.

In textile/apparel, however, many of the window-sitters were nearing retirement age. Thus attrition did a lot of the work that would require mass layoffs in other sectors.

Is the loss of a half million jobs really progress? In a growing economy, a half million workers released from textiles are liberated to enter growing, higher-productivity sectors. Textiles and food are mature industries. Even if prices fall 20 percent due to improved efficiency, consumers will not buy 20 percent more food or clothes. But they will have a lot more money to buy mobile phones, PCs, and better housing. Conversely, if telecommunication prices go down by 20 percent, people will buy, say, 40 percent or 50 percent more in telecom services and equipment. That's why almost every country that has deregulated telecom has seen a big increase in jobs within both telecom and related equipment suppliers.

Competition: The Crucial Dividing Line

The critical line dividing light from dark in the dual economy is exposure to competition. The fiercer the competition, the higher the efficiency.

In *Japan: The System That Soured* we focused on exposure to international competitive pressures. The larger a sector's ratio of exports plus imports to industry output, the better was its productivity.[15]

A recent study of seventy-seven different industries focused on domestic competition. It was conducted by competitiveness guru Michael Porter and Mariko Sakakibara, a former METI official now teaching at UCLA's business school.[16] Industries with fierce competition are marked by a lot of fluctuation in market ranking and market share among the leaders. These industries, such as cameras and semiconductors, are efficient, and their efficiency has been rewarded with success on the export front (Figure 3.4, top panel). Now take a look at industries where a market share chart is a flat-liner, the telltale sign of cozy cooperation among oligopolies (Figure 3.4, bottom panel). In these industries, such as chocolate and polyethylene film, efficiency is poor and so is export performance.

During the 1973–90 period covered by the study, the biggest beneficiaries of import protection were these inefficient industries with weak domestic competition. Moreover, the authors found, the import protection made them even less competitive on the export front. This coheres with our findings in *Japan: The System That Soured*.[17]

A third dividing line is regulation. In general, the more regulation, the lower the efficiency.

During 1960–85, according to economist David Weinstein, TFP increased 29 percent in manufacturing but only 3 percent in the rest of the economy (Figure 3.5). In the United States, by contrast, TFP grew at more or less the same rate in manufacturing and nonmanufacturing sectors. The worst performance occurred in the most highly regulated and protected sectors: farming, construction, utilities, transportation, and communication. In farming, Japanese TFP actually *fell* 26 percent during 1960–85, compared to a 47 percent increase in the United States. In construction, Japanese TFP fell by 24 percent. Utilities hit their peak productivity in 1970 and then fell back 23 percent by 1995. In the transport/telecommunications sector, U.S. TFP grew as deregulation took hold, whereas it flattened out in Japan, except for a one-shot boost in the late 1980s. These four laggard sectors make up almost a third of the nonmanufacturing portion of the Japanese economy.[18]

Such widespread TFP declines are stunning in a modern economy. We're talking not just about slower growth but about sizeable deterioration. With each passing year the same amount of labor and capital produces less and less output. If that occurred in the economy as a whole, it would shrink. In Japan's case, the bright side of the dual economy saved it from that fate, but with less and less success. This terrible TFP performance in the dark side of the dual economy is why overall Japanese growth hit the wall.

Industrial Policy, Exports, and the Dual Economy

There is one big difference between our findings and those of Porter, Sakakibara, and a third author, Hirotaka Takeuchi, who co-wrote *Can Japan Compete?*[19] We believe that Japan's industrial policy was tremendously successful and beneficial during the 1955–73 high-growth period and only turned counterproductive beginning in the 1970s.

Figure 3.4 **Lots of Competition in Efficient Sectors . . .**

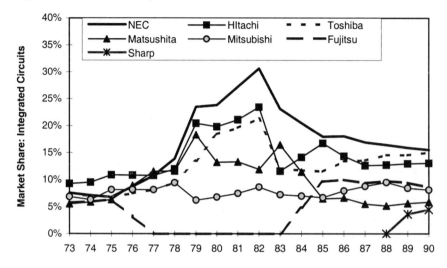

. . . But Not in the Inefficient

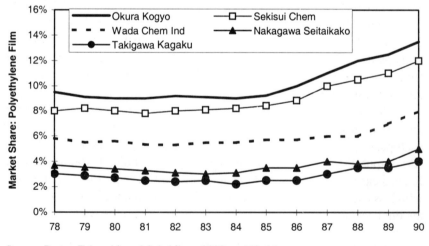

Source: Porter, Takeuchi, and Sakakibara 2000, p. 113–14.

Figure 3.5 **Regulations Stifle Japanese TFP Growth in Services**

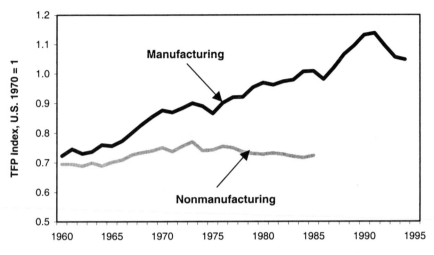

Source: Weinstein 2001b.
Note: The chart compares the level of TFP in Japanese manufacturing and nonmanufacturing to the U.S. level of 1970. It took Japanese manufacturing until 1984 to catch up to the level the United States had reached in 1970. The rest of Japan's economy never caught up even to that level.

For example, while Japan protected its backward sectors during 1973–90, it did the opposite during the high-growth era. During the 1950s and 1960s, the industries receiving the biggest import protection were, in fact, the efficient sectors that either already enjoyed comparative advantage or were gaining it. Indeed, the industries receiving the most help ended up enjoying the biggest trade surpluses a decade or two later.[20]

In an earlier book, *The Competitive Advantage of Nations,* Porter also took the view that industrial policy helped propel Japan's industrial takeoff and only became counterproductive later.[21] In the new book, by contrast, he and his coauthors argue that, even in the catch-up era, the government played a prominent role only in the inefficient industries, while it "was almost entirely absent" in competitive exporting industries like autos, machinery, materials, computer chips, and consumer electronics.[22]

This is simply inaccurate. In reality, as we documented throughout Chapter 6 of *Japan: The System That Soured,* governmental protection and promotion played a pivotal role in the takeoff of virtually every one of these industries. Japan protected the nascent car industry with stiff import quotas until 1965, and then tariffs as high as 40 percent for a few additional years. The auto industry was granted tariff exemptions on imported machinery needed to build the cars. At the same time, Tokyo gave huge subsidies to both machinery makers and their customers. Consumer electronics were also protected by quotas and then tariffs, with color TVs enjoying tariffs up to 30 percent between 1965 and 1970. The government permitted an illegal cartel in televisions, enabling the industry to charge domestic prices twice as high as the export price—a huge profit subsidy. The TV industry, in turn, was the major initial market for semiconductors, which also enjoyed direct import protection.[23]

1990s: Deflation and the Unraveling of the Dual Economy

Up till 1990 or so, it was possible for the dual economy and growth to coexist, but not afterward. One of the two had to give way. Growth lost.

Growth and dualism were compatible only as long as the efficient sectors could afford to subsidize the inefficient. By the 1990s, the need for subsidy had grown too big, while the capacity to provide that subsidy had grown too small.

For one thing, the efficient industries were a small, and dwindling, share of the entire economy—too small to carry the rest on their back.

The real coup de grâce, however, came with deflation. The price mechanism—for example, the high prices that Toyota pays for inputs—is the indispensable means by which income is covertly transferred from the efficient to the inefficient. A drop in prices means a drop in these covert subsidies. Under those circumstances, even the most shielded sectors can no longer sustain hidden unemployment without transparent subsidies from the government, whether it be public works or loan guarantees. Such transparent support being more difficult politically, job losses and bankruptcies have soared. That is one reason why the defenders of Japan's backward industries have pounded so hard on the deflation issue. (Of course, others have pounded on the deflation issue with more sincere motivations.)

The breaking point came with the 1997–98 recession. Even the previously invulnerable food industry was suddenly forced to shed 6 percent of its workforce. Overall, 2.5 million jobs disappeared in Japan from 1997 through mid-2002.

Deflation is proving to be the straw that breaks the camel's back of the dual economy. Deprived of their ability to siphon income from the efficient sectors, the inefficient cannot stand on their own. This process is analyzed in a Bank of Japan report entitled *Stagnation and Structural Adjustments of Nonmanufacturing Industries During the 1990s.*[24]

The study divides the source of profits (called "operating surplus") into three factors: increased output, higher productivity, and prices. More output (i.e., more sales) produces more profits. Enhanced efficiency will add to the bottom line even if the top line (sales) remains stagnant. As Figure 3.6 shows, there was a lot of productivity growth in manufacturing but little in nonmanufacturing. But it is the third factor, price, that unveils the parasitic relationship in the dual economy. On average, manufacturers have lowered their prices relative to their costs. That detracts from their profits. By contrast, the nonmanufacturers have—at least until 1993 or so—been able to raise their prices far more than their costs, thereby padding profits. During the period 1975–93 price hikes accounted for about *half* of the entire increase in nonmanufacturing profits.

In effect, profits are transferred from manufacturers to services via the price mechanism. The BOJ's "price factor" measures a kind of "terms of trade" among different sectors of the economy. Manufacturers pay high prices for inputs from the service sector—for example, for electricity, wholesale distribution, the use of port facilities, construction of plants, and long-distance calls—while lowering the prices of items it sells to those service sectors. This is a disguised subsidy. But that's just one layer of the onion. Japanese households pay 23 percent of their income for food—partly due to the subsidies for, and protection of, Japanese farmers. Consequently, Japanese manufacturers have to pay higher wages to their workers so that the latter can afford high food prices. That, too, is a subsidy from the manufacturers to the farmers. The wages are merely the conveyer belt.

The degree of subsidy was immense. Even though productivity performance was better in manufacturing, profits in manufacturing were 6.4 percent of sales; they were more than double that, 13 percent, in nonmanufacturing.[25]

Of course, not all the inefficient sectors lie outside of manufacturing, but that's how the BOJ data divide it.

As long as the manufacturers' productivity gains outweighed their subsidy to the nonmanufacturers, manufacturers' profits could still increase. But after 1991–92, manufacturing productivity leveled off. The price drain now outweighed any productivity increases. Besides, under new pressure to maintain profits, manufacturing firms started cutting their overhead expenses, thereby reducing their subsidy to the service sector. The price of business services peaked in 1993 and then fell by 8 percent through the year 2000.

Meanwhile, the price deflation produced by the slump weakened the service sector's bargaining power. Consequently, price gains for the nonmanufacturers stopped growing after 1993. The nonmanufacturers could

Figure 3.6 **Manufacturers Lose Ability to Subsidize Service Sector**

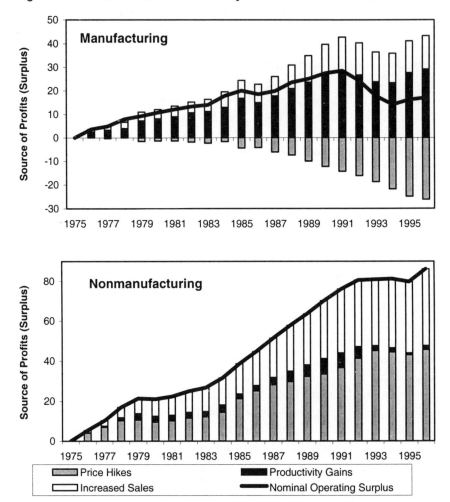

Source: Oyama 1999.

Note: 1975 is the base, so a level of 40 means that the operating surplus, or one of its components, is 40 percent higher than the level of 1975. The chart outlines how much of the profits (nominal operating surplus) comes from price hikes, improved productivity, or increased sales (output). The negative numbers for price hikes in manufacturing reflect price drops. The leveling off of price hikes in nonmanufacturing after 1993 means that prices were no longer rising.

no longer extract profit from the productivity improvements generated within manufacturing.

These data highlight the critical political point we made in Chapter 1: Japan cannot learn to live with low growth. Too many of its institutions, including debt-ridden inefficient firms, depend on a decent level of real and nominal growth for their very survival.

"Good Deflation" Stemming from Initial Reforms

Some of the inefficient sectors' loss of pricing power is the product of good developments: deregulation and globalization. In fact, looking at sectoral price trends is a fairly good indicator of how much reform has taken place. The BOJ study found the greatest price declines in sectors where globalization and deregulation had increased competition.[26]

As we'll discuss further in Chapter 4, when price drops stem from competition, that's good for growth. Such price drops add to consumer purchasing power and thus economic growth. Hence they've been nicknamed "good deflation."

Consider telecommunications, where Japanese labor productivity in the early 1990s languished at only 77 percent of U.S. levels and productivity of capital at only half the U.S. level. Long-distance phone rates fell 80 percent between 1987 and 1998 as more competitors, both Japanese and foreign, were allowed into the field. From 1990 through 2000 overall telecommunication prices—while still very high by global standards—have nonetheless fallen by almost half (see Figure 18.1 in Chapter 18).[27]

Then there is the shakeup of the distribution sector since the reform of the Large-Scale Retail Store Law *(Daiten-ho)* in the early 1990s. This, too, is a notoriously inefficient sector, with productivity at 44 percent of U.S. levels in the early 1990s. One reason is the small scale of operations. As of 1997 half of all retail stores employed only one or two people. Nearly half of all wholesalers employed four people or less. Moreover, these wholesalers did *two-thirds* of their business with *other* wholesalers. Layers and layers of unnecessary middlemen stand between maker and retailer.

This inefficiency is driven by political protection of an important voter base: the mom-and-pop operation. Until the reform, such small stores had the legal power to delay and even prevent the opening of large stores in a particular neighborhood in order to prevent "excess competition." Under the pressure of the Structural Impediments Initiative negotiations with the United States, Japan reformed that law. Once it did, both foreign and Japanese large stores, including discounters, expanded operations.

Toy prices have fallen by an estimated 20 percent since the arrival of Toys R Us, now Japan's biggest toy retailer.

Daiten-ho reform catalyzed the spread of Japanese discount stores, which used the reform to launch extensive investments—excess investments in many cases. From 1991 to 1997, sales at traditional department stores fell 12 percent while sales at "superstores" increased 25 percent.

This had several benefits. First, it weakened the power of manufacturers over retailers and thus over retail prices. For example, Toys R Us wanted to buy directly from the toy makers, outflanking the traditional middlemen. This caused great controversy at first but has now taken hold. Lewis Cohen, a Washington trade consultant who does work for Toys R Us, points to evidence from a 1994 report of the Japan Fair Trade Commission (JFTC). Before Toys R Us's entrance, 80 percent of toy retailers sold at prices equal to or above manufacturers' suggested list prices. By the mid-1990s this had dropped like a rock to only 30 percent, as Japanese retailers were forced to discount in order to compete with Toys R Us.

As this pattern spread to other product lines, whole layers of middlemen were cut out of the system, forcing wholesalers to cut prices. According to Ken Okamura, formerly the chief equity strategist at the Tokyo office of Dresdner Kleinwort Wasserstein, between 1991 and 1997 wholesale sales fell 16 percent even as retail sales increased 4 percent. Whereas it used to take 4 or even 4.5 yen of wholesale sales for every yen of retail sales, that has now fallen to a bit more than 3 yen. A lot of middlemen have been purged from the system. The number of wholesale establishments fell 15 percent, while the number of retail establishments fell 12 percent. As this process unfolded, monopolistic prices came under pressure. The price deflator for the wholesale sector has fallen 9 percent since 1990.

By contrast, in unreformed sectors, already high prices have continued to rise even further. The most notorious, not surprisingly, is construction, where prices peaked in 1998 at 17 percent above the 1990 level. In the transport sector, prices in 2000 were 12 percent above the 1990 level.

The BOJ concludes (rightly, in our opinion) that the only way out is to accelerate reform:

> [T]hese structural pressures on the non-manufacturing industry, which were partly triggered by deregulation measures, cannot be avoided if the Japanese economy is to achieve balanced growth over the long term. An ever-increasing gap in service prices between Japan and foreign countries due to the low productivity of the non-manufacturing industry will only lead to a further weakening of the manufacturing industry's competitiveness. In this sense, what the Japanese economy needs now is to expedite the process of deregulation rather than slow it down,

Figure 3.7 **Manufacturing Workforce Plummets**

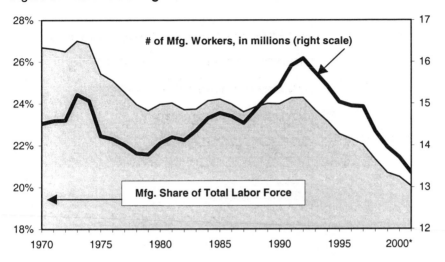

Source: For 1970–98, Cabinet Office 2000. For 1999–2001, Statistics Bureau 2002b.
Note: The Statistics Bureau numbers for 1999–2001 were adjusted by the author to make them commensurate with the Economic Planning Agency series.

and thereby motivate the non-manufacturing industry to improve its productivity in a more competitive environment and expand its business frontiers.[28]

Hollowing Out Accelerates

Given Japan's reputation as a manufacturing superpower, one of the most remarkable developments of the last decade was the complete stagnation of industrial output.

By mid-2002 industrial production was almost 10 percent *below* the 1991 peak it had reached at the end of the "bubble." The much-hyped IT boom proved to be a flash in the pan.

The number of manufacturing workers, which had peaked at 16.1 million in 1992, plunged by almost 4 million to 12.3 million as of December 2001. As a share of the total workforce, manufacturing workers fell from 24 percent in 1990 to 20 percent by 2001 (Figure 3.7).

Mostly this reflected the general economic slump. But a significant chunk of it was due to "hollowing out." Fleeing high input costs at home, Japanese manufacturers found it better to produce abroad, whether to meet domestic or foreign markets. Nippon Chemi-Con, a producer of aluminum

Figure 3.8 **Export Stars Lead Flight Abroad**

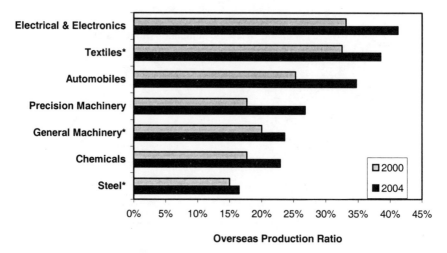

Overseas Production Ratio

Source: Japan Bank for International Cooperation 2001.

Note: The overseas production ratio is the ratio of overseas production to total production (both domestic and offshore). Hence, a ratio above 50 percent means more production is conducted offshore than at home. This is the response among eight hundred multinational companies. Data reflect actual results for fiscal year 2000 and plans for fiscal year 2004.
*FY 2003 instead of FY 2004.

electrolytic capacitors for cars and IT equipment, sends the capacitors to Washington State in the United States for part of the processing due to high electricity prices in Japan. Transport costs are less than the differential in electricity costs.

In many cases, the greatest increase in overseas production has been in industries such as autos and electronics, which used to be Japan's greatest source of exports (Figure 3.8).

Already almost 40 percent of all Japanese automobiles are made outside of Japan, up from a third in 1994.[29] In 2001 Toshiba stopped making TVs in Japan and shifted all production to China. Of the 1.5 million units to be made each year in China, 800,000 will be imported back to Japan. Aiwa, an electronics subsidiary of Sony, announced it would close all but one of its nine factories, reduce its workforce by half, and start outsourcing from other parts of Asia. Within a few years, half of Matsushita's entire global output will be produced overseas, up from about a third now.[30]

By 1999 Japanese multinational firms (MNCs)—that is, firms with at least some production overseas—produced 35 percent of their total output,

Figure 3.9 **1990s: Manufacturing Slows at Home, Soars Abroad**

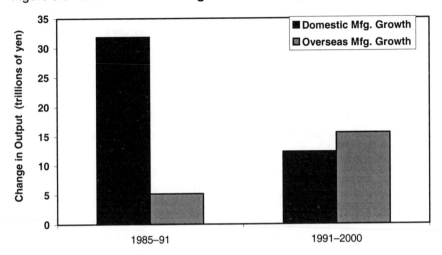

Source: Ministry of International Trade and Industry 2000.

employed 40 percent of their workers, and made 19 percent of their capital investment overseas. These figures were all double or triple the levels of the mid-1980s. By 1999 sales of these overseas affiliates outweighed exports from the home islands.

Looking at all of manufacturing, not just the MNCs, the ratio of overseas manufacturing to total manufacturing zoomed from a negligible 3 percent in 1985 to 14 percent by 1999. Indeed, in the 1990s the growth in manufacturing overseas dwarfed the minimal growth at home (Figure 3.9).

At first blush it might seem as if Japan is simply converging on global patterns. After all, America's overseas production ratio is even higher. But there is a big difference. In the U.S. case, overseas production *complemented* exports. Exports, domestic production, and sales by overseas affiliates all rose in tandem. The United States maintained its share of world exports at a high 12 percent between 1982 and 2000.

In Japan's case, by contrast, overseas production substituted for, and detracted from, both exports and domestic production. Japan's exports, which had hit a high point of 10.5 percent of world exports in 1986, when the yen was relatively low, fell to 7.5 percent by 2000 (Figure 2.3 in Chapter 2). Moreover, with every passing year, more and more of these exports go to Japan's own affiliates overseas—27 percent in 1998 compared to 13 percent in 1986.[31] Hence if we consider only exports to truly independent customers, Japan's share of the global export market has fallen even more sharply.

Japanese firms can still compete very powerfully on the global stage, but they can no longer do so from the Japanese home base. Japan's most efficient firms are being pushed out of Japan by the high cost structure at home rather than pulled out by the natural division of labor in a mature economy.

By 1996 (after which METI stopped publishing the figures), hollowing out had become a drag on domestic output. Partly this was because imports from the affiliates substituted for domestic output, and partly it was because sales by the affiliates substituted for exports from Japan. Overall, the activities of foreign affiliates subtracted 6 trillion yen from domestic manufacturing production in 1997, about 1.2 percent of GDP. Such activities also eliminated 225,000 jobs.[32]

Since many of the exiles had been Japan's most efficient industries, "hollowing out" contributed to the shift that we saw earlier: a smaller proportion of workers in the most efficient industries. Protecting glass, steel, and cement drives away autos and electronics, causing Japan to specialize in what it does worst. The whole convoy slows to the pace of the weakest boat.

—— 4 ——

Overcoming Anorexia

The Labors of Sisyphus

The past decade proved one thing: Japan can enjoy growth spurts as long as those spurts are driven by the powerful tailwinds of massive macroeconomic stimulus—budget deficits approaching 10 percent of GDP, interest rates close to zero, and an expanding trade surplus. However, Japan has a very difficult time sustaining growth once such artificial life support is withdrawn.

During 1999–2000, as in 1995–96, Tokyo repeatedly promised that injections of macroeconomic stimulus would allow it to "pass the baton" to self-sustaining, private-led growth by 2001. In line with that theory, Tokyo stopped adding to fiscal stimulus in mid-2000. It got the same result as in 1997, when it raised taxes. Once again the economy plopped back down. It did so this time after one of the weakest recoveries on record. Private demand had not even recovered its January–March 1997 peak (Figure 4.1).

Japan is suffering the worst of both worlds. On the one hand, its malady of "economic anorexia"—a chronic shortfall in domestic private demand— is worse than ever. On the other hand, the traditional macroeconomic nostrums that used to be able to counter anorexia have lost much of their punch. Worse yet, repeated use of short-term fixes has exacerbated the underlying maladies. It has left a terrible legacy of excess physical capacity and its financial mirror, a mountain of bad bank debt and government debt. In addition, near-zero interest rates have decimated what had been a major source of consumer income. These legacies act as an anchor on growth and create diminishing returns to future applications of macroeconomic stimulus. IMF economists have found that, for both fiscal and monetary stimulus, excess capacity and bad debt have reduced the "multipliers," that is, how much GDP will increase for a given amount of stimulus.[1]

No longer can massive macroeconomic stimulus make up for even more massive structural defects.

Figure 4.1 **Private Demand Still Below 1997 Peak**

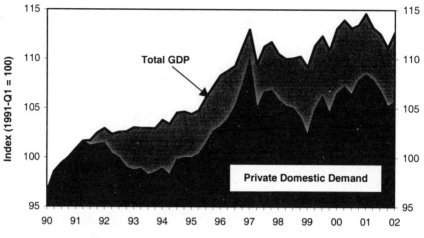

Source: Cabinet Office 2002b.
Note: Real (1995) yen.

Anemic Consumers: Lack of Wallet, Not Will

How can private growth replace stimulus-led growth unless both personal consumption and business investment rise at a sustained and healthy clip? Yet there are serious obstacles to growth on both counts.

Personal consumption, which amounts to about 55 percent of real GDP, has been flat since 1997. New housing, which used to amount to another 6 percent of GDP, has fallen 30 percent since 1990. As home construction plunges, so do sales of new refrigerators, rugs, and furniture.

There are those who put the blame on consumers too anxious or frugal to spend. However, a look at the data shows that the problem is not consumer psychology but consumer reality. Not lack of will but lack of wallet.

The ups and downs of consumer spending track the ups and downs of employee income (Figure 4.2a). As the combined compensation of all employees rose about 15 percent from 1990 to 1997, so did consumer spending. As compensation flattened after 1997, once again, so did spending. During 2001, real income of the total labor force was up a tiny 1 percent from the 1997 average; and personal consumption did a little better: 2 percent. Spending stagnated because income stagnated.

Companies have tried to improve their bottom line by cutting bonuses, wages and benefits, including moving workers to subsidiaries that pay lower

Figure 4.2a **Sluggish Consumption Caused by Sluggish Income**

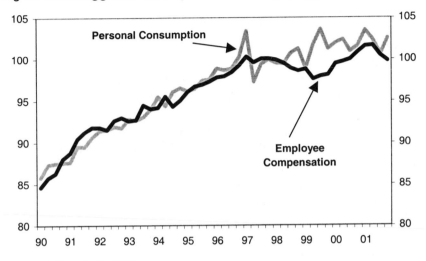

Source: Cabinet Office 2002b.
Note: Both income and consumption are in real (1995) yen.

Figure 4.2b **Real Wages Falling Again**

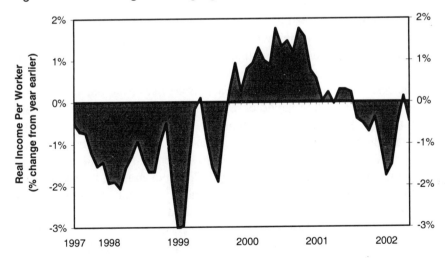

Source: Author's calculations based on Ministry of Health, Labor, and Welfare 2002a, 2002b.
"Consumer Price Index, Reference Table 2" and "Monthly Labor Survey, Table T-1."
Note: The figure is a three-month moving average.

wages. As a consequence, real wages per employee have fallen during most of the past four years (Figure 4.2b).

In a classic fallacy of composition, the effort of each firm to improve its bottom line by cutting wages ended up reducing overall consumer income. As I cut my costs, I cut your sales.

Retirees, who normally provide a good chunk of consumer spending, suffered even more than workers. When the Bank of Japan slashed interest rates to stimulate business investment, it also slashed the income of retirees and other savers. Walk into a bank and plunk down $5,000 for a ten-year certificate of deposit and all you will get is a measly 0.2 percent to 0.3 percent. A retiree with $100,000 in the bank who was getting $4,000 a year in interest income back in the early 1990s now had to make ends meet with only $200 or $300 on a ten-year CD and $60 on a one-year deposit.[2]

As a result, net interest income (receipts minus payments) plummeted, from almost 9 percent of national income during the 1980s to only 4.4 percent by 1998 (Figure 4.3).[3] It was a huge transfer of income from households to banks and their borrowers.

In the United States, a big cut in interest rates spurs a flood of housing mortgage refinancing, thus adding to consumer cash flow. But in Japan, where households save so much more than they borrow, what they have lost as savers was not made up for them as borrowers. The hit to consumer income should have been offset by permanent tax cuts. Instead, the consumption tax was raised in 1997.

It is not only current income that has come under attack. So has future income.

The zero interest rate policy (ZIRP) used to save the banks and their borrowers has wreaked havoc on life insurers and pension funds. From 1980 through 1992, life insurers guaranteed a return of around 6 percent a year on new policies. Then, as bond market interest rates and the stock market tumbled, the insurers steadily lowered their guaranteed payout, reaching a low of 1.5 percent in 2001. Indications are that it may be lowered to 0.75 percent in 2002. Currently, these reductions affect only new policies. The firms are still obliged to pay the contracted amount on policies already in force. However, the negative interest-rate spread between the benefits that the insurers are obliged to pay and what they can earn these days has sent several insurers to bankruptcy court. Once they fail, they (or their purchaser) can lower the payout rate on existing policies. In mid-2001 the Financial Services Agency announced it might recommend legislative changes that would permit life insurers to cut payout rates below the contracted amount before they go bankrupt.

Figure 4.3 **Low Interest Rates Depress Household Income**

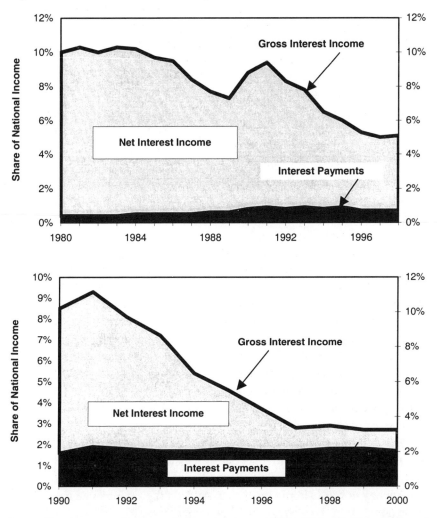

Source: For the top panel, Economic Planning Agency 1999, Table 3.2, "Distribution of National Income and National Disposable Income." For the bottom panel, Cabinet Office 2001b, Table 4.2, "National Income and Its Uses."

Note: All figures are current yen, share of national income. The top panel (covering 1980–98) is based on the old SNA 68 database. The bottom panel (covering 1990–2000) is based on the new SNA 93 database but does not go back before 1990. There are big discrepancies in the two series in terms of absolute numbers but not the trend.

Either way—insurer bankruptcy or a de facto default on the contract—policyholders face a good chance of not receiving the retirement income they were counting on and for which they paid so much.

Not surprisingly, then, households have fled in droves. The value of life insurance policies in force plunged 17 percent from a peak of 1.58 quadrillion yen ($1.27 trillion) as of March 1997 to 1.31 quadrillion yen ($1.05 trillion) as of March 2001.[4]

Meanwhile, 1,800 corporate pension funds with combined assets of 55 trillion yen ($443 billion) suffer similar problems. As of March 2001, these pension funds suffered an unfunded liability of about 8 trillion yen ($64 billion). Accounting rule changes enacted in fiscal 2000 require corporations to list such unfunded liabilities on their balance sheet. This lowered corporate profits in the affected firms by 35 percent in 2000. In fiscal 2000, a record 29 corporate pension funds simply dissolved, the fourth consecutive year of double-digit dissolutions.[5]

In response to these pressures, the government changed the rules in 1997, allowing firms to cut already-promised payouts in their defined-benefit plans. Sixteen funds did so in 1998, 52 in 1999, and 177 in 2000—all with the approval of their labor unions (as required by law). Given a choice between losing their job or losing part of their future income, workers have chosen the latter.

With almost a third of total household financial assets tied up in life insurance and pension plans, these hits to future income loom quite large.

Then there are rising premiums for the national medical and health insurance programs (which we'll detail below). Such premium hikes cut into disposable income.

Given all this, the wonder is that consumer spending is not even weaker. If it were really true that anxious consumers were refusing to spend money that they have, evidence of this should show up in a higher savings rate. The money doesn't simply disappear. And yet the savings rate has actually gone down: from an average of 14 percent in the early 1990s to around 10 percent since 1997 (Figure 4.4).

A recent lunch conversation in Tokyo illustrates that what everybody "knows" sometimes just isn't so. One of the dozen Japanese businessmen in attendance said that demand was low because Japanese were afraid to spend and already owned everything they needed. Tax cuts wouldn't work because they would just put any extra money into savings. Just about everyone agreed. Then I asked them about their own personal experience. Were they individually saving at a higher rate than ten years ago? All but one—the exception being a professional financial manager—laughingly

Figure 4.4 **Savings Rates Go Down, Not Up, in Recent Years**

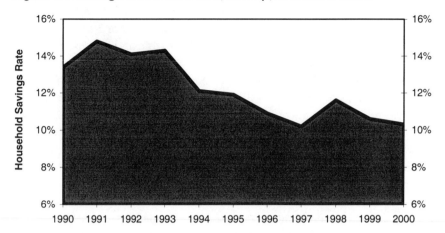

Source: Cabinet Office 2001b, Table 2.5. "National Disposable Income, Households."
Note: The household savings rate is household savings divided by household disposable income.

admitted that they spent what they needed to on household needs. If anything was left over, they saved it. And yet, having read the newspapers, they all believed that they were the exception.

Investment Cannot Lead the Recovery

In 1999–2001, as in 1995–96, business investment experienced a temporary boomlet. But, as in the previous instance, it eventually collapsed of its own weight. As of 2001, total business investment had yet to regain the peak it first reached ten years earlier. Rather than still more investment, what Japan really needs is a big reduction of excess capacity. While there may be some new investment in certain areas, such as IT, this will be offset by reduced investment elsewhere.

Manufacturers, operating way below capacity and more sensitive to cost pressures than other sectors, have already reduced capacity by 5 percent from its 1997 peak. Other industries will join them.

Japan faces the classic problem of the "liquidity trap." Why would auto or steel companies facing the burden of 30 percent too much equipment lying around go even deeper into debt to build even more useless capacity just because interest rates are low? The biggest obstacle to current investment is the excess of past investment.

Falling asset prices also limit new investment. During the late-1980s bubble, when a building could be built for, say, $50 million and then sold for $100 million to someone who in turn could sell it for $150 million, it paid to erect lots of buildings festooned with marble and ornaments. Floor space increased a whopping 50 percent between 1986 and 1990. But once prices plummeted—the same building could now be sold for only $40 million today, and perhaps $30 million tomorrow—developers retreated. As of 1999, construction of buildings was 34 percent below the 1990 level. The government's Price Keeping Operations, which prevent stock and real estate prices from hitting bottom, only prolong the pain. Buyers hold back since they can never feel confident that another ratchet downward isn't just around the next corner.

As we noted in Chapter 3, decreased business investment was the single biggest factor in anemic demand during the lost decade. Since the investment slump was primarily caused by structural factors—excess capacity, excess debt, and falling asset prices—business investment has been, according to the IMF, far less responsive than is normal to cuts in the real interest rate.[6] The scenario of an investment-led recovery is a chimera.

In this area, as in so many others, Japan suffers the worst of both worlds. Its investment is not growing fast enough to fuel self-sustaining recovery. And yet it is still so high that firms continue adding to capacity, making the excess even greater. *Net* investment—the amount of investment above and beyond that needed simply to replace worn-out buildings and machines—added up to 5 percent of GDP in 2001. While that is down from net investment of 10 percent of GDP a decade earlier, it's still too much to be profitable or sustainable.[7]

By 1998, the ratio of capital stock (factories, machinery stores, office buildings, public infrastructure, and housing—but not land) to GDP had risen to a record high of 2.9. Thirteen percent of this is excess (Figure 4.5a). For companies to work off all their excess, they'd have stop every yen of investment for eight months (Figure 4.5b).[8]

Automakers have the capacity to build 14–15 million vehicles a year. Yet not since 1993 have they sold as many as 11 million units, domestic sales and exports combined. These days, sales are closer to 10 million. Now factor in that two-thirds of the auto industry's market is overseas, and that this market is increasingly being reached via overseas production instead of exports. In fact, exports in the year 2000 (4.4 million) were down about a third from the 1985 peak (6.7 million). The industry will never sell anything close to 15 million units. But only recently have automakers begun reducing capacity, as the firms with the highest level of

Figure 4.5a **Excess Capacity Mounts . . .**

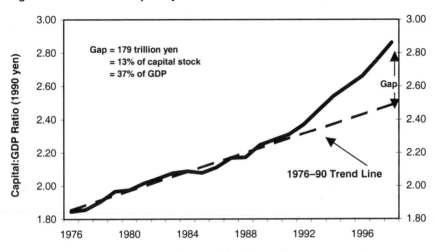

Source: Cabinet Office 2000, Table 6.1 "Net Fixed Assets."

Note: Capital stock is measured by net fixed assets excluding land. Capital stock includes all sectors: business, government, and households. Net fixed assets, given in nominal yen, were deflated using the deflator for gross fixed capital formation. All data are in 1990 yen.

Figure 4.5b **. . . Including in Business Sector**

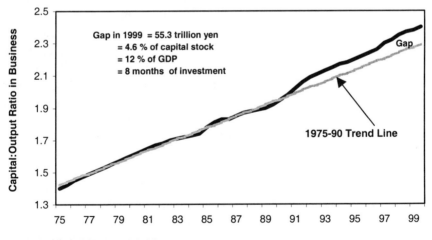

Source: OECD 2000b, p. 34–35.

Note: This chart measures the ratio of capital stock to potential output in the business sector alone.

foreign management—Nissan (controlled by Renault), Mazda (controlled by Ford), and Mitsubishi (heavily influenced by Daimler-Chrysler)—announced plans to close some domestic plants.[9]

Then there is integrated steel. While steelmakers can produce over 110 million tons a year, not once in the past two decades have they sold more than 80 million tons. As of 2001, capacity was down a mere 5 percent from the 1996 peak. After all, with imports kept to only 7 percent of domestic consumption, the steel oligopoly can offset low volume by charging monopolistic prices in the home market while matching the market abroad. Political scientist Mark Elder reports that for hot-rolled coil, a widely used steel product, the Japanese domestic price was twice the Japanese export price in 1998. For hot-dipped galvanized steel, the domestic price was 37 percent higher than the Japanese export price. Why do automakers and other big buyers tolerate monopolistic prices despite their own financial strains? Because, as Elder points out, they see this as the price of membership in a system that gives them nonmarket edges: from inspections that force Japanese consumers to buy new cars more often than their American counterparts to exclusive dealership arrangements that limit competition.[10]

How about retail? Once again we find the odd combination of falling sales and rising capacity. Since 1997 same-store sales at large stores have been falling at a 3–4 percent annual clip. Yet, propelled by the drive for market share and protected by their banks against failure, these retailers kept expanding floor space at a 5–6 percent rate since 1993. But, even in Japan, the law of gravity eventually prevails. The past couple years have seen multibillion-dollar bankruptcies and near-bankruptcies of such industry giants as Sogo, Daiei, Seiyo (a real estate branch of the Seibu retail conglomerate), and Mycal. Perhaps that is why, in the year 2000, the pace of expansion finally slowed to 1 percent. In 2001, supermarkets finally reduced floor space for the first time, albeit by a miniscule 0.5 percent.[11]

Thus, when it is alleged that the Bank of Japan can engender an investment boom just by expanding the monetary base, we have to ask: Exactly what industries are supposed to do all this investing?

True, via zero interest rates and the IT hype, Tokyo temporarily drove corporate investment back up to 17.4 percent of GDP in the year 2000 (Figure 4.6). But an economy with a growth rate of only 1–2 percent, not to mention a shrinking labor force, cannot profitably use all the new capacity created by so much investment. This rate is "more appropriate for an economy whose trend growth is 4 per cent per year than 1," in the words of the OECD. By early 2002, investment was back down to 15 percent. Sooner or later, investment will have to settle down to something more like 13–14

Figure 4.6 **Investment Rate Falls, but Still Unsustainably High**

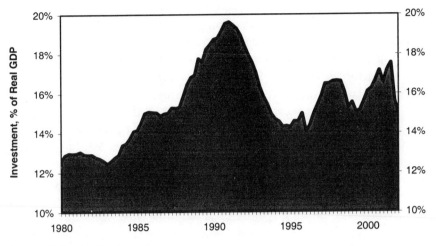

Source: Cabinet Office 2002b.

percent of GDP, according to Robert Feldman, chief economist at Morgan Stanley Dean Witter's Tokyo office.[12]

Sooner would be better than later. To the degree that firms keep piling on new investments, we must surmise that, despite ostentatious hymns at the altar of profitability, managers are still fixated on market share, herd instinct ("we've got to get into IT because everyone else is"), and the presumption that, in the end, the government and banks will somehow rescue them from their own folly. That just sets Japan up for more excess capacity and bad debt, leading to another round of collapsing investment and economic downturn.

Stimulative policies that hinge on investment-led growth are doomed to fail. Japan needs to shift to consumer-led demand. That's a big part of structural reform.

Anorexia Index Plunges to Record Low

In a healthy economy, temporary slumps in consumption and investment gradually work themselves out. Why, then, are they so intractable in Japan? The reason is that they are part and parcel of a chronic shortfall in demand we have termed "economic anorexia." In other words, Japan cannot consume all it produces.

By 1998, Japan's "anorexia index"—our measure of the shortfall in private demand—had plunged to an astounding −13 percent of GDP (Figure 4.7a). Had this shortfall not been offset by government demand and external demand—that is, a total budget deficit at nearly 11 percent of GDP plus a trade surplus of about 2.5 percent of GDP—then Japan's deep recession would have turned into Depression (Figure 4.8).[13]

What we call "anorexia" is what the textbooks call "excess savings," or the "investment-savings gap," or the "paradox of thrift." Too much savings equals too little spending. Hence, for an economy to operate at full capacity, one person's savings must be balanced by someone else's spending. Otherwise, total demand in the economy does not keep up with total supply. Usually it is business borrowing to finance investment that balances household savings. However, if businesses and individuals all try to hike their savings, i.e. cut their spending, at the same time, then the economy sinks into recession.

Naturally, then, in investigating Japan's stagnation, analysts ask who is saving too much. Many mistakenly point the finger at consumers. Yes, households did temporarily tighten their belts a bit in 1998, but nowhere near enough to account for Japan's deep downturn (Figures 4.4 and 4.7b).

The real rise in savings—and commensurate drop in spending—came from Japan's corporate sector. Look at the area of Figure 4.7b labeled "Net Corporate Borrowing to Invest." In 1998 this figure plunged from 2 percent of GDP to −5 percent. That swing represents a drop in demand equal to 7 percent of GDP. That is the primary source of the downturn.

Just like households, businesses save. Business saving equals cash flow, that is, the sum of retained profits and depreciation. Most capital investment is financed by that internal cash flow. Normally, however, that does not suffice. Companies need to borrow additional money.

In the late 1990s this changed. Firms cut investment so much that they had little need to borrow. On the contrary, in 1998, for the first time on record, Japan's corporations became net savers—to the tune of 5 percent of GDP. They had much more free cash flow than they could invest.

How does this square with all the reports of debt-strapped firms facing bankruptcy?

That is precisely the "paradox of thrift." Debt-ridden firms cut expenses (such as wages and investment) to hoard cash, commercial paper, and so forth. But what makes sense for each firm by itself turns into disaster when everyone does it at the same time. Each firm's cutback in spending hurts the sales of other firms, leading to even more belt-tightening and cash hoarding in a vicious cycle.

Figure 4.7a **"Anorexia Index" Plunges . . .**

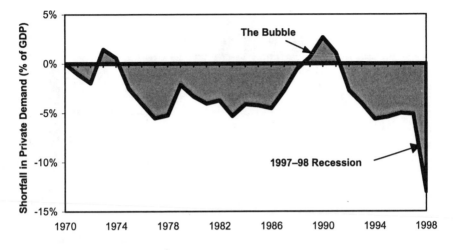

Figure 4.7b **. . . As Firms Become Net Lenders Instead of Borrowers**

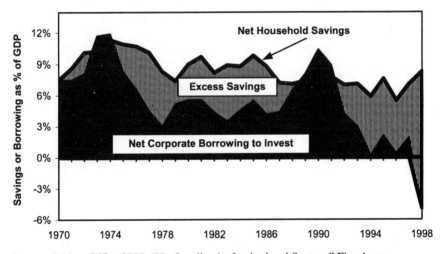

Source: Cabinet Office 2000, "Net Lending by Institutional Sectors." Fiscal year.

Note: The "shortfall in private demand" in Figure 4.7a equals the "excess savings" in Figure 4.7b. See text for further explanation. The figure goes only to 1998 because it is based on the old SNA 68 system. The newer SNA 93 data do not go back before 1990 and show large discrepancies from SNA 68.

Figure 4.8 **Budget Deficit Explodes to Prevent Depression**

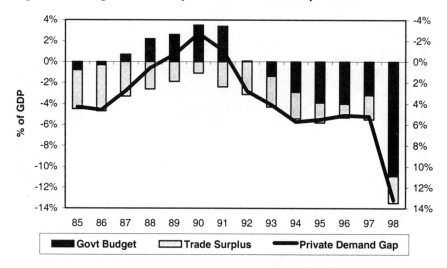

Source: Cabinet Office 2000, "Net Lending by Institutional Sectors." Fiscal year.

Note: As anorexia worsened in the 1990s, the budget balance changed from a surplus to an ever-larger deficit. The trade surplus expanded somewhat but never again became as large as in the mid-1980s.

The solid black line (measured on the left-hand scale in the chart above) is the same as the "anorexia index" in Figure 4.6a. It measures the "excess savings" or shortfall in private demand, as explained in the text. A negative figure means a shortfall in private demand; a positive figure, as in the "bubble," means an excess of private demand.

The budget deficit and trade surplus are measured on the right-hand scale. Both a budget deficit and the trade surplus are represented as positive numbers since they add to demand. The solid black bar is the government budget balance. A bar above the zero axis represents a budget surplus (as in the late 1980s), which detracts from demand. A descending bar means a budget deficit. The gray bar is the trade balance. A descending bar means a trade surplus.

Even in the investment resurgence of 1999–2000, corporations were careful not to invest an amount greater than their internal cash flow. That's why bank loans are falling so much (Figure 7.4a in Chapter 7). Solvent firms are reducing their bank debt, not borrowing more to finance investment.[14]

The Structural Roots of Anorexia

As with many of Japan's current maladies, the source of anorexia is sticking with economic patterns that made sense in the high-growth era but no longer do.

Japan's miraculous 10 percent annual growth rate from 1955 to 1973 was driven by high rates of corporate investment that, in turn, required equally high levels of savings. Some of this savings came from households, but even more originated in corporate cash flow. In fact, virtually the entire *increase* in private savings as a share of GDP, from 16 percent in 1955 to 30 percent in 1970, came from increased corporate savings.[15]

With investment and savings roughly balancing each other, the economy was in macroeconomic balance.

The situation changed dramatically once Japan matured in the mid-1970s. GDP growth halved to 4 percent. Consequently, the need to expand capacity slowed and total corporate investment in plant, equipment, land, and inventories fell from 24 percent of nominal GDP in 1960–73 to 15 percent after 1975—except during the bubble (Figure 4.9).

All would have been well if national savings had dropped proportionally—that is, if reduced business investment had been replaced by increased personal consumption as in most countries at this stage of development. But that did not happen.

The household savings rate did drop in Japan, just as it does in other countries as they reach maturity. From 22 percent of household income in the mid-1970s, it fell to 15 percent in the 1980s and 13 percent in the 1990s. As a share of GDP, household savings fell from 11 percent of GDP in the mid-1970s to 8 percent in the 1980s and 7 percent in the 1990s.

What made Japan unusual was that companies kept raking in as much cash flow as in the high-growth era—as much as 12–14 percent of GDP. The combination of high cash flow and reduced investment meant that business borrowing steadily dropped—from 10 percent of GDP in the early 1970s to 5 percent in the 1980s and 2 percent during 1992–97, and then businesses became net savers (look again at Figure 4.7b). There was no longer enough business borrowing and investing to absorb even reduced levels of consumer saving.

In a typical year, the gap between what households saved and what companies could profitably use—the so-called investment-savings gap—ranged as high as 4–5 percent of GDP. That is the size of anorexia, as measured by our "anorexia index" in Figure 4.7a.

The only lasting solution would be for personal consumption to rise to take the place of decreased investment demand, as in other countries.[16] Instead, the opposite happened. Consumption kept falling from 60 percent of price-adjusted GDP in the early 1960s to 55 percent in the 1980s and 1990s (Figure 4.10). In a typical rich country, the average is more like 60 percent. In the United States, it's about 66 percent.

Figure 4.9 **Investment Rate Drops with the End of High-Growth**

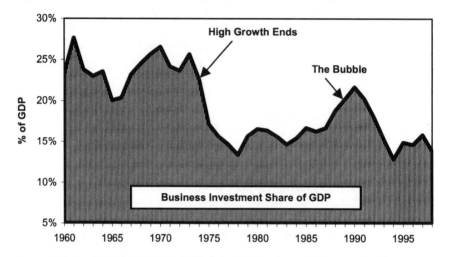

Source: Cabinet Office 2000, Table 2.2.1 "Capital, Nonfinancial Corporations."

Note: Business investment includes plant and equipment, land, and inventories. This is based on nominal yen, whereas Figure 4.5 is based on price-adjusted yen. The figure is a three-year moving average.

Figure 4.10 **Consumption Fails to Rebound with Maturity**

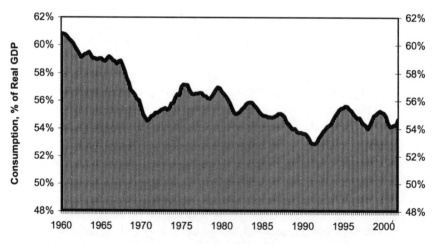

Source: For 1960–79, Cabinet Office 2000; for 1980–2001, Cabinet Office 2002b.

Note: All data are in 1995 yen. The data for 1960–79 (originally in 1990 yen) were converted to 1995 yen by the author.

Japan's consumption shortfall is the heart of anorexia. The problem was *not* that the consumption-to-GDP ratio fell in the 1960s. On the contrary, as in other newly industrializing countries, it had to fall to make room for the investment boom that propelled industrial takeoff. The problem was the failure of the consumption share to rebound once the industrial takeoff was complete.[17]

Too Little Income Means Too Little Spending

All this just begs the question of why the consumption rate in Japan didn't rebound. The reason is that people can't spend what they don't earn. Shifting to consumer-led growth requires an increase in the household share of national income. That is achieved via sufficient hikes in inflation-adjusted wages, dividends, and interest. In producer-oriented Japan, this customary shift never happened. The same cartelization and protective regulations that stifled productivity also led to sky-high consumer prices. That, in turn, limited the growth of real consumer income.

Indeed, once we adjust for Japan's monopolistic prices, total household income is a smaller share of national income today than two decades ago (Figure 4.11). Real income certainly increased a great deal in absolute terms. However, as a share of real GDP, household income fell from 65 percent in the early 1980s to less than 58 percent in 2000—a fall equal to 7 percent of GDP. While perhaps a quarter of this fall was due to a wage squeeze, by far the majority of the fall was caused by the failure of households to get anything close to a fair return on their savings.

Compare Japan to a company. If Microsoft earns a 25 percent return on assets (ROA), it can plow these profits back into the company to expand assets by 25 percent. That's because its sales are also growing 25 percent. Stockholders willingly forgo dividends because the value of their shares will skyrocket along with sales and profits. Now take a mature firm such as GM. Sales growth is, at best, only a few percent a year. If GM tried to plow a 25 percent ROA back into the firm, it could only do so by making grossly unproductive investments. ROA would plummet and so would the stock price.

The capital markets compel GM to return most of its profits to shareholders, bondholders, and bank depositors. Households can then use these proceeds in two different ways. They can invest in new, more profitable companies. This process steadily shifts capital from low-return firms and industries into higher-return ones, helping supply-side productivity. Or the households can spend the earnings on consumption. This improves aggregate demand.

Figure 4.11a **Falling Household Share of National Income**

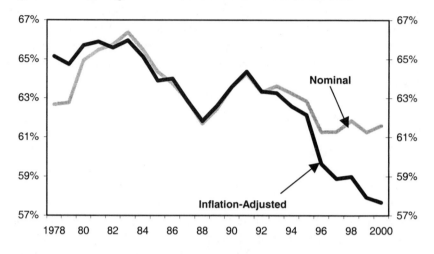

Figure 4.11b **Real Wage Share of GDP Fell**

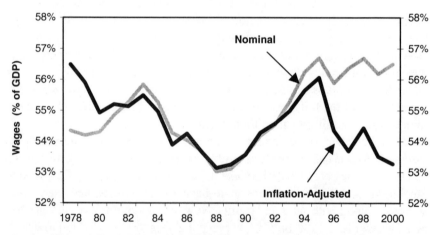

Source: Cabinet Office 2000 for 1978–98; Cabinet Office 2001b for 1999–2000. The 1999–2000 data (SNA 93) were adjusted by the author to make them commensurate with the 1978–98 data (SNA 68).

Note: Wages includes all employee compensation, including bonuses and fringe benefits. All are in 1990 yen.

In Japan, however, nothing forces firms to return their excess cash flow to the household savers/investors. Due to the cross-shareholding system, dividends are negligible (see Chapter 15). Meanwhile, interest rates, regulated until the early 1990s, were deliberately kept below the rate of inflation in order to subsidize business investment. For almost the entire post–World War II era, the inflation-adjusted return on consumer savings was *negative.*

The cumulative wealth lost by households added up to an astonishing one-third of everything they saved between 1970 and 1998, according to Albert Ando of the University of Pennsylvania. While households saved a total of 1,250 trillion yen (about $11.4 trillion in 1990 prices) during those three decades, the cumulative increase in their net worth was only 860 trillion yen. Where did the other 390 trillion yen ($3.4 trillion) go? Much of that was a disguised transfer to the corporate sector. Between 1995 and 1998 inflation-adjusted household net worth actually fell. There is much talk about the "wealth effect" of the stock market in explaining why Americans consume so much. Ando suggests that a wealth destruction effect helps explain why Japanese consume so little.[18]

The bottom line: Household spending is too low, not because households save too much, but because they earn too little.

How Did Japan Manage to Grow?

If we're right that Japan has been anorexic since the mid-1970s, then how did it manage to grow 4 percent a year between 1975 and 1990? What sources of demand substituted for investment and consumption? Why can't it still grow?

As we detailed in Chapter 8 of *Japan: The System That Soured,* during the 1970s and 1980s Japan was able to use a variety of artificial stimulants.

In the 1970s the key was a rising budget deficit and a rising trade surplus. The budget deficit rose to a height of 5.5 percent of GDP by 1978 and accounted for about 17 percent of all GDP growth during the period 1974–79. A rising trade surplus accounted for about 40 percent of all GDP growth from 1973 to 1977.

In the early 1980s, when the U.S. trade deficit soared, Japan was able to cut its budget deficit while relying on a still-growing trade surplus to feed demand. By 1985–86 Japan's budget deficits turned into balance while the trade surplus rose to a record 4.5 percent of GDP. Once again, a rising trade surplus accounted for 40 percent of all GDP growth.

Then came the Plaza Accord of 1985, which sent the yen soaring. Japanese exports were priced out of the market and the trade surplus began to shrink, falling to less than 1 percent of GDP by 1989.

As the trade surplus and budget deficit kept shrinking in the late 1980s, Japan needed an alternative source of demand. The famous Maekawa Commission of 1986 recommended reforms that would shift the economy to consumer-led growth. Instead, Japan's leaders used monetary steroids to promote private investment as a kind of disguised public works, thereby inadvertently creating the "bubble." Private investment soared to nearly 20 percent by 1991, an even higher investment rate than in the high-growth era. The rise in private investment accounted for 40 percent of all GDP growth in 1975–91 and wiped out the investment-savings gap (see again Figure 4.7b).

Because so much of this investment had little economic value, its legacy was excess capacity, unpayable debts, and intractable economic stagnation.

Today, Japan is like a drug addict who needs ever-bigger doses just to get the same hit. No dose will ever be big enough. It's time for reform.

Don't Raise the Floor, Lower the Ceiling

Understanding anorexia makes it clear why Japan's macroeconomic stimulus efforts have failed. There are only two ways to erase the gap between private investment and savings: either lower excess business savings or raise business investment. Japan has repeatedly tried the latter, most recently with the zero interest rate policy. It's time for the former: getting rid of excess business savings in order to raise household consumption.

Real reform would induce firms to return their excess cash flow to the household savers via reform of corporate governance and finance. (We'll discuss how to do this in Part Four.) Real reform would bring down high consumer prices by cartel-busting and deregulation.

Poor corporate governance is a macroeconomic issue in Japan. To fix poor demand, Japan must fix its corporate and financial system. Ando reaches the same policy conclusion:

> The liquidity trap [argument for monetary ease as a means of stimulating more investment], however, presupposes a very low level of investment as the basic cause of a recession. In Japan, on the other hand, investment appears to be too large if anything and it is the deficiency of spending by households that is the basic problem. This in turn appears to be caused at least partly by hoarding of resources by business firms rather than distributing them to households. . . . The [proper] policy package must include the means of inducing business firms to

distribute more of their cash flow to households, and this would involve serious structural reforms.[19]

One reason for wrongheaded policies is that real reforms would undermine vested interests. A second reason is that anorexia is simply not understood very widely, even among many would-be reformers. Instead, they exhort consumers to spend more while, as we'll see immediately below, taking away their means of doing so.

"Reforms" That Make a Bad Situation Worse

Many policies being conducted in the name of reform, or as a supposed unavoidable response to aging, actually worsen anorexia.

In 1997 Japan raised the consumption tax from 3 percent to 5 percent, thereby triggering its worst recession to date. There is now talk among the Ministry of Finance (MOF), the Ministry of Health, Labor, and Welfare (MHLW), and some on the Koizumi team about raising it again as soon as the economy is strong enough, gradually bringing it to 11 percent, or higher, by 2010.[20]

Meanwhile, public pension premiums are to be lifted from the current 17 percent of salaries to at least 20 percent, perhaps 24 percent, in 2004. Half of these premiums are paid by employers and half by employees.

In addition, the medical care "reforms" passed by the Diet in the spring of 2002 raise the premium for workers in small and midsize companies from 7.5 percent of their annual income to 8.2 percent. At the same time, the out-of-pocket burden for medical costs is being raised from 20 percent to 30 percent for those under age seventy. The actual amount involved so far is a tiny $40 a year since the ceiling for co-payments is so low. However, politically, this is the proverbial camel's nose in the tent toward larger hikes down the road. While much of the LDP and the doctors' lobby oppose the co-pay increases, arguing that this would reduce visits, their alternative is to raise insurance premiums.

Put it all together and consumers face imminent tax and premium hikes that will cut disposable income drastically.

The first step in this process was scheduled to take place in fiscal 2003 as hikes in health care and pension premium hikes take another 2.5 trillion yen ($20 billion) a year out of the pockets of workers and employers starting in fiscal 2003. This adds up to an effective *permanent* tax hike of 0.5 percent of GDP—a considerable drag on growth in a weak economy. As of this writing, Tokyo was planning to briefly offset this by a *temporary* tax cut ranging from 1 trillion to 2.5 trillion. However, while the majority of the premium hikes come out of consumers' pockets, the lion's share of the planned tax cuts will go to the companies (see more on this in Chapter 19). Meanwhile, beginning in fiscal 2003, the government planned to start *reducing* pension benefits linked to the consumer price index on the grounds that consumer prices have fallen. Put it all together and even more money is being indirectly transferred from consumers to firms.

This is just the beginning. Further hikes in consumer taxes, fees, and premiums are expected in coming years.

Yet, says Tokyo, they are unavoidable. With fewer workers to support more aged, how else can social security and health care be paid for? It already costs 10 trillion yen ($80 billion) a year just to support health care for those over seventy. That cost is going to soar in the coming decade and someone has to pay for it.

Even reformers have bought into this line, acting as if being "responsible" equals willingness to inflict more belt-tightening on an already beleaguered population. The opposition Minshuto party has proposed lowering the minimum income required to pay income taxes—in other words, a tax hike on the lower middle class. Then they wonder why they lose elections. LDP reformer Yasuhisa Shiozaki argues that the "only" solution to Japan's pension and social security crisis is to lower the benefits and raise the premiums.

But, as we'll detail in Chapter 14 (p. 202), this is yet another case of "what everybody knows just ain't so." What has turned a difficult pension burden into an outright crisis is not aging, but poor returns on investment.

As for health care, before raising premiums, why not lower costs? The Koizumi administration talks of lowering payouts to providers by 2 or 3 percent, but, as we'll detail in Chapter 18, that hardly scratches the surface of the incredible inefficiency and overcharging in the health field. With health care expenditures at 8 percent of GDP, lowering costs would be a truly significant part of curing anorexia.

The Koizumi approach on this front is not reform. It is instead a recipe for worsening anorexia.

5

The Banking Crisis
Dead Firms Walking

In the former Soviet Union, a crisis of the system looked like droves of people waiting in line for hours only to find nothing on the shelves. In the United States, a crisis appeared as simultaneous 13 percent inflation, 20 percent interest rates, and 10 percent unemployment. In Japan, it's a bank debt crisis.

Japan's banks have been used as a kind of public utility, forced to keep rolling over loans at ultracheap rates to insolvent firms so as to avoid mass unemployment. Seventeen percent of all loans carry an interest charge under 1 percent, 7 percent less than 0.5 percent—hardly enough to pay the clerks who collect the cash and count it.[1]

When firms cannot pay even these rates, they get debt forgiveness—if they're big enough. In January 2002 Prime Minister Koizumi pressured the banks to give retailing giant Daiei yet another bailout, including debt forgiveness of 400 billion yen ($3.2 billion), on the explicit grounds that a firm employing a hundred thousand people is too big to fail. What such arguments miss is that, in the United States, IBM laid off twice that number, thereby saving the jobs of the rest.

The root of the problem is not the nonperforming loans (NPLs) alone but the nonperforming borrowers (NPBs) behind each loan—firms that cannot afford their interest bills even at today's superlow interest rates. Sixteen percent of all corporate debt is owed by such firms (see p. 90).

As of March 2002, the total official figure for nonperforming loans at all lenders (not just the banks) added up to 52.4 trillion yen ($422 billion). That's more than 10 percent of GDP. Overall problematic bank debt—which includes loans still being serviced on time, but where the borrower is shaky—is commonly estimated at around 100 trillion yen ($806 billion).

That's 20 percent of GDP. No other populous rich country has ever had a banking crisis approaching that magnitude.

In the United States, at the height of the banking and savings-and-loan crisis of the early 1990s, NPLs added up to about 5 percent of GDP, and ultimate losses ended up totaling less than 2 percent of GDP.

To really solve the banking crisis, Japan would have to foreclose on the bad borrowers. As in any bankruptcy, some firms would be reorganized, others liquidated. Three to four million people, 5–7 percent of the labor force, would lose their jobs, not even counting multiplier effects (see details below).

Rather than getting ready to offset this political and social cost, Tokyo prefers denial, delay, and dithering. It minimizes the size of the problem. When it does move, it acts as if the problem were mere numbers on the books of the banks. Change the numbers and you erase the problem. Thus in March 1999, as Japan was in the midst of spending 26.5 trillion yen ($226 billion)—5 percent of GDP—to bail out the banks, Tokyo promised the world that "Japan's banking crisis is over."[2]

Yet by early 2002 another dose of government money was no longer a question of if, but only a matter of when and under what conditions. Unfortunately, as of this writing, it looks as if another futile bailout is more likely than a real solution to the borrower problem.

What Tokyo fails to recognize is that, until it addresses the bad-borrower problem, the banking crisis will keep coming back again and again—even bigger each time. New bad debt keeps rising even faster than old bad debt is disposed of. The bad debt is not a legacy of the "bubble," as Tokyo says; most of it arose in the decade after the bubble popped.

While Koizumi talks of biting the bullet, his plans are limited to the worst-off NPLs at the major banks, about 18 trillion yen as of September 2001. But that's only one-fifth of the problem. What about the other 80 percent? Without a policy change, the NPLs in three years will be greater than today.

How Big Is the Problem?

How big is Japan's bad debt problem? Moody's says it is so big that NPLs (including ones not recognized by the authorities) exceed the banks' capital. In other words, the banking system is technically insolvent.

Even using official figures, the total of problematic debt adds up to 20 or 30 percent of GDP, depending on whether your interest is the vulnerability of the lenders or the viability of the borrowers. The former problem adds up to 100 trillion yen, the latter to 140 trillion yen.

The Financial Services Agency (FSA) puts debt into four categories. But there is a confusing wrinkle: separate ratings for the quality of the borrower and the quality of the debt (Table 5.1).

Problematic borrowers are those already in arrears at least three months or those at risk of defaulting in the future. The latter, sometimes called the "watch list," are currently paying on time, but they've shown red ink over a lengthy period of time. Borrowers at risk or in arrears—labeled, in ascending order of severity, Class 2, 3, and 4—owe a mind-boggling 108 trillion yen ($871 billion) to the banks and an astronomical 141 trillion yen ($1.1 trillion) when we include nonbank lenders (such as credit cooperatives).

However, the FSA deducts about 60 trillion yen from this 141 trillion yen total because these loans are covered by "superior collateral," such as cash and government bonds, or because the loan is backed by guarantees from the government or a parent firm. The reasoning is that such collateral could easily be seized by the bank. So, no matter how shaky the *borrower*, the *loan* itself is classified as sound—Class 1. And yet 14 trillion yen ($113 billion) of these Class 1 loans—a whopping 3 percent of GDP—are owed by bankrupt and near-bankrupt borrowers.

The FSA's focus is the vulnerability of the banks, but, from the standpoint of economic growth, deadbeat borrowers don't cease to be a drag just because their lenders have some protection.

Then there are the official nonperforming loans (NPLs), which are a different subset of the original 141 trillion yen in problematic debt. NPLs include all loans at least three months in arrears as well as "restructured loans," which are loans where the lender has forgiven some interest or principal. They do not include the "watch list" loans. This translates into all the debt of Class 2a, 3, and 4 borrowers—even the debt covered by superior collateral. In 2001, this amounted to 44 trillion yen ($354 billion)—almost 10 percent of GDP (37 trillion yen at just the banks).

The FSA claims the banks can grow out of the bad debt using operating profits and sales of stock they hold in other firms.

In reality, the FSA's system is a highly inaccurate predictor of bank vulnerability. Among all the firms that went bankrupt during April–September 2000, only 30 percent of their debt was on the NPL list. Giant retailers Sogo and Mycal were still rated Class 1 (sound) and 2 (minimally risky) when they went belly-up.[3]

The banks have good incentives to underestimate risk. The riskier the category, the larger the required loan loss reserves, and thus the bigger the deduction from bank profits. Since the banks figure they're too big to fail

Table 5.1

Problematic Loans Total 100–150 Trillion Yen (in trillions of yen)

Classification of borrower[2]	Classification of loan[1]				Total
	1	2	3	4	
All deposit-taking financial institutions (March 2001)					
1. Normal borrowers	515.2				515
2. Borrowers needing attention	44.2	65.4			110
2a: Borrowers requiring special attention[2]					13
3. Borrowers in danger of bankruptcy	8.7	7.6	3.1		19
4. Bankrupt or technically bankrupt borrowers	5.3	6.5			12
Total loans	573.4	80.0	3.1		656
Problematic loans (class 2, 3, 4 borrowers)					141
Of which: not covered by superior collateral[3]					83
Nonperforming loans (class 2a, 3, 4 borrowers)[4]					44

Major and regional banks (September 2001)				
1. Normal borrowers	407.0			407
2. Borrowers needing attention	29.9	54.7		85
2a: Borrowers requiring special attention[2]				14
3. Borrowers in danger of bankruptcy	7.1	6.0	2.6	16
4. Bankrupt or technically bankrupt borrowers	2.8	4.6	2.6	7
Total Loans	447.0	65		515
Problematic loans (class 2, 3, 4 borrowers)				108
Of which: not covered by superior collateral[3]				69
Nonperforming loans (class 2a, 3, 4 borrowers)[4]				37

Source: Financial Services Agency 2002 (only on the Japanese-language site).

Notes:

[1] Class 1 loans include all loans to normal borrowers, as well as other loans that are covered by superior collateral or guarantees (see note 3). Class 2 loans include all remaining loans to borrowers requiring attention, as well as loans to borrowers in, or in danger of, bankruptcy that are covered by ordinary collateral. Class 3 loans include all remaining loans to borrowers in danger of bankruptcy, as well as remaining loans to bankrupt borrowers with doubtful recovery value. Class 4 loans are regarded as unrecoverable.

[2] Borrowers requiring attention are not in arrears but show low profitability and are at risk of becoming in arrears. Borrowers requiring special attention are those in default at least three months, or with "restructured" loans, i.e., loans where part of the principal and/or interest has been forgiven. Borrowers in danger of bankruptcy are those in arrears at least six months.

[3] Superior collateral consists of cash or government bonds deposited at the bank by the borrower. Guarantees can be by the government or by a parent firm.

[4] Nonperforming loans are the total of loans to bankrupt borrowers, those in danger of bankruptcy, or those requiring special attention. In other words, those in arrears at least three months or "restructured" loans (see note 2). These are all loans to class 2a, 3, and 4 borrowers.

and will get another bailout, why make their books look bad in the meantime? Ultimately taxpayers, not stockholders, get stuck with the bill.[4]

But part of the problem is the FSA definitions. Given ultralow interest rates and the pervasive practice of "evergreening" (making new loans that enable borrowers to service old ones), many firms pay interest bills right up to the eve of bankruptcy. Hence, under current rules, they are defined as Category 2—minimal risk.

Behind the Curve

Every year we are told that the banks need just three more years to eliminate the NPLs. Nonsense. The truth is, in the entire past decade, there has been only *one* year, 1996, when the banks substantially reduced outstanding NPLs (Figure 5.1a).

By March 2002, official NPLs at the banks alone stood at a record 42 trillion yen ($339 billion), 10 percent of all loans. Despite a write-off of 35 trillion yen ($284 billion) worth of bad debt over the past decade—7 percent of GDP—the remaining pile of NPLs is larger than ever.

Not only does a weak economy keeps generating new bad debt even faster than old bad debt is written off, but, ever since the big bailout in 1999, bank efforts have flagged (Figure 5.1b). Despite repeated promises of "new aggressiveness," the numbers tell quite a different story.

Actual write-offs by the banks—that is, cases in which the banks eliminate the loan from the balance sheet and, one hopes, foreclose on the debtor—amounted to a meager 3.9 trillion yen during fiscal 2001 (which ended March 2002). At just 9 percent of outstanding NPLs, this matched fiscal 2000 as the lowest rate of write-offs since 1992. Meanwhile, loan loss reserves have fallen to only 32 percent of NPLs, also the lowest rate since 1992.

The ZIRP has compounded the incentives for the banks to avoid tough action. As former Citicorp chairman John Reed told the New York Japan Society, the interest rate is the cost of time. If banks have to pay their depositors 4 percent, they've got to have loans that generate the needed cash. If borrowers can't pay, they've got to foreclose and generate cash from the sale of assets—even if it's twenty cents on the dollar. However, if banks only have to pay depositors 0.3 percent interest, then they can afford to keep the bad loans on the books for quite a long time. Why foreclose on a longtime friend? Why resist when LDP politicians say a constituent needs a loan rollover? Why not keep hoping that growth will return and solve the problem?[5]

Figure 5.1a **NPLs Keep Rising . . .**

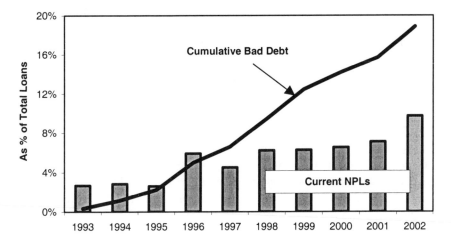

Figure 5.1b **As Banks Slacken on Disposal**

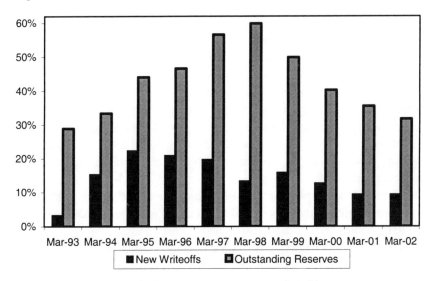

Source: Financial Services Agency 2001 for the size of NPLs, write-offs, and reserves. For the total loans outstanding, see Bank of Japan 2002a.

Note: NPLs are nonperforming loans. March of the year indicated. Cumulative bad debt equals current NPLs plus all NPLs written off since fiscal 1992. These figures are just for banks, not other lenders such as credit cooperatives.

In any case, the real test of aggressiveness is not whether the banks are doing more than in the past—though they're not—but whether they do enough to reduce the NPL total. On this test, the banks and the government fail miserably.

FSA promises about future NPL reduction defy credulity. Somehow NPLs at the big banks are supposed to shrink from 18 trillion yen today to 7–10 trillion by 2004–07. How can this be done when the FSA also says that banks' disposal efforts (the total of write-offs plus new reserves) will have fallen from 2.7 percent of loans in 1998 to only 1 percent a year during 2001–03 and then a miniscule 0.3 percent during 2004–07? How can the banks get better results than ever before with even less effort? It appears to be a number designed to keep the banks' credit costs under their operating profits. The projection is untenable and will, sooner or later, be scrapped (Figure 5.2).

Zombie Borrowers

Every nonperforming loan requires a nonperforming borrower. The banking crisis is, at its core, the financial mirror of the dual economy: huge numbers of firms that lose money year after year because their products are not worth what it costs to make them. They are commonly called zombies—the walking dead.

When it costs steelmakers $500 to produce a ton of steel that can only be sold for $450, that means society has poured $500 worth of buildings, machinery, materials, and labor into making steel but only gets back $450 when it uses that steel as an input. The more steel that is produced, the faster the economy shrinks! So it is with all the "zombies." No wonder Japan can't grow.

Were all the bad debt wiped off the banks' books today, the problem of the nonperforming borrowers would still remain. And then the NPLs would eventually return.

New light on the severity of the problem has been shed by groundbreaking reports from David Atkinson of Goldman Sachs' Tokyo office.[6]

Since interest payments are financed out of operating profits, Atkinson measured the debt-paying ability of firms by comparing their operating profits to their total debt. The 2,800 listed corporations he examined paid an average interest rate of only 2.2 percent. Hence any firm with operating profits below 2.2 percent of outstanding debt cannot even pay today's ultralow interest rates without bleeding red ink.

Figure 5.2 **FSA Plan Calls for Less Action Than Ever**

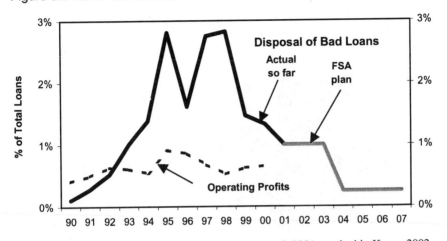

Source: Report of Minister Hakuo Yanagisawa, August 16, 2001, as cited in Kanno 2002.
Note: Fiscal year.

A full 4 percent of corporate debt is owed by firms that regularly run operating losses (Figure 5.3). These are not good firms caught in a bad neighborhood. Most have been in the red for four years, some for as long as ten. Yet the system keeps them alive. Another 8 percent of the debt is owed by firms whose operating profits are less than 1 percent of their debt.

Altogether, 16 percent of the debt is owed by firms that can't jump over the 2.2 percent interest rate hurdle. While many are in construction, real estate, and retail, there are plenty of others in steel, chemicals, textiles, low-value-added parts makers, and the like.

If the same 16 percent proportion holds true for all Japanese borrowers, not just the big corporations, then the total debt of those who can't afford even today's ultralow rates adds up to 96 trillion yen—almost 20 percent of GDP.[7]

The dualism that we found in the real economy—a hybrid of supereffi-cient and superinefficient firms—is mirrored in finance. Twenty-five per-cent of all debt is owed by firms that could be profitable even if interest rates rose to 10 percent. At the other pole, 25 percent of the debt is owed by firms that would go into the red if interest rates rose slightly to 3 percent. Yet most of the uncreditworthy firms are charged a *lower* interest rate than healthy firms—the opposite of the practice in most industrialized countries.

Figure 5.3 **Twenty-five Percent of Debt Held by Firms That Cannot Pay**

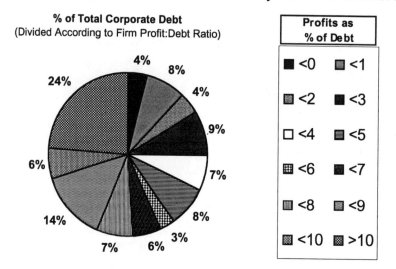

Source: Atkinson 2001a.

Over the past decade, the dualism has worsened, with the weak getting even weaker (low profits turning into chronic losses) but the strong improving their balance sheets. The worst-off firms have received the most debt forgiveness, which has been used not as a breathing space to reorganize but to keep the "walking dead" walking.

How Many Jobs at Risk?

Almost one-fifth of the entire workforce—12 million people—are employed in firms that Atkinson rates as bankrupt, near-bankrupt, or troubled. Eight percent, 5.2 million workers, are in firms that are already effectively bankrupt (with operating profits less than 1 percent of debt) but that are kept on artificial life support through ultralow interest rates and debt forgiveness.

This is a huge level of disguised unemployment. Historically, when Japanese firms went bankrupt, half the employees lost their jobs, and, of those, only 40 percent eventually found new jobs. Atkinson calculates that liquidating and reorganizing all the bad borrowers would cause 3.6 million people to lose their jobs, of which 2 million would not find new jobs.[8] And that does not even count the multiplier effects as these newly unemployed cut their spending and their firms cut their purchases of supplies.

No wonder Tokyo is loath to tackle the problem. But the longer Tokyo waits, the bigger the problem becomes, and the bigger the ultimate job loss. In addition, retraining and other measures could be used to up the re-employment rate.

Zero Interest Rates and the Zombies

Japan's leaders could have combined the ZIRP, intended as monetary stimulus, with aggressive demands for corporate restructuring. In this case, the ZIRP would have provided a critical breathing space for reform. Instead, they have used ZIRP to help companies, especially well-connected companies, avoid restructuring. As the IMF, Standard & Poors (S&P) and others rightly point out:

> Low interest rates have further undermined incentives for corporations to restructure. Despite poor underlying profitability, low-rated companies have been able to cover interest payments. . . . The real test of restructuring plans will therefore come when interest rates rise.[9]

> Easy financing has led too many corporates to postpone difficult restructuring decisions. . . . Instead of slimming down their operations, these companies have used easy money and government initiatives such as the loan-guarantee program to continue business as usual. . . . Shaking out the weakest players in Japan's corporate sector might be just what the doctor ordered.[10]

Indeed, to the extent that ZIRP keeps the zombies alive, it ironically adds to *de*flationary pressures, as pointed out by Atsushi Mizuno of Deutsche Bank:

> Firms or industries that have overborrowed are no longer able to undertake the investment necessary for their very survival, and deteriorate slowly but surely as their customers go elsewhere. Struggling firms with low competitiveness or productivity often try to survive through low-price strategies akin to dumping, ignoring profitability in a desperate bid for market share. This forces healthy firms to cut their prices to unreasonable levels, preventing them from obtaining appropriate profit margins. This sparks deflationary pressures and ruins corporate profits.[11]

Anorexia, the Collateral System, and the Banking Crisis

Why did the banking crisis become so severe in the first place? In our view, it took the interaction of two forces: the macroeconomics of anorexia and the microeconomics of a banking system that used collateral, not creditworthiness, as the basis for making loans.

Due to the excess-savings syndrome, every year trillions of yen of unneeded deposits flooded into the banks, premiums into the insurance companies, and investment funds into the securities houses. The financiers frantically searched for a way to invest that money in order to meet the interest and dividend payments. Figuring that more was better, the banks expanded their commercial loans from 73 percent to 97 percent of GDP in the five short years from 1987 to 1992.

When there is so much superfluous money to invest, it is not likely to be allocated wisely. Add to that a Finance Ministry guarantee under the "convoy system" that no bank could fail, and you have a recipe for disaster. As Eugene Dattel demonstrated in *The Sun That Never Rose,* the banks had no system for screening customer creditworthiness anything like their American counterparts did.[12] Nor did banks charge different rates according to the riskiness of the loan. Bank loans were based not on projections of future company cash flow but on collateral. If a would-be borrower—particularly an established customer whose stock the bank owned, or who owned some bank stock—had real estate or stock holdings, it could borrow based on that collateral. In some cases, banks pressured companies to borrow more than they wanted to.

Once the late 1980s bubble reached critical mass, such a system was virtually calculated to pour oil on the flames. As monetary ease raised the value of real estate and stocks, companies could then go back to their banks, pointing out that the value of their collateral had risen. They borrowed still more—not to make their normal products, but to buy even more real estate and stocks. That raised the values of those assets even higher, fueling still more borrowing to buy still more assets, ad infinitum.

In 1987, 40 percent of Toyota's profits came not from auto production but from nonoperating revenues including financial speculation. At Matsushita the ratio was 60 percent. It was 65 percent at Nissan, 63 percent at Sony, and 134 percent at Sanyo.[13]

Via this process, stock prices were geared up to one hundred times corporate earnings. The land underneath the Imperial Palace in Tokyo was said to be worth more than the entire state of California. Companies also borrowed to construct new buildings, stores, and factories. But those investments could pay off only if the bubble's high asset prices and rapid GDP growth could be maintained for years to come.

From the standpoint of the entire financial system, this was a house of cards. Yet as far as each individual bank loan officer could tell, there was no problem. After all, the borrower had the collateral.[14]

Cover-up and Corruption

Many industrialized nations have gone through banking crises. What distinguishes Japan is not only the unparalleled size of the problem but the adamant refusal of policy-makers to either acknowledge its size or solve the problem a decade after its emergence.

While some delay is typical in most countries, it's hard to find any other industrialized country that matches Japan's record of denial and delay, cover-up and criminal fraud.

Every time a bank failed, its bad debts turned out to be far higher than the banks and the authorities had claimed only months earlier. The Long-Term Credit Bank (LTCB), one of Japan's largest and most prestigious banks, went belly-up in late 1998 only months after the MOF promised everyone that it was sound. Magazine articles questioning the LTCB's viability were dismissed as scurrilous gossip. Once the LTCB failed, some of the truth came out. A few LTCB executives were convicted of cooking the books, shifting funds to cover up bad debts, and making illegal dividend payments.

In their courtroom defense, the execs claimed they were following MOF guidance.[15] The MOF denies that it knew or approved of anything illegal. Yet the finance minister, Kiichi Miyazawa, admitted that when the MOF asked banks and taxpayers to put more money into Nippon Credit Bank (NCB) in 1998, claiming its assets exceeded its liabilities, this was not really true. NCB failed shortly thereafter, and the other banks and the government lost all their money. Yet even as NCB executives were hauled off to jail, MOF Vice Minister Nobuaki Usui insisted that the MOF itself had done nothing illegal. Miyazawa claimed the cover-up was necessary because to let NCB fail before a safety net had been established would have shaken global finances. In yet another case of a bankrupt bank where officials were arrested, Hokkaido Takushoku, MOF inspectors discovered illegal practices as early as 1994 and reported them to their superiors. But the MOF never filed any accusation against the bank.[16]

One reason for the MOF's laxness may have been the lavish wining and dining of MOF bank examiners, and those of the BOJ, received from the very banks they were supposedly scrutinizing. These were the notorious parties at the "no-pan shabu shabu" restaurants (restaurants at which the waitresses wear no panties), for which several MOF and BOJ officials were arrested.[17]

Corruption is hardly unique to Japan. It has been the constant companion of financial euphoria for centuries. The corporate fraud scandals unveiled in the United States during 2002 are a classic example. Usually, however, there are plenty of arrests and convictions and jail time once the bubble pops. More than 1,600 bank and S&L executives were convicted of criminal offenses in the United States in the aftermath of the 1990s S&L crisis.[18]

What is surprising in Japan's far larger crisis is how few arrests and convictions, let alone jail sentences, have been seen—only one hundred indictments as of 2001. What is also surprising is that the cover-up continues to this very day.

For example, in its March 2000 report, Sumitomo Bank calculated its problem loans to the construction industry at only 265 billion yen ($2.4 billion). Yet Sumitomo's exposure to near-bankrupt Kumagai Gumi construction firm alone was 500 billion yen. Sumitomo even had to lend the firm the money it used to pay interest. Nonetheless, Sumitomo rated 290 billion yen of its 500 billion yen in loans to Kumagai as healthy loans, and it set aside loan loss reserves of only 110 billion yen on the remainder. When, only a few months later, Sumitomo had to organize a debt forgiveness package for Kumagai Gumi to prevent bankruptcy, it was forced to cough up another 130 billion yen in loan loss reserves.[19]

Accounting gimmicks hide the true value of bank exposure. The market value of real estate is much lower than official numbers used to judge the value of collateral. Consequently, many loans, even some in the supposedly safe Class 1, are no longer really collateralized. When the banks revalue the collateral downward, they do so only in line with official government numbers, not actual market values. This problem made headlines in the spring of 2001 when a small bank, Wakashio, tried to clean up its NPLs, only to find that the money it could recoup by selling collateral was worth only one-tenth the value it had used in its NPL calculations. The coup de grâce came when Sakura, Fuji, and other big banks lent Wakashio more money to keep it from failing. Why did they do so? Because if Wakashio failed, they'd have to acknowledge that their own subordinated loans to Wakashio were worthless. Once again, good money is thrown after bad to hide the truth.[20]

Naturally, the FSA denies that it is hiding anything. When asked why the lion's share of debt at bankrupt firms was labeled Class 1 or 2, a leading FSA official replied, "Who foresaw the failure of Polaroid or Enron a year before they went under?" In other words, the FSA's stance is that it can't be expected to do any better.

But this is clearly false. The difficulties of Japan's biggest failures were known far in advance. As early as 1998, Mycal—which failed in September 2001 with 1.75 trillion yen ($14 billion) in debt—was rated as junk, that is, BB– by S&P and BB by Moody's. In the spring of 2000, S&P further lowered the rating to B, a rating that means a 16 percent chance of bankruptcy within three years, 25 percent within seven years. Yet Mycal was rated much higher by the Japanese rating agencies—and by the FSA credit risk standards. In fact, among all the rated corporations and banks that went bankrupt in recent years, almost none had been rated A or higher by S&P during any point since 1991. The life insurers that defaulted were initially rated BB or lower by S&P.[21]

The common feeling in the markets is that the FSA has little interest in reporting the true size of the NPL problem, since it would undermine the fiction that the banks can handle the problems without any additional government money. The credibility gap hurts the banks themselves, since they have to pay larger risk premiums when they issue bank debentures.[22]

Convoy Capitalism

It would be nice if all the blame for bank and regulator malfeasance could be pinned on corruption, bureaucratic blinders, or, as some say, *yakuza* (gangster) investments in real estate. If so, the problems could be fixed more easily. However, the chief culprit is Japan's "convoy capitalism."

Just as no ship in a convoy can travel faster than the slowest boat, so the "convoy system" dictated that, from 1955 through the late 1990s, not a single bank was allowed to fail. When a bank got into trouble, the MOF convinced a larger, healthier bank to buy it out.

The situation changed with the 1995 failure of Hyogo, a second-tier regional bank, and then in 1997 with the rapid succession of failures at Nissan Life Insurance, Sanyo Securities, Yamaichi Securities, and the Hokkaido Takushoku bank. These failed, not because of any change in mind-set, but simply because the MOF could no longer prevent it. The MOF tried, and failed, to find "white knights" willing to sacrifice their own health. Having been discredited by its own lies, corruption, and incompetence, the MOF no longer packed the clout needed to bend big banks to its will.

While the term *convoy* was originally coined in regard to the bank system, the entire dual economy is a kind of "convoy capitalism." After all, if no bank can fail, then not too many borrowers can be allowed to fail either.

Thus, when the crisis began in the early 1990s, the MOF, acting under the convoy paradigm, actually *prevented* banks from recognizing their losses. As Peter Hartcher disclosed in *The Ministry,* back in 1992, a few of the biggest banks went to the MOF with plans to dispose of NPLs held by their housing loan subsidiaries, known as *jusen.* They wanted to liquidate the worst-off *jusen* and write down the losses. The MOF was appalled. After all, if even the strongest banks had such losses, what would depositors think about the weaker ones? Besides, a former MOF man headed up one of the leading *jusen*. The MOF instructed the banks to begin a regime of debt waivers and stretch-outs. When the plan flopped and the *jusen* went bankrupt in 1995, the government spent 1.3 trillion yen ($10.4 billion) of taxpayer money to clean up the problem. Not a single yen went to depositors, since the *jusen* didn't have any. Instead, it went to creditors, especially the farmers' cooperative (Nokyo), a big vote-getting machine for the LDP.[23]

With rare exceptions, the pattern set in 1992 has continued to the present day. One exception was the rapid nationalization of the Nippon Credit Bank in late 1998, but that was only because the newly created FSA was led by since-purged hard-line reformers such as Sakura Shiga, the third in command.

Officially, of course, Tokyo says the "convoy system" is yesterday's news. The reality is otherwise. In the summer of 2000 the banks and government agreed to forgive the Sogo department store chain an astonishing 630 billion yen ($5.1 billion) worth of debt to keep it afloat. The deal fell through only when taxpayers objected to 97 billion yen ($780 million) of their money being used and started boycotting Sogo stores. Sogo ended up failing with 1.9 trillion yen ($15 billion) in liabilities. Within days Seiyo Corporation, a real estate firm and an arm of the Seibu conglomerate, failed with about 500 billion yen ($4 billion) in debt.

To preclude further failures, the banks arranged huge debt forgiveness packages—this time without new public funds. Debt forgiveness for the construction sector alone amounted to 2 trillion yen ($16 billion). Altogether, fifty-seven large firms were graced with debt forgiveness by their banks during the first eleven months of the year 2000. Out of the four hundred firms that had received debt waivers in the past decade, a quarter had gone bankrupt, been liquidated, or been absorbed by other firms by the end of 2001. More have failed since then.[24]

The government itself directly supports moribund firms via credit guarantees that now cover 10 percent of all bank loans (Figure 5.4). Although the recipients of these guarantees are supposedly worthy firms victimized by an alleged "credit crunch," many of them are, in fact, highly risky. In fact, of the 30 trillion yen in loans given guarantees, only 5 percent had been repaid by the end of 2001, compared to a target of 50 percent. By late 2001, credit associations had to shell out 40 billion yen ($322 million) each month to cover defaults by guaranteed firms. As the malaise continues, more defaults on these guarantees lie in store. Hence the LDP is trying to make repayment terms even easier.

Far from ending the convoy system, Tokyo has applied pressure, sometimes quite crudely, on banks to keep lending to the deadbeats. One par-

Figure 5.4 **Loan Guarantees by Government Soar**

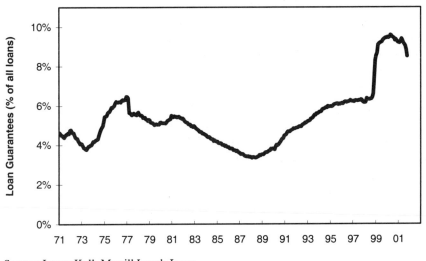

Source: Jesper Koll, Merrill Lynch Japan.
Note: Government guarantees to banks in case of default by private borrower.

ticularly blunt example was direct pressure on Shinsei Bank. Shinsei is the new name given to the bankrupt Long-Term Credit Bank when it was bought by an American investment group, Ripplewood. In early 2001 Shinsei began refusing to roll over loans to a few hundred small and medium-sized firms with Class 2 status. Shinsei's actions left other banks with a dilemma: either let these borrowers fail and suffer big losses or else buy up the loans from Shinsei and increase their own vulnerability. Many banks felt compelled to choose the latter, but they issued loud complaints of "un-Japanese" behavior that resounded in the media and the Diet.

On August 10, FSA Commissioner Shoji Mori, a stalwart of the old regime, met with Shinsei President Masamoto Yashiro, telling him that Diet members wanted Shinsei to keep lending to these firms. According to Shinsei documents obtained by the *Asia Wall Street Journal,* Mori instructed Yashiro to start behaving like other Japanese bankers, and the FSA issued a "business improvement order" instructing Shinsei to lend more to small and medium-sized companies. To comply, Shinsei would have to make profitless loans. Feeling the heat, Yashiro issued an apologetic letter on September 8, conceding that there was a "hasty element" in its actions. Yet the documents and Shinsei's behavior show that it is still trying to cut back on loans to uncreditworthy customers.[25]

Further pressure—or perhaps retaliation—against the foreign-owned Shinsei came in 2002 following the government-pressured bailout of the giant Daiei supermarket chain. Yashiro announced at a press conference that Daiei had repaid 72 percent of its short-term loans to Japanese banks, even those not among its main banks, while refusing repeated requests for repayments from Daiei.[26]

Shinsei is hardly the only case of FSA pressure. In the few months prior to supermarket giant Mycal's failure, banks made new loans of 120 billion yen ($1 billion) in a vain effort to keep it afloat. They did this despite credit rating downgrades that assigned Mycal debt junk status. Word on the street is that one reason for the bank action was pressure from the FSA.

Not all firms get protection. Aoki Construction, associated with the Hashimoto faction, had been receiving debt waivers, but then was allowed to fail when Koizumi took power. In an unusually undiplomatic slap, the IMF noted:

> Sogo's political connections may have played an important role in the rescue [attempt]. Nagasakiya, another department store with twice the sales of Sogo and one-third more staff, had been allowed to go bankrupt earlier in 2000.[27]

From time to time, the banks announce new "aggressiveness" on NPL cleanup and the FSA announces tougher inspections. Each time, on closer examination, little has changed. For example, at the end of 2001, Tokyo spread rumors that Koizumi had decided to pressure the banks to close the loan spigot for thirty big shaky borrowers by the spring of 2002. The failure of Aoki—one of the thirty—lent the story credibility. It never happened. Instead, Daiei was bailed out.

We'll know such rumors are true only when Tokyo takes action on the prerequisites that make aggressive loan clean-up possible: e.g. a new, conditional injection of government money into the banks; a beefing up of the institutions involved in foreclosure and resale of the bad assets; a big hike in the budget for unemployment compensation; and a consumer tax cut.

Reformers Arise but Still Lack Critical Mass

Just as there are vested interests trying to block a solution, so there are many important interests that need a genuine solution: all the healthier firms being dragged down by the zombies. Inevitably, then, calls for genuine solutions arise from bureaucrats, businessmen, academics, and politicians. So far, however, the reformers have never reached critical mass.

One brief window of opportunity arose during the recession of 1997–98. While the opportunity was lost, the episode had some lasting consequences, including a big loss of power for the MOF.

What provoked the crisis was that the global financial markets, no longer trusting either the MOF or the banks, imposed a "Japan premium"—an extra charge on interbank loans. By the fall of 1998, even highly rated Japanese banks had to pay 0.7 percent more than non-Japanese banks with the same credit rating. That margin made it prohibitive for banks to operate internationally.

As the LTCB and then the NCB teetered toward bankruptcy, with the prospect of others in their wake, the Obuchi administration tried to push a financial bailout through the Diet.

Because the opposition parties controlled the Upper House of the Diet, the LDP could not just ram through its own proposals. At first there were negotiations between two false choices. Prime Minister Obuchi basically proposed money for the banks with no conditions. Initially, this was countered by "no money under almost any conditions" by the leading opposition party, the Minshuto (Democrats). Soon, however, through a series of negotiations begun between urban-oriented reformers in the LDP, such as Yasuhisa Shiozaki, and wiser heads in the Minshuto, such as Naoto Kan, the reformers inside and outside the LDP began to coalesce around "money with conditions."

Three issues intersected in this struggle:

1. Forcing the banks to clean up lingering bad assets versus a simple bailout.
2. The national interest versus the special interests. As the Democrats pointed out, Obuchi's scheme to bail out the bankrupt LTCB would have used city dwellers' tax money to salvage the investments of LDP-allied farmer cooperatives in an LTCB subsidiary, Japan Leasing.
3. Rule by the elected Diet versus the bureaucracy. Using open debate instead of back-room deals, the Diet seized control of the issue, forced Obuchi to accept some conditions for bank loans, removed jurisdiction from the discredited MOF, and created the FSA, which initially proved to be far more aggressive than the MOF. It authorized the nationalization of failed banks and provided for a massive capital injection into the solvent banks, allocating 70 trillion yen ($600 billion), of which 26 trillion yen was used.

But the opportunity for a thorough solution was lost. Many sincere people in Japan, fearful of a financial meltdown, caved to the notion of a quick bailout, figuring conditionality could be applied later. The Clinton administration decided to shore up Obuchi against the reformers for similar reasons (to be discussed in Chapter 22, p. 301). Ichiro Ozawa, the leader of the Liberal Party, defected from the opposition coalition and allied his party with Obuchi.

The window of opportunity was shut. The banks received their bailout, and zombies continued to get ultralow-interest loans plus government guarantees. The FSA gradually lost its most reform-minded personnel and its aggressiveness. Today, with a few exceptions, it is hardly distinguishable from the old MOF, whence it obtained most of its staff.

Where Do We Stand Today?

As of the beginning of 2002, there is another window of opportunity. As the banks head into another episode of turmoil, key parts of the powerful bureaucracy clearly recognize the need to grab the bull by the horns.

The chief institutional actors in favor of strong action are the BOJ, some parts of the FSA, and parts of METI.

Reformers are particularly strong in sections of the METI secretariat as well as the METI-associated think tank, the Research Institute on Economy, Trade, and Industry (RIETI), and among officials who have spent some time in overseas postings.

METI officials met with their counterparts in the Ministry of Health, Labor, and Welfare (MHLW) to suggest upping the budget for unemployment compensation, in anticipation of all those who would lose their jobs in a true cleanup of the bad borrowers. But the MHLW refused.

Moreover, even METI is not united, with many in the Distribution Bureau, whose turf includes the retail sector, worried about measures that could put many of their clients out of business. In the fall of 2001, METI minister Takeo Hiranuma, a veteran LDP pol, called on the banks to delay further write-offs and foreclosure on real-estate-backed bad debt of supposedly healthy small firms.

The BOJ has offered the government a deal: It would provide all the liquidity needed to support the system if the government would compel the banks to write off all the bad debt and address the "bad debtors." In a February 2001 speech, BOJ Policy Board member Teizo Taya made the general outline of the conditions public:

We have to do something to speed up the process of bad debt disposal and reach a final solution. However, while efforts by financial institutions are a given, this will also require a comprehensive restructuring, consolidation and breakup among corporate borrowers. The process of debt disposal will intensify deflationary pressures, and if this process is accelerated, the BOJ will have to seek an appropriate response in order to ensure that the credit creation function of financial institutions operates normally. I believe that such a response would have a positive effect.[28]

The FSA is divided between genuine reformers and true conservative die-hards such as former commissioner Shoji Mori. The thinking of state minister Hakuo Yanagisawa, an ex-MOF official, was very much shaped by seeing the crisis of Citibank when he was posted in New York in the early 1990s. He was impressed both by how the regulators pressed CEO John Reed and by Reed's response.

Since Yanagisawa's return to the FSA post in 2001, he has played both positive and negative roles. In the spring of 2001 Yanagisawa said it was finally time for the banks to write off all their bad debt—and do so within two or three years. Yet the banks cannot do so without a new injection of government money—this time with stricter conditions than in 1999. As the man who presided over the 1999 bailout, Yanagisawa would have to own up to his mistake, and so he opposes a new injection, even one with proper conditions. For that reason, reformers at METI and the BOJ find him an obstacle. On the other hand, he has stopped the worst kind of bailouts being pushed by LDP apparatchiks, such as a scheme to use government money to buy stocks held by the banks at a guaranteed price, or a scheme to buy much of their loans at face value, not market value. If even Yanagisawa, one of the more reform-minded of Japan's politicians, is so unwilling to bite the bullet, it seems unlikely the political system as a whole is ready to do so.[29]

What is missing from the policy balance is the politicians. In a democracy, such a drastic program entailing so much dislocation for so many people cannot be implemented without decisive political leadership. The bureaucracy can propose a program, but it must be carried out by the political world. At that level there is a vacuum. Much of the LDP opposes reform. Koizumi, as discussed in Chapter 1, has other priorities. And, unlike in 1998, the opposition has no leverage because the LDP-led coalition controls both houses of the Diet.

Yet something will have to be done. Sooner or later, probably by 2003, Tokyo will have to accede to a new injection of government money just to stave off meltdown. It may be done in stealth fashion rather than explicitly, for example, virtually free loans to the banks by the BOJ or an increase in loan guarantees to the borrowers, or the purchase of NPLs from the banks at above-market prices by the governmental Resolution and Collection Corporation (RCC), or Price-Keeping Operations to boost stock prices using government-controlled pension funds.

The problem is that, under current political conditions, this is likely to be reactive, not proactive. Once again Tokyo will throw enough money at the problem to prevent chaos, but it will not do enough to solve the underlying malady of the nonperforming borrowers.

While it is possible that a real crisis would shake up the Koizumi team and force a change in priorities to really address the bad borrower problem, this is not very probable in the near term.

On the other hand, since the economy will never return to vibrant growth until the debt/borrower problem is cleaned up, this issue will keep returning to the top of the political agenda.

Part Two

Macroeconomic Policy Debates

6

Fiscal Dilemmas

Saying Japan needs fiscal and monetary stimulus to grow is like saying a car needs gasoline to run. It's certainly true, but it would be nice if the car also had an engine. The engine is structural reform. Neither stimulus nor reform is sufficient; both are necessary. Rather than alternatives, they should be seen as partners. Unfortunately, Japan has fallen victim to a false debate.

On one side, the "gasoline is enough" faction says that fiscal stimulus can substitute for reform. Some in this camp, such as Richard Koo, chief economist of Nomura Securities, even suggest that cracking down on bad borrowers be delayed until after recovery on the grounds that this would worsen the contraction.[1] With less sincere motivations, the construction lobby has seized on the "recovery first, reform later" argument to extract bigger budgets for more "bridges to nowhere" (see Chapter 18, p. 263).

No one says that the fiscal remedy hasn't been given a fair chance. On the contrary, it has been tried on a massive scale—and it has failed. Starting from a surplus equal to 3 percent of GDP in 1991, the deficit grew to a peak of 8 percent of GDP by the year 2000 (Figure 6.1). By other measures, the deficit was even higher—for example, 11 percent of GDP in 1998 on a national accounts basis (go back to Figure 4.7). Some of the deficit simply reflected the recession (decreased tax revenues, for example), but the majority of it—referred to as the "policy effect" in Figure 6.1—represented increases in spending or cuts in taxes aimed at stimulating demand.

While all this effort has prevented depression and catalyzed temporary rebounds, not once in the past decade has it led to a self-sustaining recovery in private demand. And yet the price for keeping the economy above water has been a growing, potentially destabilizing mountain of public debt, now at 140 percent of GDP.

At the other pole, we have the proponents of fiscal austerity: the MOF Budget Bureau, Prime Minister Hashimoto in 1996–98, the opposition Minshuto party, the current Koizumi team. They say, in effect, "We tried

Figure 6.1 **Addicted to Deficits**

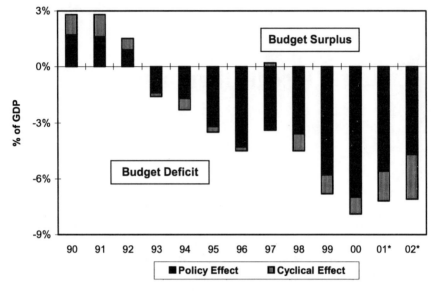

Source: IMF 2001b and previous issues of the IMF *World Economic Outlook.*

Note: The budget deficit figures exclude social security (including social security would show even larger deficits). The figures for 2001 and 2002 are IMF projections made in December 2001 based on their predictions for GDP declines in 2001 and 2002 as well as Koizumi's contractionary budget policies. See note to Figure 6.5.

The black solid bar (policy effect) shows much of the total budget deficit is due to policy changes such as tax cuts or spending hikes. It is often called the "structural balance" or "full-employment balance" in that it measures what the budget deficit or surplus would be at full-employment. The portion of the bar with horizontal stripes (cyclical effect) shows how much the deficit or surplus is due to the automatic effects on tax revenues and spending from the business cycle. In the late 1980s rapid growth automatically raised income tax revenue, whereas the deep recession of the late 1990s automatically decreased revenues— even aside from any deliberate tax cuts. The cyclical effect is one the "automatic stabilizers" of the economy.

lots of gasoline, but the car didn't run. This proves cars don't need gasoline." Pointing to the genuine problem of public debt and the futility of more public works, they have shortsightedly cut deficits, thereby triggering and/or worsening recessions. In 1996–97 the Hashimoto administration cut spending and then, in April 1997, raised the consumption tax from 3 percent to 5 percent. The result in 1997–98 was Japan's worst postwar recession to that point. In 2001 the Koizumi administration imposed spending cuts just as the economy was reentering recession, applying a fiscal tourniquet nearly as tight as Hashimoto's.

In a particularly strange twist, some macroeconomists advocate raising the consumption tax yet again—not just to close the deficit, but supposedly as a way of getting consumers to spend more. One such economist noted that Japan's fastest growth in the past decade came in the fifteen months prior to the consumption tax hike of April 1997. He neglected to point out what happened in the fifteen months *after* the tax hike. Not to be dissuaded, these economists say that a series of tax hikes will keep consumers spending as they perpetually rush to spend before the next tax hike. Somehow, in their minds, leaving consumers with less money to spend will get them to spend more.

Japan's stop-go fiscal policy has been an unintended real-world experiment, one whose results are very clear. Fiscal stimulus helps growth when it is applied and hurts when it is withdrawn. The ups and downs of GDP growth mirror the application and removal of fiscal stimulus. In fact, there is a fairly high 61 percent correlation between the change in the deficit in one year and GDP growth the following year (Figure 6.2).

The upshot is that Japan needs repeated injections of fiscal stimulus just to avoid chronic recession. And herein lies the dilemma. No budget deficit, no matter how big, directly adds to new growth. It is only *increases* in the deficit that stimulate new growth. A deficit increase equal to 1 percent of GDP, whether from 3 to 4 or from 6 to 7, provides equal stimulus. Conversely, a budget deficit that is very large but shrinking, such as from 9 percent of GDP to 8 percent, detracts from growth. Hence, just to sustain a constant amount of stimulus, say 1 percent of GDP, the overall size of the deficit has to keep increasing year by year. That's how Japan became addicted to ever-larger deficits. And that, in turn, led to increases in the public debt at exponential rates.

The only exit from this dilemma is growth-enhancing reforms that raise the tax base.

What Fiscal Stimulus Can and Cannot Do

In a healthy economy, fiscal stimulus works by giving the economy a temporary boost sufficient to bring it close to full capacity. At that point, companies find it profitable to make new investments, which leads to new hiring, expanded personal consumption, and self-sustaining growth.

Were it not for Japan's endemic excess capacity and deeply entrenched anorexia, the traditional fiscal remedy should have worked long ago. That's why so many neoclassical economists, who shy away from institutional explanations of performance, used to be so confident of its potency.

Figure 6.2 **Ups and Downs of Fiscal Stimulus Lead GDP Ups and Downs**

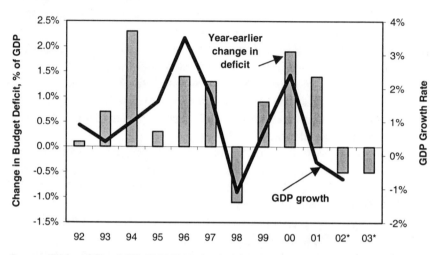

Source: Cabinet Office 2002; IMF 2002 plus previous issues of the IMF's *World Economic Outlook.*

Note: Calendar years. GDP for 2002 is consensus estimate. Deficits for 2001 and 2002 are estimates by IMF.

Stimulus added or removed is measured by the size of the *change* in the deficit as a percent of GDP. We have included only changes due to deliberate policy changes such as tax cuts or spending hikes, i.e., changes in the structural balance. On the left-hand scale, positive 1 percent means an increase of the deficit by 1 percent of GDP, say from 4 percent to 5 percent, or from 7 percent to 8 percent. That's an application of stimulus. Negative 1 percent means a decrease in the deficit, e.g., from 7 percent to 6 percent. That's a withdrawal of stimulus; it's a contractionary policy. Since fiscal stimulus operates with a lag, the chart compares changes in GDP growth to changes in the budget deficit one year *earlier.* For example, 1998 shows the drop in GDP in 1998 and the drop in the budget deficit one year *earlier* in 1997. The budget figures for 2001 and 2002 are IMF projections made in December 2001 based on announcements by the Koizumi administration. They show a very contractionary policy.

Indeed, in a 1998 book, Washington economist Adam Posen called for a single big dose of fiscal stimulus, about 4 percent of GDP. Posen was sure it would do the trick, especially if it were done through tax cuts rather than public works and if it were accompanied by additional monetary stimulus and a resolution of the banking crisis. Three years later, he contended, it would be safe for Japan to sharply reduce deficits via spending cuts. The MOF's main mistake in 1996–97 was introducing budget cuts and the consumption tax a year or so too soon.[2]

By the spring of 1999, when the Obuchi administration applied large doses of fiscal largesse and a huge bank bailout, Posen declared that, aside from monetary policy, Japan had done enough to secure recovery. He predicted a 1 percent rise in GDP in 1999, followed by 3 percent each in 2000 and 2001. Initially, during Japan's short-lived recovery, Posen's theories gained credibility. Then the recovery imploded.[3]

When asked about Japan's disappointing response, Posen replied:

1. Fiscal policy has been contractionary since spring 1997 except for the first six months of 1999.
2. Monetary policy has been deflationary for over four years.
3. Bad loans were left to accumulate for so long.
4. Points 2 and 3 interact in a vicious spiral.
5. I was over-optimistic in 1999 because of political naiveté, overestimating the degree and duration of change on all positive three fronts.
6. In my opinion, events do nothing to disprove my interpretation that macro policy plus bank clean up is enough to restore Japan's economic growth even today.[4]

We disagree with Posen on the basic facts. For one thing, keeping overnight interest rates at virtually zero for six years is hardly tight money (see Chapter 7). Second, Posen has repeatedly understated the amount of fiscal stimulus, saying the only sizeable packages were in the fall of 1995 and the first half of 1999. In reality, Japan has applied huge amounts of fiscal stimulus year after year. From 1991 to 1996, Japan's structural balance went from a surplus of 1.6 percent of GDP to a deficit of 4.3 percent, a huge swing that added up to stimulus worth 6 percent of GDP. Between 1998 and 2000, the deficit increased another 3.4 percent.

The real issue is why all this stimulus failed to do the job. How did the United States thrive even as it reduced its structural deficit by 4 percent of GDP during 1993–98, whereas Japan was sent reeling by its much smaller cutbacks in 1997?

The answer is this: Fiscal fixes stand or fall on their ability to jump-start private investment, which, in turn, fuels consumer income and spending. But for that to occur, Japan's investment rate would have to return to bubble-era heights, and, as discussed in Chapter 4, that is not in the cards. (In the United States, by the way, budget cuts led to lower interest rates, which triggered an investment and consumer boom.)

The failure of fiscal policy to provide a permanent cure should not lead us to adopt the opposite extreme: that fiscal stimulus was totally impotent and unnecessary. That's the dangerous reasoning that led to the Hashimoto and Koizumi errors.

Study after study shows that fiscal stimulus can give the economy a temporary boost, enough to provide a macroeconomic safety net while reform is undertaken. They differ only on how much impact it will have, that is, how much GDP will grow for every 100 yen of fiscal stimulus A multiplier of 1.2 would mean 120 yen of additional GDP per 100 yen of stimulus.

The IMF found that, in the 1990s, GDP increased only 65 yen for every 100 yen increase in government spending. This is about half the multiplier of 1 to 1.2 the IMF has found in its large economic models for most rich countries. In explaining this, the IMF pointed to the low "real water" content of packages, their stop-and-start manner, and the choice of projects with a low return. It found a very low 0.2 multiplier for tax cuts, citing, in part, the use of temporary rather than permanent cuts.[5]

Adam Posen and coauthor Kenneth Kuttner found higher multipliers using a different methodology. Kuttner and Posen point out that when GDP increases, so does tax revenue, thereby reducing the deficit and the ultimate impact of the spending hike. Taking that into account, they found that GDP increases by 175 yen for every 100 yen in new spending. For every 100 yen cut in taxes, they estimated a 484 yen hike in GDP.[6]

Given the wide discrepancy between the IMF's numbers and those of Posen and Kuttner, neither magnitude seems reliable. But the main point is clear: Put money in consumers' pockets via tax cuts and they will spend. Consumer surveys bear this out. Households spent at least 50 percent of recent temporary tax cuts just to pay day-to-day bills; without the tax cut they would have had to cut other spending.

Public Debt Trap

Unfortunately, fiscal stimulus is not costless. Gross government debt has soared from 60 percent of GDP in 1990 to an estimated 140 percent in 2002. Japan is now number one in its debt burden (Figure 6.3). Even with reductions in the size of the annual deficit, the cumulative debt load will keep on rising for years to come, hitting 150 percent in 2003 and possibly topping 200 percent by the middle of the decade.

The arithmetic of debt dictates the following:

- Even if the primary budget (i.e., the whole budget other than interest payments) is in balance, the debt-to-GDP ratio will still rise if the interest rate is higher than the growth rate of nominal GDP. In that situation, more money is borrowed just to pay the interest.

Figure 6.3 **"Japan As Number One" in Government Debt**

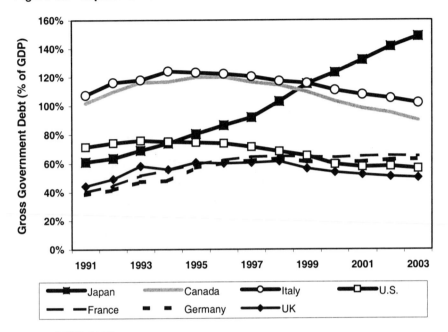

Source: OECD 2001b.
Note: Refers to gross government debt as a ratio of nominal GDP.

- If, as in Japan's case, the interest rate is higher than the growth rate of nominal GDP and the primary budget is in large deficit, then the debt-to-GDP ratio will skyrocket.

Consequently, just to stabilize Japan's debt-to-GDP ratio at 180 percent of GDP by 2010, Japan would have to put the primary budget into a large surplus, requiring budget cuts as large as 10 percent of GDP over the coming half decade or so.[7] But without a restoration of self-sustaining private growth, the economy cannot tolerate such huge cuts. There are no pleasant options.

The only reason this explosion of debt has been financially sustainable so far is Japan's ultralow interest rates. They've kept the total interest paid by the government flat despite the mounting level of debt (Figure 6.4). In fact, interest rates have fallen so much that, in 2002, the government's interest payments amounted to only 1.9 percent of GDP, far lower than in the mid-1980s, when they averaged 3 percent of GDP.

Figure 6.4 **Government Debt Soars, But Interest Burden Is Held Down . . .**

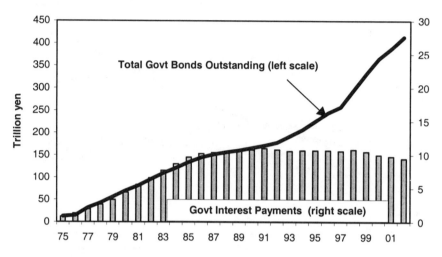

. . . By Superlow Interest Rates

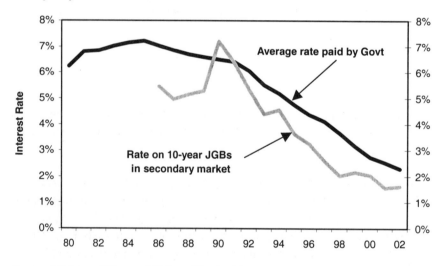

Source: Ministry of Finance 2001b and Bank of Japan 2002c.

Note: In the bottom panel, the solid black line shows the average interest rate paid by the government. It is calculated—using the data in the top panel—by dividing the total interest paid by the total bonds outstanding. The figure for 2002 is an MOF projection. One reason this figure is higher than the average rate in the secondary market is that much of the government debt was contracted when interest rates were higher. The average rate paid by the government still has some room to fall to match current rates. But at some point the average rate will stop dropping and the interest burden will rise with the total of outstanding loans.

Eventually, however interest rates will bottom out and the debt service burden will rise. At that point, bond investors will recognize that only inflation will enable the government to pay the interest burden. Today, inflation is hardly a threat. But investors being asked to buy ten-year bonds will demand an inflation premium. Interest rates will rise, making the debt burden even more difficult to pay. For example, if net debt were 50 percent of GDP, every 1 percent rise in interest rates would hike the annual budget deficit to the tune of 0.5 percent of GDP. As the net-debt-to-GDP ratio rises, so does the impact of every new rise in interest rates. This creates even more pressure for monetizing the debt (i.e., inflating it away), and the vicious spiral takes off.

Recognizing this, credit rating agencies such as Moody's and Standard & Poor's have downgraded the *domestic* credit rating of Japanese government bonds (JGBs) to AA– and A2, respectively, with further downgrades likely. This recognizes the tiny, but no longer inconceivable, possibility that Tokyo will impose a default, stretch-out, et cetera on Japanese citizens, but not foreign lenders, over the next decade or so. The risk of default at an A2 rating is, for example, 0.5 percent over five years, up from 0.14 percent for an Aa3 rating.

Meanwhile, since the value of existing bonds drops when interest rates rise, the holders of JGBs, such as the already fragile banks, will suffer a large capital loss. To preclude this hit to the banks, the BOJ will face even greater pressure to keep long-term nominal rates very low by monetizing the growing government debt. How long it can do so, no one can reliably say. But, increasingly, the BOJ will, in effect, lose its independence. It will have no choice but to feed the debt machine to avoid financial meltdown. When the bond market will revolt—and whether it will do so gradually or abruptly—no one can reliably predict.

A Public Debt Volcano?

A famous May 2000 report entitled *Could Japan's Financial Mount Fuji Blow Its Top?* warned that "a truly historic downside risk is emerging in Japan today, posing a threat to global economic stability that makes crises in Mexico in 1994, Russia in 1995, and South East Asia in 1997 pale in comparison." The authors—David Asher of the American Enterprise Institute and Robert Dugger of Tudor Investments—contended that in the event of a U.S. slowdown, "Japan's debt volcano would be left open to erupt." In a July 2000 interview Asher, who later joined the State Department under the Bush administration, envisioned this eruption by mid-2002 or mid-2003.

In a May 2002 piece, Adam Posen—previously known for his advocacy of fiscal stimulus—predicted that the fiscal debt bomb would explode by September of 2002, saying, "the Japanese economy is likely to tumble into crisis sometime before the Diet's supplemental budget process begins in September 2002. This reflects Japan's increasing vulnerability to shocks, now that it is caught in the tightening vise of debt-deflation and fiscal erosion."[8]

We disagree. Japan still has lots of safety valves that can carry it for the medium term. Unlike the other countries in the Asher/Dugger sample of fiscal crises, Japan does not suffer a simultaneous balance of payments deficit (see Chapter 1, p. 13). Of course, the debt-to-GDP ratio cannot grow indefinitely; at some point there will be a break. But where that is, no one can say, because it is based in part on subjective factors.

The problem is not the size of the debt per se. The United States came out of World War II with a debt-to-GDP ratio of approximately 140 percent, the same ratio as Japan's today, while Great Britain's debt-to-GDP ratio was 270 percent in the same period. Yet the financial markets did not revolt because these were seen as temporary results of the war. In Japan, however, there is no end in sight. As Moody's points out:

> After surveying the historical record, one is almost tempted to conclude that debt levels, in and of themselves, have not always been an indicator of potential default on debt. What appears to have been very important was investor acceptance of the reasons behind the debt build-up and the domestic policy response to dealing with the existing debt. [9]

The reality is that the mounting public debt is not the *cause* of Japan's problems but a *symptom,* caused primarily by falling tax revenues in a weak economy as well as the need to pump up deficits to avoid depression. Tax revenues in fiscal 2002 were projected to be only 46 trillion yen, down 22 percent from 1990. As a result, relative to GDP, taxes were down by almost 4 percent of GDP from 1990. While spending did rise, it did so by only half as much relative to GDP (Figure 6.5).

Without faster growth in the private sector that improves the tax base, there is no solution to the budget dilemma.

Reformers in the Trap

Unfortunately, reformers have let the LDP conservatives and the Ministry of Finance set the terms of the debate: Either accept more useless public works or risk recession. Some opposition parties, such as Minshuto, as

Figure 6.5 **Weak Private Economy Lowers Tax Revenue**

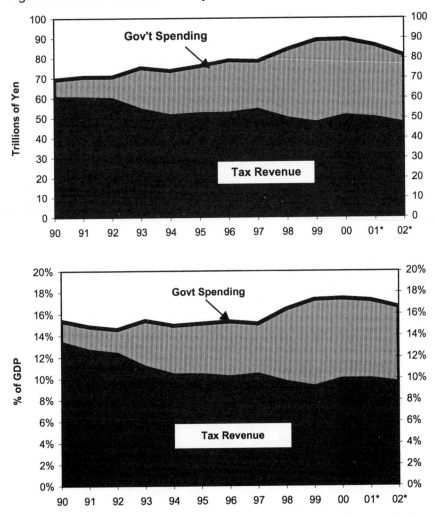

Source: Ministry of Finance 2001b for budget; OECD 2001b for nominal GDP projections for 2001–02.

Note: Fiscal years. FY 2001 is a projection by the MOF. FY 2002 is the budget plan. It is the initial budget, with no supplementals and assumes 0 percent real GDP growth and –0.9 percent nominal growth in FY 2002, much more optimistic than private forecasts. The reason for the discrepancy between Figure 6.5 and Figure 6.1 is that Figure 6.5 includes only the general account taxes and spending of the national government, not local budgets, the Fiscal Investment and Loan Program, or semigovernmental agencies.

well as reformers within the LDP focus on the deficit as if it were public enemy number one.

The Minshuto has called for an actual tax hike, by lowering the minimum income that is taxable (see Chapter 19). To its credit, the Liberal Party, led by Ichiro Ozawa, has bucked the trend by calling for permanent tax cuts to accompany spending cuts.

The Koizumi administration says that downgrades by credit rating agencies leave it no choice but to prune the debt. Not so. As the credit agencies themselves recognize, not all budget deficits are created equal. The financial markets will digest deficits that are used to finance reforms that raise the tax base down the road. We asked representatives of Standard & Poor's the following. Suppose Japan used higher deficits to solve the banking problem. What would be the effect on the credit rating? The answer was favorable.

The way out is to change the terms of the debate: to use budget stimulus as a macroeconomic safety net while growth-boosting reforms are carried out. In doing so, Tokyo's primary tool should not be more spending. It should be tax cuts for consumers, who will spend the extra cash, not companies, because the latter won't. But keep in mind that safety nets don't last forever.

———— 7 ————

Monetary Magic Bullets Are Blanks

Wouldn't it be wonderful if Japan could cure its chronically weak private demand the easy way: just by declaring an inflation target and printing lots of money (so-called quantitative easing)?

Backed by some monetarist economists, many in the LDP and MOF insist that this is exactly the cure and are pressuring the BOJ to go along. Some Diet members (led by ex-MOF bureaucrat and current LDP Dietman Kozo Yamamoto) have even threatened to retract the legal independence that the BOJ gained in 1998 unless it concedes.

Backed by other economists and some influential figures within METI, the BOJ denies that there are any monetary magic bullets. It views weak demand as a product of structural problems, particularly the bank debt crisis. In the words of the BOJ, "Monetary policy cannot substitute for structural policy."[1] Some critics claim the BOJ's resistance is simply due to one stubborn old man, BOJ governor Masaru Hayami. In reality, it is the consensus view of most of the senior BOJ staff. When Koizumi's chief economic adviser Heizo Takenaka declared that, "Unless banks make progress on bad-debt disposal, the monetary easing by the Bank of Japan will not produce results, making it impossible to beat deflation," he was saying nothing different from what the BOJ has said all along: as long as banks continue to prop up unproductive borrowers, the economy cannot return to vibrancy.[2]

Pushing on a String

If it were possible for monetary stimulus alone to revive growth, it would have done so long ago. For more than six years so far, the BOJ has kept overnight interest rates at less than 0.5 percent. Since early 1999, except for a brief interruption, they have been pushed to virtually zero: 0.001 percent (Figure 7.1). The ten-year government bond rate has been under 2

Figure 7.1 **Years of Near-Zero Rates Fail to Reinflate the Economy**

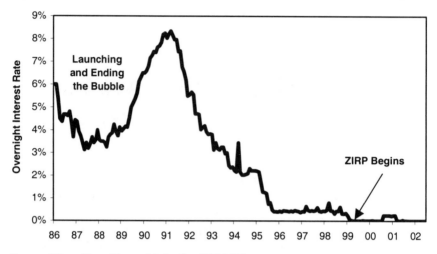

Source: "Short-Term Money Market" at BOJ 2002c.
Note: This is the rate on collateralized overnight loans. ZIRP is zero interest rate policy.

percent since 1998 and during 2001 averaged 1.4 percent. These low rates themselves are proof positive that lack of liquidity is not the constraint on growth. If the economy were demanding more money than the BOJ was supplying, interest rates would have shot up.

In a healthy economy, low rates induce companies to buy more machinery and consumers to buy more cars and houses. Once rates hit zero, however, a central bank starts running out of bullets. The next step is to extend low rates to instruments of longer and longer maturities (a tactic known as "flattening the yield curve"). The BOJ has done that. By mid-2002, three-month Treasury bills were at 0.04 percent, while the five-year bond had been pushed down to around 0.4 percent. Searching all the way back to the Babylonian Empire, it's hard to find a precedent.

Having done all that, the BOJ argues that any additional money printing would have only marginal impact. The proponents of quantitative easing retort that the economy responds to the sheer quantity of money printed by the BOJ regardless of the interest rate. But how? Unlike a tax cut, money creation by a central bank does not directly put a single yen of real money in people's pockets. All that happens is that the BOJ buys existing financial instruments (usually short-term government bills) from those who already own them. This has a direct effect on interest rates in the capital markets. But it has no effect on people's wallets—unless businesses and banks and consumers respond to those lower rates. As BOJ Policy Board member Kazuo Ueda pointed out, "Unless one believes that provision of liquidity has a direct impact on the demand for goods and services, money-supply targeting also works through interest rates."[3] This stance attracted attention, because when interest rates were still positive, Ueda had been one of the most outspoken proponents of further monetary easing.

Contrary to accusations that Hayami has been a tightwad, the BOJ has been trying to create money at a pell-mell rate. Quantitative easing has been tried—and it has failed. From late 1998 through late 2001, the BOJ pumped up the so-called monetary base at a 9 percent annual rate, the highest since the late 1980s bubble. In 2001, the BOJ monetized much of the government debt, buying 40 percent of all newly issued bonds. While its efforts pushed interest rates to the floor, the economy proved incapable of responding in a normal fashion. The broader money supply (M2 + CDs)— which reflects the economy's need for money—limped along at only a 2.7 percent pace, bank loans fell 2.3 percent each year, and prices fell at a 1.5 percent clip (Figure 7.2). The BOJ faced the classic case of trying to "push on a string," a situation where monetary policy acting by itself is very weak (although in combination with tax cuts and bank reform it could be quite powerful). This is the much-discussed "liquidity trap."

In 2002, the BOJ pushed the proverbial string even harder, expanding the monetary base at a virtually unprecedented 20–30 percent annual rate. Even U.S. Council of Economic Advisers chairman Glenn Hubbard, a critic of the BOJ, proclaimed, "As long as policy remains on this course, it will no longer be possible to claim that the Bank of Japan is ignoring the problem of deflation."[4] Nonetheless, in defiance of monetarist prediction, the broader money supply hardly responded. As of August, its growth was still limping along at 3.2 percent while bank loans continued to decline at a 2–3 percent pace. (Look ahead to Figure 7.7 on p. 135.)

Why, then, is the BOJ under such strong attack from LDP politicians and accused of pursuing a deflationary policy? The real dispute is not over technical issues of monetary policy, but whether or not the BOJ will be forced to finance "convoy capitalism." Just as some politicians wanted to use public works to substitute for reform, so some see the same role for monetary easing that raises the price of stocks and real estate, and that finances the rollover of bank loans for the "zombies."

Naturally, not all who support inflation targeting and quantitative easing do so for such unsavory motives. Many respected economists support additional monetary ease. However, unless care is taken to link monetary ease with reform, such arguments are seized upon by the anti-reformers.

Figure 7.2 **BOJ Printing Lots of Money, but Response Is Weak**

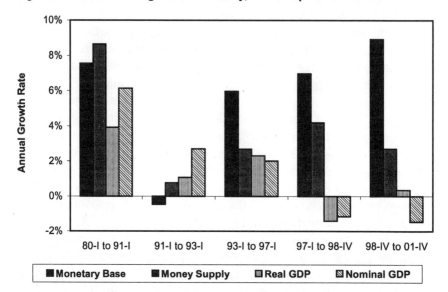

Source: "Money Stock" and "Bank of Japan Accounts" tables at BOJ 2002d.
Note: All at annualized rates. Money supply equals M2 + CDs.

This is worsened when some prominent economists, such as Paul Krugman, join the LDP in opposing reform and even liken reformers to Herbert Hoover:

> Japan isn't limited by its capacity. It is plagued by chronic insufficiency of demand. . . . And in such an economy, attempts to increase efficiency often do more harm than good. Freeing capital by reducing the budget deficit and closing down unprofitable businesses sounds great—but if that freed capital is simply put under the mattress (or stored in a bank vault), the result is not faster growth but a deeper slump. . . .
>
> Banks, in particular, are already awash in cash, but cannot find good new loans to make. Why would forcing them to write off bad old loans make any difference?[5]

Often disagreements among officials in Japan are muted in public. But on this issue, the two sides fought it out in the world's op-ed pages.

Writing in the London *Financial Times,* Takatoshi Ito, an internationally renowned economist who had just become a vice minister at the MOF, declared:

> The Bank of Japan could commit to an inflation target of, say, 1 to 3 percent, to be achieved in two years. . . . [This would] define the parameters of its independence . . . the Diet and the government would be able to hold the BOJ responsible only if results were not consistent with the announced target.[6]

The reality is that the BOJ has no way to guarantee such a target. Central banks can no more create inflation at the snap of a finger than they can reduce it at will. If they could, then U.S. Fed chairman Paul Volcker could have cured America's double-digit inflation of the early 1980s without putting the country through the wringer of double-digit unemployment. Consequently, the MOF proposal would end up compelling the BOJ to buy whatever asset the government asked it to. Already, the BOJ has been asked to buy everything from long-term government bonds to stocks, foreign exchange, and buildings—all the way to refrigerators and TVs.[7] In short, the MOF's notorious "price-keeping operations" for stocks and real estate, not to mention all the "bridges to nowhere" used to buy votes for the LDP, would now be supported by unlimited money printing.

For most of 1999 and 2000 the BOJ stood alone, under attack from the LDP, the MOF, and at times Washington. But in the spring of 2001 other forces in Japan, notably parts of METI, began to publicly ally with the BOJ. The most explicit early example was the "morphine-versus-anesthesia" argument put out by METI's Tatsuya Terazawa (see Chapter 1, p. 20). Noboru Hatakeyama, a former vice minister of METI who now chairs the Japan External Trade Organization (JETRO), wrote an op-ed piece in *Mainichi Shimbun* implicitly defending the BOJ and arguing that some of the deflation reflected the process of weeding out excess capacity.[8] Added backup came from Naoki Tanaka, a Koizumi adviser who is president of 21st Century Public Policy Institute, a think tank associated with the big business federation Nippon Keidanren. Tanaka told the *Nihon Keizai Shimbun:*

> In the future when we look back to today's prices going down, we can place this time as a positive step for the Japanese economy. One of the reasons why lowering prices became possible is because of globalization. That is, imports from overseas of inexpensive raw materials. Another reason is falling land prices. There may be cases of excessive competition and landslide price declines but using monetary policy for this kind of micro price declines is not appropriate.[9]

Less important than the technical analysis was the beginnings of an "anesthesia faction" that wanted to finally get out of Japan's false stimulus-versus-reform debate by making the two partners, beginning with the bad debt problem.[10]

Deflation Is a Symptom, Not a Cause, of Weak Demand; No Deflationary Spiral

Deflation is a dragon that breathes little fire. Yes, Japan has some deflation—that is, a slow decline in prices—but there is no "deflationary spiral." What's the difference? It's the difference between Japan today and the United States in the 1930s.

In America's Great Depression, weak demand and falling prices fed each other. The stock market crash led firms to slash investment and lay off workers in order to hoard cash. That weakened demand further, pushing down both commodity and asset prices. Rapidly falling prices made it harder for firms and people to pay their bills, so they cut spending even more. By 1933, prices were down 25 percent, real GDP had plunged 35 percent, and one-quarter of America's workers were on the street.

Nothing remotely like this is happening in Japan, partly because of massive fiscal and monetary stimulus.

Japan's deflation is mild, with the GDP deflator falling at a 1.5 to 2 percent clip from 1999 to mid-2002, and consumer prices falling even less, at a 0.5 percent rate. In the United States, by the way, wholesale prices fell 2.6 percent in 2001, yet that didn't block recovery in 2002.

The key point is this: While weak demand is causing prices to fall in Japan, those falling prices are not, in turn, causing demand to weaken further.

During the past decade, the best predictor of inflation or deflation has not been monetary policy but the demand-supply gap (or output gap) in the real economy. This is the gap between supply, that is, what the economy could produce at full capacity (potential GDP) and the demand for goods and services on the part of businesses, government, and households (actual GDP). When demand is below supply, prices soften. When a boom causes demand to become so strong as to stretch the economy's capacity, inflation results.

Japan's recent deflation is primarily a symptom of a weak economy, one where actual GDP is now 5 percent or so below full capacity. In fact, over the entire fourteen-year period from 1987 through 2001, there was an extremely high 88 percent correlation between the demand-supply gap in one quarter and inflation or deflation four quarters later. During 1998–2001, the correlation was even higher, 93 percent (Figure 7.3). This result is a variation of the famous Phillips Curve of economics.

If deflation were, in turn, exerting a backlash on demand, we should see a similar correlation, with deflation in one year leading to weaker demand

Figure 7.3a **Ups and Downs of Inflation Stem from Real Demand**

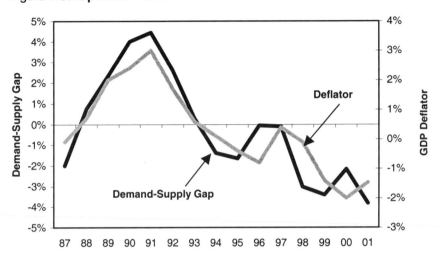

Figure 7.3b **In 1990s, Demand Gap Leads to Deflation One Year Later**

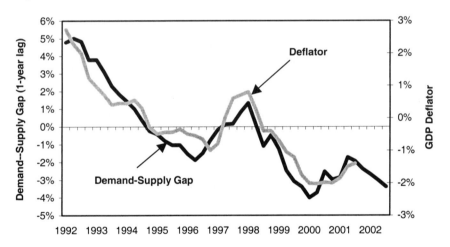

Source: Cabinet Office 2002b for GDP deflator. Demand-supply gap was calculated by author using data on potential growth in Bayoumi 2000a.

Note: The top panel shows annual figures with both prices and the output gap in the same year. By the mid-1990s, however, deflation began to lag the output gap by a year. The bottom panel shows quarterly figures and takes into account the lag. It shows how an output gap today affects inflation or deflation a year later. So the year 2000 shows the deflator in 2000 and the demand-supply gap in 1999.

a year or two later. But we do not. During the years from 1995 to 2001 the correlation between deflation in one quarter and the demand-supply gap four quarters later was *negative* (it would be positive if deflation were weakening demand). But it was statistically insignificant, so there is no real correlation at all. In short, there is no sign whatsoever that deflation is weakening demand. That's very good news for Japan.[11]

Deflation and the NPL Problem

Some economists worry that deflation makes it harder for companies to pay their debts, thus worsening the NPL problem. If prices, and hence a company's revenues, fall 5 percent, its debt remains the same. Hence there is 5 percent less revenue to finance interest payments.

What this argument ignores is that the company's costs are also falling by 5 percent. A company's ability to pay debt depends on the ratio of operating profits to debt. Suppose a firm's debt and its sales revenue both equal 100 yen and its costs are 95 yen. Thus operating profits are 5 yen, and they equal 5 percent of its debt. If interest rates are 3 percent, it can easily pay its debts. Suppose deflation means prices fall 10 percent. Then sales revenue, costs, and profits each fall by 10 percent. Revenue drops to 90 yen and costs drop to 85.5 yen, pushing operating profits down to 4.5 yen. As a result, operating profits now equal 4.5 percent of debt. With interest rates still at 3 percent, the company can still easily pay its interest bill.

Of course, some costs are fixed and so deflation does hurt. There is also a lag between the time inputs are purchased and sales are made. But all this is small potatoes compared to the biggest hit to profits: the weak economy. Deflation was actually milder in 2001 than in 2000. Yet profits were up 25 percent in 2000 because the economy was growing, and down 11 percent in the first three quarters of 2001 because the economy was slowing.

Good Deflation and Bad Deflation

In defending its policies, the BOJ distinguishes between "good deflation" and "bad deflation."

Good deflation, previously called "price destruction," comes when monopolistic prices are brought down to earth due to deregulation or globalization. A drop of 80 percent in long-distance call rates or the halving of fleece jacket prices due to imports from China are examples. In this case, a drop in prices actually adds to demand by increasing real consumer purchasing power. In economic jargon, it is a falling *supply* curve, which should stimulate growth in GDP, whereas bad deflation reflects a falling *demand* curve. We discussed some of this good deflation in Chapter 3, p. 53.

According to economist Robert Feldman, almost all of the decline in the consumer price index (CPI) is concentrated in a few items subject to increased competition or deregulation, mainly clothing, telephone charges, fresh food, and personal computers. Ken Okamura, formerly of Dresdner Kleinwort Wasserstein, reports that of all the consumer deflation from 1998 to February 2001, 84 percent came from just food and clothing. In the wholesale price index, falls in communications, a newly deregulated sector, stand out. Feldman comments, "In one sense, there is no comfort in the fact that price declines are concentrated. If technology and globalization are pushing some relative prices down . . . there is no necessary reason for the aggregate price level to fall. . . . Thus, there is a macroeconomic problem. Having said that, the macro camp cannot find full justification for hand-wringing in these numbers either."[12]

At times, good deflation and bad deflation are intertwined, as when weak demand, rather than deregulation or globalization, makes it impossible to sustain monopolistic prices.

In any case, while elements of good deflation are present, and more would be welcome, we believe the lion's share of deflation reflects the unraveling of an unsustainable system.

The Liquidity Trap and Monetary Policy

The BOJ's monetarist critics claim that, even in a zero-interest-rate environment, the combination of quantitative easing and inflation targeting would succeed in raising prices and elevating real demand. Yet they have offered little empirical evidence to justify these assertions. On the contrary, a look at the evidence shows the opposite.

Normally, monetary stimulus induces both consumers and companies to buy more. That's not working in today's Japan, and not just because interest rates have already hit zero. More fundamentally, as we pointed out in Chapter 4, neither firms plagued with excess capacity nor consumers finding their incomes under siege want to get deeper into hock just because interest rates are low, or because the BOJ might promise 3 percent inflation, or because the money supply is rising.

Beyond that, monetary stimulus has a tough time working when bank loans are dropping due to little demand for them. Normally, monetary stimulus increases demand, at least initially, because it creates additional lending capacity in the banking system. Indeed, the very measure of the money supply—known as M2 + CDs—is the amount of checking and savings deposits and certificates of deposit (CDs) at the banks. That, in turn, provides the basis of bank lending capacity. In order for monetary stimulus to lift GDP, the banking system must turn central bank-created bank reserves (the lion's share of the monetary base) into credit in the real economy.

But with bank loans dropping like a rock, the normal monetary mechanism has been short-circuited. The banks are awash in liquidity, but they have few takers. Total loans at the banks are far less than total deposits. Consequently, banks are putting these deposits into government bonds (Figure 7.4). An IMF study concluded that

> banks play a crucial role in transmitting monetary shocks [either stimulus or tightening—RK] to economic actors . . . We conclude that policy measures to strengthen banks are a *prerequisite* to restoring the effectiveness of the monetary transmission mechanism. [Emphasis added][13]

In short, monetary stimulus works when a dearth of liquidity means that borrowers are unable to get the loans they want and banks are unable to make the loans they would like to provide. It is evidenced by a rise in interest rates as demand for funds outweighs supply. But Japan is not constrained by lack of liquidity. Hence the central bank's powers to propel further economic growth are limited.

To make matters worse, a liquidity trap means the central bank can no longer easily expand the money supply at will. The BOJ, like any central bank, does not directly control the size of the overall money supply (M2 + CDs), but only a narrow segment of the money supply, the monetary base, which consists of currency (cash) and bank reserves held at the BOJ. Normally the BOJ expands the money supply via so-called open-market operations in which it fabricates money to buy government notes. The sellers of these government securities deposit their proceeds into their banks. That, in turn, increases bank reserves, enabling the banks to lend more. When the borrowers spend the money and their vendors deposit their receipts into their own banks, bank reserves expand still further, leading to even more loans. Through this process, the increase in the monetary base becomes multiplied into a big increase in the broad money supply.

However, with loan demand falling, the multiplier process breaks down. Instead, excess reserves pile up in the banks. At times, 75 percent of these excess reserves were being sent back to the BOJ via fund brokers, known as *tanshi*. As the BOJ sent more money out, even more came back. As

Figure 7.4a **Plenty of Deposits, Fewer Loans**

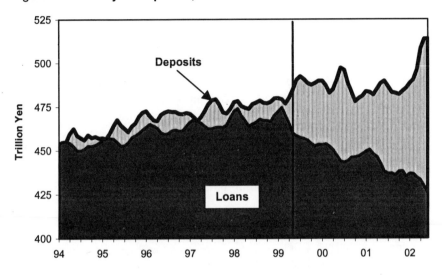

Figure 7.4b **As Bank Loans Tumble, Gov't Bond Purchases Soar**

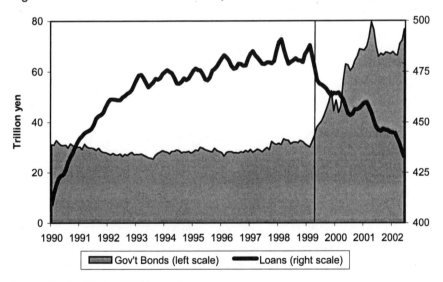

Source: Bank of Japan 2002a.

Note: The top panel shows deposits and loans, both in three-month moving averages. The bottom panel shows the amount of government bonds and loans plus discounts, with the latter in a three-month moving average. The vertical line in both panels marks the simultaneous injection of government money into the banks and the initiation of zero interest rates in February–March of 1999.

Kazuo Ueda noted, "Once the zero rate is reached . . . attempts to expand the money supply themselves may become unsuccessful."[14]

Consequently, whereas the growth of the monetary base reflects the BOJ's attempts to supply more money, M2 + CDs and bank lending reflect the economy's demand for money. In the 1980s the monetary base and the broader money supply grew in tandem. But not in the 1990s (look again at Figure 7.2). As the saying goes, "You can lead a horse to water but you can't make him drink." The BOJ was able to put a floor underneath the economy, but it couldn't make it grow.

Economists at the IMF tested the theory of quantitative easing—the notion that simply expanding the monetary base would automatically translate into faster growth—and found that, in the case of current-day Japan, it's just not true:

> Thus far, we have assumed that monetary policy acts only through interest rates. . . . To address this issue of whether base money is also important for aggregate demand when interest rates are held constant, we added base money to the basic model. The impulse response of real demand to base money is small and insignificant. . . . This suggests that, at least in normal circumstances, quantitative easing may have only limited effects on activity.[15]

Even Adam Posen and his colleague Kenneth Kuttner have conceded that, in the absence of other moves—such as fiscal policy and a bank cleanup—quantitative easing is weak tea. This is particularly significant since Posen has been one of the most fervent advocates of monetary stimulus. Reporting the results of their econometric regressions, they write:

> The monetary shock . . . initially increases prices, but the effect is reversed after a few quarters. . . . In addition, given the weak link between M0 [the monetary base] and M2 (and thus between M0 and prices), an increase in high-powered money [another name for the monetary base] will have only a limited effect if banks are unable or unwilling to lend the additional reserves. . . .
>
> Under conditions of a liquidity trap, even more than under normal conditions . . . , it would appear that interest rates are what matter, not monetary aggregates. . . .
>
> To some degree, however, the monetary policy question is moot. If the Bank of Japan *can print money without causing inflation* over some large range of values . . . it can monetize large quantities of government debt. . . . *If fiscal stimulus is effective, then ultimately the role of monetary policy should be to accommodate expansionary fiscal policy.* [Emphasis added][16]

In short: by itself in today's Japan, monetary stimulus is weak. When combined with other measures, it can be very powerful.

The Chimera of "Inflation Targeting"

Paul Krugman, too, acknowledges that quantitative easing by itself doesn't work. So, he says, it must be accompanied by the promise of inflation:

> Many people apparently read my previous note as saying simply that Japan should print money like crazy. I have indeed said this in the past. . . . But I now believe . . . that even a very large current monetary expansion will probably be ineffective. What is needed is a credible commitment to future monetary expansion, so as to generate expectations of inflation.[17]

His reasoning is this: Normally there is some interest rate low enough to cause households to save less (i.e., spend more) and businesses to invest more. In Japan's case, that interest rate is negative. It's as if you could borrow $100 and pay back only $95. Of course no bank would agree to such a deal. So, how to solve the dilemma? The key is *real* interest rates, that is, nominal rates adjusted for expected inflation. If the bank charges 2 percent but inflation is 5 percent, then the real interest rate is *minus* 3 percent. Thus Krugman argues that the BOJ should declare a target of 3–4 percent inflation over the next fifteen years and back it up by printing tons of money. This combination of quantitative easing and inflation targeting will get people to spend and "cure Japan's ills."[18]

In effect, Krugman is proposing that Japan adopt negative interest rates for fifteen years, thereby promoting capital investments with a negative real return—investments that cannot pay for themselves. But wasn't that exactly what led to today's debt crisis?

As economist J.A. Kregel has pointed out, Krugman proposes exactly the failed policy that classical economist Irving Fisher proposed to Franklin Roosevelt during the 1930s Depression, a policy that Keynes correctly criticized as impotent.[19] It is just as wrong for Japan now as it was for the United States back then.

The chain of logic of the inflation-targeting-cum-quantitative-easing faction is this:

1. The BOJ can create inflation at will.
2. Higher inflation will lead to lower real rates of interest.
3. Expectations of inflation and negative real interest rates will lead people and businesses to spend now before prices go up.

All three links in the chain fail, refuted by theory as well as decades of data.

For one thing, central banks cannot create inflation at will—certainly not over the one- to two-year time frame proposed by Takatoshi Ito, Paul Krugman and others, as we'll demonstrate below.

As for the second point above, this necessarily presumes that only households and companies will alter their behavior in light of promised inflation, but that bondholders will not. It presumes that bondholders will happily agree to get back less than they lent out and that they won't raise nominal rates to compensate for higher inflation.

Nonetheless, suppose for the sake of argument that the BOJ could create inflation and negative real interest rates at will. Who exactly is supposed to do all this buying in response?

Why would companies add more excess capacity just because prices are going up? And if they did, the whole process would be self-defeating, as the additional excess would add to deflationary pressures.

How about consumers? The inflation faction contends that if consumers expect prices to go down, they will delay purchasing items, just as people sometimes delay buying a personal computer while waiting for further price declines. But if they expect prices to go up, they will want to buy things now. There is an opposite reaction, however, that could be even more powerful in hurting demand.

Inflation that creates negative real interest rates of 3 percent means a decline in the real value of household savings accounts by 3 percent. To make up for the loss, households might save more rather than spend more. Suppose a family has thirty years to accumulate a retirement nest egg of $100,000. If the interest rate is 4 percent, then it needs to save $1,800 a year. If the interest rate drops to zero, the family must sock away $3,333. And should the rate turn to *negative* 3 percent, then its savings must rise to $5,000.

In fact, a recent study by the BOJ shows that because of this negative effect on income, a drop in real interest rates has an ambiguous effect in Japan. In the United States, where households borrow a lot, a drop in interest rates sends householders scurrying to refinance their mortgages, garnering lots of cash to spend. But, in Japan, where household borrowing is so much less, a drop in rates hurts consumers as savers without giving them that much relief as borrowers. The net result is a sharp drop in household income (as we saw in Figure 4.2 in Chapter 4). In normal times, this problem is more than offset by the positive effect of lower interest rates on business investment and hiring. But not these days.[20]

Given these contradictory effects, one would think the "inflation faction" would back up their promises with some evidence. Yet in his major academic paper on this topic, Krugman did not provide a single regression testing whether either Japanese consumers or companies spend more due to inflation, not one regression testing whether increased inflation causes Japanese GDP to go up or down, not even one trying to demonstrate that deflation is the cause of Japan's low growth.[21]

Inflation, Deflation, and GDP Growth

If higher inflation truly spurred higher GDP growth, then the ups and downs of inflation in one year should lead to ups and downs in GDP growth a year or two later. But the opposite is shown in the data. It is not higher inflation that leads to faster growth; rather, faster growth sometimes leads to higher inflation. Conversely, as we'll see, deflation is a symptom of weak growth, not its cause.

Faster GDP growth can lead to higher inflation because faster growth reduces the so-called output gap or demand-supply gap.

This is seen in Figure 7.5. The top panel tests whether higher inflation today leads to higher GDP growth two years down the road. The answer is no. As often as not, the two curves move in opposite directions. In fact, a regression produces a fascinating result. During the period 1982–90, when the economy was operating around full capacity, each 1 percent rise in inflation today was followed by a 0.32 *decline* in GDP two years later. Inflation hurt growth. What about 1992–2000, when the economy went soft? Did deflation lead to weaker GDP later? The regression shows no significant relationship. Deflation neither hurt nor helped growth over the past decade.

By contrast, the bottom panel shows that higher GDP growth today does lead to higher inflation later on. During the whole period 1982–2000, each 1 percent *rise* in GDP was followed eight quarters later by a 0.35 percent *rise* in inflation. During the 1990s, each 1 percent up and down of GDP growth led to 0.29 percent up or down in inflation or deflation.

The conclusion is clear: Over medium-term periods (two to three years), higher inflation is not the *cause* of higher GDP growth but its *result*.[22]

The inflation faction has got cause and effect backward. Inflation does not cause higher growth; it *reflects* it. Trying to elevate growth by raising inflation is like trying to make October feel like July by boiling your thermometer.

Imported Inflation

One bizarre notion now making the academic rounds is that Japan can import inflation through a depreciation of the yen. The logic is this: A

Figure 7.5 **Higher Inflation Does *Not* Lead to Higher GDP Growth . . .**

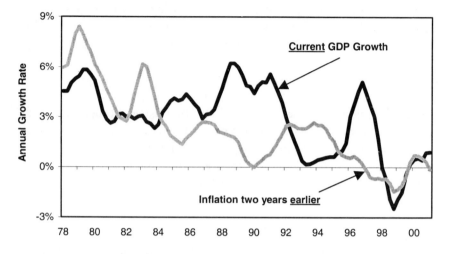

. . . Rather, Higher GDP Growth Leads to Higher Inflation

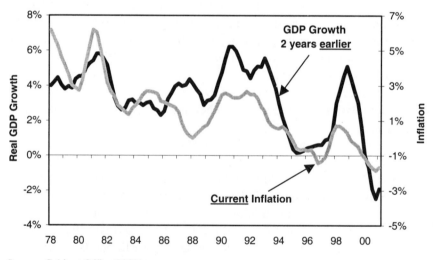

Source: Cabinet Office 2002b.

Note: In order to have data going back to the late 1970s, this is the old SNA 68 basis data.
GDP growth and inflation are both four-quarter moving averages of the year-to-year change.
Inflation is the GDP deflator. In the top panel, GDP growth in each quarter is compared to
inflation eight quarters earlier—e.g., the data point for the first quarter of 2000 shows GDP
in that quarter and inflation during the first quarter of 1998. In the bottom panel, inflation in
each quarter is compared to GDP growth eight quarters earlier—e.g., the data point for the
first quarter of 2000 shows inflation in that quarter and GDP growth during the first quarter
of 1998.

weak yen buys less, forcing Japan to pay more for everything it imports, from oil to food to clothes to machinery. Rising import prices will help feed more general inflation.

It is certainly true that higher import prices mean higher domestic prices. A 20 percent hike in import prices tends to raise Japanese inflation by about 1 percent. But to believe that this kind of inflation will spur growth is to believe that Japan would grow faster if OPEC quadrupled oil prices. No nation (or individual) has ever benefited by paying more to get less. On the contrary, higher import prices transfer spending power from domestic consumers to foreign producers. Higher import prices are the sacrifice a nation makes in order to gain the real demand-side benefit of currency depreciation: more exports.

The BOJ Cannot Create Inflation at Will

Nor is there any evidence for the novel theory that the BOJ can create inflation in a weak economy just by "raising expectations" and then printing money. This is something that Krugman himself used to stress. In a *Nikkei* article where he first proposed quantitative easing alone—rather than inflation—as Japan's panacea, he wrote: "Printing money is only inflationary if people spend it, and if that spending exceeds the economy's capacity to produce."[23] While Krugman later reversed himself, we think he got it right the first time.

Although monetarists are wont to say that inflation and deflation are purely monetary phenomena, it's just not so. Money does matter, but so do the price of oil and the output gap; sometimes the latter matter even more. Otherwise why would Alan Greenspan pore so carefully over figures for unemployment, factory utilization, and productivity growth in measuring inflationary pressure? Why do central banks rely on the awkwardly named nonaccelerating inflation rate of unemployment (NAIRU) as a predictor of inflation? Indeed, while we can explain about half of the ups and downs of Japanese inflation from 1977 to 1990 just by looking at the ups and downs of money supply, we can explain almost 90 percent if we also consider GDP growth and import prices.

As Krugman originally stressed, printing more money does not translate directly into higher inflation. Only if monetary stimulus raises GDP growth and narrows the output gap does inflation result. It's the mirror image of slashing inflation through recession and unemployment.

Figure 7.6 **Money and Deflator Move in Different Directions**

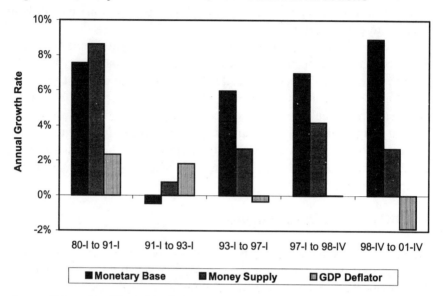

Source: "Money Stock" at BOJ (2002d), and Cabinet Office (2002b)
Note: All at annualized rates.

Consequently, the link between monetary ease and inflation hinges on the strength of the economy. From 1977 to 1990, when the economy was operating close to, and sometimes above, long-term potential, each 1 percent hike in money supply growth led to a 0.17 percent hike in inflation two years later. (Incidentally, each 1 percent rise in real GDP growth led to a 0.27 percent hike in inflation a year later.) That's because easy money stimulated demand beyond the capacity of the economy to respond. So it accelerated both real growth and inflation.[24]

By contrast, in the period 1991–2000, when the economy was operating far below capacity, money lost its inflationary power. Taking GDP growth and other factors into account, a regression shows that accelerated money growth had no *independent* power to accelerate inflation. What influenced inflation most was growth in real GDP.[25]

We are not saying that monetary policy was useless. What we are saying is that to the extent monetary ease promoted inflation in the past decade, it did so only indirectly: via its power to raise real GDP growth. In a period such as the 1990s, when the ability of monetary stimulus to improve real growth is limited, so is its ability to promote inflation. The BOJ's power to

Figure 7.7 **Pushing on a String: Monetary Base vs. Money Supply**

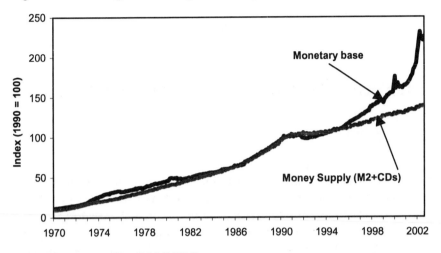

Source: "Money Stock" at BOJ (2002d)

Note: Up through 1996, whenever the BOJ increased the monetary base, the broader money supply expanded in tandem, as the textbooks say it should. After 1996, the normal linkage did not work. Money supply growth did not respond to even astronomical increases in the monetary base. For definitions of terms and explanation, see text p. 119.

create inflation is most impotent just when the "inflationists" say it is most needed.

This contrast between BOJ action and prices in the late 1990s compared to the 1980s is illustrated in Figure 7.6.

Of course, monetary stimulus is needed—but as part of a package, including tax cuts, bank cleanup, and other reforms. By itself, monetary stimulus can do little more; in combination with other measures, it can do a lot.

8

Japan Cannot Export Its Way Out

As Japan scurries from pillar to post, searching for a painless quick fix, it keeps returning to the dream that it can export its way out of trouble. If only the Bank of Japan printed enough money to drive the yen to 150 to the dollar, or even 200 to the dollar, proponents claim, then exports would soar, providing a big market for domestic production and investment. Unfortunately, this is yet another of the unending chimeras du jour.

Yes, back in 1973–77 and again during 1980–85, Tokyo did indeed use a rising trade surplus to propel about 40 percent of Japan's GDP growth.[1] But never again has Japan's trade surplus in goods and services come anywhere close to the record 4 percent of GDP it hit in mid-1985 (Figure 8.1). The soaring yen that followed the 1985 Plaza Accord, the rise of new competitors in Asia, the hollowing out of Japan's most competitive export sectors, and the sheer size of anorexia have all taken their toll. In 2001, despite a relatively cheap yen, the merchandise surplus was the lowest in eighteen years. Never again will Japan be able to use an expanding surplus to solve its problems.

Trade's impact on demand growth is a function of the trade balance, with a surplus adding to demand and a deficit subtracting from it. What's important is not the size of the surplus per se, but whether it is growing or shrinking. Even a very large surplus, if it is shrinking, still subtracts from growth. With all the ups and downs of the surplus, the net effect since 1990 has been a wash.

Sorry, No More Room

There are some economists who say Japan could run a trade surplus as big as it wanted to—even 10 percent of GDP—if only it drove the yen down enough. But the truth is that Japan cannot run a surplus of, say, $300 billion unless the rest of the world runs an offsetting deficit of $300 billion. And

Figure 8.1 **Trade Surplus Will Never Again Come Close to 1985 Peak**

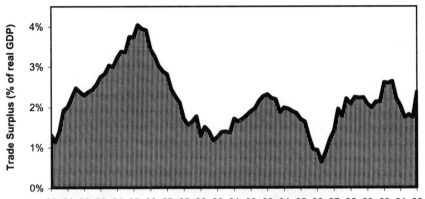

Source: Cabinet Office 2002b.
Note: Includes goods and services. All data in four-quarter moving averages at an annualized rate.

the latter depends on conditions in those countries, not just Japan. If their economies are slowing, they are not going to rush to buy more Japanese exports even if the yen is somewhat cheaper. For almost twenty years— from the mid-1970s to the mid-1990s—the ups and downs of Japan's *trade* surplus were a function of the ups and downs of America's *budget* deficit.[2]

Compare Japan with South Korea. In 1998, when both countries strove for export-led recoveries, Japan's trade surplus equaled $73 billion, not quite twice Korea's surplus of $42 billion. Together, they accounted for 25 percent of all the trade surpluses in the entire world. But Korea's surplus amounted to a whopping 13 percent of its GDP, whereas Japan's surplus was only 2 percent of its GDP. With only half the burden on the world's absorption capacity, Korea obtained six times the boost to growth.

Suppose Japan tried to pull off Korea's achievement, replacing a budget deficit of 8 percent of GDP with a trade surplus that size. While currency fluctuations preclude us from directly translating this into a dollar amount, a rough guesstimate is that Japan's trade surplus would have to triple to about $250 billion.

In 1999, the combined trade surpluses of all the world's surplus countries totaled $451 billion. Japan's share was 14 percent—way down from 34 percent in 1986. To hit $250 billion, Japan would have to gobble up at least half of the entire global surplus, reversing years of decline (Figure 8.2a). The

Figure 8.2a **Japan's Falling Share of Global Trade Surpluses**

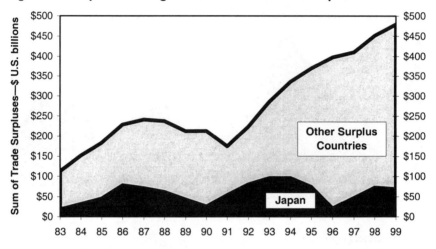

Source: World Bank 2002.

Note: The chart shows the combined trade surplus of all of the surplus countries. For example, in 1999, 60 out of 174 countries ran trade surpluses, and these surpluses added up to $479 billion. Includes goods and services.

Figure 8.2b **Japan's Falling Share of U.S Trade Deficit**

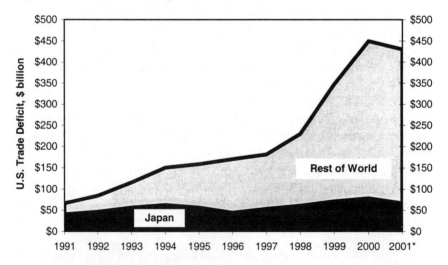

Source: Census Bureau 2002.

Note: This includes only trade in goods, whereas the chart in Figure 8.2a includes goods and services. In 1999, the U.S. deficit in goods alone was $345 billion, much larger than the $261 billion deficit in goods and services combined.

surpluses of China, Korea, France, and Germany would have to dwindle. East Asia, which used growing surpluses to recover from the 1997–98 debacle, would have to reverse course. It's not in the cards.

Alternatively, one could posit that the U.S. deficit would soar so high that it could absorb it all. Even if that were possible, which it is not, Japan has hardly been the beneficiary of America's growing deficits. On the contrary, in 2000, only 18 percent of America's merchandise trade deficit was with Japan, way down from 65 percent in 1991. China's bilateral surplus is bigger (Figure 8.2b).

The verdict is clear: Quite aside from any protectionism, the pure economics of the situation veto Japan's efforts.

Hollowing Out Diminishes the Export Route

One must also consider the hollowing out of Japan's most powerful export industries. To the extent that people want to buy Japanese cars or TVs or machine tools, they increasingly buy them from factories outside of Japan. Hence, a given yen level no longer packs as much punch.

Besides, the same yen depreciation that helps factories in the home islands hurts Japanese-owned factories overseas, creating mixed emotions among big exporting firms. There is a growing conflict of interest between the needs of Japan's home islands—and those who live there—and the needs of its big multinationals. Squaring that circle is getting tougher.

Tokyo Cannot Control the Yen Rate

Even if a cheaper yen could send the surplus skyward, Tokyo does not have fingertip control over the yen rate.

The yen rate is a price. Like all prices, it is determined by the forces of supply and demand. When the BOJ buys dollars and other foreign currencies—evidenced by an increase in Japan's foreign exchange reserves—that adds to demand for those foreign currencies. All else being equal, that should cheapen the yen. But all else is never equal. Hence Tokyo can influence the yen rate, but actual control is beyond its powers.

From the spring of 1999 to the spring of 2000, the BOJ increased its foreign exchange reserves by 50 percent, about $120 billion. That huge intervention was almost equal to Japan's entire current account surplus during that period. And yet the yen actually strengthened from 120 to 106 (a lower number equals a stronger yen). All the BOJ could do was to limit its rise. Then, as the yen weakened again in late 2000, the BOJ continued to buy dollars. This added to the weakening trend, but it didn't create it.

What really determines the ups and downs of the yen over the medium term are basic trends in capital and trade flows.

Japan's trade surplus creates *demand* for the yen. Foreign buyers have to exchange dollars, euros, or another currency to purchase yen in order to buy Japanese products. That pushes the yen upward. (Since the yen rise, in turn, makes Japanese exports more expensive, the expansion of the trade surplus is somewhat self-correcting.)

Conversely, a net outflow of capital from Japan creates a *supply* of yen. Japanese investors use the yen to buy other currencies and invest in overseas assets. A net outflow means that Japanese investors are investing a lot more in the stocks, bonds, and real estate of foreign countries than foreigners are investing in Japan. Japan almost always has a net capital outflow. But the size gyrates. The most important factors in this gyration are prospects for economic growth and profits in Japan compared to the rest of the world, together with interest rate differentials. All other things being equal, higher interest rates and more optimistic profit projections in the United States would attract money from Japan to the United States.

For the yen to remain stable, the inflow of money via the trade surplus has to be matched by an equal outflow of money via net capital flows.

However, except during the 1998 financial crisis, the net capital outflows have almost always been too small to match the current account surplus (Figure 8.3a). Consequently, demand for the yen almost always outstrips supply. In more technical terms, the private balance of payments is usually positive. The black area in Figure 8.3a shows the size of this excess demand.

As we see in Figure 8.3b, the ups and downs of the private balance of payments are the most important factor in the ups and downs of the yen.

In recent years, the swing factor has been foreign sentiment about Japan, which changes in sync with Japan's economic and financial fortunes.

In short, there is a constant struggle between two conflicting forces. Japan's perpetual trade surplus, unmatched by equivalent capital outflows, creates continual pressure for the yen to rise. By contrast, disenchantment with Japan's economic prospects leads to capital flight and a falling yen, as in 1998 and 2001.

The overall result is an oscillation of both the yen and the trade surplus. When the yen is strengthening, the BOJ tries to limit the rise. Certainly, had it not been for massive BOJ purchases of dollars throughout the decade, the yen would have risen to an even higher level during its episodes

Figure 8.3a **Gyrations of Capital Flows . . .**

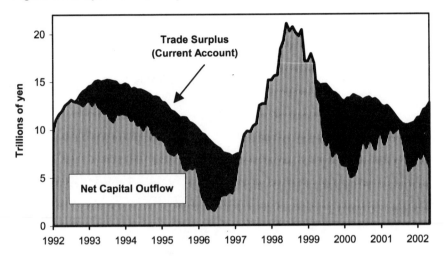

Figure 8.3b **. . . Create Gyrations of Yen**

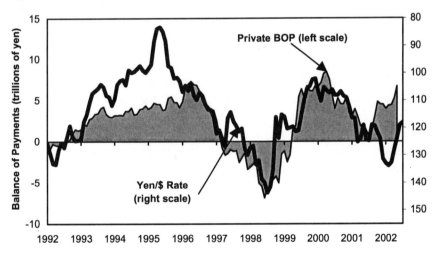

Source: Ministry of Finance 2002b.
Note: All balance of payments data are presented in a twelve-month moving sum. The yen-to-dollar rate is a monthly average. The data go through November 2001. In the top panel, a rise in the capital outflow means more capital is leaving Japan. It includes only private flows by both Japanese and foreigners. In the bottom panel, the private balance of payments figures equal the black area of the top panel. That is, it is the net capital outflow minus the current account surplus. A negative number means more money is leaving Japan than is coming in. The yen scale is inverted so that a rise in the line means a rise in the value of the yen.

Figure 8.4 **Dancing Partners: The Yen and Stocks**

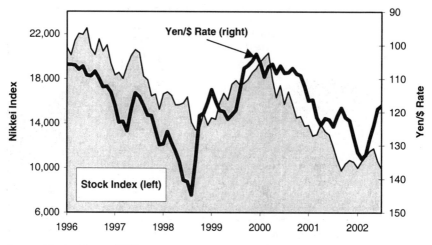

Source: Bank of Japan 2002e.
Note: The yen rate is inverted so that a rising line means a more valuable yen.

of strength. However, the BOJ has no power to set a target and meet it when private market forces are going the opposite way.

Nor are neighbors such as Korea and Taiwan likely to stand idly by while their export competitiveness is undermined. Almost half of Korea's exports directly compete with Japanese goods. As Tokyo launched a campaign to weaken the yen in early 2002, its neighbors issued stern warnings, warnings that were joined by the Bush administration. A determined effort to weaken the yen could set off a destabilizing round of competitive depreciations throughout Asia, leaving everyone worse off.

Be Careful What You Wish For: The Yen and the Stock Market

Promising that Tokyo will drive the yen down by, say, 20 percent is also telling foreign investors that Japanese stocks and bonds are going to drop 20 percent in value when measured in dollars. It tells Japanese investors that any American securities will rise 20 percent when measured in yen. Why not just hang "Sell Japanese Stocks" signs on the MOF doors?

If the Japanese stock market were still a domestic affair, as in days of old, a weakening yen would not lead to falling share prices. But these days, foreign investors account for up to half of all trades. They have become the key swing factor. When they lose confidence in Japan, or when they expect the yen to drop, they sell Japan—and the market tumbles. Starting in the late 1990s, stock prices and the yen began moving in tandem. From 1996 through mid-2002, there was a 43 percent correlation between monthly ups and downs of the stock market and the monthly ups and downs of the yen (Figure 8.4).

As in the summer of 1998, when the yen briefly dropped to 146 amid financial turmoil, a plunging yen cannot be separated from a flight from Japanese financial assets. It is not a pretty sight.

Part Three

Globalization: A Progress Report

9

Globalization

The Linchpin of Reform

If Japan is to reform, increased globalization will have to play a critical role. We say that for three reasons:

1. All across the world, where reform has succeeded, increased globalization—that is, an increase in competing imports and foreign direct investment (FDI)—has been indispensable.
2. Since insufficient globalization is at the heart of Japan's problems, increased globalization must be at the heart of the solution.
3. The politics of reform become much easier under the pressure of globalization.

Without increased globalization, it is hard to see how reform can succeed, either economically or politically. The good news is that on some fronts—especially FDI and financial integration—we see progress. Unfortunately, this progress does not extend to competing imports.

Openness, Growth, and Reform

The link between openness and growth is clear (Chapter 9 in *Japan: The System That Soured*). Countries that are more open—that is, with a higher trade-to-GDP ratio and more inward FDI—grow faster. They do so because competition and economies of scale breed faster productivity growth.

Increased trade and FDI were critical in the successful transitions to market economies in Poland, China, and now India. President Kim Dae Jung of South Korea promoted a rapid increase of FDI as a means of "locking in" his economic reform program. Increased trade was critical to America's shift from the "rust belt" economy to the information age, as well as in the upgrade of heavy manufacturing itself.

All countries get into trouble from time to time. When they do, the more open countries usually respond and reform more quickly. Witness South Korea's rather rapid recovery from the 1997–98 calamity. And whenever reform has failed, failure to expose the market to international competition was usually present. Since Asia apart from Japan is far more open to trade and FDI than Japan, we wrote back in 1998:

> [W]hen the new millennium dawns, most of Asia will probably be well on its way to full recovery. But when it comes to Japan . . . we will still be waiting for the sun to rise.[1]

Globalization Is Particularly Important in Japan's Case

Insufficient globalization has been at the heart of Japan's problems, as we detailed in Chapter 3. But globalization is also important politically. The entry of new players not tied to the cozy cartels breaks down those cartels. Foreign players offer the "countervailing institutions" so deficient in Japan. In the process of political "creative destruction," globalization offers both destruction and creation. It eliminates some of the safety valves of the old regime and adds new pressure to undertake reforms.

It is not that globalization is more important than domestic reforms. Rather, domestic reform is more likely to occur if Japan experiences more globalization. We already discussed in Chapter 3 how reform of the Large-Scale Retail Store Law *(Daiten-ho)* led to big changes in the way that Japanese retailers operated. Later we'll discuss further examples, from mobile phones to the "Big Bang."

Therefore, in measuring progress toward structural reform, it is vital to examine the globalization front, specifically, competing imports, foreign direct investment, and financial integration.

The most important role of imports in reform is competitive pressures, as discussed in Chapter 3 (p. 43). In addition, they allow Japan to specialize in what it does best. There is no reason for Japan to import a single drop of crude oil, since its refiners are incredibly inefficient. It should instead import petroleum products, as most countries do.

Sometimes FDI can be even more powerful than imports because of the demonstration effect, such as in the case of Renault's takeover of Nissan. Japan is hardly unique. It was not until Japanese automakers established plants on U.S. soil that the American Big Three began to change their own practices in emulation.

Financial integration is critical because it increases the odds that money will be allocated according to its most efficient use, not outdated ties. The foreign presence in Japan's stock market has made it harder for banks to cover up their NPL problems with stock price manipulation.

Globalization and the Asian Economic Crisis of 1997–98

Some in Japan resist globalization, pointing to the Asian calamity of 1997–98. In our view, that crisis was 90 percent unnecessary—the result of tragic and correctable policy errors rather than either globalization per se or internal structural flaws (as in Japan).

It's amazing how Asia's history has been rewritten. The "East Asian miracle" has been metamorphosed into the land of "crony capitalism," a case study in the "failed Japanese model of development." In reality, Asia's development approach was neither Japanese nor failed.

Failure? The truth is that, for three long decades from 1965 to 1995, Asia's "miracle economies" (South Korea, Taiwan, Hong Kong, Singapore, Malaysia, Indonesia, Thailand) averaged 8 percent growth a year. The twenty-year-olds of 1965 saw real GDP per person grow *five times* by their fiftieth birthday. No other group of countries has grown so fast for so long.

Unstable? Then why was it that, throughout these three decades, two of the crisis countries suffered not a single year of economic downturn and two experienced only a single year?

In 1960 South Korea's per capita GDP ranked with Zambia's; by 1997, it had reached the level of 1986 Japan. Where once the ambition was just to fill the belly, today in South Korea, it's to get a color TV or a car.

The fruits of all this growth were so widely shared that millennia of poverty were wiped out in the blink of an eye. Three decades ago, few in Southeast Asia had access to safe drinking water. Today nearly everyone does. No wonder life expectancy has risen from fifty-six years in 1975 to seventy-one today.

Twenty-five years ago, six out of every ten people in developing Asia (including China) had to survive on less than $1 per day. By 1995, that was down to two in ten and was falling rapidly.

Naturally, as the countries of Asia developed, they have had to shift gears, just like Japan before them. Efficiency requires giving far greater sway to markets, including financial markets. Asia began liberalizing in the late 1980s. But markets do not function without market institutions. This includes strong banks and banking supervision, transparent accounting procedures, credit rating agencies, and a mature legal structure. These take time to build. Exposing countries to short-term international money flows should be, as economist Barry Bosworth pointed out, "the last stage in a complex process of financial liberalization and growth."[2]

Alexis de Tocqueville wrote that the most dangerous time for a bad regime is when it starts to reform itself. The same is true for regulated financial regimes. Deregulation was the harbinger of America's savings-and-loan crisis, Japan's bubble economy, Asia's 1997–98 depression, and other banking crises around the world. From this, some people conclude that financial systems should not be deregulated. That's the wrong conclusion. The right conclusion is that, under the best of circumstances, the transition is a very delicate process. Proper sequencing is critical.

Asia was bound to hit some bumps in the road. But prematurely exposing Asia to hot money flows turned these bumps into an unnecessary cataclysm.

What really happened in Asia was a good old-fashioned boom-and-bust-cycle depression such as Europe and the United States suffered in their industrialization heydays. But Asia had its boom-bust cycle amidst the maelstrom of turbocharged global financial flows.

Worse yet, in the years leading up to 1997, rigid IMF-Treasury policies prevented Asia from applying the same techniques that rich nations use to dampen boom-bust cycles. In addition to built-in stabilizers such as deposit insurance, unemployment compensation, and government budgets, central banks actively adjust the economy's thermostat. By preventing booms from overheating, they prevent a bust.

In much of Asia, by contrast, the boom-bust cycle was amplified by a witch's brew of fixed currency rates and hot money flows. Grafting Latin American experiences onto Asia, the IMF advised pegged currencies as a barrier against inflation, together with abolition of controls on short-term international capital flows as a supposed route to market efficiency. The combination was an accident waiting to happen.

Asia's economic boom lured more foreign money than its underdeveloped financial systems could digest. A third came from Japan. The money gusher fed an investment boom far beyond any genuine need. From 1986–90 to 1991–95, the ratio of investment to GDP soared from 23 percent to 39 percent in Malaysia, from 33 percent to 41 percent in Thailand, and from 32 percent to 37 percent in South Korea. Inevitably, investment switched from manufacturing to real estate. Cash went into buildings for which there were no renters, factories in industries already suffering over-capacity, unscreened bank loans, overvalued stocks, and so forth. Japanese, European, and American funds all joined the party. All of this raised asset prices, drawing in even more money.

The boom sucked in imports and trade deficits soared. From 1989 to 1996, Korea's trade balance (current account) swung from a surplus equal to 2.5 percent of GDP to a deficit of 5 percent. In Malaysia, a surplus of 1 percent in 1989 became a deficit of 8.5 percent by 1995. In Thailand, the deficit grew from 3.5 percent to 8 percent. Debt mushroomed, but not a commensurate ability to service that debt. To top it off, most of the borrowings were short-term funds easily withdrawn at the first sign of panic.

In industrialized countries, a central bank would forestall such overheating by raising interest rates. However, this doesn't work when guaranteed currency rates mean foreign investors fear no currency risk. In that case, higher interest rates just attract even more money. The central bank is impotent. The bubble keeps growing until it finally pops.

That is why Hong Kong, with its inflexible currency board, suffered a 5 percent GDP decline in 1998 and another 1 percent in 1999, while Taiwan, with its managed float, barely took a breather. The 2001 crisis in Argentina, which kept a frozen currency too long, is another example.

When the yen weakened in 1996–97, it started the first domino falling. Since these currencies were pegged to the dollar, the weakening yen hurt their exports and began to send investors to the exits. But some other trigger could have done so just as well.

The risks of combining fixed currencies with that volume of cross-border capital flows should have been known in advance. After the crisis, Robert Mundell was given the Nobel prize for work performed decades earlier that predicted the consequence of this combination.

Once the panic hit, the U-turn in capital flows—amounting to 10 percent of the crisis countries' GDP—whipsawed the economies. Imagine Alan Greenspan lowering U.S. interest rates to zero and then abruptly hiking them to 40 percent.

Then the IMF-Treasury team turned recession into depression by imposing big budget cuts and stratospheric interest rates. They dismissed warnings from World Bank chief economist Joseph Stiglitz and Harvard professor Jeffrey Sachs. Later on, the IMF offered the excuse that, had it known the depression was going to be so bad, it never would have imposed such big budget cuts. But, had it not imposed the cuts, the downturn would never have been that bad in the first place. Once the IMF relented and let countries such as South Korea use fiscal stimulus, these economies quickly recovered.

Guided by the premise that bringing back international investors was the key to restoring growth, the IMF insisted on *raising* interest rates in a recession—the exact opposite of what any central bank does in a rich country. The IMF contended that higher rates would draw in money and stop the currency depreciation, which made it difficult for companies in these countries to pay their international bills. But the reality is that higher interest rates caused more bankruptcies and more chaos, making it even harder for these countries to pay their bills. That further discouraged foreign investors. The majority of nonperforming loans in these countries arose after, not before, the crisis.

Interestingly enough, despite all the IMF's errors, reformers in some Asian countries seized on the crisis to use IMF power to enforce needed domestic reforms. It was Indonesian technocrats, not IMF officials, who added to IMF conditionality the dismantling of the Suharto family's costly boondoggles.

The lesson should be clear. Just as capitalism does not mean laissez faire, so globalization should not mean hot money flows. But neither do the horrible mistakes of the IMF justify opposition to market reforms and increased globalization in Japan.

—— 10 ——

Imports

Too Many Captives, Not Enough Competitors

Civil Trade War

In the fall of 2000, one industry after another petitioned Tokyo to use "safeguard clauses" and other legal techniques to restrict mushrooming imports from China and other Asian countries. Producers of mushrooms, tatami mats, scallions, towels, fleece jackets, wood products, socks, ties, and bicycles all joined the fray. Computer chip producers discussed launching antidumping suits against Korea.

In the end, the agricultural lobby got its temporary safeguard protection, but no one else did. In response, China slapped 100 percent tariffs on imports of Japanese cars, mobile phones, and air conditioners, thereby pitting Japan's exporters against Japan's farmers.

Strange as it may seem, all this is very good news. Why? Because in the past, imports would never have loomed as large in the first place. Some might have been blocked at the loading dock. Distributors and retailers would have kept others off the shelf, either on their own or under duress. There would have been no newspaper articles, no public debate, no public knowledge.

Instead, covert protectionism became overt. When it did, Japan got a very healthy public debate. The Japan Chain Store Association condemned the curbs on farm goods and asked that they not be applied to other products. Nikkeiren, the employer association, took the same tack, noting the danger of Chinese retaliation against Japanese manufactures. *Nikkei Weekly* editorialized, "If Japanese companies seek to be protected, they will lose international competitiveness."[1]

The textile industry was internally divided, with small domestic producers demanding protection but larger multinationals, as well as retailers, opposing it. When the LDP set up a Special Committee on Textiles, the Japan Textile Federation conceded that it was unable to offer a unified view.[2]

While the Agriculture Ministry supported protection for farmers, METI, with its constituents divided, held back. One reform-minded METI official, upon learning that an American journalist was going to have dinner with some Diet members, said, "Tell the Dietmen not to support any import curbs."

What initially looked like a Japan-China trade war was really a civil trade war within Japan.

Some of the farm products were cultivated on behalf of Japanese trading companies, using Japanese seeds and spores. Many of the apparel and textile imports from China came from Japanese companies located there. Originally, apparel retailers such as Uniqlo subcontracted manufacturing to firms in China. That compelled Japanese manufacturers to go to China to compete. Who, then, is demanding protection? It's the smaller firms that remain at home and can no longer compete.[3]

A classic debate has thus ensued in Japan. In most industrialized countries, the fight for free trade is not led by disorganized consumers but by powerful multinationals and exporters anxious to break down foreign barriers to their own products, or to access low-cost inputs from abroad. That process has been delayed in Japan, partly because Japan's exporters received protection themselves. But now, for the big retailers and manufacturers, the costs of protectionism have started to outweigh the benefits. So the internal fight long seen in other countries is finally appearing in embryonic form within Japan.[4]

It's been a long time coming. The Economic Planning Agency was a lonely voice in 1996 when it declared that "an increase in imports would stimulate incentives to raise productivity of domestic industries."[5] Now, at long last, others are getting the point. Some METI officials say a series of bilateral free trade agreements with countries such as Singapore and South Korea could put pressure on Japan's less competitive service industries, such as port operations and telecommunications.

Falling Behind by Standing Still

While these political developments are very welcome, they have yet to translate into greater openness on the ground. With some exceptions, notably apparel and textiles, Japan has shown disappointingly little progress in recent years.

Since World War II, trade interdependence—that is, the ratio of trade (exports plus imports) to GDP—has increased dramatically for virtually every major industrial country except Japan. It is virtually the only rich country that traded less, relative to GDP, in 2000 than it had in 1955 (Figure 10.1).

In Germany and the United States, by contrast, the trade-to-GDP ratios more than doubled in recent decades, in the U.S. case from 9 percent to 26 percent. Normally, more populous countries trade less than small countries.[6] And yet today the United States not only imports more than Japan relative to its GDP but also exports more.

By standing still while the rest of the world moved ahead, Japan fell behind global trends. In the 1950s and 1960s Japan's trade-to-GDP ratio was about 45 percent of the average among a group of twenty-five countries. By 2000 Japan's ratio was down to 25 percent of the group average (Figure 10.2). If Japan had simply kept up with global trends, both its exports and its imports would be almost twice as high as they actually are.

At times in the late 1980s and again in the mid-1990s, imports rose quickly for a while, and some analysts rushed to claim that past patterns had been broken. In reality, these were mere gyrations in a flat secular trend, a temporary product of a spurt of growth and/or a rising yen. Moreover, as we'll detail below, most of the increase in imports came from Japan's own affiliates overseas rather than from competing firms.

Manufactured Imports: Half Full . . .

By some measures, it does seem as if big changes are occurring. Imports of manufactured goods, which hovered for years at only 12 percent of total consumption of manufactured goods, suddenly rose in the 1990s, virtually doubling to 23 percent by 1999. Moreover, economist Edward Lincoln reports a significant improvement in "intra-industry trade" between 1986 and 1998. Intra-industry trade—where a country both exports and imports autos, steel, or cars—is a standard measure of openness to products that compete with domestic production.[7]

Additionally, machinery—everything from electric fans and bicycles to computer chips and cars—has soared from only 7 percent of Japan's total imports in 1980 to 32 percent by 2000. Even if we discount the misleading effect of lowered oil prices in the late 1980s, this is still a major sea change, most of which occurred in the 1990s.[8]

The rise in machinery imports belies the notion that Japan's "resource endowment" and the economics of comparative advantage doom it to import

Figure 10.1 **Imports, Exports Still Flat Vis-à-Vis GDP**

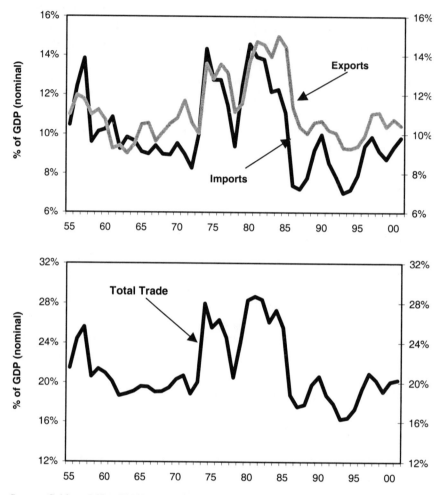

Source: Cabinet Office 2002b.

Note: All figures in nominal yen. Includes goods and services. The 2000 figure is for the first three quarters. In order to have figures going back to 1955 we had to use the SNA 68 numbers, which end in mid-2000. The bulge during 1973–86 reflects higher oil prices. Gyrations of import-dependence reflect gyrations in the growth rate of Japan's GDP and the lagged effects of gyrations of the yen.

Figure 10.2 **Japan Falls Behind World Trade Trends**

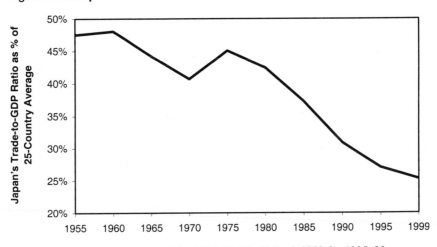

Source: Summers and Heston 1995 for 1955–90, World Bank 2002 for 1995–99.
Note: The chart compares Japan's trade-to-GDP ratio as a percentage of the average trade-to-GDP among a group of twenty-five countries.

mostly raw materials rather than manufactures. The obstacles to greater manufactured imports have never been the laws of comparative advantage but anticompetitive activities by Japanese firms.[9]

The rise in clothing imports equally belies the notion that consumer taste, rather than lack of consumer power, kept imports low. Few imports were sold because few could make it to the store shelves. But once imports were brought in, initially by maverick retailers, Japanese, like consumers elsewhere, showed they like quality goods at low prices—no matter where they are made.[10]

... Or Half Empty?

Given all these significant improvements, why is our overall conclusion so downbeat? The reason is this: While these changes indicate the potential, a closer look shows how far Japan stands from that potential. The glass truly is half empty rather than half full.

Take the ratio of imported manufactures to total consumption of manufactured goods. While Japan's ratio did increase, it was chasing a rapidly moving target. By 1997 the average OECD country imported 67 percent of the manufactured goods that it consumed while exporting 69 percent of the

Figure 10.3 **Share of Manufactured Imports in Manufacturing Consumption**

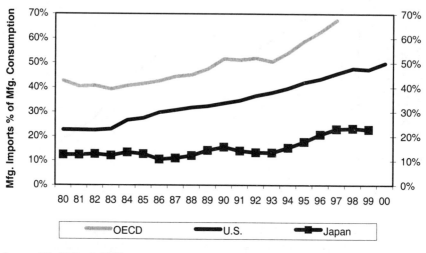

Source: World Bank 2000.
Note: All in current prices.

manufactured goods that it produced. The dividing line between domestic and foreign production was disappearing as a true international division of labor emerged.

Against this global trend, Japan's improvement was minor. In the early 1980s, the import share of manufactured goods consumed in Japan was about 31 percent of the OECD level. By 1999, Japan had risen to 35 percent. That's an improvement, but not by much (Figure 10.3). We find a similar pattern if we look at imports relative to GDP.[11]

Too Few Exports

That Japan is an underimporter by global standards is well known. Many economists have written about it, and it is the subject of great controversy. What is hardly discussed is that Japan is a remarkable under*exporter* as well. So much attention has been paid to Japan's chronic trade surpluses that few have looked at the *volume* of exports. Like Japan's imports, its exports also were lower relative to GDP in 2000 than in 1955. Japan's surplus is the difference between low exports and even lower imports. Indeed, for reasons discussed elsewhere, the biggest barrier to Japan's exports is its own low level of imports.[12]

Figure 10.4 **Share of Manufactured Exports in Manufacturing Production**

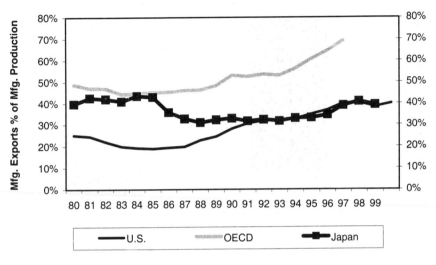

Source: World Bank 2000.
Note: All in current prices.

Worse yet, the share of manufactured output that Japan has been able to export has actually stagnated over the past few decades, while racing forward in the rest of the OECD. Consequently, Japan's export performance has plunged compared to international trends (Figure 10.4).

Importing from, and Exporting to, the "Captives"

The biggest disappointment in Japan's import trends is that, during the last decade, all of the increase in manufactured imports was provided by Japanese affiliates operating overseas, mostly in Asia. A typical example is Matsushita importing the TVs or air conditioners it makes in Malaysia. By contrast, manufactured imports from non-Japanese sources actually fell (Figure 10.5). As a result, such "captive imports"—called "reverse imports" by METI—rose from 4 percent of total imports in 1990 to 14 percent as of 1998.

Why should we care? What difference does it make if an imported TV is made by Matsushita in Malaysia or by Lucky Goldstar in South Korea? The answer is that the Matsushita TV is not designed to challenge the price structure and cozy ties of the Japanese electronics industry. A South Korean TV is. And it is competition that provides the productivity kick Japan

Figure 10.5a **1990s: All Import Growth Is from "Captive Imports"**

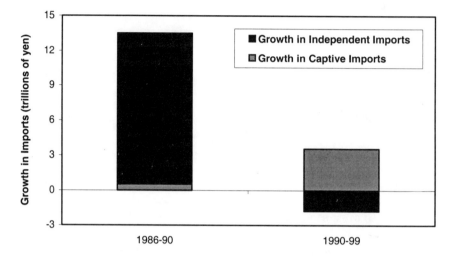

Figure 10.5b **Share of Captive Imports Soars**

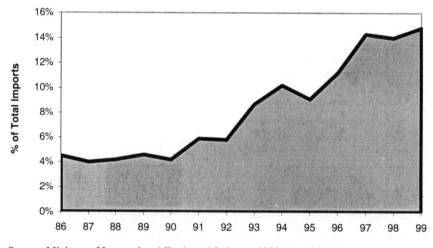

Source: Ministry of International Trade and Industry 1999a, pp. 16–17.

Note: "Captive imports" means imports from Japanese-owned affiliates overseas. "Independent" means all other imports. All in current prices.

Figure 10.6 **1990s: Export Growth Is to "Captive Customers"**

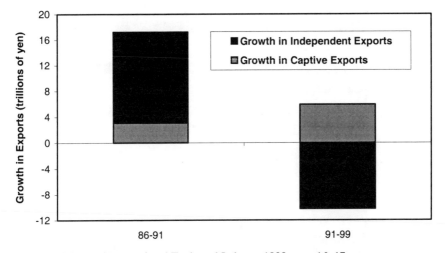

Source: Ministry of International Trade and Industry 1999a, pp. 16–17.

Note: "Captive customers" means exports to overseas affiliates. Independent exports means all other exports. All in current prices.

so desperately needs. Moreover, competing imports change the behavior of Japanese players.

It was not until Compaq unveiled its discount PCs in Japan in 1992 that Fujitsu launched its own price war against Nippon Electric Company (NEC). At the time, NEC owned a 53 percent share of the market. Within months, PC prices dropped by a third and NEC's share fell below 40 percent. Within a few years, NEC's share fell to 30 percent and continuing price drops fueled a PC boom.

What about Uniqlo's import of clothing from China? That is the exception that proves the rule. A buccaneer *retailer* imported clothing that competed with Japanese *manufacturers* by offering cut-rate prices.

What is equally remarkable is that the entire growth in *exports* went to these same overseas affiliates (Figure 10.6), once again in stark contrast to the late 1980s.

Thus, what we see in the past decade is not greater Japanese trade integration with the rest of the world, but simply a geographical expansion of Japanese manufacturing from the home islands to the home islands plus overseas affiliates. Rather than true international trade, this is just a vertical division of labor between Japanese parent firms and their overseas affiliates.

Figure 10.7 **Japan's Asian Imports Less Than U.S., Sometimes EU**

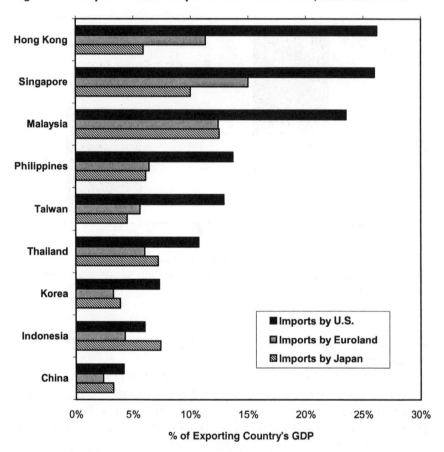

Source: Morgan Stanley Dean Witter, *Global Economic Forum,* December 11, 2000.
Note: This covers mostly 1999 data. It includes only merchandise trade, not services.

True, interfirm trade is important elsewhere. However, in most industrial countries, interfirm trade supplements and stimulates their overall trade. In Japan these days, interfirm trade is, to a considerable degree, substituting for other trade.

The Japan-Asia Link

About 80 percent of Japan's captive imports are from Asia.[13] Consequently, much of Japan's trade is shifting to Asia.

Figure 10.8 **Price Drops and Import Growth**

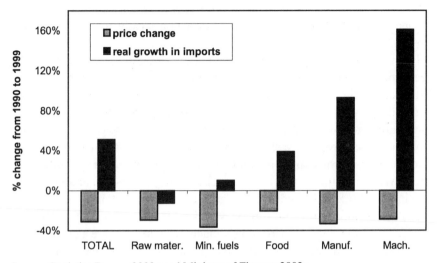

Source: Statistics Bureau 2002c and Ministry of Finance 2002c.

Note: Import growth is measured in terms of physical volume, e.g., tons of oil, numbers of TVs, etc.

In 2000, for the first time ever, Japan's imports from Asia were larger than imports from the United States and the European Union combined. China is now the second largest exporter to Japan after the United States.

However, since 60 percent of the entire increase in Japan's imports from Asia were "captive imports," this does little to help Asia's export-led industrialization. Japan's share of Asian exports is still surprisingly small. The U.S. imports far more than Japan from almost every East Asian country except Indonesia (Figure 10.7). America's imports from Taiwan amount to 13 percent of Taiwan's GDP, compared to 4.5 percent in imports by Japan. For South Korea, 7 percent of GDP goes to the United States but only 4 percent to Japan; for Malaysia, it's 23 percent to the United States and 12 percent to Japan. Moreover, in half the countries, even imports by faraway Europe outweigh those by neighboring Japan.

Do Japan's Imports Respond to Price Changes?

One of the great tests of whether market forces prevail is sensitivity to prices. If the price of Korean steel falls below Japanese steel, then Japanese imports from Korea should soar. Traditionally, Japan's imports were not very price-sensitive at all. Following the "yen shock" of 1985–86, imports did become more price-sensitive, but less so than in other countries.[14] So one measure of the progress of reform is a steady increase in price sensitivity (Figure 10.8).

Even in a completely free market, not all products are price-sensitive. If steel production is flat, steelmakers aren't going to buy a lot more iron ore just because the price has dropped. Naturally, then, as manufacturing slumped, the volume of raw material imports dropped, and petroleum imports barely rose despite big price drops. Food imports did grow in response to price drops as well as population growth, but nowhere near as much as one might expect in light of Japan's extraordinarily high food prices. With consumers in Tokyo compelled to pay prices 50 percent higher than in New York and London, 70 percent higher than in Paris and twice as high as in Berlin, the real question is why there is not a torrent of imports.[15]

Manufactured imports, particularly machinery imports, are a good news/ bad news story. Imports are now much more price-sensitive than ever. That's good. The bad news is that with captive imports predominating, price changes now lead to changes in where the machinery is produced, but not in the identity of the producer.

——— 11 ———

Foreign Direct Investment

A Sea Change

Changes on the Ground and in Attitudes

When it comes to inward foreign direct investment, events inconceivable a decade ago have now become commonplace. To cite just a few examples:

Retailing. As late as 1989, Toys R Us was legally obstructed from setting up so much as a single store. Today it is Japan's largest toy retailer, with more than a hundred stores and 14 percent of the market.[1]

Acquisition in autos and banking. A decade ago foreign acquisition of any large Japanese firm was unheard of. Today just about every auto firm other than Toyota and Honda is now under the effective control of foreigners: Nissan by Renault, Mazda by Ford, Mitsubishi Motors by Daimler-Chrysler, and Suzuki and Isuzu by General Motors. Foreign executives now run Nissan and Mazda and Mitsubishi, while having a heavy influence in Isuzu. After one of Japan's largest banks, the Long-Term Credit Bank (LTCB), went bankrupt, the Japanese government sold it off to a U.S.-based investment consortium, Ripplewood.

Contested takeover in telecom. In one of the first contested bids for control of a firm—by either domestic or foreign suitors—Britain's Cable & Wireless (C&W) beat out Nippon Telegraph and Telephone (NTT) for control of Japan's International Data Communications (IDC) in 1999. Initially, IDC's board took twenty minutes to sell themselves to NTT. Then minority shareholders in IDC, such as Toyota, pointed out that C&W's bid was higher and that C&W promised to protect the jobs of existing employees. IDC's board was forced to concede, lest it be subject to shareholder suits. Instead of helping out NTT, the government stayed neutral, a new and important precedent. By contrast, after Ripplewood bought LTCB, the government acted to prevent bankrupt Nippon Credit Bank from also being taken over by a foreign player.

These dramatic cases are just the tip of a growing iceberg. Overall, FDI into Japan has multiplied from about $4 billion a year and 0.1 percent of GDP in the early 1990s to $18 billion and 0.4 percent of GDP by fiscal 2001 (Figure 11.1). The fields of finance, autos, electronics, telecommunications, and retail/wholesale head the list of investments (Figure 11.2).

These changes on the ground both reflect and reinforce a sea change in attitudes.

Tip of the Iceberg

Pessimists could easily point out that Japan has a long way to go to reach international standards. In 1999, inward FDI in the typical OECD country was 2.7 percent of GDP, nine times as much as in Japan (Figure 11.3a). On a cumulative basis, the comparison was even worse: 0.7 percent of Japanese GDP in 1998, compared to 16 percent in the United States and 26 percent in France, with similar patterns in manufacturing (Figure 11.3b and Table 11.1).[2]

The comparisons look even worse if we compare the growth of the foreign share in Japanese manufacturing to the growth of Japanese production overseas (Figure 11.4).

Skeptics also point out—correctly—that almost all the acquisitions so far have been rescue operations for distressed firms. If inward FDI is to take off, it must become easier for foreigners to buy healthier firms, either parts of them or entire companies.

Nonetheless, such depictions present an accurate view only of the past, not necessarily of the future. If, as we expect, current trends continue or even accelerate, a decade hence Japan will be much closer to international norms.

The annual inflow of new FDI has now reached a critical mass that can lead to a big cumulative change over time. Even if the annual inflow goes no higher than the peak 0.6 percent of GDP attained in fiscal 2000, cumulative FDI would still rise to almost 6 percent of GDP by 2010. That's ten times today's level.

Why is there so much progress in FDI compared to imports? The biggest factor is that imports are widely seen as threat to jobs, whereas people hope FDI will add, or at least preserve, jobs. When Merrill Lynch agreed to take over Yamaichi Securities after its 1997 bankruptcy, most press coverage focused on the two thousand jobs Merrill pledged to save, not the fifty-five hundred that it could not. Carlos Ghosn, the Renault executive now running Nissan, is lionized, a far different reaction than the xenophobic

Figure 11.1a **Foreign Direct Investment into Japan Starting to Rise**

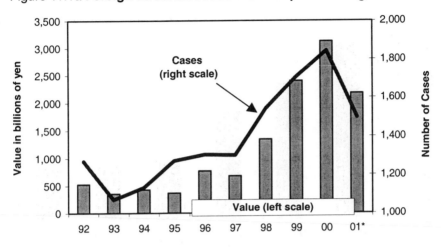

Fig. 11.1b **Flow of New FDI Rises Relative to GDP**

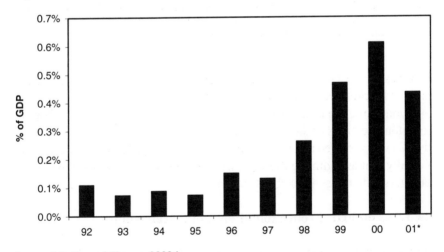

Source: Ministry of Finance 2002d.
Note: Fiscal years. Fiscal 2001 shows an annualized rate for figures from the first half of the year.

Figure 11.2 **FDI: Autos, Finance, Telecom, Distribution Stand Out**

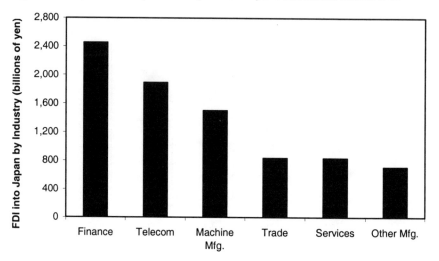

Source: Ministry of Finance 2002d.
Note: These data include the total from 1998 through the first half of 2001, all fiscal years.
Machinery manufacturing is primarily autos and electronics. Other manufacturing is every-
thing other than machinery. Trade means wholesale and retail trade.

headlines in the United States that greeted Mitsubishi Real Estate's purchase of Rockefeller Center in the 1980s.

Beyond that, the past decade has produced a dramatic reversal of opinion among sections of Japan's bureaucratic and corporate elite. Traditionally FDI was rebuffed as a threat to national autonomy. Today it is welcomed
as an ally—at least among those growing numbers of officials and business
managers who are serious about reform.

The Laws on FDI: From Prohibition to Liberalization

Unlike postwar Europe, which welcomed FDI as an alternative to imports,
Tokyo legally restricted both imports and FDI for years. During the post–
World War II occupation, the U.S. authorities had promoted FDI. However, as soon as Tokyo regained control over the issue, it reimposed
restrictions via the 1949 Foreign Exchange and Foreign Trade Control Law
(FEFTCL) and the 1950 Law Concerning Foreign Investment (LCFI). Each
investment had to be individually approved by the Finance Ministry as
well as the ministry responsible for the individual sector (for example,
METI for most manufacturing).

Figure 11.3a **Japan's Higher Levels Still Tiny by International Standards**

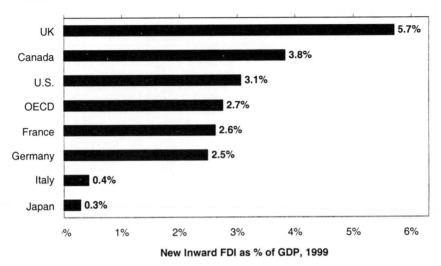

New Inward FDI as % of GDP, 1999

Source: OECD 2000d, Table 1.

Note: All data for 1999 based on OECD definition. Note that while current flows into Italy are tiny, cumulative foreign presence in Italy is much higher, as seen in Figure 11.3b.

Fig. 11.3b **Japan Lags in Share of Mfg. Under Foreign Control**

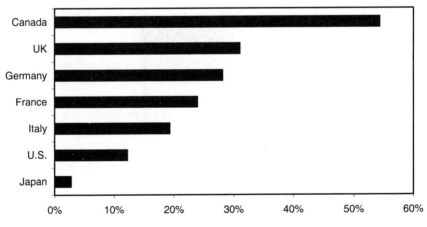

% of Manuf. Under Foreign Control.

Source: Hatzichronoglou 1999, p. 21.

Note: Data cover the year 1995.

Table 11.1

Foreign Share of Manufacturing in the United States and Japan

	United States	Japan
Food	9.0%	0.6%
Textiles	6.9%	0.2%
Wood, furniture	2.1%	0.5%
Paper, printing, publishing	9.9%	0.1%
Basic chemicals (except drugs)	21.8%	8.4%
Drugs	34.8%	21.9%
Petroleum refining	13.5%	43.8%
Rubber, plastics	16.0%	0.6%
Nonmetal mineral products	27.3%	4.7%
Basic metals	20.2%	0.0%
Metal products	8.1%	—
Nonelectrical machinery	10.4%	1.2%
Computers	6.4%	—
Electrical machinery	25.5%	4.4%
Electronics	8.6%	—
Motor vehicles	8.4%	0.6%
Other transport	4.6%	—
Instruments	13.0%	7.9%
Other manufacturing	4.5%	1.3%

Source: Hatzichronoglou 1999, pp. 42–43.

Note: 1995 data. In the case of Japan, nonelectrical machinery includes computers. Electrical machinery includes electronics. Motor vehicles include other transportation equipment (such as airplanes and ships) as well.

Initially Tokyo blocked all FDI except in cases where it offered an "essential contribution" to domestic industries. In 1959 Tokyo agreed to allow investments that did not "seriously impede the domestic development of industrial techniques." Still, approvals were a meager twenty per year. Foreign firms seeking to sell in Japan had little choice but to license their technology to Japanese firms or to joint ventures.

Until 1967 Tokyo rarely permitted either acquisitions of existing Japanese firms or even majority ownership of new affiliates. In the 1950s foreign ownership in joint ventures was usually limited to 49 percent. By 1960 fifty-fifty companies started to become common. Even then, Tokyo normally insisted that the Japanese partner have the majority of directors and executives.

In 1964, when Japan joined the OECD, it was obliged to phase out most restrictions. But not until 1967 did the business-dominated Foreign Invest-

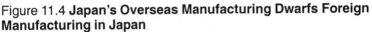

Figure 11.4 **Japan's Overseas Manufacturing Dwarfs Foreign Manufacturing in Japan**

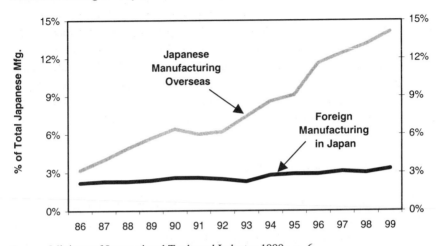

Source: Ministry of International Trade and Industry 1999a, p. 6.

Note: The production ratio includes only the manufacturing sector. Foreign affiliates in Japan include firms in which the foreign ownership share is at least one-third, and in which the firm has filed a report on inward direct investment with MITI (now called METI).

ment Council (FIC) present its plan to the MOF. Until this point, all investments had been forbidden unless specifically approved. Liberalization meant that all investments would be automatically approved unless specifically forbidden. Phased in on an industry-by-industry basis, liberalization began with those needing the least protection. Acquisition was not liberalized until the end. The process did not finish until 1976 and was not codified into law until 1980.

At the same time, METI set up its Capital Transactions Liberalization Countermeasures Special Committee. Countermeasures ranged from development aid (e.g., $140 million for the computer industry) and rationalization plans that divided up some industries among particular companies to forged mergers in others. METI was particularly protective in "strategic" sectors such as computers, semiconductors, machine tools, and autos.

A final countermeasure was promoting cross-shareholding so as to make hostile takeovers impossible. METI even persuaded the Diet to change the Commercial Code so that corporate boards could issue new shares and place them with other corporations without requiring the approval of current shareholders, mostly households, who might object to the dilution of their ownership. Rather quickly, the shares held by "stable shareholder" allies jumped from 42 percent in 1964 to 62 percent by 1973. Conversely, the share of stock owned by households fell from 55–60 percent to 20 percent. With as few as 15–25 percent of the shares publicly traded, there were not enough on the market for any would-be acquirer to acquire a majority via a tender offer, as is commonly done in the United States. This made a foreign—or domestic—takeover virtually impossible. Both Japanese government officials and Japanese lawyers have confirmed that stopping foreign takeovers was the primary purpose in encouraging greater cross-shareholding.[3]

Structural Impediments to FDI

For two decades now, there have been virtually no overt governmental restrictions on inward FDI beyond the sort seen in other countries. Yet FDI remained low due to lingering structural impediments.

In most countries, acquiring an existing company is the favored way of establishing a beachhead, since the buyout carries a built-in support base of customers, employees, suppliers, distributors, reputation, and so forth. Acquisition was American firms' favorite route of entry into Europe, and it accounted for 80 percent of all FDI into the United States in the 1980s and early 1990s.

In Japan, however, institutional obstacles made acquisition extremely difficult and rare—for foreigners and Japanese alike. The main impediment is the cross-shareholding system cited above. "Absent the stable shareholding system," says Arthur Mitchell, head of the Japan practice at the New York law firm of Coudert Brothers, "Japanese firms would be quite naked to takeovers."

As recently as February 2000, the support of entrenched management by shareholder allies such as Canon and Fuji Bank foiled Japan's first-ever full-scale attempted hostile takeover. This was the effort of Yoshiaki Murakami, a former METI official turned mergers and acquisitions (M&A) specialist to buy out Shoei. Murakami complained that the stable shareholders were not willing to sell at any price. There have been a few successful exceptions since then—e.g. Vodaphone's successful bid for controlling shares of Japan Telecom in 2001—but they can be counted on one hand. In fact, the word for hostile takeover, *nottori,* means "hijacking."

This left foreigners with the famous Groucho Marx joke, not caring to buy any of the firms willing to be bought out. Even among Japanese firms, friendly acquisitions occurred mainly to rationalize an industry; rescue a sick firm; or keep a small firm going when the family owners retired. As late as 1988, Merck's buyout of Banyu remained the only foreign buyout of a publicly listed corporation.

If Japanese firms couldn't be bought, and joint ventures were undesirable to foreigners seeking to control their own operations, then the only choice was to set up new facilities from the ground up. That meant hiring a complete labor force, which for many firms was a tougher problem than winning sales.[4]

The lifetime employment system meant it was difficult to recruit middle managers with experience. The potential employee worried he could not get a new comparable job if the foreign firm failed or downsized, as many did. Newly minted college grads likewise hesitated to work for low-prestige foreign firms. By the late 1980s, big-name firms who had been in Japan for a long time—such as Texas Instruments or IBM—found the recruitment problems shrinking. Unknowns had much greater problems.

The 1990s Crisis Changes Attitudes and Practice

Then came the 1990s economic crisis, and long-held attitudes rapidly melted away. More firms needed a knight in shining armor and cared little whether that armor was made at home or abroad. The majority of the publicized cases involved rescues of failed or near-failing entities. Nissan, before being taken over by Renault, had lost money year after year. Mitsubishi Motors and Mazda are similarly firms in big trouble. Merrill bought Yamaichi Securities after it went bankrupt, as was the case with Ripplewood's purchase of LTCB (since renamed Shinsei) and GE Capital's purchase of Toho Life.

Not all firms, particularly smaller ones, waited until they crashed before selling themselves. With M&A in general and foreign takeovers in particular becoming more respectable, foreign acquisitions soared in the late 1990s—from 40 in 1996 to about 100 in 1999 to an annualized rate of 150 during the first nine months of 2000 (Figure 11.5). In 1999, the $16 billion worth of acquisitions accounted for three-quarters of the entire $21 billion in inward FDI that year.[5]

While friendly rescues have soared, hostile takeovers are still well nigh impossible for either foreigners or Japanese. Ultimately, that will put a ceiling on the scale of FDI, as well as the pressure for corporate restructuring.

Today the hiring problems are much fewer, particularly for well-known firms. In surveys, college students reportedly list Goldman Sachs as among the most desirable firms, especially among educated women, who face thick glass ceilings at traditional Japanese companies.

Figure 11.5 **Foreign Buyouts of Japanese Firms Soar**

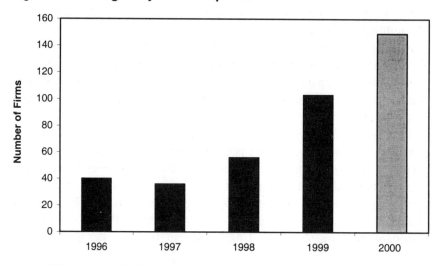

Source: Nihon Keizai Shimbun 2001a.
Note: The figure for 2000 is the annual rate based on actual results from January to September.

FDI Promotes Corporate Reform

The *Nikkei Weekly* headline "Foreigners Breathe Life into Japan Inc." reflects not only new attitudes but also new realities.[6]

The most celebrated example is, of course, Renault's rescue of Nissan after it became the company's largest shareholder, with 37 percent of the shares. The problem at Nissan was not just poor management but the refusal of the entire industry to downsize. During the period 1991–98, Nissan, once Japan's second-largest automaker, had lost money in every year but one, with the total losses adding up to 467 billion yen ($4 billion).

The hope was that foreign managers would be willing to make the tough decisions that tradition-bound Japanese counterparts couldn't or wouldn't. Moreover, as Mazda president Mark Fields (a Ford executive) noted, tough actions taken by foreign owners seemed more palatable to Japanese workers and suppliers than those same actions when taken by longtime Japanese owners.[7]

Carlos Ghosn, nicknamed "the cost-cutter," developed a plan to bring Nissan back to profitability—even with zero growth in global sales—through a program of harsh downsizing: a 16 percent cut in the workforce, a 30 percent cut in capacity, a 50 percent cut in debt, a 20 percent cut in materials costs, reductions in the number of suppliers, elimination of cross-shareholding, and other drastic reforms. After years of losses, the firm earned more than 180 billion yen ($1.5 billion) in net profit in both fiscal 2000 and 2001 (years ending in March 2001 and March 2002, respectively). There are now entire sections of bookstores devoted to Ghosn's exploits and an adult-oriented comic book celebrating his life from boy to corporate exec.

Not all cases involve downsizing. In many cases, all that is needed is managers who understand the business. A classic along this line is Nippon Foundry, a semiconductor subsidiary of Nippon Steel that was bought out in 1998 by Taiwan's United Microelectronics Corporation (UMC). Under Nippon Steel, the subsidiary languished. Under UMC, it is flourishing. Sales were up, costs were down, and so were defects (defect-free levels reached 99 percent under UMC compared to only 80 percent under Nippon Steel). It earned record profits in 2000 (but went into the red in 2001 due to the global chip slump).

In the long run, the most important effect of FDI will be the changes that improved performance in acquired firms catalyzes in other Japanese players. If Nissan continues to prosper, the demonstration effect will ripple throughout Japanese manufacturing.

The poster boy for the competitive effect of FDI on Japanese firms is Toys R Us (see Chapter 3, p. 54).

METI Says FDI Is Reform's Ally

One of the more hopeful signs in Japan is the "FDI initiative" launched by METI. Vice Minister Hidehiro Konno speaks of the mutually reinforcing quality of FDI and structural reform. In the past, such METI efforts were limited to marginal issues as finding land or aiding with financing. But now, partly in cooperation with the U.S. government, METI is engaging in a bit of a search-and-destroy mission to find those aspects of Japanese corporate governance and labor practices that limit inward FDI.[8] It is encouraging to hear some METI officials speak not of how far Japan has come but of how far it has to go.

In many cases, the remaining impediments concern issues that affect the flexibility of the entire economy, not just FDI. These issues (to be discussed in Chapter 15) range from M&A, holding companies, and stock options to consolidated accounting and taxation and portable pensions. For that reason, METI's FDI initiative really consists of these broader changes in corporate practice.

The latter approach is not sufficient, in the view of both the American Chamber of Commerce in Japan (ACCJ) and the New York Council on Foreign Relations Task Force on Japan. Some current provisions of Japan's tax code disadvantage FDI in ways that need to be addressed specifically.[9] Some of them sound very arcane, but in combination they can make a big difference in what happens on the ground. Some examples include:

- Capital gains from stock options are taxed at a rate of 26 percent in Japan, considerably below the ordinary income tax. However, an individual employee can receive stock options only from his or her direct employer, not its parent. Thus even though a foreign parent of a Japanese affiliate would like to provide stock options in the parent to lure good talent, Japan's tax laws make it hard to provide this incentive.
- Japanese employees of foreign firms in Japan are not allowed to put their pension money in the pension plans of foreign parent companies. Employees can invest only in registered pension plans in Japan, and they can almost never take their pension funds with them when they leave a company. There are also issues of double-taxation that employees of foreign firms face in the 401(K)-style plans now being introduced into Japan.
- Stock-for-stock swaps, the most common way of financing M&As, are given favorable tax treatment for transactions within Japan, but not for cross-border transactions. This hinders not only foreign acquisition of Japanese firms but also Japanese acquisitions abroad. Thus, some Japanese firms also want the system changed.

The ACCJ is not charging that the tax laws are, in and of themselves, discriminatory. But they do have the "collateral damage" impact of putting tacks in the road of more FDI. In some cases, the changes that the ACCJ, the U.S. government, and others are seeking are changes also sought by some officials in Japan. There is no doubt that, among at least these Japanese officials, the feelings that FDI is an ally of reform are genuine. It is not just public relations fluff, as in the past.

Given political resistance in Japan, not to mention pure inertia, translating good intentions into practice will take time. Nonetheless, the train of increased FDI has left the station, and the pace of improvement is accelerating. Ten years from now, the situation will be radically different from today.

—————12—————

Financial Integration
The Iceberg Cracks

If we had to name the most important sectors where a sizeable foreign presence could generate systemic ripple effects, finance would, along with retail, head the list. Control over finance dictates what industries and companies and jobs exist. Thus the increased foreign presence in stock ownership and underwriting, asset management, investment banking, and insurance has truly momentous potential.

Theoretically, one could envision the following several-step scenario.

1. Foreign financial institutions gain a critical mass in investment, asset management, and so forth.
2. Rather than operating in Rome as the Romans do, the foreign players place higher emphasis on profitability than on outdated corporate ties. They earn higher, more secure returns for investors, pension funds, holders of insurance policies, and others.
3. Higher returns lure money from Japanese players to the foreign ones.
4. The growing market share of foreign firms pressures Japanese financial intermediaries to match the behavior of the foreigners.
5. Nonfinancial firms have to improve their own profitability in order to attract investment funds.

So far, at least, we are seeing only the beginnings of Step 1: a truly significant increase in the foreign presence. It remains to be seen whether the foreign players will truly operate differently than Japanese firms and whether that will lead to broader changes. Nonetheless, the former insulation of Japanese finance from global trends is largely ended. That alone increases the odds of a more fundamental overhaul.

Conspiracy Theories About Foreign Financial Firms

All this progress hardly means Japan is a bed of roses for the foreign financial firms. On the contrary, they face several problems. Sometimes these problems are of their own making, as in the case of retail brokerage and mutual funds, where they overestimated the market potential. However, at times, in the view of some foreign brokers and investment bankers, the Financial Services Agency has discriminated against the foreign firms. They charge it has meted out harsher punishments to foreigners, including Lehman Brothers, ING Barings, Deutsche Bank, Commerz Bank, Morgan Stanley, Bear Stearns, and Credit Lyonnais than it has in the case of similar infractions by Japanese firms.

Both foreigners and some Japanese believe it's a classic case of punishing the messenger, with the authorities blaming "overly pessimistic" views by the foreign institutions, as well as devices like short-selling and derivatives trading, for the problems of Japan's stock market. As *Nikkei Weekly* reported:

> Regulators are also believed to be under pressure from politicians to "do something about foreign brokerages," as the view is spreading among politicians that the dim outlook held by foreign securities houses should be blamed for a steep decline in stock prices. . . . As the Mycal incident indicates, analysts at foreign securities companies were proved correct in analyzing the state of things in the financial sector.[1]

Some of the harshest punishments have been meted out to institutions whose analysts have been strongly critical of the FSA's actions and inactions on the bad loan front. In 2001, the FSA appeared to make an example of James Fiorillo, a bank analyst at ING Barings who has been a prominent critic of the FSA. In mid-August, the FSA decided to investigate ING Barings for a mistake made back in May. At that time, Fiorillo sharply downgraded the shares of Daiwa Bank. In reporting the bank's "Tier 1" capital, Fiorillo's report contained a typographical error that transposed two digits, thereby presenting it as only 4.79 percent of assets, rather than the correct figure of 7.49 percent. On June 5, long before the FSA got involved, ING Barings published a note publicizing, and apologizing for, the error.

Meanwhile, in what turned out to be sheer coincidence, a trader at ING Barings sold 250,000 shares of Daiwa two hours before the report came out, buying them back for a profit five days later. This led to accusations of insider trading by some of the Japanese press. However, the FSA investigated the incident, and found that the trader had no advance knowledge of Fiorillo's report. But the FSA did accuse ING Barings of lax procedures, both in regard to preventing such typos and in internal procedures that would frustrate any would-be insider traders. The FSA demanded that ING Barings come up with a "business improvement plan."

Soon after the FSA issued its order, almost all Japanese firms stopped doing business with ING. Some clients were visited by the FSA and there are suspicions that the FSA urged the de facto boycott. In addition, FSA officials made it clear that they wanted Fiorillo dismissed. Instead, ING cut Fiorillo's salary 20 percent for two months. In addition, Fiorillo was effectively barred from making any public comments or speaking to investors or to the press while the FSA investigated. Finally, in late September, ING submitted its business plan and it was accepted.

Around the same time, Goldman Sachs was barred from participating in government bond auctions for four weeks when there was a typo in one of the several hundred bonds whose prices Goldman lists every day. Goldman Sachs' bank analyst, David Atkinson, is another vocal skeptic of the FSA's NPL numbers.

MOF/FSA officials paint a very different picture. They insist, in private, that their actions are in response to collusion by foreign securities firms to deliberately drive stocks down in hopes of making a killing. These officials argue that it was not economic fundamentals, but market manipulation by mostly foreign firms, that caused the serious stock market decline in Japan in late 2001 and early 2002. For example, when Aoki Construction went bankrupt in late 2001, officials hoped that the stock price of Asahi Bank— one of Aoki's long-suffering creditors—would rise, since this would indicate a willingness to clean up the bank's overall bad loan problem. However, Asahi's stock fell. Why? MOF officials say it is because Goldman Sachs decided to "dump" Asahi stock. In a second case, MOF and FSA officials contend that foreign brokerage houses colluded to drive down the price of Mizuho Bank group stock, hoping to lower it to a level that would trigger so-called stop-loss sales, which would lower the price even further. The alleged goal: reap big paper gains on "short" selling.

In private conversations, the minister in charge of the FSA, Hakuo Yanagisawa has reportedly accused the American-owned Shinsei Bank of calling in loans in order to drive companies into bankruptcy, so that those firms could be snapped up on the cheap by foreign investors.

Foreign brokers in Japan strongly deny any collusion occurred. And since stock manipulation is illegal in Japan, the MOF and FSA have legal methods to use if evidence of collusion really exists. But lack of evidence has not dowsed the suspicions of MOF and FSA officials. Indeed, several senior officers have communicated their concerns to senior politicians.

Nihon Keizai Shimbun reported that the FSA circulated a document to Diet members charging that the large majority of foreign securities firms in Japan will eventually pull out of the market, and "thus have the attitude of 'take the money and run'." Even worse, the memo discussed possible actions against "individual employees who have benefited." One possible form of retaliation being discussed is tax treatment of stock options, which form a significant portion of the compensation of foreign investment bankers and brokers.[2]

Peter Tasker, the popular equity strategist for Arcus Investment, summed up the problem this way:

> The market mechanism itself is coming under attack. According to a Cabinet official, Japan has become a "den of gamblers." Apparently foreign vultures are buying Japanese assets at unfairly cheap prices. Hedge funds are said to be deliberately collapsing stock prices. This kind of view is becoming increasingly common amongst the Japanese elite—bureaucrats, commentators, and businessmen. The alternative explanation—that stock prices have been falling because of repeated policy bungling by the government and the failures of unaccountable out-of-touch managements—is too dangerous to admit.[3]

Despite all this, the role and clout of foreign financial firms within Japan continues to grow dramatically. The days when the firms could simply be kept out are over, due to a series of U.S.-Japan agreements as well as deregulatory moves by Tokyo itself. Moreover, the declining prestige of the Japanese ministries means their "administrative guidance" to Japanese firms no longer packs the wallop it used to. If foreign firms can do better, they're going to get a lot of business.

Stockholding, Brokerage, Underwriting

Japan Inc. is now a joint venture, with 20 percent of it—or at least 20 percent of the value of firms listed on the Tokyo Stock Exchange—now owned by foreign investors. A decade ago, foreign ownership was 5 percent (Figure 12.1).

Change on the brokering front is even greater. Not until 1986 were foreign brokers allowed to buy seats on the Tokyo Stock Exchange. Yet only fifteen years later, foreign-affiliated brokers handle 40–50 percent of the buying and selling of Japanese stocks.

To the extent that Tokyo is interested in keeping stock prices up, it has to at least think about maintaining the confidence of foreign investors, who now account for half of all trades. Their confidence, or lack of it, is the

Figure 12.1 **Foreigners Own 20 Percent of Japanese Stocks**

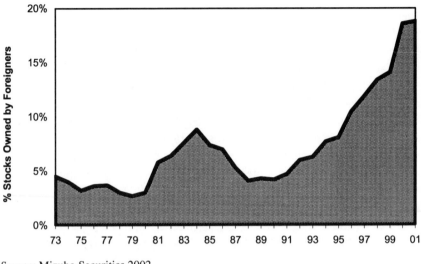

Source: Mizuho Securities 2002.
Note: As of March of the year named.

critical swing factor. If Tokyo bails out a big borrower such as Mycal or Daiei, the stock prices of these retailers' banks, and the rest of the market, could go down.

So far the foreigners' ownership presence has not translated into the influence in the corporate boardroom that would occur in other countries. One reason, according to Ken Okamura, formerly the chief equity strategist at Dresdner Kleinwort Benson's Tokyo office, is that the foreign presence is extremely concentrated. In mid-2000, almost half of the foreign holdings were focused on just twenty companies, the top six being Sony, NTT DoCoMo, NTT, Toyota, Fujitsu, and Canon.[4] Foreign investors had the most leverage where their combined share in a single company was extremely high, such as in the cases of Sony (44 percent foreign share in mid-2000) and Rohm (43 percent).

But the more basic reason is that shareholder power is still quite weak in Japan (see Chapter 15). Japanese corporate executives do make appearances before foreign investors, submitting to questions rarely raised by Japanese investor-allies. But that has yet to lead to real changes in their management of the firm.

On the other hand, the growth of foreign investment is one of the factors leading to (as well as reflecting) a decline in cross-shareholding.

Stocks, the Yen, and the Constraints on Muddling Through

One measure of Japan's increased sensitivity to global trends is the close correlation between movements of the yen and the Japanese stock market (review Figure 8.4). This correlation constrains Tokyo's ability to use palliative actions to substitute for reform.

For example, if Tokyo uses government money in so-called price-keeping operations to lift the stock market, the rise in share prices may lure foreign investors. Since the latter have to buy yen to buy the stocks, the yen goes up. But a rise in the yen depresses Japanese exports, offsetting the benefits from higher stock prices. Conversely, if Tokyo tries to cheapen the yen to help exporters, this depresses stock prices, thereby hurting the banks (see Chapter 8, pp. 142–43). The bottom line is that financial integration constrains the usual "muddling through" options by exacting a higher trade-off for any action.

Movements of money in and out has a much weaker effect in the bond market because, as of late 2001, foreigners owned only about 6.5 percent of outstanding Japanese government bonds (JGBs).

Asset Management, Pension Funds

Asset management, particularly pension fund management, is an enormous business, with all the public and private pension funds adding up to more than 300 trillion yen ($2.4 trillion). That's a fifth of total household assets. Wielding clout in asset management means wielding clout in Japanese finance, and therefore the corporate world, more generally. Just by going about their normal business of seeking the highest returns and pressuring management to target shareholder value, foreign asset managers are putting themselves in a position to shake up the traditional corporate governance system of Japan. That's one reason market access to the pension fund market was a U.S. goal in the 1984 Yen-Dollar Agreement.

But the effort did not bear fruit until quite recently. As late as 1995, foreign presence in the pension fund market was negligible. But by 1998, there was a quantum leap. Foreign trust banks (such as Bankers Trust, CitiTrust, and Credit Suisse) and investment advisers (such as Schroder, Merrill Lynch, and Goldman Sachs) managed 6 percent of the 51 trillion yen ($410 billion) in the corporate-run employee benefit plans, a share that rose to 15 percent by March 2000. In 1998, they managed an even higher 12 percent (26 trillion yen, or $210 billion) of the privately managed portion of public pension plans. Their share soared to 22 percent by March

Figure 12.2 **Foreign Share of Pension Fund Management Rises**

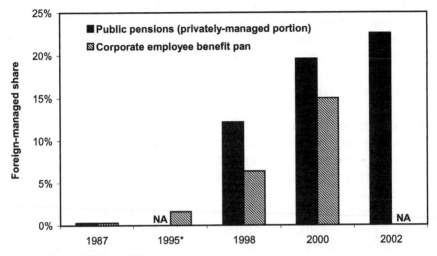

Source: Harner 2000, p. 103.

Note: 1995 data on public pension assets not available. Data for 2000 and 2002 are from industry sources.

2000 (Figure 12.2). If the early momentum will continue, it will help change the shape of Japanese finance.[5]

The increased foreign role was a product of two interacting forces: a series of regulatory changes together with the ultralow rates.

Until 1986, almost all government social security funds were managed by the Ministry of Finance's Trust Fund Bureau. They were used mainly to finance the government's Fiscal Investment and Loan Program (FILP). Then the MOF gradually turned some 20 percent of the funds over to private management by the same life insurers and domestic trust banks who monopolized the private pension funds. Their performance was miserable, not only due to bad management but also because of regulations that limited investments to low-risk, low-return instruments such as government bonds.

It eventually became apparent that neither private nor governmental pension funds could ever meet their obligations unless they obtained better returns from their asset managers. That was the context in which a series of U.S.-Japan financial services agreements plus the Hashimoto Administration's "Big Bang" opened the market.[6]

The change was dramatic. Investment advisers (Japanese and foreign alike) had virtually no share of the governmental pension funds in 1995. Today their share is 25 percent. Their share of the corporate funds rose from 2 percent in 1995 to 17 percent by 1999. Of the top ten investment advisers in 1998, half were foreign or foreign-Japanese joint ventures.

Ongoing reforms mean that even more of the social security funds will be turned over to private managers. Hence the foreign firms will likely get a larger slice of a rapidly growing pie.

Mutual Fund Management

The foreign share of stock mutual funds—known in Japan as investment trusts—has also risen quite sharply, from 4 percent in the mid-1990s to a peak of 13 percent in 1998. The number of foreign investment trust managers (ITMs) rose from only two in 1990 and seven as late as 1995 to thirty-three by mid-2000.

Some foreign ITMs, such as Fidelity, have gained the reputation of providing superior results.[7] Nonetheless, once the "Big Bang" allowed Japanese banks into the ITM business, the foreign share fell back to 10 percent in 2000. Foreign ITMs must often rely on Japanese firms as distributors, which limits their marketing independence as well as their ability to differentiate their products. Some firms have experienced sizeable setbacks. Chase Investment Trust Management withdrew from Japan after only about a year and a half. Cerulli Associates, a consulting firm, estimates that the foreign share may continue to drop.[8]

With the poor performance of Japanese stocks scaring off small investors, foreign firms are finding it hard to make money in the retail market and are deciding to focus on institutional investors. In late 2001 and early 2002, a number of foreign brokers reduced or closed altogether the retail side of their brokerage operations in Japan, including Merrill Lynch, Morgan Stanley, Société Générale, and Charles Schwab.

Investment Banking; Purchase/Sale of NPLs

Investment banking plays to the strength of foreign investment banks.

In 2000, foreign firms won the top three positions in M&A deals, and five of the top ten spots. Goldman Sachs came in first, advising on $33.5 billion out of about $100 billion worth of deals, whereas Merrill Lynch was second with $31 billion.[9]

On the underwriting side, the Nikko Salomon Smith Barney joint venture captured a 40 percent market share in new issues of Japanese stocks in 2000 and again in 2001. Indeed, foreign firms captured five of the top ten spots in stock underwriting in 2000 (Figure 12.3).[10]

Figure 12.3 **Foreign Share of Stock Underwriting**

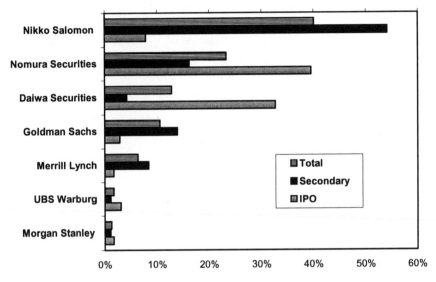

Source: Nihon Keizai Shimbun 2001p.
Note: Japanese firms were leaders in IPOs, but foreigners were leaders in secondary issues.

Foreign investment banks are just beginning to play a role in underwriting domestic bond issues, a market that dwarfs international issues. In 1998, foreign firms underwrote just 0.5 percent of the $75 billion in bonds issued that year. By 1999, their share was up to 3 percent.[11]

Just a few recent high-profile deals:

- Goldman Sachs was joint global coordinator for an international equity issue by Japan Tobacco (JT) and a "Yankee bond" issue by NTT.
- In the Renault takeover of Nissan, Merrill Lynch advised Renault, while Nissan retained Nikko Salomon Smith Barney.
- In the 1999 sale of $11 billion in U.S. assets held by the former Long-Term Credit Bank (LTCB), the Japanese government used Goldman Sachs as its adviser.
- Goldman joined Nikko Securities as global coordinator for NTT DoCoMo's $18 billion initial public offering (IPO).
- In a $2.6 billion deal in March 1999 whereby Sony used its stock to buy three of its own affiliates—the first such swap transaction under revisions in the law—Sony used Merrill as its adviser; the affiliates hired Morgan Stanley.

The foreign investment banks are also playing a big role in a new business in Japan: the purchase and sale of commercial banks' nonperforming assets, including both the loans and the real estate used as collateral. In March 1999 Japan saw its first securitization of commercial real estate that had been used as collateral for a bank loan. In a deal worth 10 billion yen, Morgan Stanley Real Estate Fund purchased condominiums from Daikyo, financing this with the issue of new bonds. Sale of the real estate will finance the repayment of the bonds.[12]

Despite the problems of the Japanese economy and the Japanese securities firms, the foreign investment banks have been making money hand over fist on their corporate business in Japan. Nikko Salomon Smith Barney earned $1.6 billion in operating profit in fiscal 2000, while Morgan Stanley earned $1.1 billion.

Commercial Banking

The heart of Japan's financial system is banking. In this sector, even aside from Ripplewood's purchase of the failed Long-Term Credit Bank (now known as Shinsei), the foreign penetration has also risen sharply.

More sharply, it seems, than Japan's authorities would like. They don't trust foreign owners to treat deadbeat borrowers with kid gloves (see Chapter 5, page 97). Although Ripplewood, a U.S. investment consortium, was allowed to buy the nationalized bankrupt Long-Term Credit Bank, political pressure made sure that, when Nippon Credit also failed and had to be nationalized, it was sold to Japanese buyers, led by Softbank. Cerberus, another U.S. investment consortium, which already owned 11 percent of the shares, was interested in buying the bank, now renamed Azora, but Diet members raised objections. Furthermore, when Softbank decided to sell its 49 percent stake in Azora, politicians summoned Softbank president Masayoshi Son to register their objections. Minister Hakuo Yanagisawa made it clear that he preferred the shares be sold to a Japanese buyer. When yet another U.S. fund tried to buy the bankrupt regional bank, Ishikawa, the Deposit Insurance Corporation said it would sell it to foreigners only if no Japanese buyer made a good offer.[13]

Nonetheless, through the expansion of their existing branches in Japan, the foreign banks are growing dramatically. They are not concentrating on plain-vanilla loans, where it's hard to make any money. Loans are only 17 percent of assets among foreign banks, compared to 60 percent for domestic banks. Instead, foreign banks have emphasized various lucrative (sometimes fee-based) niches: foreign exchange trading, private banking, loan

Figure 12.4 **Foreign Share of Bank Assets Grows . . .**

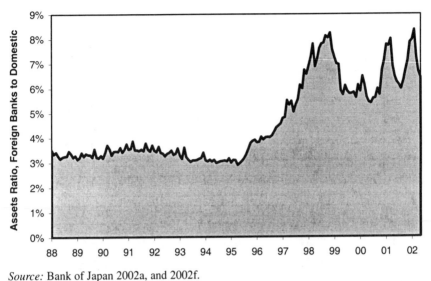

Source: Bank of Japan 2002a, and 2002f.

Note: This is an undercount because "foreign banks" does *not* include domestic banks that were bought out by foreigners such as Shinsei (formerly Long-Term Credit Bank).

syndication, foreign currency deposits, and so on. In 2001, Japan accounted for 8 percent of Citigroup's entire global profits, half of which came from its consumer operations.

For years the foreign share of banking assets hovered at 3 percent. In the mid-1990s, however, the banks took advantage of new regulatory freedoms and their market share jumped up. By mid-2002, their share had more than doubled, to almost 8 percent (Figure 12.4). This does not even count the operations of Shinsei, the former Long-Term Credit Bank.

Shinsei and Kansai Sawayaka Banks

When Ripplewood first bought the bankrupt LTCB in 2000, some expected it to be something of a maverick. That has proved true. It cut back loans to less creditworthy customers and charged higher interest to riskier customers—often in the face of heavy-handed political pressure. Meanwhile, it beefed up its investment banking section and based employee bonuses on performance.

As a result, Ripplewood turned a perennial money-loser into a profitable enterprise by fiscal 2000 (ending March 2001), only two years after it

Table 12.1

Foreign Takeovers of Japanese Life Insurers

Firm	Foreign Purchaser	Condition Prior to Purchase	FY 1999 Assets (in trillions of yen)	% of Assets of Top 14 Insurers*
Chiyoda	AIG (USA)	Failed	3.4	2.1%
Kyoei	Prudential (USA)	Failed	4.6	2.8%
Daihakyu	Manulife (Canada)	Failed	1.7	1.0%
Toho*	GE Capital (USA)	Failed	3.0	1.8%
Nisshin	Artemis (France)	Failed		
Nichidan	AXA (France)	Weakened	3.4	2.1%
Heiwa*	Aetna (USA)	Weakened	0.5	0.3
Nicos	Winterthur			
Orico	Prudential			
TOTAL			16.6 +	10.2% +
Top 14			**162.7**	

Source: Prof. Mitsuhiro Fukao, Keio University.

Note: The assets of the top fourteen insurers total 162.7 trillion yen (about $1.4 trillion)—the overwhelming majority of industry assets. In fiscal 1998, the assets of the top eighteen firms amounted to 94 percent of total industry assets of 193 trillion yen ($1.67 trillion). Fiscal year 1999 ended in March 2000, except where noted by an asterisk. Heiwa and Toho figures are from fiscal 1998.

bought it. In fiscal 2001, it upped those net profits to 59 billion yen ($530 million).

While NPLs remain high—and difficult to reduce speedily due to government pressure—Shinsei is now so profitable that it is planning on going public again, launching an IPO. That would enable the government, if it chose, to sell its preferred shares, thus recovering all taxpayer money put into the bankrupt LTCB, something it has been unable to do at the other Japanese banks.

Although Ripplewood's takeover of LTCB is the most celebrated of foreign takeovers, it is not the only one. There have also been a few buyouts of failed or failing regional banks. Wilbur Ross's Asia Recovery Fund bought out the failed Osaka-area Kofuku Bank, now renamed Kansai Sawayaka Bank (KSB). Billions of public funds were used to strip the failed bank of NPLs. In the fiscal year ending September 2000, KSB earned profits of 2.2 billion yen, a 16 percent return-on-equity.[14]

Life Insurance

By 2001, nine major Japanese life insurers had either failed or come close to it, and then been bought out by foreign investors. Overall, with nineteen of Japan's forty-two life insurers now affiliates of foreign firms, the foreigners gained a 13 percent market share by 2001 (Table 12.1). This is a remarkable change from the 1.6 percent market share they had in 1997.[15] (Market share in the non-life business remains low.)

In most cases, the foreign firms have been able to negotiate deals that don't saddle them with the target's worst liabilities. More failures and takeovers can be expected given the ongoing zero interest rate environment.

Depending on how well the newcomers perform, their presence could be catalytic since the industry is such a large institutional investor. The 163 trillion yen of assets held by the fourteen largest life insurers are equivalent to about 20 percent of the total assets held by all banks.

Part Four

Structural Reform: A Progress Report

——— 13 ———

What Is Structural Reform?

Structural reform is a high-sounding name. But what it boils down to in practice is hundreds of measures, some exceedingly arcane, affecting a wide variety of activities: politics, finance, business practices, labor, competition policy, regulations, state enterprises, taxation, and so forth.

Both the government and companies have already taken so many of these steps—the financial "Big Bang," assorted deregulatory measures, corporate downsizing, mergers—that they claim to be implementing widespread reform in rapid fashion.

How can we measure whether all this appearance of hustle and bustle adds up to real progress? Our test is whether the actions substantially reduce both of Japan's obstacles to growth: supply-side inefficiency and demand-side anorexia. Reforms that address only one or the other won't do the trick. In the following chapters, we'll apply this test in the areas of finance, corporate practices, competition policy, labor, deregulation, taxes, and state enterprise reform. Here's what we found:

- In many areas, the reforms are both real and the right steps to take. Yet because of offsetting factors, these reforms have not yet been allowed to do their work. "Big Bang" reforms are offset by financial socialism. That is the predominant pattern.
- In other cases, such as competition policy, there has been almost no progress at all, and even some backsliding.
- In still other cases, what passes for reform is actually movement in the wrong direction. On the health care and taxation front, the measures being considered actually worsen anorexia while doing little to address the high costs and inefficiency of producers.

The Tapestry

Why have the efforts undertaken so far created such a small result? One reason is that the various strands of the Japanese political economy are interwoven so tightly that it is hard to fix just one part at a time. Even a few examples highlight the problem.

Solving the bank debt problem requires foreclosing on bad borrowers. But that would cause the loss of millions of jobs in a country without fluid labor markets. Thus, without reforming the labor markets, how can the bad debt problem be fixed? Yet this is a problem of collective action. Individual workers and firms won't change their behavior unless they know that other firms and workers will act in the same way. A forty-five-year-old worker needs assurance that if one firm lays him off, another firm will be willing to hire him.

Corporate reform that gives firms more freedoms needs to be balanced by a big increase in antitrust enforcement and shareholder power. Otherwise we'll just see stronger oligopolies. Shareholder power requires increased ownership by institutions and individuals. Yet who wants to invest in a market that can't get off the floor?

Deregulation gives firms freer entry into new fields. Yet unless the moribund firms are forced out, such deregulation only leads to excess capacity, making life tougher for everyone. However, the government is reluctant to see too many firms fail, lest it bring down the banking system.

The upshot is that each reform by itself seems to have only marginal impact. Worse yet, piecemeal reforms seem to threaten chaos, increasing the resistance to reform. It is only when reforms are all applied in a comprehensive, coordinated manner that they will work well. That's why bottom-up, incremental change won't suffice. Achieving consensus for a comprehensive program will take time and political leadership.

Sectoral Priorities

Politically, the reform process may well bring the destruction of the old regime before the creation of the new. In this process, certain sectors should be given priority because of their systemic ripple effects. Since the reformers' political capital is limited, they need to expend it where it is most likely to have a snowball effect on further change.

Finance and retail are the two ends of the daisy chain of cartels that hobble Japanese growth. To the extent that these two are opened up to competition, the links in between will tend to crumble. Finance dictates who gets to produce what. Retail is critical because cartels cannot be sustained if high costs cannot be passed on to the final customer. Telecommunications is critical because the Internet revolution can cut through layer upon layer of middlemen while clearing out bloated back offices.

It's Just the Second Round

Much of what follows makes for discouraging reading. In the war between reform and resistance, the resistance seems to be winning most of the battles so far. How, then, can we be so optimistic that, within a decade or so, reform will have won? It is this: while inertia is on the side of the resistance, time—for all the reasons we laid out in Chapter 1—is on the side of reform. The myriad changes already undertaken, inadequate as they are, are proof of that.

The notion that reform is indispensable has already captured the imagination of many Japanese, among both the elite and the "man on the street." What is lacking is the specific program, the institutional-political vehicles, and credible assurances that the long-run gain is worth all the short-run pain. The day-to-day skirmishes that we read about in the newspapers are moments in the time-consuming process of creating these needed ingredients.

Even the failure of Koizumi to fulfill popular expectations is part of the process of reform. After all, why should the public accept the need for new institutions until the existing ones have been given a fair chance to show what they can do? The public wants reform and it wants the LDP to carry it out. It cannot have both.

In the battle between reform and resistance, Japan is now in just the second round of a fifteen-round match.

—— 14 ——

Financial Reform
"Big Bang" Versus Financial Socialism

Many people believe the financial "Big Bang" ushered in a new era. Others call it a "wee whimper." How can we judge among these opposing views? To us, the test of reform is whether or not it improves the financial system's ability to perform its two primary tasks:

- On the supply side: mobilizing capital, allocating it to its most efficient use, and disciplining nonfinancial corporations
- On the demand side: providing a fair return to the original providers of that capital, household saver/investors so they have more money to spend

Japan's bank-dominated financial system doesn't do either job very well. While the banks suck up savings like a vacuum cleaner, they've never been all that good at allocating capital. Meanwhile, for most of the postwar era, the inflation-adjusted returns to savers have been negative.

So far, any help the "Big Bang" could provide has been more than offset by negative trends, from the poor macroeconomy to the protection of "zombie" borrowers to the growth of "financial socialism." Let's look at the record.

Financial Socialism

Government bodies take in 46 percent of all deposits, up from 35 percent in 1990. They provide an astonishing 35 percent of all loans in Japan, up from 23 percent in 1990 (Figure 14.1). Not only does the postal savings system account for a third of all banking deposits, but postal life insurance accounts for a third of all life insurance.[1]

Figure 14.1a **Financial Socialism: Government Share of All Deposits**

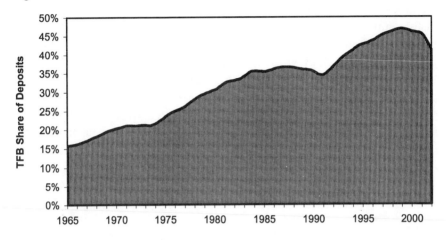

Figure 14.1b **Financial Socialism: Government Share of All Loans**

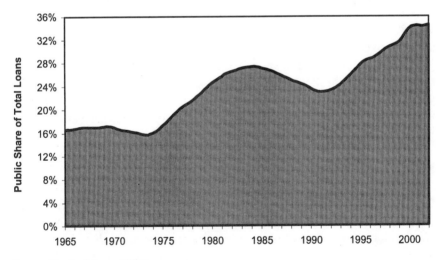

Source: Bank of Japan 2001b.

Note: The top panel is a total of deposits at the Ministry of Finance's Trust Fund Bureau (TFB) as a share of all deposits in all financial institutions. The bottom panel is lending by all government-related institutions as a share of total lending by all institutions, including banks, insurance companies, pension funds, credit cooperatives, etc. Since the BOJ series changed in 1999, the author has adjusted the figures for 1999–2002 to make them commensurate with pre-1999 figures. This shows a four-quarter moving average.

Bankers and insurers complain that the government's cut-rate programs are destroying their profits, since they must cut their own margins to stay in the game. The postal savings system offers a state guarantee that no private bank can match. On the loan side, to take one example, the Housing Loan Corporation (HLC) provided 42 percent of the 160 trillion yen ($1.3 trillion) in home loans as of March 2001. Since its money comes from the postal savings system, via the MOF's Fiscal Investment and Loan Program (FILP), the HLC can undercut private bank mortgage rates by 1.2 percent. Other government banks, such as the Development Bank of Japan, are still big lenders to corporations, at lower rates. Reportedly, the DBJ accounts for 96 percent of borrowing at Japan Telecom, 76 percent at Tokyo Gas, 60 percent at All Nippon Airways, and 53 percent at Odakyu Electric Railway.[2] Overall, government banks account for about 10 percent of all corporate loans.

Some reform has occurred. Starting in the year 2001, postal savings and life insurance receipts stopped being turned over automatically to the FILP. Koizumi has suggested privatizing the postal savings system. But, as economist Ed Lincoln points out, simply privatizing it would turn it into the world's largest private bank, headed by bureaucrats with even less understanding of banking than Japan's private bankers. Instead, it should be abolished. The maximum term of a deposit is ten years. If the postal savings system were prohibited from taking in any new deposits, then over ten years its deposit base would gradually turn to zero. Savers who redeemed their deposits would have to turn them over to the private banks, bond funds, and so on.[3]

Price Keeping Operations

Despite pledges in the Big Bang that markets would be "fair, free, and global," Tokyo continues to engage in stock market manipulation. Not only was it widely suspected of using government pension funds to buy stocks to start a rally in the ramp-up to the March 31 book closing in 2002, but government agencies and the Tokyo Stock Exchange reportedly engaged in direct intimidation of brokers who sold stocks on client orders.

Fearing that low stock prices would cause damage to the banks ahead of the March 31 closing, the Financial Services Agency (FSA) and Ministry of Finance tightened the rules on short-selling (making it illegal to short stocks except when they are rising) and clamped down on foreign securities houses that engaged in short-selling. Firms like Morgan Stanley, Bear Stearns, and Credit Lyonnais had their trading licenses suspended for a couple of weeks for minor infractions usually overlooked at their Japanese counterparts.[4]

Worse yet, according to *Nikkei Business*, selling of any kind began to elicit intimidation:

> Indeed a phone rang at an executive suite at Nomura Securities headquarters one day, the call was from an official with the MOF's Minister's Secretariat. "I heard that you were opposed to our restricting short-sellings, were you not?" the caller said. A classic example of governmental harassment, it has to be said.
>
> Harassment becomes all the more real when one sells bank shares. As soon as the sell-deal is done, the trading desk (be it at a domestic or foreign firm) gets a call from Tokyo Stock Exchange, which in principle acts as a market watchdog for the sake of enhancing fairness of the entire market. But hear what they inquire: "Who are the three biggest customers that placed the sell orders? Are they individuals, trust accounts, or foreigners? Was it a spot trading, margin, or short-selling?"[5]

Household Finance

By saving so much, Japanese households are, in effect, lending firms vast sums to invest in new equipment, factories, stores, and so forth. As of the year 2000, household savings reached 1,418 trillion yen ($11.4 trillion)—almost four years worth of total household income. While the companies using that capital have made lots of money, they have returned very little of their profits back to the households.

Despite the Big Bang, the situation has gotten worse. Household property income (mostly net interest, insurance benefits, rent, and dividends) halved during the 1990s, from 13.5 percent of total national income to only 6 percent. Indeed, returns and capital gains have gotten so bad since 1999 that, despite all the new money being socked away, the total value of household assets actually fell 1 percent from 1999 to 2001 (Figure 14.2). Consequently, in addition to poor income, a stagnant "wealth effect" also stunts consumer spending.

The chief reason for such low returns is that the vast majority of Japan's household savings are invested in low-return instruments such as bank deposits (51 percent) or life insurance and pensions (another 28 percent). Only 9 percent is invested in stocks. In the United States, the reverse is true (Figure 14.3).

Bank deposits have long been a sucker's game, with regulated rates deliberately held below the rate of inflation as a subsidy to business investment.[6] Not until 1991 were rates liberalized on consumer time deposits smaller than 3 million yen (about $24,000), and not until 1994 were

Figure 14.2a **Household Income on Assets Halves in 1990s**

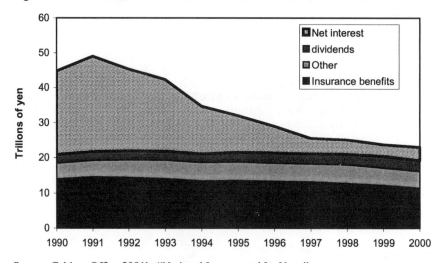

Source: Cabinet Office 2001b, "National Income and Its Uses."

Figure 14.2b **Household Assets Stop Growing After 1999**

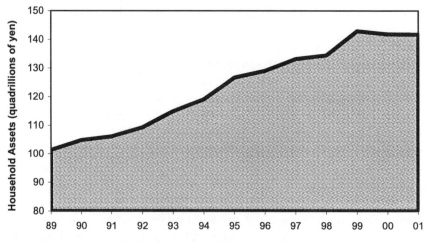

Source: Bank of Japan 2001b.

Note: This is the total value of all household *financial* assets, from bank accounts to insurance policies to stock holdings to pension accounts. Personal assets, such as a home, are not included.

Figure 14.3 **Household Finance: Bank Deposits, Not Stocks**

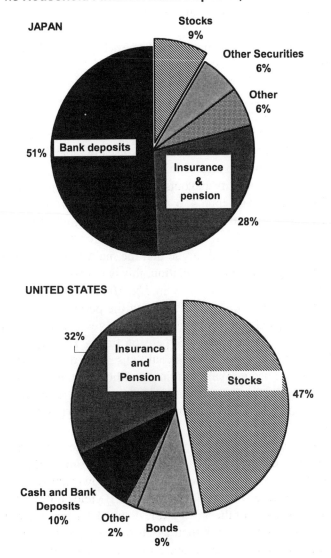

Source: BOJ (2001b) for Japan and Daiwa Research Institute for the United States.

interest rates freed up on demand deposits. If not for U.S. pressure via the 1984 U.S.-Japan Yen-Dollar Agreement, deregulation would have taken even longer.

With deregulation, real returns finally turned positive for a few years. Then came the zero interest rate policy (ZIRP). Even before the ZIRP, explicit collusion by the banks still kept depositor rates below free market levels. On demand deposits, amounting to about a fifth of consumer deposits in the early 1990s, the interest rate was kept at around 0.25 percent. Despite reports that banks were meeting together to collude on rates through the City Bank Discussion Council *(Tonginkon)*, the Japan Fair Trade Commission (JFTC) refused to intervene.[7]

Meanwhile, with annuity payouts from the life insurers dropping toward 0.75 percent (see Chapter 4, p. 62), total income from insurance benefits fell from 4 percent of national income in 1990 to 3 percent by 2000. Pension funds are likewise reducing benefits and/or dissolving.

While government officials argue that the main reason for the pension crisis is the aging of Japan's population, this is not so. The real reason, as Peter Hartcher argues convincingly in *The Ministry*, is a long history of poor returns even before the ZIRP. During the period 1985–95 Japanese pension funds earned an average of 5 percent a year, only one-third of the 15 percent return averaged by U.S. pension funds. Yet, says the Nomura Research Institute, if pension funds could raise their returns to 8.5 percent a year, they would become self-sustaining without further premium hikes.[8]

Without meaningful financial reform that increases return on assets, no amount of tax and premium hikes will enable Japan to pay for its growing host of aged.

One reason that returns have traditionally been so low is Finance Ministry regulations—the so-called 5-3-3-2 rule—that forced funds to put 50 percent of their money into low-risk (but also low-return) fixed-income assets such as Japan government bonds. As JGB yields fell, so did pension fund earnings. The rest of the 5-3-3-2 rule dictated that pension funds could put no more than 30 percent of their assets overseas, no more than 30 percent in domestic stocks, and no more than 20 percent in real estate. By contrast, nearly 60 percent of the assets of American pension funds are invested in stocks.

For years the Pension Fund Association urged the MOF to loosen up, to no avail. While the Big Bang began to loosen these strictures, these days the Japanese stock market hardly seems like a winner.

Beyond regulations there is the cartel problem, a problem that recent reforms have alleviated. Until the U.S.-Japan Financial Services Agreement of 1995, 95 percent of Japan's $1.7 trillion in pension funds could only be invested in either the MOF's Trust Fund Bureau, Japan's trust banks, or Japan's insurance companies. The 1995 agreement, combined with Big Bang reforms, allowed investment advisers into the game. Within only a few months of the regulatory change, Japanese pension fund managers took a reported $20 billion away from life insurance firms and put it into the hands of foreign managers. In 1996, when the insurance companies lowered their guaranteed return to 2.5 percent, Nenpuku, the national employee insurance system, withdrew $50 billion from the insurance companies and turned it over to investment management firms, including foreign ones (see Chapter 12, p. 182).

Theoretically, the best long-term investment for households is stocks. Households used to own 55–60 percent of stocks back in the 1950s, but as cross-shareholding increased, the household share plummeted to only 20 percent. In addition, as cross-shareholding increased, dividend payout plunged: from 4 percent of the share price in 1970 to less 2 percent by the late 1970s to a negligible 0.5 percent by the end of the 1980s (see Figure 15.6 in Chapter 15).

Other facets of the system discouraged household ownership as cross-shareholding was built up. Most stocks must be bought in lots of a thousand, which, given high prices on some stocks—one share of the Mizuho bank holding company costs $3,000 compared to $30 for a share of Toyota—means a minimal outlay of tens of thousands of dollars. Unlike in the United States, firms rarely split their stocks to attract small shareholders.[9]

Still other practices, sometimes illegal ones, disadvantaged the small shareholder. Fixed commissions (finally ended by the Big Bang) were high. "Churn-and-burn" activities by brokers gave these brokers commissions at the expense of the shareholders. Then there was the illegal practice of *tobashi*—brokers guaranteed the investment of large stockholders at the expense of small ones. As scandals regarding *tobashi* became public in the early 1990s, the public naturally turned away from stocks.

The most fundamental problem in attracting householders to stocks is that, if capital gains are the only benefit, then there is no benefit in a market where prices are 75 percent below where they were a decade earlier.

The first step in bringing householders back into the market and giving them some income is to use tax incentives to induce firms to make higher dividend payout rates out of profits (see Chapter 19). There is nothing "un-Japanese" about high dividend rates. Back in 1931–35, Japanese firms paid out 69 of their profits in dividends, until they came under ideological attack during the mobilization for war. By 1966–70, as cross-shareholding took off, the payout rate was down to 42 percent, steadily descending from there to 33 percent in 1985 and 24 percent in 1990.[10]

Japan faces a terrible catch-22. Until Japan solves the problem of meager returns to household assets, it will have a tough time overcoming economic anorexia. However, it will be hard to improve financial returns until anorexia is overcome, demand recovers, and financial markets return to normal.

Corporate Finance

For the financial system to allocate capital to its most efficient use, two links in the chain are required:

- Financiers—banks, investment banks, institutional investors, and so on—must have an interest in seeking the highest return instead of handing out money to corporate allies.
- Companies have to be dependent on those financiers so that they too are obliged to take an interest in efficiency and profitability.

Neither link is yet very strong in Japan, and current trends are not promising.

The corporate world is *self*-financing to a greater degree than ever before, enabling it to evade external financial discipline. Back in the 1930s, internal financing accounted for only 20 percent of corporate fund-raising. But this changed in the high-growth era as the profit share of national income increased and as low interest payments and low dividends enabled firms to retain these profits. During the years from 1965 to 1991, firms financed half of their plant and equipment investment with their own internal cash flow, that is, profits plus depreciation (Table 14.1). U.S. firms, by contrast, traditionally relied on external financing (bank loans, bonds, stocks) for two-thirds of their investment funds.

These days, with investment so low, the need for external financing has all but disappeared. By 1992–94 it was down to 15 percent, and by 1995–97 to 4 percent. Now firms are deliberately investing less than their cash flow so that they can pay back loans.

These are, of course, aggregate figures. Many firms, particularly small to medium-sized ones and the less profitable ones, still need bank credit. Moreover, whatever their current borrowing needs, all firms still hold a lot of accumulated past debt, which in theory should give creditors some leverage.

Table 14.1

Corporations Become Self-Financing (% of corporate investment financed by method)

	Internal Financing	Total External Financing	Private Loans	Government Loans	Stocks	Bonds
1965–67	39%	61%	46%	6%	4%	3%
1968–70	44%	56%	41%	4%	4%	2%
1971–73	29%	71%	56%	4%	4%	2%
1974–76	53%	47%	35%	5%	3%	2%
1977–79	67%	33%	21%	4%	3%	2%
1980–82	60%	40%	29%	4%	3%	1%
1983–85	54%	46%	33%	2%	3%	1%
1986–88	39%	61%	36%	3%	5%	2%
1989–91	44%	56%	32%	6%	5%	3%
1992–94	84%	16%	7%	8%	1%	4%
1995–97*	97%	3%	0%	0%	2%	4%
1998–00*	111%	–11%	–16%	1%	4%	1%

Source: Author's calculation based on BOJ 2001b and Cabinet Office 2002b.

Note: Corporate investment figures from the GDP tables. Corporate financing figures come from the BOJ flow-of-funds figures. Because of a change in the BOJ data series, there is a small discrepancy between the data for 1965–94 and those for 1995–2000. It does not materially change the results. The 1995–2000 data are calculated from the BOJ annual data series that begins in 1990 based on the 1993 SNA series. The 1965–94 data use the quarterly data based on the 1968 SNA series.

But the upshot is that financial markets have less leverage over corporate managers than ever before. As long as firms are making some profit, they can make their investment plans according to their own notions of empire building or employee security or any other target they choose, not profitability.

A second problem is that Japan's financial system remains dominated by banks, with capital markets still playing a very small role. Little has changed on that front. During 1965–91, of all the external financing used by corporations, 70 percent came from bank loans and another 8 percent from government loans. Only 7 percent came from the stock market. Why should managers worry about maximizing stock prices if they don't need the stock market for financing? (When a firm does raise money by issuing new shares, a higher stock price is equivalent to a lower interest rate on a loan.)

Bank domination is hardly a Japanese predisposition. In the 1920s, stock and bond markets played quite a substantial role New stock issues provided about 40 percent of external financing until as late as 1935. But beginning in the aftermath of the 1927 financial crash and then even more so in the run-up to World War II, the government deliberately minimized the capital markets and created the "bankers' kingdom" as a mechanism of control.[11]

These days, healthier big firms are paying back bank loans and seeking financing on the Eurobond market instead. But, with overall external financing so meager, that's a marginal change in the big picture.

Unfortunately, the banks are not very good allocators of capital—and never have been. Screening for creditworthiness was honored mainly in the breach. They rarely charged higher rates of interest to less creditworthy customers. Hence, the cost and availability of capital had little relationship to firm profitability.

The claim of the system was that each commercial borrower had a "main bank," which carefully monitored firm management and intervened if necessary, even sending its own personnel to manage firms in trouble. Thus, it is said, Japanese banks served the same function that shareholders serve in the United States. Perhaps they served it even better, since they knew the firm so intimately and could intervene more powerfully.

Yet careful research by economists Masaharu Hanazaki and Akiyoshi Horiuchi shows that, even during the high-growth era, firms with a main bank performed no better than firms without one. And, in the 1980s, firms with a main bank actually performed *worse*. The reason the main bank system appeared to work in the high-growth era, they say, is that most of the big banks' primary customers back then were manufacturers with in-

ternational exposure. Trade competition, not bank monitoring, differenti-
ated the good and bad performers.[12]

Once financial deregulation in the 1980s allowed these big exporters to
tap cheaper sources of funds, such as the Euromarket, the banks were left
trying to push all the excess savings onto less creditworthy customers.
Whereas manufacturers took up half of all bank loans in the 1960s and
1970s, by 1980 it was down to a third and by 1990, down to 15 percent.
Conversely, real estate, construction, and finance (like the *jusen* we discussed in Chapter 5) rose from only 5 percent of all bank loans in 1960 to
40 percent by 1990. These are the sectors, along with retail, that owe most
of today's bad debt.

Why should banks take care? After all, until 1995 the government's "convoy" policy made sure that no bank failed (see Chapter 5, p. 95). Feeling
invulnerable, banks sometimes used their monitoring power to push unneeded loans onto customers, exploiting them rather than aiding them. Professor Mamoru Ishida, a former board member of the Itochu trading
company, tells how the Industrial Bank of Japan (IBJ) used its control to
get the Sogo department store chain to borrow and expand, a policy that
contributed to Sogo's 1.9 trillion yen ($15 billion) bankruptcy:

> Here is a typical example of a main bank's failure. Mr. Hiroo Mizushima, presi-
> dent of Sogo Department Store, was sent by the Industrial Bank of Japan. Appar-
> ently with his support, the bank increased its loans to Sogo so much. . . . In the
> process, Mr. Mizushima established over 20 new department stores all over Ja-
> pan, of which about half have turned out to be money-losing projects. Mr.
> Mizushima demanded the Industrial Bank of Japan and other banks to renounce
> a substantial part of their claim against Sogo on the ground that they forced Sogo
> to borrow loans he did not want to borrow.
>
> When Mr. Masao Nishimura, president of Industrial Bank of Japan was sum-
> moned to the Parliament, he testified that . . . he had known in 1994 that Sogo's
> net equity was negative. Clearly, the capital market had been left in the dark. . . .
> The lesson is that a main bank, which cannot monitor its own recklessness, can-
> not monitor its customer's recklessness.[13]

Today, in the effort to avoid writing off too much bad debt, the banks
have granted the most debt forgiveness to the least creditworthy debtors
(Chapter 5, pp. 89–90).

Banks Versus Capital Markets

Even were the banks doing a better job, it is now widely recognized that
Japan needs to move from the "bankers' kingdom" to a more balanced

financial system with a larger role for capital markets. A bank-centered system is simply inadequate for the era of innovation-led growth. Back in the high-growth era, it sufficed to vacuum up savings and allocate them to industries with standardized technologies and economies of scale. No longer. Bank incentives don't apply as well to the world of untried new technologies and entrepreneurial firms. If a start-up fails, the bank loses most of the principal. But even if the start-up skyrockets to success, the most the bank can earn is the standard rate of interest. Besides, Japanese banks traditionally rely on collateral as the main criteria for extending loans. A new firm has little collateral.

By contrast, venture capital and stock markets are tailor-made for start-ups. The most one can lose is the entire investment, but the upside is unlimited. The risk-reward ratio favors taking a chance.

The bank-centered financial system is one reason Japan is so bad at fostering new firms relative to North America and Europe (see Chapter 15, p. 223).

Recently, Japan has created two new stock exchanges devoted to start-ups: NASDAQ Japan and MOTHERS, an offshoot of the Tokyo Stock Exchange. NASDAQ is on the verge of closing, and it's too early to tell whether MOTHERS will significantly change the picture.

There is also a danger to watch for. With the Big Bang allowing banks to get into the securities business, Japan's big banks might come to dominate the capital markets. There are two dangers here. To have powerful commercial banking and investment banking powers invested in just a few companies invites significant conflicts of interest. We have already seen this in the recent corporate scandals in the United States, where commercial banks made unwise loans to shore up deals for their investment banking divisions. Precisely the kind of conflict that the Glass-Steagall law of the 1930s was created to preclude has returned with Glass-Steagall's abolition. Second, if the banks bring their traditional mind-set into the capital markets, it is not clear how well the capital markets will perform.

Capital markets are not perfect. While banks make the error of keeping too many unsalvageable firms alive, fickle capital markets sometimes abandon troubled firms that should be salvaged. But surely Japan needs a better balance than it has today.

Prelude to the Big Bang

The Big Bang, initiated in 1996 by Prime Minister Hashimoto, has been widely hailed as a major, almost revolutionary step in increasing the ability of market forces, rather than government edicts or outdated corporate alliances, to direct financial flows.

To our mind, the Big Bang, while certainly important and positive, is hardly revolutionary. It is the latest in a series of deregulatory milestones that began in the 1970s, forced by the end of the high-growth era. Back in the 1950s and 1960s, the state together with the banks rationed scarce capital and dictated the price (i.e., interest rates). The BOJ issued "window guidance" to individual banks on their total volume of loans as well as allocation to various business sectors. Such a system was possible only under two conditions: scarcity of capital and insulation from global flows and rates. With demand for capital higher than supply, directing it to favored borrowers was possible. But scarce capital also meant that Japanese interest rates were higher than global ones. Had international flows not been restricted, borrowers other than favored ones could have obtained cheaper capital outside of Japan. The ups and downs of interest rates overseas would have influenced rates inside Japan. Neither rationing of credit nor regulated interest rates would have been feasible.

During the mid-1970s, as capital moved from scarce to excessive, this system inevitably broke down. Economist Hugh Patrick argues that during the entire transition prior to the Big Bang, the Finance Ministry responded in an ad hoc, reactive manner as each pressure emerged. There was no grand design. Moreover, internal pressures for change often had to be aided by external pressure from Washington before the MOF would move. However, with the Big Bang, Patrick suggests, authorities finally adopted a new "regulatory vision, at least for capital markets."[14] We would argue that, rhetoric aside, Patrick's verdict on earlier steps applies to the Big Bang as well. It is yet another incremental, reactive adaptation.

To place the Big Bang in context, let us review the most important of previous deregulatory steps.

Interest Rate Deregulation

The regulated system began to unravel in the mid-1970s as islands of freedom developed that caused disintermediation from the regulated system. Corporations with excess funds to lend and that were unhappy with the low regulated rates developed a short-term repurchase agreement market (*gensaki*), where free market rates prevailed. At the same time that this was happening, the government, for the first time, was compelled to run big budget deficits to overcome the 1973–75 downturn. In order to raise funds successfully, Tokyo had to tolerate the development of a secondary market in government bonds (JGBs). Since investors could obtain higher rates in the latter, the government had to free up rates in the primary market as well. Interest rate deregulation became a matter of when, not if.[15] Finally, as we'll detail below, granting Japanese corporations access to the Euro-bond market made it impossible to retain controls at home.

However, the MOF dragged out the process. Large firms and investors benefited first, while households faced discrimination until 1994, when the last bastion of interest rate regulation was finally ended.

Internationalization of Financial Markets

Since insulation from global capital flows and rates was indispensable to the control regime at home, Tokyo restricted the free movement of capital in and out of Japan via the Foreign Exchange and Foreign Trade Control Law from 1949 until 1980, when the law was replaced. In the old law, everything was forbidden except for those things explicitly permitted; in the new law, everything was permitted except for things explicitly forbidden.

In practice, the transition was more gradual. In the old regime, Japanese firms were forbidden to issue bonds overseas, while foreign firms were forbidden to issue yen bonds in Japan. The first such issuance, by Sears, didn't occur until 1979. Japanese financial institutions faced severe limits on investing in foreign stocks and bonds. Overseas branches of Japanese banks were subject to limits on their operations. Until 1984, Japanese firms could not buy or sell foreign currencies forward unless such transactions matched an underlying commercial transaction, for example, an export or import. That hindered speculation in the yen, which was important, since influencing the yen/dollar rate was part of the control regime.[16]

The spark for change was the 1973 oil shock. The ensuing combination of big budget deficits and relatively tight money sent Japanese interest rates upward. To compete globally, Japanese industrialists demanded access to the cheaper Eurobond market. Beyond that, Japan's chronic trade surpluses had turned the country into a massive exporter of capital. From 1980 to 1990, the net overseas assets of Japanese investors rose from a meager $11 billion to $400 billion. The era of insulation was over. The only question was the conditions under which international integration would be made.

Once again, adjustment to new conditions was protracted. Not until 1984 were all the restrictions lifted on Japanese participation in the Euromarket as issuers and underwriters. Not until the mid-1990s did regulations limiting the overseas assets of some big categories of investors, such as the pension funds, start being lifted.[17]

New Capital Market Instruments Erode Banks' Monopoly

To maintain the "bankers' kingdom," regulators in the high-growth era continued the strict limits on corporate bond issuance initiated back in the 1930s. Except for utilities, very few companies, even topflight ones, were permitted to issue bonds. Even then, collateral was required—no unsecured bonds. Commercial paper and similar instruments were nonexistent. As for bond issuance, oversight of eligibility and rates rested with an MOF advisory body, the Bond Council, on which bankers were prominent members.

Once corporations were allowed to tap the less regulated Eurobond market, these domestic restrictions became untenable. After all, the main purchasers of Japanese Eurobonds were *Japanese* investors. Regulations driving issuers and investors alike to London and Frankfurt meant less business in Tokyo for Japanese securities houses.

The MOF responded in the usual incremental fashion. Though the process began in 1979, as late as 1988 only 180 companies were permitted to issue straight unsecured bonds. Not until 1996 were all restrictions lifted.[18]

Did Deregulation Cause the 1980s Bubble?

Some analysts blame all this *de*regulation for the bubble. In their view, not only was government leverage over firms reduced, but also, once big firms could tap nonbank sources of finance, the banks' disciplinary tools were weakened. And yet the capital markets were not yet developed sufficiently to provide a substitute source of discipline. Meanwhile, to gain customers, banks turned to weaker sectors, such as real estate. The net result was that no one was disciplining either banks or borrowers.

The inevitable result was that newly unshackled firms went wild. From 1978 through 1991, the combination of internal and external financing was far above any investment needs—50 percent more in the early 1980s and twice as much by the end of the bubble. Firms borrowed money just to speculate in stocks and real estate, so-called *zai-tech* (see Chapter 5, p. 92). In fact, the firms that issued the most equity-linked bonds during the bubble showed the most drastic profit falls after the bubble popped. The issuers had counted on stocks continuing to rise, but once they fell, investors wanted to be repaid in real money, not stock.[19]

Many countries run into trouble in the process of deregulating. Japan was unique, however. Financiers and borrowers were given more freedom but, due to the convoy system, were never held accountable for their errors. Deregulated financial systems need even more supervision and stricter accounting, ingredients sadly lacking in Japan. To paraphrase political scientist Steven Vogel, freer markets require more rules.

What Did the Big Bang Add to the Menu?

In all the deregulation through the early 1990s, one vital ingredient was left out of the recipe: competition among financial firms. Hardly a new bank, insurance company, or securities house was permitted to enter the arena in all these decades—except for foreign ones. Similarly, licensing requirements meant that few, if any, new firms entered securities or insurance. Nor, until the mid-1990s, was any bank or life insurer allowed to fail. Finally, under Article 65 (Japan's version of Glass-Steagall), banks, securities houses, and insurers were kept out of each other's turf. New products, which required licenses, were often delayed. The Big Bang ended many of these restrictions.

The *tatamae* (official story) was to create a new financial market, one that was "free, fair, and global." The *honne* (actual intentions) were less high-flown. There were three:

1. To give the struggling banks access to new, more lucrative areas of business at a time when their most creditworthy customers were abandoning them for the capital markets. To this end, the Big Bang broke down the strict segmentation among commercial, banks, long-term banks, trust banks, brokers, life insurers, non-life insurers, and so on dictated by Article 65. It also allowed freer entry and exit into the financial industry.
2. To make the financial industry somewhat "leaner and meaner" via somewhat greater competition, including freer entry and exit of new firms and new products.
3. To foster world-class financial conglomerates, thereby making Tokyo a global financial center like New York and London.

Since the 1980s, the banks had been seeking entry into the securities business. They were the ones lobbying for ending Article 65 barriers, while securities houses were resistant. As Steven Vogel notes, the banks had more to gain by entering securities than vice versa. Indeed, some analysts predicted that if the big banks were allowed into securities, half of Japan's 235 securities firms might go under. Beginning with a 1985 report by the MOF Banking Bureau's Financial System Research Council, the MOF's banking and securities bureaus battled over the speed and modality of desegmentation. Thus the Big Bang reforms were the outcome of a long process that happened to come to a head when the banks' need for more-profitable business lines had became acute.[20]

The Big Bang also freed up pricing. The purpose was to end the "hollowing out" of the financial sector. Due to high fixed commissions, the Tokyo Stock Exchange (TSE) was losing out to London, where trading in Japanese stocks was 30–40 percent of the levels in Tokyo itself. Foreign exchange trading volume stagnated in high-priced Tokyo as Hong Kong and Singapore business away. Syndicated loans and corporate bonds were often executed in Singapore rather than Tokyo. If Japan's beleaguered securities firms were to survive, reform was vital.

While the intentions of the Big Bang's designers thus seem rather limited, the law of unintended consequences is making the "Big Bang" more consequential than intended. When the "Big Bang" was launched in 1996, most of Japan's elite had convinced themselves that the country's financial crisis was over. They were wrong. Hashimoto himself said that, had he known how dire were the straits of the banks, he would not have introduced the Big Bang. As a result, rules intended to produce limited entry have, in the event, allowed a great deal of entry by new players, particularly foreign players. Their presence could turn mere formal changes in regulations into genuine changes on the ground.

With this background in mind, let's review the chief reforms of the Big Bang.

Ending Industry Segmentation

Beginning in 1993, well before the Big Bang, step-by-step reforms gradually enabled banks, trust banks, securities firms, and insurance firms to invade each other's turf. Each step required protracted negotiation, since all players wanted to retain their own drawbridges while lifting those of others. The main phases of desegmentation were:

- The 1993 Financial Reform Law abolished in principle the firewall between banks and investment houses. Securities houses were permitted to offer some products with features like bank accounts, such as automatic deposit, demand deposits, and automatic payments. However, strenuous MOF licensing procedures ensured that actual entry remained slow and controllable.

- In December 1997, investment trust companies (i.e., mutual funds) were allowed to sell their products at banks.
- In March 1998, financial firms were allowed to create holding companies for "one-stop shopping" financial conglomerates (i.e., a bank, a broker, and an insurer all under one roof).
- During 1998, banks were allowed to sell their own investment trusts, while securities firms were allowed to expand their asset management services.
- During 1999, there was further reduction of the barriers preventing banks, trust banks, and securities firms from entering each other's markets. Special subsidiaries under a general holding company are the permitted route.
- During 2000, insurance firms were allowed to enter banking. Life and non-life insurers (mainly property, casualty, and health) were allowed to invade each other's turf.
- In March 2001, banks and securities firms were allowed to enter some types of insurance business, but there are still many limitations.

Reducing Barriers to Entry and Exit

Traditionally, the authorities restricted both entry and exit in the financial industry, thus effectively prohibiting Darwinian shakeout.

The MOF sometimes used its licensing powers to retaliate against firms that it deemed were undermining stability. For example, while the MOF was unable to prevent Daiwa Bank from setting up a trust bank subsidiary, it retaliated by being stingy in granting Daiwa's requests to open up new branches.[21]

The Big Bang greatly reduced the barriers to entry. Since 1999, almost seventy new firms have entered the securities business, including subsidiaries of big industrial firms such as Hitachi. Nonfinancial firms were also allowed to enter banking, and both Ito-Yakodo (a retailer that owns Japan's 7–Eleven) and Sony have set up Internet banks.

While the Big Bang did allow freer entry, exit was a different story. The Big Bang did not end the convoy system in banking, despite claims to the contrary (see Chapter 5, p. 95). In the securities field, almost sixty firms have ceased being independent since the mid-1990s, but mostly because they were merged into larger firms, not through closure.

Deregulation of New Products

Traditionally, new products required MOF approval, and the ministry was reluctant to let one firm get much ahead of others. For example, until the mid-1990s, all changes in insurance rates or products had to be approved by the MOF, usually with the advice of industry leaders. In effect, a firm trying to improve its position had to seek the approval of its competitors. Not surprisingly, competition on both price and products languished.

Moreover, the ministry frowned on certain types of products, such as financial derivatives, that it felt would disrupt orderly markets. In 1997 the ban on securities derivatives was lifted, and banks were allowed to engage in the trading of such derivatives.

Not all barriers to new products were so transparent. In many cases, new products were blocked by "administrative guidance." Despite liberalization in principle, domestic and foreign firms seeking to introduce new products knew they had to go to the MOF to get tacit approval. Otherwise they would suffer retaliation on other fronts, such as a license to open a new branch. Often this approval was delayed or no answer was given.

Since the Big Bang, things have greatly eased up. Firms seeking to introduce a new product find it helpful to go to the MOF and FSA to make sure it does not violate any regulation—just as in the United States. In practice, industry sources report that there is little of the obstruction that often occurred in the past as a matter of course. New product entry—a major competitive advantage—has been greatly freed up.

Lowering Transaction Costs Through Price Deregulation

One of the big successes of the Big Bang is alleviating the high-price syndrome afflicting the financial industry.

Until 1998 the insurance industry cartel was authorized by the MOF to set rates on non-life (e.g., property and casualty) insurance. Now firms set their own rates, and discount insurers have arrived on the scene.

In 1998 fixed commissions on stock buying ended, leading to the rise of online discount brokers. Back in 1999, brokers charged a fee of 11,500 yen ($92) on trades of one million yen ($8,000). By the fall of 2001, commissions on these "small-lot" transactions were as little as 480 yen ($4) over the Internet.[22]

As a result of this new freedom, online broker Matsui Securities jumped from thirty-first place in trading volume in 1998 to fifth place in the handling of stock margin trades in fiscal 2000. Reportedly, 40 percent of all trading by individuals is now done over the Internet due to lowered fees.

Meanwhile, changes in foreign exchange regulations should eventually lower transaction costs for multinational firms. Until the Big Bang, only banks could conduct foreign exchange trading. A trading company or industrial company was forbidden to net out its purchases and sales of foreign exchange and had to go through a bank, at considerable expense. The margin at Japanese banks was 10 to 15 percent higher than elsewhere.

Other Foreign Exchange Liberalization

While there have been some other changes affecting international capital flows, none really adds to the freedoms that already exist. Individuals can now buy foreign stocks directly on a foreign stock exchange, but they could already buy a foreign stock listed in Japan or as part of a Japanese-registered mutual fund. They can also make foreign currency deposits in an overseas bank, as opposed to in a Citibank branch in Japan. But few will do so, just as few Americans do. Most capital flows in and out will be mediated through institutions such as mutual funds, banks, and insurance companies.

The Verdict

Were all these changes allowed to do their work, the Big Bang would have had a marked beneficial effect on the allocation of capital in Japan. However, as stated at this chapter's outset, any benefits from financial reform have been more than offset by other, more negative trends: the expansion of financial socialism, the continued protection of "zombie" borrowers, and the ZIRP's effect on the household income.

——— 15 ———

Corporate Reform

No Competitiveness Without
More Competition

Role-Playing and Reality

Downsizing. Spin-offs. Holding companies. Merit pay. Profitability targets. Mergers and acquisitions. Sale of cross-held shares.

On the surface, it certainly looks as if corporate restructuring is finally under way. Under intense financial pressure, firm after firm has announced reorganization plans. Meanwhile, regulatory changes both impose new obligations, such as consolidated accounting, and grant new freedoms, such as tax relief for spin-offs and mergers. Seemingly, there are both more pressure on firms to restructure and more tools and incentives enabling them to comply.

But does all this helter-skelter motion add up to improved efficiency and profitability? Or is this a repeat of 1999, when investors bought into the hype of rapid corporate restructuring and imminent IT revolution? All too often, unfortunately, the new mantras proclaimed by corporate executives conform to what is expected of them rather than their actual intention.

Take the issue of outside corporate directors. Currently, virtually all corporate directors are the same executives that the board is supposedly overseeing, even though some studies show that firms with outside directors do better on sales and profits.[1] The Ministry of Justice has even proposed requiring at least one outside director at large companies. While Nippon Keidanren, the big business federation, bitterly opposes making this obligatory, many of its members recognize that the financial markets see the presence of outside directors as a litmus test of corporate governance reform. Yet when business professor Christine Ahmadjian looked at thirty-seven firms claiming to have appointed sixty outside directors, it took her just fifteen minutes to discover that half of these "outsiders" were from another firm in the same *keiretsu* or from one of the firm's stable shareholder allies, such as a life insurance company.[2]

A few exceptional firms appear to have given outside directors some real power. One is Hoya Corporation, a supplier of high-tech glass parts, which in 2001 was one of four winners of the Michael Porter Prize. This prize is awarded by *Toyo Keizai* magazine for firms with outstanding competitive strategies. Perhaps not coincidentally, foreigners own about 30 percent of Hoya's shares.

Incidentally, rule by internal directors is another of the many wartime and postwar innovations now falsely portrayed as long-standing artifacts of Japanese business culture. Back in 1935, only 30 percent of the directors at the top *zaibatsu* and non-*zaibatsu* firms were company executives. By 1951, the ratio was 90 percent.[3]

By no means can all changes be dismissed as a sham. That's not only cynical but inaccurate as well. Many reforms in regulations and corporate attitudes are both real and consequential. But the most progress is being made by the same group of internationally exposed big firms that have always been in the forefront of improvement. It is good that Sony and Toshiba are trying to make changes, but if all of Japan had problems on the same level as Sony and Toshiba, the country would still be growing 5–6 percent a year.

The object, then, is not only to distinguish hype from real progress, but also to see who is reforming and who is not.

The Obstacles to Efficiency

Why do so many Japanese firms operate so inefficiently? There are at least three reasons:

- The mentality of empire building
- The labor system
- A dearth of competition and shareholder power

Equity strategist Alex Kinmont of Nikko Salomon Smith Barney tells the story of a firm that produced three hundred widely variegated products. Company executives had no idea which ones made money and which lost it. They didn't care; the firm as a whole made money and could pay its staff—until recently. Now, to survive, the firm had to get rid of the money-losing products. When the company president asked his subordinates to identify them, he got the bad news. Never having asked itself this question before, the company didn't even have the systems in place to provide the answer. It had to start from scratch.

The same story is writ large in electrical machinery giants such as Hitachi, Fujitsu, Matsushita, NEC, and Toshiba. Together, these firms employ more than one million people producing tens of thousands of products. Hitachi actually consists of 1,069 firms; Fujitsu is a combine of 517. And that does not even count the host of suppliers and distributors in their production and distribution *keiretsu*.

As business professor Michael Porter stresses, strategy consists not only of knowing what to do, but also what *not* to do. General Electric gets out of businesses where it is not one of the very top players. And yet, under the "full-set" mentality, Japan's "general electrics" (*sogo denki*) still want to be all things to all people.[4] Matsushita, which suffered net after-tax losses totaling 290 billion yen ($2.3 billion) during 1999–2001, makes everything from refrigerators and toasters to computer chips and cell phones. While Tadashi Okamura, Toshiba's president, talked in mid-2001 of eliminating twenty thousand jobs through attrition, he still insisted there was tremendous "synergy" among his 323 group firms.[5] His firm lost $1.5 billion during 1999–2001. Instead of specializing, execs at these firms offer to do the same things, simply at lower cost. Certainly cost cutting is necessary, but when that's the only answer, it's a strategy for presiding over decline, not for paving the way to future growth.

It is no accident that some of the best performers in electrical machinery are companies such as Canon and Ricoh, which have put focus before empire building. Canon tries to ensure a synergy among its products, for example, the optical technology that underlies superb products in lenses, cameras, FAX machines, photocopiers, and laser printers. Focus does not make Canon small. On the contrary, its sales are about half the size of Toshiba and NEC, and about a third the size of Hitachi and Matsushita. But Canon shows that large does not have to mean sprawling. It earned $3.1 billion during 1999–2001, even as the sprawling conglomerates hemorrhaged cash. Moreover, while the rest of the stocks in the *Nikkei* 225 fell 50 percent in the decade from 1992 to 2002, Canon's shares rose 250 percent.[6]

Empire building is directly related to the labor system, where custom and law make it difficult to lay off redundant workers. In tough times, wages and bonuses are cut, but it's difficult to move workers from moribund firms to healthier ones (see Chapter 17). Since the workers must be paid regardless, firms search for ways to generate some revenue. Nippon Steel set up semiconductor plants, amusement parks, flower shops, and now the latest fad—an IT subsidiary. As long as the revenue from the flower shops surpasses the cost of setting them up, then any additional revenue cuts Nippon Steel's losses—even if the flower shop itself loses money. For the economy as a whole, however, the resources poured down these drains take away from potential growth.

The fastest way to get more output and sales per worker is to give each worker more tools to work with. And that's what firms did. In the past twenty-five years they've tripled tangible fixed assets per employee (Figure 15.1a). By this we mean just the plant, equipment, and other physical assets, but not land or financial assets. However, that route to labor productivity has a built-in problem: diminishing returns. In the mid-1970s each yen of assets produced 1.5 yen in sales, but this was down to only 1 yen in sales by early 2002 (Figure 15.1b). The inevitable result was plunging returns (profits) on those assets, from 5.5 percent ROA during 1976 through 1985 to only 3.1 percent in the past decade (Figure 15.2).

Japanese firms' strategy elevated labor productivity, or sales per worker, at the expense of total factor productivity, or the productivity of labor and capital combined. Over the long haul, profits are what TFP looks like to a firm. Why do we care? Because, as discussed in Chapter 2 (p. 32), without continuous increases in TFP, growth in labor productivity and GDP eventually slows to a crawl. This is what happened in Japan.

Empire building and inattention to profits are, in turn, directly related to the incestuous system of cross-shareholding and stable shareholding. The majority of a firm's shares are owned by its banks, insurers, *keiretsu* partners, suppliers, customers, and sometimes even competitors. *Cross-shareholding* refers to a case where Company A and Company B own shares of each other; *stable* shareholding refers to cases where shares of Company A are held long term by financial and nonfinancial corporations regardless of whether Company A owns their shares in return. Stable shareholding encompasses a larger portion of the shares.

As long as firms are not losing money, the major shareholders don't complain. Firms accumulate not only excess workers but also excess cash flow. Instead of returning excess cash to household investors via dividends, they reinvest it in low-profit or even money-losing enterprises.

Among the 1,500 corporations in the first section of the Tokyo Stock Exchange, a full two-thirds are so unprofitable that the stock market rates their value at less than their breakup value (net equity plus unrealized gains on land and stocks), and in 40 percent of the cases, the market value is less than half of the breakup value. They are destroying society's capital, not adding to it. The best thing the managers could do is to sell off the wasted

Figure 15.1a **Assets per Employee Triple . . .**

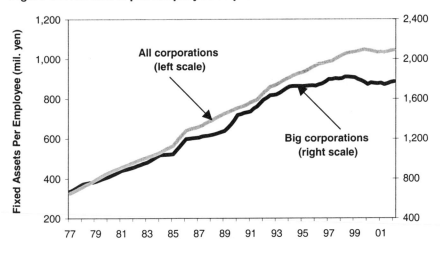

Figure 15.1b **. . . While Sales Produced by Each Yen of Assets Tumble**

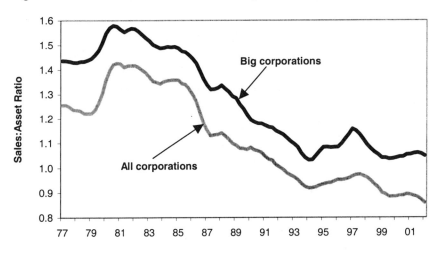

Source: Ministry of Finance 2001a.

Note: "All corporations" includes about 1.2 million firms with 33 million employees. "Big corporations" includes about 5,300 firms with 7 million employees. Four-quarter moving average.

Figure 15.2 **Excess Assets Leads to Plunging Return on Assets**

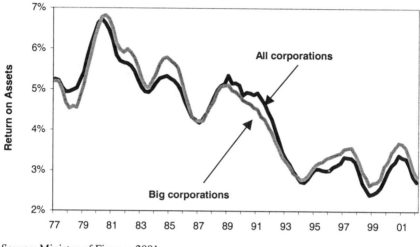

Source: Ministry of Finance 2001a.

assets, or even fold up shop. But they don't. Moreover, hundreds of these firms are sitting on mountains of unused cash—retained earnings equal to at least half of their market capitalization. These retained earnings could be used to pay dividends, but they are not. Cash and assets are hoarded, not exploited.[7]

What enables firms to get away with such counterproductive behavior? It's the fact that the two main things that hold firms' feet to the fire—competition and shareholder power—are sadly deficient in Japan.

Our Barometers of Progress

Thus, in measuring whether all the hustle and bustle genuinely mean progress, we would pose these tests:

- Are competitive pressures increasing, as measured by market share fluctuations, industry concentration, and other standard measures?
- Is shareholder power increasing, as seen in a decrease in stable share-holding, the genuine ability of shareholders to influence management policies, and an increase in dividend payout ratios?
- Are firms spinning off divisions and reducing the number of products in order to specialize in what they do best?

- Are excess assets shrinking?
- Are firms increasing authentic productivity (output per worker), or are they just cutting costs through wage reduction?

The answers to these questions are the leading indicators for a revival of efficiency, profitability, and GDP growth down the line.

The Birth and Death of Firms: Economic Natural Selection

Just as families are the basic building block of society, firms are the basic building block of the economy. Sounds obvious enough. Yet the ability of an economy to engender productivity growth requires a system in which new firms continuously replace older firms. Firms are not just a collection of resources—managers, labor, equipment, and so on. They are organic institutions in which the whole is greater (sometimes less) than the sum of the parts.

Often, introducing a new generation of technology requires a new generation of firms. In the United States, the companies that dominated air travel in the propeller days were replaced when jet engines came on the scene. Something similar happened when semiconductors supplanted vacuum tubes. In Japan, by contrast, when a new technology comes down the pike, an established firm typically develops a new division or offshoot to commercialize it.

Japan's system certainly has its advantages, deep pockets being one. In the era of standard technologies, when economies of scale spelled success or failure, this was very helpful. But in the information age, when nimbleness is prized, the Japanese system has its disadvantages as well.

To a surprisingly large degree, productivity growth is a by-product of new firms replacing older firms. Thus it is highly significant that in Japan, the birth and death of firms is so low. In the average OECD country the turnover of firms averages 20 percent a year. In Japan it averaged only 6 percent in the 1990s, and that was way down from 10 percent in the 1970s.[8] The rigidity has gotten worse. The only change in the late 1990s was a big increase in firm closings to a level still below the OECD average. This reflects a weak economy, not greater mobility. The birth rate of new firms continued to fall (Figure 15.3).

It's stunning how important new firms are to productivity growth. Looking at ten industrialized countries (unfortunately, not including Japan), the OECD broke down overall productivity growth into three sources: increased productivity within existing firms; a shift in output from low-productivity

Figure 15.3a **Business Turnover in Japan Slows**

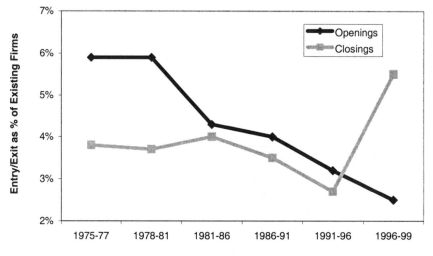

Source: Management and Coordination Agency, and White Paper on Small Business.

Figure 15.3b **Japan Firm Mobility Lags Far Behind G7**

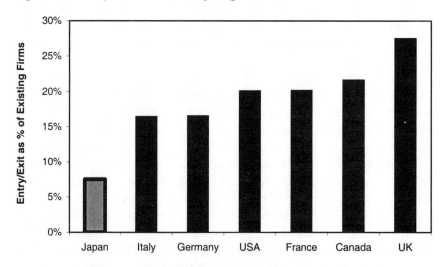

Source: OECD 2001a and Management and Coordination Agency.

incumbent firms to higher-productivity incumbent firms; and firm turn-over (i.e., low-productivity firms being pushed out of business as new firms with higher productivity replaced them).[9]

What they found is this: When it comes to growth in *labor* productivity, as much as two-thirds or even three-quarters comes from the effort of each firm to improve its operations by adding new equipment or shedding excess workers. This is particularly true of mature industries. Hence it is not surprising that Japan has traditionally been so good at labor productivity.

However, that route to labor productivity often came at the expense of total factor productivity (TFP). When it comes to TFP, improvements *within* each firm account for only half of TFP growth. The other half is provided by competition *among* firms. Specifically, nearly 40 percent of TFP growth results from newer firms displacing older firms. Another 13 percent results from firms that are more efficient taking away market share from less efficient firms within the same industry (Figure 15.4). These figures may underestimate the role played by firm turnover, since, as noted in Chapter 3 (p. 46), much of the improvement achieved by incumbent firms is done under the duress of competition. New firms pressure old firms to change their ways.[10]

Why is this so? In part it is because new firms more easily bring new technology, new attitudes, fresh blood. To the extent that new technologies are embedded in new capital, older firms may be reluctant to move too fast, since they have lots of sunk costs in the old capital. But the death of old, inefficient firms is equally critical. Moribund firms trap capital and labor in low-TFP-growth institutions. In the United Kingdom the exit of old moribund firms was at least as important for TFP growth as the entry of new firms, and in France the exit of old firms was dominant.

This is why Japan's "convoy capitalism" is so harmful. A barrier to the exit of old firms is a barrier to the entry of new ones.

The birth and death of firms is the economy's version of Darwinian experimentation and natural selection. Most new firms do not succeed. But those that do succeed change the "economic ecology" around them.

Making Japan Safe for "Gazelles"

For Japan to revive, it has to become safe for "gazelles." This is the nickname given to the newer, more entrepreneurial firms in the United States by David Birch of Cognetics, a Waltham, Massachusetts, research firm. Birch speaks of three kinds of firms: mice, elephants, and gazelles. Mice are your corner drugstore, beauty parlor, or mom-and-pop shop. They will always be

Figure 15.4 **Competition and Firm Mobility Breed TFP Growth**

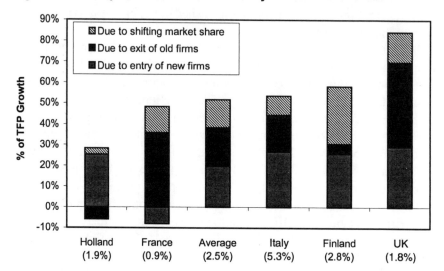

Source: OECD 2001a, p. 215.
Note: Numbers in parentheses are annual average TFP growth.

mice. Elephants are the old-line, decades-old giant firms such as General Motors or DuPont or IBM, some with hundreds of thousands of employees. Since the late 1970s, the role of the two thousand or so biggest multinational firms in the United States has been shrinking. Back then their U.S. sales were equivalent to 72 percent of U.S. GDP. By the mid-1990s it was down to 55 percent of GDP. Meanwhile, after years of cutting their payrolls, their share of the U.S. workforce dropped from 23 percent to 16 percent.

The real growth in both jobs and GDP has come from the gazelles. These are firms only ten or twenty years old, or at most thirty, usually with just a few dozen or a few hundred employees. Some have become household names in their own right: Intel, Microsoft, MCI-WorldCom, Home Depot, Wal-Mart, Kindercare, America Online, and CNN. Most remain anonymous. But they are the source of jobs, productivity, and GDP growth because they embody new technologies, new attitudes, and new ways of doing things.

It's very easy to be a gazelle in the United States. Any entrepreneur with a good idea can find financing, whether from individual "angels" or the venture capital market or, eventually, the stock market. It's also easy to hire talented managers and staff away from other firms. And certainly, with aggressive enforcement of antitrust laws, no entrenched firm can block a newcomer from gaining access to distributors and final customers.

In Japan, by contrast, all of these basics are hard. In a system where the banks own, and are owned by, old-line firms, it's hard for upstarts to find financing. As a percent of GDP, venture capital in Japan is the lowest in the OECD. While some firms have managed to get listed on the MOTHERS exchange in just a few years, on average, it takes nineteen years to get listed on Japan's stock market. That's an improvement only in comparison to the thirty years it used to take. In the land of lifetime employment, hiring talented management and staff is also hard. When entrenched firms use bully-boy tactics to keep newcomers' products off the shelves, the Japan Fair Trade Commission (JFTC) does little to interfere. There are exceptions, of course—look at Fast Retailing (Uniglo). But its success was, in part, due to its ability to ally with Itochu, one of the big trading companies. Put it all together and entry is difficult.

Then there are all the factors that put tacks in the road of firms leaving or shrinking, from well-meaning but misguided labor laws to loan guarantees for the insolvent.

Risk Aversion: A Problem of Institutions, Not Culture

There are those who say Japan's problem is cultural: a national psychology of risk aversion. We disagree. Consider two contrasting stories.

A cousin of mine worked as a mechanical engineer at Hewlett-Packard (HP). When a colleague developed a new Web server technology and wanted to leave HP to found his own firm, he asked my cousin to join him. HP agreed to buy 10 percent of the new firm and told the staff that if their venture failed, they were welcome to come back. So if the firm succeeds, he'll be a millionaire. If it fails, he'll go out and get a job at HP or some other firm.

What about Japan? An acquaintance there wanted to leave a big-name firm for a start-up. As is typical, the firm argued that leaving was betrayal. The firm even pressured the man's in-laws, warning that the man was risking the welfare of his children. The in-laws in turn pressured him, pointing out, correctly, that if the new venture failed, it would be tough to get a new job anything like the one he had given up. And if he succeeded, his financial rewards would not be that big. They told him, "We allowed our daughter to marry you precisely because you worked for [a big-name firm]."

Then there is the promotion system. At many big firms, young employees on the fast track start off with 100 points. For any mistake, points get deducted. Those with the highest scores get preference for promotion. Of course, the best way to avoid mistakes is to avoid taking a chance. The system doesn't reward achievement; it rewards risk aversion. This, however, is not an artifact of age-old Japanese culture but of the mid-1960s.

Alexander Hamilton once commented that the worst thing about monarchy was not that it engendered bad kings but that it taught citizens to think like subjects. The same is true in Japan. Change the institutions and the risk-to-reward calculus, and, over time, you will change in attitudes and behavior.

Regulatory Changes Affecting Corporate Mobility

Those who claim that there is rapid reform in Japan point to a remarkable series of changes in the commercial code and other regulations. Some are already enacted and some have yet to be. At least on paper, most of these changes seem groundbreaking:

Accounting: During fiscal years 1999–2001, Japan phased in consolidated accounting as well as mark-to-market accounting. Consolidated accounting makes it much more difficult for big firms to hide losses or problems by shunting them off to subsidiaries. Proponents say it will also encourage firms to divest themselves of money-losing operations that others might manage better. Mark-to-market accounting compels firms to revalue the land they hold for investment purposes, or stocks they hold in other firms, at market value. Once again, this gives investors a more accurate picture.

Consider Mycal, a big retailer that went bankrupt in 2001 with 1.75 trillion yen ($14 billion) in debt. In fiscal 1997, Mycal claimed 11.1 billion yen ($92 million) in net income. Had consolidated accounting been in force then, it would have revealed its actual loss of 67 billion yen ($558 million). In early 2001, in anticipation of consolidated accounting, Mycal began trying to raise cash by selling off subsidiaries. In Mycal's case, it was too late. The hope is that the new rules will cause other firms to take the proper steps in time.

Consolidated taxation. Consolidated taxation is to accompany consolidated accounting, but, as of this writing, the MOF is still stalling full implementation, fearing a loss of tax revenue.[11] Proponents say that, among other things, consolidated taxation would encourage more divestiture. A would-be acquirer could buy a currently unprofitable division of a firm and gain tax write-offs while it rehabilitated its new acquisition.

Holding company form. A firm can separate its different divisions into separate firms owned by a single holding company. Then it could differentiate wages according to the profits and skill levels of each unit. It could also more easily sell off units that chronically lose money.

Corporate spin-offs. Hitherto, firms trying to spin off unneeded divisions faced several tax disadvantages, including capital gains taxes. As of April 2001 those have now been removed. In addition, Tokyo has removed tax disadvantages for stock-for-stock swaps, which are often used as the currency for mergers and acquisitions (though there are still obstacles to cross-border stock-for-stock swaps). Proponents say that this will reduce meaningless diversification.

Defined contribution pension plans. Similar to the 401(K) plans in the United States, these pension plans have the firm and the employee put a set amount of money into a pension plan. The returns to the employee depend on how well the investments do. Currently, most pension plans are of the defined-benefit type, where the firm is obliged to pay the pensioner a certain amount of money. The presumed advantage of defined-contribution plans is that it makes it easier for an employee to switch firms. He simply rolls over his pension plan into the new firm. Whether it will also increase worker risk and lower pension benefits, as the Enron case brought to light in the United States, remains to be seen.

Let us review how well these reforms have achieved their desired results.

Reliable Accounting Needs Reliable Counters

We yield to no one in our enthusiasm for accounting reforms. But someone has to do the counting. And therein lies the rub.

There are only 13,000 auditors in Japan, compared to 350,000 in the United States and 120,000 in the United Kingdom. Worse yet, in all too many cases their numbers don't add up. Sooner or later we'll learn how common the practices revealed in the Enron–Arthur Andersen scandal are in the United States. But it already appears that prettifying the books is commonplace in Japan. Each time a large firm such as Sogo or Chiyoda Life or LTCB failed, investors discovered that assets had been systematically overstated. "In most of the recent bankruptcies," charged Mamoru Ishida, a former board member of the giant Itochu trading company, "it has been revealed that both corporate auditors and accounting auditors have failed in their duty. They are partly responsible for having provided the capital market with inaccurate information."[12] When Mita Kogyo's accounting auditor was arrested—

a new and still unusual enforcement of the law—he pleaded that he would have lost business if he had defied the company president's request to overlook certain data.

The good news is that there is some progress toward truth in accounting. Some shareholders of Nippon Credit Bank (NCB), which went bankrupt in 1998, have sued its directors and accounting auditors for compensation, arguing that they relied on the certified financial statements. Should the accountants be held liable in this case, it will shake things up. In 2001 the Business Accounting Council, an advisory panel to the Financial Services Agency (FSA), called on the government to require auditing firms to clearly state their views about whether a corporate client is likely to go bankrupt in the foreseeable future. Japan is virtually the only developed country without this rule.

In the United States, malfeasance by accountants has already led to the prosecution and bankruptcy of Arthur Andersen. Further arrests are likely. But the revelation of problems in the United States hardly justifies the continuation of lax accounting in Japan. Both countries require a shake-up.

Corporate M&A: Less Competition

Is the recent explosion of mergers and acquisitions (M&A) the harbinger of rapid reform? Yes, answers Jesper Koll, chief economist at Merrill Lynch's Tokyo office.

> M&A activity is one of our favorite leading indicators of corporate restructuring. Typically, M&A triggers change at the boardroom level, and thus the need to present a credible leadership strategy to shareholders and regulators. M&A raises the probability that corporate governance is changing, and that corporate priorities towards shareholder value will not just be talked about, but actually be implemented.[13]

No one denies that M&As, corporate spin-offs, and associated practices have exploded of late. In 1990 there were only 341 cases. But in both 1999 and 2000, there were more than 2,000 cases each year. The value has also exploded (Figure 15.5).

However, as competitiveness expert Michael Porter points out, M&A per se does not mean restructuring if it's just a way for corporate giants to get even bigger and to reduce competition even further:

> Much of the M&A activity is more of the same old-style approach. It's the mentality that being big and having the biggest market share is what makes you successful. Sure, there are some Japanese industries that are much too fragmented

Figure 15.5 **Mergers and Acquisitions Activity**

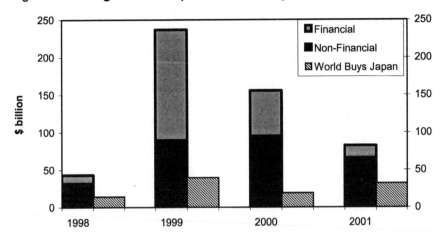

Source: Koll 2001.

Note: Data for 2001 annualized from January–August figures. In each year, the left-hand column is the total of mergers and acquisitions activity, divided between the financial and nonfinancial sectors. The right-hand column is the portion in which foreign firms bought Japanese firms, or parts thereof.

and which need to consolidate. But, overall, mergers *per se* are not strategy. Getting bigger is not a strategy. Consolidating the industry is not a strategy. Strategy is carving out a distinctive position based on some genuine competitive advantage. Some of the first round of mergers is perhaps an example of companies clinging to the old mindset.[14]

If we look at the U.S. corporate restructuring in the 1980s and 1990s, many of the most successful cases involved diversified companies selling off divisions, or firms breaking themselves into two or three parts.

The record in Japan is, at best, mixed. We've seen a plethora of troubled firms in weak industries getting together to form even bigger oligopolies that can jack up prices. This is not reform, but resistance.

More than half of all M&A activity in 1999 consisted of $138 billion in deals that created four mega bank groupings out of ten big banks. Despite initial PR about cutting operating expenses and breaking down *keiretsu* ties, the real deal was to create entities "far too big to fail." Investors who bought the PR now wish they hadn't.

Then there is the steel industry. This is already very concentrated, with the top three producers accounting for over half of Japan's output, and the top five accounting for two-thirds. This concentration, combined with low imports, allows these oligopolists to charge their Japanese customers prices far above world levels (see Chapter 4, p. 68). How can it possibly enhance efficiency for the industry to become even more concentrated? Yet that is exactly what's going on. In mid-2001 the second and third largest producers, Nippon Kokkan and Kawasaki, announced that they would merge as of late 2002. The combined firm would produce about a quarter of Japan's steel output. Meanwhile, Itochu and Marubeni, two of the top five giant trading companies, will use a new company spin-off clause to merge their steel product divisions.

Beyond these outright mergers, some of the big steel companies, prodded in part by METI, are swapping product lines. Thus, even if the concentration within steel as a whole didn't appear to change, such swaps would reduce competition within individual products.

The same process has been seen in other industries where profits and efficiency are low and debt is high.

Sumitomo Chemical and Mitsui Chemical announced they would use the new holding company law to merge their operations as of 2003. That would make the combined entity Japan's largest chemical firm and the fifth largest chemical firm in the world. Mitsubishi Chemical and Showa Denko announced plans to integrate their polyethylene businesses in mid-2002.

In the paper industry, Nippon Paper and Daishowa Paper are using a holding company to integrate their operations under the name Nippon Unipac, following which three firms will dominate the market for paper products such as newsprint.

Mergers have raised the share of the three top firms from 43 percent to 50 percent in gasoline, and from 57 percent to 81 percent in cement.

Overall, during 1997–99, the top three companies increased their market share in the *majority* of industries surveyed—forty-seven out of eighty.[15]

Nor are the supposed spin-offs quite as advertised. Since the change in the spin-off law in April 2001, forty-five big corporations have announced dozens of supposed spin-offs. However, according to a survey of the Daiwa Institute of Research, in very few instances has the parent really severed its ties with the new firm, as occurs in the United States. Instead, these spin-offs are being turned into wholly owned subsidiaries—a simple shell game—or else joint ventures with another company.[16]

Certainly, there are exceptions, such as Nippon Steel's wise decision to sell its money-losing chip division to a Taiwanese firm (see Chapter 11, p. 175). But they are just that—exceptions.

No Easier to Displace Market Leaders

One of the best measures of competitive pressure is the ability of newcomers to displace industry leaders. As yet, there are no clear signs that the situation is improving.

Make a list of Japan's top forty-five largest industrial firms for 1987 and one for 1997. Every name, except for six, will be the same. In the United States, on the other hand, as economist Douglas Ostrom points out, seventeen of 1987's leaders were displaced by 1997. Japan's top ten retailers in 1984 were still the top ten in 1994.[17]

Far from improving, corporate mobility appears to be slowing, says Ostrom. In the 1977–87 decade, 29 percent of the top forty-five firms were replaced. But in the more recent 1987–97 decade, the replacement rate dropped to 13 percent.

A study of one hundred industries during 1997–99 showed that in only ten was the number-one firm replaced by another contender. In only twenty-four out of the hundred did a new player even enter the ranks of the top five.

Certainly there are exceptions. Fast Retailing (Uniqlo) in apparel and Matsui in online brokerage spring to mind. But, unfortunately, like Honda and Sony before them, they are the exceptions that prove the rule.

METI and JFTC Support the "Bigger-Is-Stronger" Approach

Disappointingly, both METI and the Japan Fair Trade Commission (JFTC) are encouraging the merger trend, on the spurious grounds that bigger is stronger.

The JFTC has even changed its rules to facilitate such mergers. Now, in judging whether a firm has monopolistic bargaining power, it will consider its share of the world market rather than the Japanese market. In markets where imports loom large, that makes sense, but with imports so low in so many of Japan's inefficient sectors (see Chapter 10), it is the domestic market that counts for bargaining power. Due to this rule change and other factors, the JFTC reviewed 90 percent fewer M&A cases in 1999 than in 1998 (325 vs. 3,813).[18]

Moreover, the JFTC wants to lift restrictions on the amount of stock that very big firms can have in other firms. Those restrictions were originally put in place in 1977, when trading houses and major manufacturers bought big stakes in retailers to stifle competition. Today, says the JFTC, those restrictions limit Japanese competitiveness in the global arena.

Size Doesn't Always Count

Asked about the growing concentration of industry, a senior METI official offered the following justification: "We have to think about the competitiveness of Japanese companies in the world market. With economies of scale, making Japanese companies bigger will make them more competitive in exporting."[19]

This thinking is a vestige of the high-growth era, when it was more appropriate.[20] To be sure, there are exceptions where fragmented industries would do better with some consolidation, as long it was used for efficiency purposes rather than price control. Petroleum refining springs to mind. For the most part, however, any advantages from economies of scale are far outweighed by the damage caused by insufficient competition.

Michael Porter and Mariko Sakakibara have tested out the "bigger-is-stronger" thesis. It's not true.[21] The single most important factor in an industry's success in the export market is the degree of rivalry at home, as measured by fluctuations in market ranking and market share among the leaders (see Figure 3.4 and the accompanying discussion in Chapter 3). The more competitive pressure at home, the better an industry does overseas. Conversely, protection from imports hurts an industry's export performance. And finally, they found no significant impact from economies of scale. Industries did *not* perform better when the firms became larger. METI's conventional wisdom is wrong.

While Porter and Sakakibara themselves found no direct impact of industry concentration on export performance, they cite a previous study on Japanese exports to the United States that showed that increased industry concentration had a significant *negative* effect on export performance.[22]

Decline in Stable Shareholding: A Move in the Right Direction

Currently, independent shareholders have almost no power over management. With all, or almost all, members of the company board being company executives, management supervises itself. With companies obtaining so little funding from the stock market, there is little financial leverage, either. And with the majority of shares held by corporate allies, those who'd like to challenge management can't buy enough shares at any price.

A drastic decline in cross-shareholding and stable shareholding is absolutely necessary, though hardly sufficient, to make room for genuine shareholder power. Not until there is a real market for corporate control—where

Figure 15.6 **Stable Shareholding Means Lower Dividends**

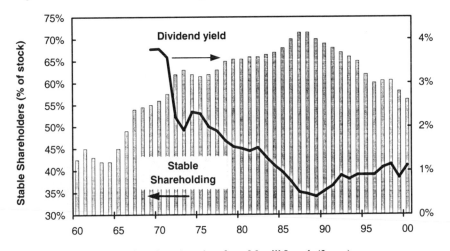

Source: Author's calculations based on data from Merrill Lynch (Japan).
Note: Stable shareholding equals the percentage of shares (by value) held by financial institutions and nonfinancial corporations.

shareholders can kick out failing management—will shareholders wield power. That will never happen as long as managers from different firms have sufficient shares in each other to protect each other.

Corporate governance is not just an issue of efficiency but also one of macroeconomic demand. As we see in Figure 15.6, as cross-shareholding increased beginning in the mid-1960s, the dividend payout ratio decreased. Households will not get their rightful income flows until they directly or indirectly own enough of the shares to compel firms to return their excess cash.

There has been some progress. By one measure, *stable* shareholding has gone down from 70 percent of all ownership in 1990 to 53 percent in 2001, as banks, insurers, and corporate allies sold stocks to raise cash (Figure 15.7, top panel). *Cross*-shareholding is estimated to have fallen from 50 percent in 1994 to 31 percent as of early 2002.[23] This is a trend that will continue, perhaps even accelerate. The combination of consolidated accounting, mark-to-market accounting, and a change in the *zeitgeist* is making it difficult for firms to hold shares that chronically decline.

Most of the shares sold by the stable shareholders were bought up by foreigners. Individuals and mutual funds (investment trusts) actually lowered their share slightly, from 25 percent to 23 percent.

Figure 15.7 **Stable Shareholding Decreases . . .**

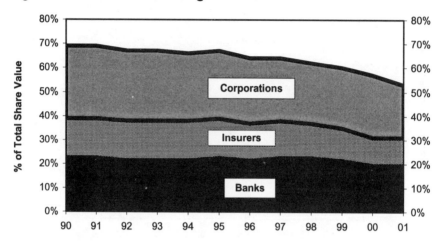

. . . While Foreign Ownership Rises

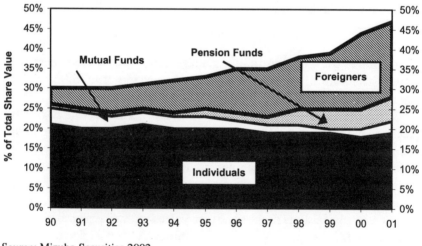

Source: Mizuho Securities 2002.

Japan has a long way to go before independent stockholders hold the overwhelming majority of shares. Given that one-third ownership provides veto power over major decisions, stable shareholding must be reduced to far less than one-third.

Do Managers Have to Care About the Share Price?

Corporate governance does seem to matter for stock prices; according to Kathy Matsui, equity strategist at Goldman Sachs, firms ranking higher on her corporate governance scorecard tended to show better performance on the stock market.[24] However, until managers have compelling reasons to care about the price of their company stock, shareholder power will be minimal.

There are several reasons why managers might be compelled to care, none of which have applied in Japan—at least not so far:

1. An excessively low stock price makes a firm a takeover target. There are hundreds of Japanese firms whose market value is less than their breakup value. Yet in the failed attempt at a hostile takeover of Shoei, Japan's first such attempt, none of Shoei's chief shareholders, such as Canon or Fuji Bank, were willing to sell at any price.
2. In stock for stock swaps, firms use their own shares as currency to buy targets. Having a higher share price is, in effect, having more money. Until recently M&A was negligible and stock-for-stock swaps were disadvantaged in Japan's tax laws. Both of these ingredients have changed in ways that, at least on paper, should give managers more reason to care about their share price.
3. For firms that raise money on the stock market by issuing additional shares, a high stock price is like a low interest rate.

For most firms, as long as their stock price is above a certain minimum, managers don't really have to take their share price into account in planning strategy.

Ironically, firms now have a greater interest in the share price of allies than in their own. With mark-to-market accounting, a firm's own balance sheet can be whipsawed by the ups and downs of the shares that they hold for alliance purposes. While Japanese managers don't have to maximize profit, they cannot afford to run losses year after year. Hence, many firms are being impelled to unload poorly performing shares. This is one of the major forces weakening the cross-shareholding system.

Some Positive Signs for Shareholder Power

Despite all the obstacles, there are still some hopeful signs.

One potentially significant change is the rise of shareholder suits. Traditionally, such suits were rare. Despite myths about Japanese being nonlitigious, the real obstacle was not culture but exorbitant fees.[25] As soon as the fees were lowered, the number of suits soared from 31 in 1992 to more than 280 in 1999. In the year 2000, the courts ordered eleven current and former directors of Daiwa Bank, including the bank's president, to pay the bank a total of $775 million in compensation. They had failed to oversee bond-trading activities in the bank's New York branch, thus failing to stem corruption that led to a steep fall in the share price. It was the very first time the courts had recognized directors' fiduciary responsibility to shareholders. Nippon Keidanren, the business federation, is fighting tooth and nail to reduce the liability of directors.

Pension funds are now legally obliged to exercise their right to vote. No longer can they simply hand over blank proxy cards to management. Moreover, fund directors are legally liable if they vote against the interests of the fund's beneficiaries in order to benefit the sponsoring firm. The degree to which this rule is enforced will be an important leading indicator of genuine corporate reform. One encouraging sign is that, in 2001 the Pension Fund Association (PFA) started giving guidelines to its member fund managers to help them push management decisions in the interest of shareholder value.

In 2001 Institutional Shareholder Services (ISS) started doing business in Japan. This U.S.-based firm analyzes resolutions drawn up by management firms for shareholder meetings and advises about five hundred institutional investor clients how to vote on them.

At the annual meetings in 2001, about 40 percent of the institutional investors dissented at some of the meetings. Though the dissents failed, the dissent alone is a new trend.

As of mid-2001, there were nearly 250 firms where a single institutional investor, often a foreign one, owned 5 percent or more of the shares. Consequently, top executives now travel overseas to explain their plans to these institutional investors—often for the first time. Still, if the investors don't like what they hear, all they can do is sell the stock; they can't compel managers to change their ways. Only 11 percent of the institutional investors felt management was more responsive to shareholders than before.

In 1997 a revision of the commercial code allowed firms to offer stock options, and as of March 2001, about 20 percent of firms listed on the stock market did so. However, the size of options is so limited that its impact on management behavior is questionable.

Those hoping for a shareholder revolt are watching carefully the activities of M&A Consulting (MAC) International, which is led by ex-METI official Yoshiaki Murakami and backed by leading business reformer Yoshiko Miyauchi, chief of Orix, a big leasing company. During 2001, MAC started raising 40 billion ($333 million) to invest in cash-rich firms. By December, MAC had obtained 2–4 percent shares in eight firms whose stock price is less than their net asset value per share. MAC argued that since these firms had not used their accumulated profits well and had few good investment outlets, they should distribute the excess cash to their shareholders by buying back shares and paying higher dividends. This would also boost the stock price. In one case, MAC held 9 percent of the shares of Tokyo Style, an apparel maker. Criticizing the company's plan to invest 50 million yen ($400,000) in real estate, Murakami said the excess money should be returned to shareholders rather than invested outside the firm's core business.

Given that foreign investors raised their ownership of Tokyo Style to 38 percent as of January 2002, Murakami expected to succeed. Instead, Murakami's shareholder revolt failed as stable shareholders such as Mizuho bank, Nomura Securities, Nippon Life, and Sumitomo Mitsui bank remained steadfast in support of management. Nomura even lobbied on management's behalf. Isetan, a big department store that buys a lot of dresses from Tokyo Style voted its 2.3 percent of Tokyo Style's shares in favor of management. Isetan said it feared that Tokyo Style would cut off supplies if they voted for the revolt, and it failed. Takashimaya, another department store, took the same attitude.[26]

The real news is not the revolt's failure, but how close Murakami came— about 40 percent of the vote—and how many attitudes changed during the course of the battle. Reportedly, Tomomizu Yano, managing director of the Pension Fund Association, urged some of the domestic asset managers hired by the PFA to give Murakami's ideas a fair hearing rather than blindly follow their parent bank or securities firm.[27]

We agree with the verdict of Arthur Mitchell, a lawyer who heads Coudert Brothers' Japan practice:

It is likely that this is only the first skirmish in a war against the distinctive management system that has guided Japan through good times and bad. The long accepted notion that the management of public companies should be insulated from the demands of shareholders—the very cornerstone of Japan's economic system—was openly challenged in a manner which suggests that corporate Japan itself, and not just the external world that deals with it, is at last ready for a markedly new paradigm.[28]

Not quite ready, but at least it's starting to get ready. Stay tuned.

─────16─────

Competition Policy

Not Enough Competition, Even Less Policy

Industry Associations: Between the State and the Market

It is all too often assumed that, when the government retreats, what remains is the market. Hence, many expect deregulation to automatically usher in truly competitive capitalism. However, in many countries, a third entity lies between the state and the market: self-regulation through industry associations, or cartel capitalism. In *Cooperative Capitalism,* business professor Ulrike Schaede argues:

> As Japan's postwar industrial policy regime crumbles and the regulating ministries become less potent, many industries rely more than ever on the practice of self-regulation (*jishu kisei*). . . . [M]any markets will remain as restricted as they are today, but this restriction will be based more on trade practices established by trade associations and less on government intervention in the marketplace. . . .
>
> Japan's antitrust system needs to undergo significant changes before it can contain self-regulation. . . . [U]ltimately [self-regulation's] effect on Japan's economy will be an increase in the bifurcation between primarily domestically oriented and largely inefficient sectors on the one hand, and export-oriented and internationally competitive industries on the other.[1]

The OECD agrees:

> Regulatory reform will not succeed without effective competition policies, but competition policy is not yet strong enough.[2]

Whose Side Is the JFTC On?

One piece of good news is that, due to changes in the Anti-Monopoly Act (AMA), the overt, formal, government-authorized cartels formerly exempt from the AMA have declined to virtually zero (Figure 16.1).

The other good news is that when anticompetitive activities are particularly blatant and explicit, the JFTC rules such practices illegal. In one such

Figure 16.1 **Formal Cartels Virtually Disappear**

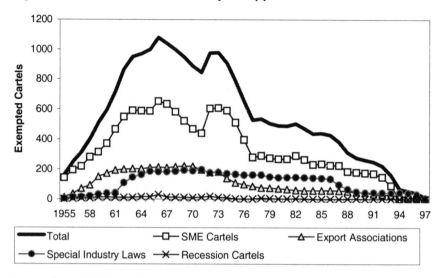

Source: Schaede 2000, p. 86.

example, the agricultural cooperative Zenno required its members to buy cardboard boxes from an affiliated manufacturer, even though another one offered the identical product more cheaply.

The bad news is that enforcement is so weak that banned activities often return in another guise. Additionally, many of the informal practices that block new entrants and stifle competition remain firmly in place beyond the reach of the JFTC.

Worst of all, sometimes the JFTC has sided *with* the informal cartels, using its powers in order to reinforce cartel activity or monopolistic prices.

When Pepsi Cola tried to increase its share by instructing its distributors to go below the price established by the Soft Drink Wholesalers Association, the association complained to the JFTC. It argued that Pepsi was bound by the agreement even though it was not a member. Using Japan's laws against excessive premiums, the JFTC threatened Pepsi with prosecution for unlawful competition.[3]

When asked about this, one otherwise reform-minded METI official commented, "This is really a dispute between Pepsi and Coca-Cola, the dominant player in Japan, and its related firms. It is not a Japanese vs. American case." There was no understanding that the victims in cases like this include not only Pepsi, but its customers and therefore consumer purchasing power.

When the highly regulated liquor and gasoline industries, both bastions of LDP support, began to undergo deregulation, prices fell sharply. More than 10 percent of the 120,000 small liquor shops closed their doors, as did many gas stations. (Deregulation had ended the limitation on the number of liquor stores, allowed convenience stores to get liquor licenses, freed up gasoline imports, and allowed self-service gas stations.)

The LDP reacted strongly to defend its base. In 1999 Kabun Muto, a former METI minister, created a caucus within the LDP to roll back deregulation of these and other sectors. It included a majority of the LDP's Lower House delegation, including one member, Yoshiro Mori, who went on to become prime minister.

Coincidentally or not, the JFTC stepped up warnings to discounters in liquor and gasoline that they were discounting too much, thus providing unlawful competition. In fiscal 2001 the JFTC issued 2,494 such warnings to liquor stores, 86 to gasoline stations, and 44 others.[4]

According to the JFTC, "unfair discounting" is discounting that, if continued for a certain period of time, could cause financial harm to rival firms. What U.S. law considers a normal shakeout in an overcrowded industry is treated by Japanese law and the JFTC as predatory pricing:

> Because selling at unjustifiable low prices in the retail business gives adverse effects to small- and medium-sized businesses seriously, the FTC intends to act on prospective unjust low-price sales swiftly. . . . [T]he FTC investigates each case on an individual basis if they are deemed to have a significant impact on retailers in the neighborhood . . . and takes strict action against cases that are deemed problematic.[5]

Competition Policy Is Even More Vital Under Deregulation

In the era of deregulation, strict competition policy is even more vital. For one thing, in case after case, firms and industry associations have reacted to government deregulation by putting in place their own self-regulation to fix prices and/or stifle competition. Second, if imports are blocked by industry association action rather than government action, there is no recourse to the World Trade Organization (WTO), whose rules apply only to government measures.[6]

When METI partially liberalized electricity, allowing large-lot users to buy electricity from suppliers other than big utilities, the utilities threatened to cut off customers who took advantage of the new freedoms. The

244 STRUCTURAL REFORM: A PROGRESS REPORT

JFTC issued a notification that this was illegal, as are more surreptitious means, such as raising cancellation fees for those who seek additional sources of supply.[7]

It's one thing for the JFTC to declare such acts illegal. It's quite another for the JFTC to prosecute those who violate its findings.

The record on the latter point is not encouraging. The JFTC is most strict in cases of outright price-fixing or bid rigging (*dango*), though even here enforcement is weak.[8] Enforcement is even more lax in instances such as the electricity example above—the boycotts, refusals to deal, and all the other intimidating practices that block new entrants and stifle competition. These are treated as violations of Section 19 governing "unfair trade practices," where the law does not allow the JFTC even to levy fines. All it can do is issue warnings and recommendations.[9]

In 1999 the JFTC found that Autoglass East Japan, a wholesaler of glass for auto repair, raised prices and decreased the frequency of delivery to retailers that actively used imported products. In addition, the JFTC found that the Tokyo Automobile Glass Association, an industry association of retailers of glass for auto repair work, instructed its members not to sell imported products. In February 2000 the JFTC found that an association of companies selling automobile repair glass restricted the number of imports to be sold by its members.[10]

In all three cases, the JFTC simply issued a "recommendation." In legal terms, this means the violator has accepted the JFTC's advice to stop the behavior. No violation of the law is listed, there is no fine, and there are no further investigations. Violators can and do find a different, less explicit means to skin the cat. An association could even add or drop a member and continue the same behavior so that a new instance is not treated as repeat behavior—generally only the latter draws financial penalties, and not always. JFTC records are replete with firms and industries that have received new warnings and recommendations with no change of behavior.

Rules of Evidence Limit Criminal Prosecution

Criminal prosecutions for antitrust violations are almost unheard of—only ten cases between the end of World War II and the late 1990s. In 1999 the JFTC filed criminal charges in two cases, more than in any previous year. In the United States there are about seventy criminal cases of antitrust violations each year. No Japanese executive has ever been jailed for violating the AMA.

In one case the JFTC issued a cease-and-desist order to Sumitomo Chemical, Japan Polychem, and five other firms, charging that they engaged in collusive price-fixing on polypropylene. The JFTC wanted to file criminal complaints but backed off after the prosecutors said there was insufficient evidence. Sounds straightforward enough—except that the rules of evidence make prosecution well nigh impossible. The AMA requires the JFTC to demonstrate not only an explicit agreement to collude and the collusion itself, but also enforcement of the collusion by some sort of penalties against would-be violators. In this Alice-in-Wonderland world, if all the firms willingly collude and hence no threat of penalty is needed, there is no evidence of collusion.

To avoid JFTC action, all that industry associations have to do is make their agreements less explicit and bury their talks in subcommittees. Warnings and fines against industry associations have declined over time as associations simply hide the evidence.[11]

Any Improvement Lately?

Beginning with the Structural Impediments Initiative (SII) of the first Bush administration, Washington pressed Tokyo to increase JFTC powers and action. Partly in response to this pressure, staffing has increased from 154 professionals dealing with anticompetitive practices in 1990 to 269 in 2001. Further staff increases are planned in the next few years, raising its total staff from 500 in 2001 to 800 by around 2005.[12] In 1999, the United States and Japan reached an agreement on cooperation in antimonopoly issues, the first such agreement for Japan.

As to actual enforcement, improvement remains exceedingly limited. In 1999 the JFTC took formal legal actions (recommendations and/or fines) in thirty-two cases. Out of these, twenty-two involved bid rigging (*dango*), while only five involved unfair trade practices, the heart of Japan's competition problem. Industry associations were involved in just two of the thirty-two cases. Fines (surcharges) have gradually increased, from 3.15 billion yen ($25 million) in sixteen cases in 1998 to 8.6 billion yen ($70 million) in the same number of cases in 2000. But the absolute amount remains tiny.[13]

Politics and Enforcement: Flat Glass and NTT

Enforcement seems to depend on the political clout of the industry. Often, dedicated career JFTC officials find their intentions hamstrung by prevailing law and/or political pressure, sometimes stemming from officials seconded to the JFTC by MOF and METI.

A notorious, and illuminating, example related to the well-connected construction sector is the flat glass oligopoly. For year after year, three firms have split the market, with virtually no change in share: Asahi gets 40 percent, Nippon Sheet gets 30 percent, and Central Glass gets 20 percent. Imports account for 7 percent of the market, many of which come from Japanese affiliates overseas. Intimidation and boycotts of wholesalers or retailers who try to bring in cheaper foreign glass are common.

While this sector has been a hearty perennial of U.S.-Japan trade disputes for decades, the chief victims are Japanese consumers, who pay more for houses; companies, which pay more for office buildings; and taxpayers, who pay more for public works.

Back in 1993, the JFTC stated that it was "unable to find evidence of Anti-Monopoly Law violation" despite the fact the JFTC itself stated:

> There were incidents of [dealers] being pressured by manufacturers or contract agencies in one form or another as a result of handling imported products, such as . . . suggestions that the supply of domestically produced goods would be terminated and others.[14]

In 1999 the JFTC issued a new report, once again finding no violations that required it to act. On the contrary, aside from some isolated problems, the JFTC concluded:

> The situation of transactions among flat glass companies has greatly changed because domestic makers have addressed the problems that were pointed out in the report on the 1993 survey. . . . [T]here are no systematic problems that adversely affect the interest of agents that deal with other companies' products. Therefore, the flat glass market has been increasingly open.[15]

In other words, the problems that failed to rise to the status of AMA violations in 1993 have now been "fixed." As often happens, problems exist only in the past, not the present.

In 2000 the JFTC issued a warning against NTT East for possible anticompetitive activity, saying it suspected NTT East of preventing new DSL (broadband Internet hookup) operators from entering the market. This was the first JFTC action against NTT. It coincided with pressure from METI and private firms, who accused NTT of blocking the information revolution due to its high phone fees. And yet the JFTC contented itself with a mere warning rather than a recommendation. The former is issued when there is suspicion of possible violations; the latter is effectively a cease-and-desist order when the JFTC is sure of a violation.

Some observers believe the JFTC tactic worked in this case, but only due to widespread political pressure on NTT. Taking advantage of the opening, in September 2001, Softbank lowered its price to 2,280 yen ($18) per month, about half of then-prevailing prices. In some cases, this is lower than prices in other countries. Consequently, not only is the number of Japanese DSL subscribers up to 3 million as of mid-2002—and expected to hit 6 or 7 million by early 2003, but NTT's market share fell sharply from 65 percent in 2001 to 40 percent as of mid-2002.

Nonetheless, rivals such as eAccess charge that NTT continues to violate the AMA in order to block challengers. An official complaint filed with the telecommunications ministry in November of 2001 charged that NTT illegally offered discounts on DSL service to those who subscribed to other NTT services where NTT is dominant.

Observers wonder how strongly the JFTC can move against NTT, considering that in the government reorganization of 2000 the JFTC was incorporated into the Ministry of Public Management, Home Affairs, Posts, and Telecommunications (MPHPT). That's the new home of the former Ministry of Posts and Telecommunications (MPT), which, as supervisor of NTT and manager of the postal savings system, has been a traditional opponent of reform.

Unlike in the United States, there is no alternative to the JFTC. Whereas in the United States there were almost thirty-two thousand private cases launched between 1945 and 1988, there were only fourteen in Japan from 1947 through 2000. The constraints in Japan are high court costs, lack of double or triple damages, and an inability to launch class action suits. In 2001 the Diet passed legislation allowing private action to seek injunctions, but obtaining financial remedies and punishments remains tough.[16]

At a time when competition policy is one of most critical ingredients of corporate reform, Japan has little in its arsenal.

——17——

Labor Reform
Mobility, Not Wage Cuts, Is the Answer

Trapped Labor

Nowhere are Japan's barriers to entry and exit more profound than in the labor market, where too many workers are trapped in moribund firms and industries. As with firm mobility (Chapter 15), labor mobility is vital to productivity growth. After all, where are new firms to find experienced staff if they are not released by older firms?

In Japan, 72 percent of male employees working for a given employer in 1990 were still there 5 years later.[1] In other rich countries, the comparable figure was only 53 percent. In Japan, male employees stayed with the same employer, on average, for 13 years. Elsewhere it was 10.4 years, and in the United States only 8 years (Figure 17.1).

Worse yet, far from labor becoming more mobile, employee tenure actually increased in the 1990s, according to economist Marcus Rebick.[2]

All of this raises a chicken-and-egg question. Across the OECD, countries with a lot of firm turnover also show good labor mobility. So is Japan's labor mobility low because there is too little exit of old firms and entry of new ones? Or does a rigid labor market block firm turnover? We suspect the two causes are mutually reinforcing, making it all the more difficult to tackle one problem at a time.

Why?

After World War II, Japan enshrined the "three sacred treasures" of "lifetime employment," company unions, and seniority pay, particularly among large firms. The workers involved in formal "lifetime employment" number about a third of the labor force, mostly male salaried workers in medium-to-big companies, but the no-layoff policy encompasses far more.

This system is not the product of centuries of culture, but of specific decisions made after World War I, and especially after World War II.

Figure 17.1 **Japanese Workers Stick with Same Job Longer**

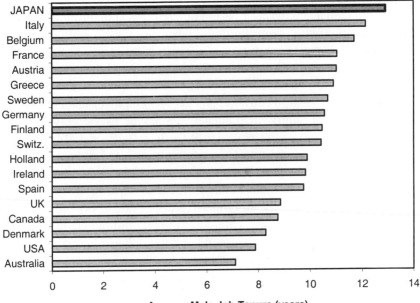

Average Male Job Tenure (years)

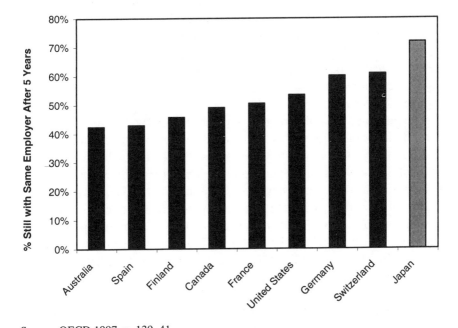

Source: OECD 1997, p. 139–41.

Lifetime employment originated in the 1920s as a company response to labor shortages. It became solidified during the mobilization for World War II, and then again during a period of labor unrest that followed World War II. Together with company unions, seniority wages, and large bonus payments, the overall system tied workers to their firms and helped suppress radical unions influenced by the Communist and Socialist Parties during the 1950s.

But the ideology shoring up these practices—"employer-labor harmony," "the company as a family," and alleged "employee sovereignty"—didn't emerge until the end of the violence of the late 1940s and 1950s. In the initial postwar years, leftist unions and employer-hired right-wing gangs repeatedly clashed in brutal scenes reminiscent of the United States in the 1930s. The same Socialist and Communist Parties leading riots against the U.S.-Japan Security Treaty in 1960 were also leading violent strikes of coal miners at the same time.[3] Only after the fact did the claim arise that the new system stemmed from age-old cultural values of community, paternalism, social harmony (*wa*) and hierarchy.[4]

The system persisted because, as long as Japan was growing, it seemed to serve both employer and employee. If his firm did well, a worker's bonus—often equal to as much as a third of total annual income—was higher. As his seniority increased, so did his wages. Other firms were loath to hire a job-hopper. So the ethic of "company loyalty" made economic sense.

From the firm's standpoint, it paid to invest in training a worker who could be counted on to stay with the firm. The firm would benefit from a better-trained worker without fear of losing company secrets if the worker "defected." Nor would workers oppose labor-saving technology, since they enjoyed job security.

The entire system of seniority pay was originally designed as an obstacle to labor mobility so that firms could hold onto valued workers—and it still functions this way. While younger workers are paid below their productivity, older workers are paid above it. That gives workers an incentive to stay with the firm. Now, suppose a forty-five-year-old leaves the firm or is laid off. For another firm to hire him at the rate appropriate for his age would not make sense. The firm is better off hiring a younger person who can work nearly as well but be paid much less. What if the forty-five-year-old is willing to work for less? No good, because it will disrupt the system for the other forty-five-year-olds at the firm.

Once growth stopped, the same system that proved a boon in good times, turned into a bane in bad times. With layoffs off the table, the main way to reduce jobs was by attrition, that is, not hiring new, younger workers as older ones retired. The consequence was a continuous rise in the average age of the workforce. Given seniority wages, this meant a rising wage bill at a time of stagnant sales.[5] Pension benefits became a huge burden. Middle-aged workers felt frustrated at the dearth of promotion slots, while younger workers felt embittered at having to swallow cuts in bonuses, sometimes even base pay, while some of the older, better-paid workers sat around doing very little.

Law, Custom, and Insecurity

Several factors were working against change in the labor system. No one entity—worker or union or firm—could effect change on its own, unless everyone else changed at the same time. And given the attitudes toward workers who left companies, was it responsible for a firm to lay off people, knowing that other firms would not hire them? Besides, law and court decisions made layoffs very difficult. Except in cases of misconduct, the courts have ruled that companies can lay off workers only when they face irresistible economic pressures, have an excess number of employees, have secured the union's agreement, selected workers on a rational basis, exhausted all other means for reducing labor costs, and put into place measures to ensure proper concern for those dismissed. These strictures apply only to permanent employees, not to temporary or contract workers.[6]

Japan is in danger of creating a European-style dual labor market, with one group of permanently employed individuals and another group who are permanently unemployed or underemployed. By early 2002, unemployment among youth (twenty to twenty-four years old) had doubled to 10 percent, as did unemployment among those sixty to sixty-four.

A rigid labor market doesn't preserve the total number of jobs; it may even reduce them, since it causes the economy to operate below capacity. But it does influence who gets to keep a job and who does not.

The Real Unemployment Rate: More than 7 Percent

A system regarded as ensuring labor security has, in fact, done the opposite. Officially the unemployment rate has risen from 2.1 percent in 1991 to 5.4 percent by August 2002. But something is clearly awry with these numbers.

From 1997 through the first half of 2002, the total number of job holders fell by 2.6 million. Yet the unemployment rolls rose only by only 1.3 million. The other 1.3 million are in statistical limbo. Neither employed nor unemployed, they are called "discouraged workers."

Normally in Japan, about 63 percent of all people over age fifteen either have a job or are actively looking for one. That 63 percent is called the labor force participation rate. The rest are students, housewives, retirees, and so forth.

Something changed suddenly in the late 1990s. As jobs abruptly turned south, so did labor force participation. From 1997 through 2002, the number of working-age people *rose* by 2.6 million. Yet the labor force (employed and officially unemployed combined) *fell* by one million.

Some of the drop was due to aging. After 1998, the number of people over sixty-five rose by three million, whereas the number of people ages twenty to sixty-four stopped growing altogether. Only 17 percent of over-65s have jobs. But, even if we adjust the participation rate for age level, the labor force in 2002 still had 1.3 million fewer people than historical patterns would dictate.

Who stopped looking for work? New high school and college graduates living with their parents. Mothers who normally go back to work once their children are old enough. Salarymen who retired from their first job at age fifty-five but couldn't find the usual postretirement job.

To get a true picture of joblessness in Japan, we should look not at the rising unemployment rate but at the falling employment rate. The latter is the percentage of working-age people with a job.

If we count the gap between those who should have had jobs and those who actually had them, it adds up to another 1.3 million jobless beyond the officially unemployed. Counting them brings the real unemployment rate to 7.3 percent (Figure 17.2).

Cutting Personnel and Wages

By 1999 it had become conventional wisdom that excessive personnel costs—too many workers with wages that were too high—were the primary culprit in falling profits.

In response, big Japanese companies did what they always do in tough times: they cut pay and workers. Firm after firm cut bonuses, sometimes even base wages. They hired part-timers and temporary workers ineligible to receive bonuses, pensions, and other fringe benefits available to full-timers. Given that bonuses can make up as much as a third of all compensation, this is a big pay cut. They cut jobs via attrition, redeployed permanent employees to various subsidiaries, and launched voluntary retirement programs. Many of these retirements were genuinely voluntary—but some

Figure 17.2 **Uncounted Unemployed: Dropouts from the Labor Force**

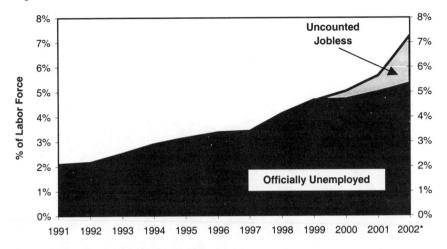

Source: Statistics Bureau 2002b, Table 2.

Note: "Uncounted jobless" measures the gap between officially unemployed and all the rest of the people who would have held jobs if the ratio of the labor force to the total age-adjusted working-age population had stayed the same as in 1995. Data for 1991 through 2001 are annual averages. Data for 2002 is the January–August average.

were the result of being kept in a room without a phone or even windows all day.

Though all of this was portrayed as corporate flexibility, the most important result was a significant drop in real wages and thus consumer purchasing power (see Figure 4.1 in Chapter 4).

The personnel cuts were also advertised as restructuring, but there is nothing new here. Given that workers, once hired, cannot be fired, the big corporations, which account for about 10 percent of all employment in Japan, have always shied away from expanding their payrolls except in boom times. Cutting payrolls in slack times is not restructuring. It's standard operating procedure and was used for years after the 1973 oil shock (Figure 17.3).[7]

What is different today is that employment in small and medium-sized firms and self-employment are not playing their usual shock absorber role.

Downsizing may be necessary but it is a far cry from true labor mobility. It is still rare for a worker leaving or losing a job in one firm to get another job in the same industry. In the United States in the 1980s, most of the firms that downsized stayed downsized. Downsizing was a recipe for survival,

Figure 17.3 **Employees at Big Firms Falling Since 1993**

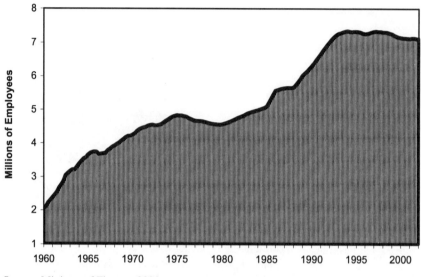

Source: Ministry of Finance 2001a.

not future growth. If restructuring means creative destruction, we are seeing the destruction long before the new creation. Rising joblessness is a sign of the old regime unraveling, not a new one arising.

Poor ROA: Excessive Wages or Excess Assets?

None of these efforts solved the corporations' low profitability problem because they didn't address the real source of their problems: excessive and unproductive assets (see Chapter 15 including Figures 15.1 and 15.2).[8]

Firms had bought into the following myth: Labor costs rose from about 10 percent of corporate sales to 14 percent in the past two decades, and that's why return on assets (ROA) declined from a peak of 6.7 percent in 1980 to 2.4 percent in 1999. Japan can no longer afford to pay these labor costs if it is to restore ROA even to the 1976–91 average of 4 percent.

Some private economists, such as Robert Feldman, as well as public organizations, such as the OECD, have called for cuts in wages and a permanent decrease in the labor share of national income. The OECD put it this way: "Poor investment returns require a sizeable reduction in labour's share of [national] income . . . by around 3 percentage points beyond cyclical changes." At least some Koizumi officials agree, including, Koichi Hamada, a renowned academic economist serving as president of the Cabinet Office's Economic and Social Research Institute. At a 2002 conference, he declared: "The Japanese economy cannot enjoy the high real income, and particularly the high real wages." Even if the NPL problem were solved, he continued, "it is difficult to believe that the lending activities will be activated without the improvement in profit opportunities in the real sectors of the economy. In order to do that, real wages should be reduced."[9]

The argument is flawed and the solution counterproductive. Wage austerity would just worsen economic anorexia. If consumer income drops, who, then, is to provide the demand to drive the economy? Private investment? Government deficits? A trade surplus? The analysis is flawed because the prime culprit is unproductive assets, not excessive wages.

To begin with, much of the apparent rise in the wage-to-sales ratio is a pure statistical illusion caused by an unadvertised change in the Ministry of Finance database. As a result of a 1990 revision of the Commercial Law, hundreds of thousands of firms had to increase their capital to 10 million yen, the minimum level for inclusion in the MOF survey.[10] Suddenly the MOF database included these new, smaller firms. Consequently, from 1990 through 1999 the average size of a firm in the MOF database dropped by 60 percent—not due to any change in the firms, but simply the inclusion of smaller firms in the database. Smaller firms have higher wage-to-sales ratios and lower profit-to-sales ratios. Hence what appeared to be an actual change over time, rising wage costs, was really just a change in the data set as it increasingly reflected the characteristics of smaller firms.

Second, if rising wages were really the cause of falling profits, then the rise in the wage-to-sales ratio should have taken place when wages were *rising*. In reality, the opposite occurred: The rise in the wage-to-sales ratio (and the fall in the profits-to-sales ratio) took place when wages were falling. Nominal wages per worker in the corporate sector were actually 4 percent *lower* in 2001 than at their 1995 peak (Figure 17.4).

Here's what's going on. Profits gyrate much more than wages in line with the ups and downs of sales. When sales boom, profits boom even more. When sales slump, profits slump even more. Consequently, in a slump, even if wages are falling, profits will fall even faster. Hence labor will appear to get a larger share.

Suppose, for example, that total corporate value-added is 100 yen, divided as 75 yen in wages and 25 yen in profits.[11] In other words, a 75–25 split. Suppose now that a recession causes profits to drop by 20 yen to 5 yen and wages to drop by 10 yen to 65 yen. In that case, total value-added has dropped from 100 to 70 yen, and the labor share of that 70 yen has

Figure 17.4 **Wages per Employee Stop Growing After 1996**

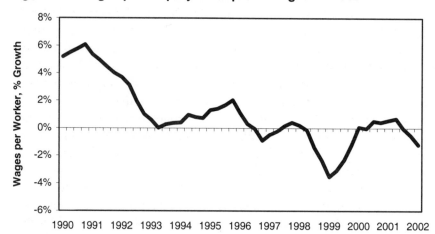

Source: Ministry of Finance 2001a.

Note: Total personnel costs per person employed in nonfinancial corporations. Four-quarter moving average. All in nominal yen.

risen to 93 percent (65 out of 70). The labor *share* rose even though actual wages fell. That is exactly what happened in Japan in the past decade.

Ironically, the profits share of value-added is highest when wages are rising quickly and profitability is lowest when wages are falling sharply. Low profits and falling wages are both products of the same cause: a no-growth economy.[12]

When sagging profits are then compared to still-rising assets, the consequence is inevitable: a fall in ROA. In fact, even if the profit share of corporate value-added had remained as high as ever, the rise in unproductive assets was so great that ROA would have fallen anyway, as we discussed in Chapter 15 (p. 220).[13]

Some people argue that the problem is not excessive wages but an excess of workers. But there is a basic fallacy of composition here. While that is true for many individual firms, is it really true for the economy as a whole?

Suppose every firm in Japan could produce the same output with 10 percent fewer workers. Would anyone advocate sacking 10 percent of Japan's total workforce? Or should we say that there is room for Japan to increase GDP by 10 percent via productivity hikes? Yes; many firms need to downsize their labor forces. But those workers should be absorbed by other firms or by new firms.

For Japan as a whole, the problem is not an excess of workers but a horrible misallocation of millions of workers. Some firms and sectors have too many workers, but cartelized prices allow them to avoid downsizing. Meanwhile other sectors and firms (including some that don't even exist yet, due to barriers to exit and entry) have too few.

Some firms and industries would even increase jobs if they raised productivity and lowered prices. In virtually every country that has deregulated telecommunications and lowered prices, jobs have increased. That's because a price drop of, say, 20 percent leads to increased sales of 30 or even 40 percent.

The McKinsey Global Institute projects that, in a reform scenario, industries such as retailing, housing construction, and food processing would lose jobs. However, health care—where productivity is now 25 percent below U.S. levels—would gain one million new jobs. The transition will be difficult, but at the end of the road lies faster growth, higher wages, and bigger profits.[14]

What Is to Be Done?

To ease the transition to greater labor mobility, the first step is to beef up Japan's social safety net.

Unfortunately, the opposite is being done. Tokyo is thinking up new ways to cut benefits even as it raises premiums because the unemployment insurance system is running out of money. During the course of 2001 and 2002, premiums were raised from 0.8 percent of pay to 1.4 percent and they are set to rise to 1.6 percent in 2003. In May 2002, the Labor Policy Council of the Ministry of Health, Labor and Welfare proposed that, for workers earning more than 10,280 yen ($83) per day, benefits be cut from 60 percent of their former base pay to 50 percent. Often, due to seniority wages, the highest-paid workers are older workers who find it most difficult to get someone else to hire them. The Ministry is also reportedly considering proposals to reduce, or even eliminate, benefits to some workers over the age of sixty. Some researchers at METI have come up with a scheme that, by adjusting benefits to age levels, could cut benefits by 30 percent with no cut in premiums.[15]

On paper, Japan would seem to have a good unemployment compensation system. People who retire or leave their jobs for personal reasons are eligible to receive 60–80 percent of their base salary (which, in turn, is about two-thirds of total income) for 90 to 180 days. In other words, they are supposed to get 50–53 percent of their total income. Employees whose companies go bankrupt or who are restructured out of a job can collect from 90 to 330 days. Three-fourths of the insurance premiums comes from employees and their employers; one-quarter from the national government.

However, there are gaping holes in the system. Only about half (34 million) of Japan's 64 million workers are even eligible. That's because it applies only to full-time employees, leaving out the self-employed, part-timers who work less than 30 hours per week, and temporary employees who have worked less than six months for that employer. Those most likely to be marginalized have the least coverage. In the United States, by contrast, out of the total labor force of 140 million, nearly 130 million were covered by the unemployment insurance system. In 2001 in Japan only 1 million people received benefits on average in any given month, even though the average number of people unemployed each month was 3.4 million.[16]

Moreover, the actual money that people receive is less generous than the nominal terms indicate. In 1997, an average recipient's benefits lasted 149 days and totaled 150,000 yen per month. That's about 36 percent of the average monthly income of an employee in a firm with at least thirty workers.

Finally, the system is woefully underfunded. In 1997 there was 4 trillion yen ($32 billion) in the unemployment account. By late 2001 it was down to 143 billion yen ($1.1 billion). Despite hikes in premiums, the system continues to run out of money.[17]

The dearth of money creates an incentive to minimize unemployment rolls. Somehow, even though the unemployment rate rose sharply from 1998 through 2001, the number of people receiving benefits did not.

Moreover, the amount of compensation is based on a worker's salary in his or her last six months on the job. Some employers have moved workers to subsidiaries that pay lower wages before finally letting them go. That lowers the unemployment benefit.

Given all this, Japan's real social safety net is the current job. The government has even subsidized firms to retain redundant labor. Some in METI have lobbied for more government funding for the unemployment insurance system, but the Labor Ministry resists. In fact, in fiscal 2002 the Labor Ministry argued for a lower unemployment forecast than METI so as to avoid asking for a higher unemployment budget.

Clearly, no country has figured out the perfect balance between security and efficiency. The United States enshrines labor mobility at the expense of worker security, particularly for the lower half of wage earners. Europe has made a social safety net so thick that it has suffered long-term double-digit unemployment. But Japan's answer—the current job is the primary safety net—surely works no longer, and it is a barrier to reform.

As for labor mobility, certain government regulations and tax rules have made things worse. Under present tax law, for example, those who retire after more than twenty years at one company receive tax deductions twenty times the size of those who stay less than that amount of time.

Private job placement agencies for temporary work (as opposed to government agencies) were legalized in 1986, but the Ministry of Health, Labor, and Welfare permitted them only in twenty-six occupations. In 1999 the rules were relaxed, but many restrictions remain. One rule highlights the genuine dilemmas. Current rules hinder the indefinite use of temporary workers so that firms cannot use them to undermine the rightful benefits (pensions, bonuses, health plans, etc.) enjoyed by full-time workers. After a year (three years in some sectors) temporaries must either be hired directly or let go. The problem for the firm is that once hired, a worker cannot easily be let go even when he or she is no longer needed. Firms say the rule stifles their flexibility, while existing employees say the rule protects their livelihood and the unemployed say it denies them a job.

A reconciliation of these conflicting needs would be easier if firms could hire employees with full bonus and pensions (portable ones) but then let them go when they're redundant. The government is looking for perfect regulations when the need is to create fluid labor markets.

Japan suffers a classic collective-action problem. Few firms or workers can change until they know others will. Just as the government and business federations actively cooperated to create the current employment system, so they, and the unions, must work together to change it. Piecemeal reforms, no matter how well designed or intentioned, won't achieve the desired result.

─── 18 ───

Deregulation and State Enterprises

The Momentum Is Clear,
the Destination Is Not

The Starting Point

The momentum is unmistakable. The overt role of the state in regulating huge swaths of the economy is receding. Even the fiercest opponents of deregulation feel compelled to pay it obeisance. They delay and dilute rather than openly oppose. It is not whether, but *how,* deregulation is carried out that will determine its meaning for economic efficiency.[1]

When the 1990s began, about 55 percent of the economy and 46 percent of the workforce were in highly regulated sectors (Table 18.1).

Naturally, some regulations offer vital protections to consumers. But in far too many cases onerous rules are designed to create an artificial market. Particularly notorious are the biannual car safety inspections that often cost almost $700 for mandated parts replacement on a domestic car (far more for a foreign car). The inspection provides almost half of the annual sales of the auto service industry. Germany has a rigorous inspection system, but the cost is only $50 to $100.[2] Japan also has land use regulations limiting the size of buildings, the main purpose of which seems to be to create an artificial scarcity of land so as to bid up prices. (The officially stated purpose is to protect access to sunshine and to prevent congestion.) This protects the value of old projects but limits developers' ability to profit from new ones.[3]

The heart of the regulatory state is that, in perhaps half the economy, such basics as entry of new firms and exit of old ones, pricing, and introduction of new products all required government approval to one degree or another. Trust in officials was such that, within broad guidelines, the Diet delegated officials to use their discretion. Consequently, defying an official in one area might lead to the denial of a vital entry license in another.

Table 18.1

Regulated Sector in 1990 Was Half of GDP

	% of GDP	% of Employment
Real estate	11.4%	1.5%
Construction	10.6%	9.6%
Health care	8.0%	4.0%
Transport and communications	6.6%	5.7%
Retail trade	5.4%	12.0%
Finance and insurance	5.4%	3.3%
Electricity, gas, and water supply	3.3%	0.8%
Agriculture, fisheries, forestry	2.9%	8.8%
Petroleum and coal products	1.1%	0.1%
TOTAL	**55.0%**	**46.0%**

Source: Cabinet Office 2001a; McKinsey 2000 for 1996 figures on health care and employment in retail trade.

Firms almost never appealed these decisions to the courts, going instead to the politicians.

While regulated firms might protest this or that decision, most enthusiastically supported the regulatory regime as a whole. Why not? One of its main purposes was to protect incumbent firms under the official rhetoric of preserving "stability" and "adjusting supply and demand." Until recently, few top firms failed in the regulated sectors.

The only way to preserve perceived stability is to prevent alleged "excessive competition." Hence, new challengers, domestic or foreign, were regularly excluded. For example, from the 1950s until 1998, not a single new airline was licensed to start operations. Regulators also limited competition among the incumbents. One mechanism was control over pricing—for example, regulated insurance rates or pharmaceutical prices. Another was control over new financial, insurance, or health care products, with a pioneer often forced to delay while others caught up.

In exchange, the regulated industries were required to act as social utilities. This goes far beyond the usual practice in most countries—for example, requiring railways and buses to provide service to unprofitable rural routes. There is a huge covert regulatory redistribution machine. The most extreme case is in farming, where the transfer from consumers to farmers is $577 per consumer in Japan, compared to $189 in the European Union and $15 in the United States.[4] Restrictions on large stores served to provide disguised unemployment and income support for the mom-and-pop retail stores. High electricity rates allowed the utilities to pay high prices to their suppliers, from construction to machinery.

Public Corporations: Moneychangers in the Temple

Junichiro Koizumi came to power vowing to destroy the iron quadrangle of politicians, bureaucrats, public corporations, construction firms. It's a worthy goal, but his temporizing actions have failed to match his fiery oaths.

The public corporation system, a labyrinth of seventy-seven different companies, is a nest of corruption, kickbacks, and waste reminiscent of the Soviet *nomenklatura*. Behind the public corporations stand three thousand subsidiaries. Often staffed by government bureaucrats on temporary leave, they receive fat contracts from the public firms that sponsored them in the first place. Then there are the construction firms doing the public works and their millions of employees. Half of all construction work in Japan is for public works. Not only does 90 percent of all public works involve rigged bids (*dango*) and profit rates sometimes as high as 17 percent, but kickbacks from the firms to bureaucrats and politicians are said to total 300 billion yen ($2.6 billion) a year.[5]

This parasitic cancer is huge. At its peak in 1997, the funding source for these corporations, the Fiscal Investment and Loan Program (FILP), amounted to 10 percent of Japanese GDP and 30 percent of all combined private and public investment in Japan.[6]

With half of Japan's coastline and most of its rivers already wrapped in concrete, Gavan McCormack reports that Tokyo plans to dissipate yet another 102 trillion yen ($630 billion) on roads and water management in a country that already has more roads and dams per square mile than the United States.[7] Many of these projects exist simply to provide work for construction firms and kickbacks to bureaucrats and politicians. Yet somehow Japan still lacks good roads in districts where the Diet member is from the "wrong" party. And in a world where infrastructure increasingly means information superhighways, Japan ranked nineteenth out of forty-nine countries, according to the Institute for Management Development. It's as if 10 percent of GDP were Enron.

If you want to know why Japan stopped growing, take a look at the Urban Development Corporation (UDC), an affiliate of the Ministry of Construction (now part of the new Ministry of Land, Infrastructure, and Transport). Since 1969, the UDC has shelled out 1.4 trillion yen ($11 billion) to build Chiba New Town. Though originally designed for 340,000 people, the town now hosts only 78,000. Due to this and other loss-making ventures, the UDC's debt totaled 15 trillion yen ($120 billion) at the end of fiscal 1999. Its interest bill was 1.7 trillion yen but its revenue only 1.4 trillion.

But behind this story is another story. When the JFTC launched a *dango* case against the UDC regarding orders for paint, it found that the UDC had slipped secret information to the paint supplier. Was it coincidence that eleven out of nineteen of the paint supplier's directors came from the UDC?[8]

Every year the UDC hands out 80 percent of its maintenance contracts to a single firm: Japan General Housing Life, known as JS. Although it's a private company, UDC officials—that is, former Construction Ministry bureaucrats—typically spend two to three years working there before going back to the UDC. Somehow, every year the UDC loses money—lots of money—that taxpayers have to make up. But every year JS makes money—lots of money—much of which finds its way into the hands of the bureaucrats who assigned the contracts as well as allied politicians. In 1995, JS earned 11 billion yen ($88 million) profit on sales of 170 billion yen, while the UDC losses of 280 billion yen ($2.2 billion) the same year had to be covered by taxpayers.

The Honsho-Shikoku Bridge Authority built three roads linking Honshu and Shikoku, two of four main islands comprising Japan. Daily traffic is just half of the levels projected to justify the project. On one route linking Hiroshima and Ehime prefectures via seven bridges, each bus averages only nine passengers all day, thus giving rise to the expression "bridges to nowhere." In 2001 the authority's interest payments of 150 billion yen ($1.2 billion) dwarfed its revenue of 87 billion yen ($700 million).

Problems extend far beyond construction. A public corporation affiliated with the Health, Labor, and Welfare Ministry has an effective monopoly on the screening of bills sent by medical institutions. And they are done manually rather than by computer as a make-work project.

The losses of these state enterprises have to be covered by the taxpayer. The reason is that the FILP is funded by the postal savings system, where one-third of the public's money is deposited. These depositors must be paid back. So in fiscal 2001 the ordinary householder in his role as taxpayer had to cough up 5.3 trillion yen ($43 billion) to pay himself in his role as saver. That equals 1 percent of GDP and 10 percent of the whole general expenditures in the budget (i.e., everything other than debt service and grants to local governments). While that's no worse than it was a decade or two ago, it's less affordable when tax revenues are shrinking.

Table 18.2

Sky-High Costs for Medical Equipment in Japan (in thousands of yen)

	Pacemaker	Balloon Catheter	Artificial Lung	Artificial Eye Lens
Japan	1,431	257	219	52
United States	783	71	143	14
Germany	370	77–147	185	17
United Kingdom	220–537	53–87	—	7–15

Source: Nikkei Weekly 2001c.

Note: When medical equipment is imported, distributors' markups can total as much as 65 percent of the price.

Today's payouts are locked in—and will be for years to come—by bad decisions made years ago (see discussion of Japan National Railway debt on p. 272).

The Incredible Cost of Health Care

Most of what passes for health care reform is focused on making users pay more rather than reducing the system's high costs (Table 18.2).

One good target would be the payments system set up by the Ministry of Health, Labor, and Welfare (MHLW), which provides incentives for unnecessary repeat visits to doctors:

> [V]isits average less than five minutes, and patients are often required to visit the doctor many times a year in order to renew routine prescriptions. The Japanese visit the doctor an average of 14 times per year. Americans, on the other hand, visit the doctor around 4 times per year, but still manage to spend more time with their physicians in a year than the Japanese.[9]

The system also provides incentives for long hospital stays. No wonder the average acute care patient is hospitalized for twenty-four days in Japan compared to eleven days in Germany and six in the United States.

Drug prices are set by an MHLW advisory council, which includes representatives of the doctors' lobby, a critical get-out-the-vote machine for the LDP. But there is a huge conflict of interests. Doctors in Japan dispense—at a profit—the medicines that they prescribe. They can even own pharmacies. The more drugs they prescribe and the higher the prices, the more they make. In 1997 for instance, the average number of drugs per prescription in Japan was 4 (compared to 1.7 in Germany and 3.2 in France). Some efforts have been made to address this conflict of interests, but they have not always been successful. When, in the 1990s, the ministry began to reduce the profit margin per pill, the doctors and hospitals simply prescribed 60 percent more drugs. The payments system is even biased against generic drugs.[10]

Sometimes the cause of high prices is not vested interests but bureaucratic inanities. When methotrexate is prescribed for cancer, the price is 130 yen ($1.04) per dose. When exactly the same drug is prescribed for rheumatism, the MHLW set the price ten times as high, 1,300 yen ($10.40) per dose. The ministry reasoned that other remedies for rheumatism carried this price.[11]

McKinsey argues that immense cost savings, with no loss of genuine care, could be made just by reforming the current payments system:

> A long-term care hospital that shifted from the traditional fee-for-service system to a recently instituted all-inclusive *per diem* system lowered its prescription drug costs by a whopping 78 percent per patient day. It is important to note that the only change in this hospital was the payment system. The type of patients, disease mix, and even the doctors were the same. The data also suggest that outcomes improved during this period. . . . [In an informal poll], Japanese doctors and hospital administrators . . . estimated that Japan's prescription levels could be cut by 40–65 percent without adverse effects on patients.[12]

Some medical reforms instituted in late 2001 would appear to remedy some of these flaws. Due to complaints from the pharmacists' lobby—only one third of drugs were sold through pharmacies—the doctor's profit was reduced from 15 percent of the drug price to 2 percent. Other changes in the determination of prices were aimed at increasing the use of generic drugs. Hopefully, these changes in rules will lead to substantial changes on the ground—fewer unnecessary drugs and lower prices. It's too soon to tell.[13]

Some defenders of Japan's current health care system point out that, despite far lower total expenditures in Japan—7 percent of Japanese GDP versus 14 percent in the United States—life expectancy in Japan is higher. Moreover, Japan provides nearly universal health care while many Americans go without insurance coverage. We would make two points. Firstly, the fact that the U.S. system is deeply flawed hardly justifies maintaining inefficiencies in Japan. Secondly, much of the cost and life expectancy difference reflects not greater efficiency in Japan, but social and behavioral differences. Drug use, auto accidents, alcoholism, AIDS, and gun wounds are far less common in Japan than in the United States. Better diet results in far less heart disease in Japan and, surprisingly, even lung cancer is less common in Japan. When these factors are taken into consideration, McKinsey estimates that, for the same types of disease and injury, the productivity of the Japanese system is 25 percent lower than in the U.S. system.[14]

Potential Gains from Regulatory Reform

With the regulated sectors exhibiting the worst productivity and most monopolistic pricing (Chapter 3, p. 47), regulatory reform could give a tremendous boost to both supply-side efficiency and demand-side household purchasing power. The OECD speaks of productivity gains of 25 percent or more in electricity, transport, telecom, and distribution. The Economic Planning Agency (now part of the Cabinet Office) estimated that deregulation alone, apart from other structural reforms, could add 1 percent a year to GDP growth for six years.[15]

Meanwhile, the Cabinet Office estimates that price cuts due to deregulation have saved consumers 15.7 trillion yen ($126 billion) from 1987 through 2000. That's equivalent to 3 percent of a year's GDP, but it is spread over so many years that the impact on consumer demand is still pretty tiny (see Table 18.3).

The Regulated Oppose Deregulation

The biggest obstacle to deregulation is not the ambitions of the regulators but anxieties among the regulated about losing their umbrella. "In 1995, when we first formulated three-year deregulation plans, our opponents were bureaucrats, but since 1996, we have been fighting industry groups," reported Yoshio Suzuki, president of the Asahi Research Center and a member of the government's Council for Regulatory Reform.[16]

In some cases, the regulatory state has created Frankenstein monsters it can no longer control. The prototypical example is Nippon Telephone and Telegraph (NTT), which has become far more powerful than the Ministry of Public Management, Home Affairs, Posts, and Telecommunications (MPHPT). In March 2001 NTT-allied Dietmen induced the Cabinet to reject a number of reform proposals made by a ministry advisory panel, including dismantling the NTT's holding company structure and its widespread control over various subsidiaries, such as DoCoMo. The Dietmen argued that weakening NTT might jeopardize Japan's "telecom sovereignty."

Table 18.3

Consumer Savings from Deregulation (in billions of yen, except per capita)

Telecommunications	Domestic calls	42,671
	International calls	3,624
Transport	Airline	3,589
	Rail	19,100
	Taxi	44
	Truck	23,648
	Car safety inspection	6,326
Energy	Electricity	19,550
	Natural gas	773
	Oil	18,999
Finance	Stock commissions	3,737
Food	Rice	8,520
	Alcohol	6,519
TOTAL		157,099
Per Capita		12,400

Source: Cabinet Office 2001c.

Note: This is the total cumulative savings between fiscal 1987 and fiscal 2000. It equals 3 percent of FY 2000 GDP, but spread out over fourteen years. The per capita savings amount to 12,400 yen or about $100 over those fourteen years.

The electric utilities, also big LDP campaign contributors, successfully resist METI's deregulatory efforts, partly because they have their own allies within METI. Consequently, when METI established yet another advisory panel on electricity reform in 2001, eleven of its twenty-six members were known to be opponents of deregulation, with only eight in favor and the other five undecided.[17]

Drivers for Regulatory Reform

Despite all this resistance, many forces combine to give momentum to deregulation.

The biggest intellectual force is the increasingly hegemonic view that the regulatory state inhibits growth.

Parts of the bureaucracy, notably sections of METI, have also become champions of deregulation, particularly when their manufacturing clients are hurt by regulations aiding other sectors.

Back in 1997, the Hashimoto administration's "Program for Economic Structure Reform" targeted four highly regulated, high-cost sectors: energy, transport, distribution, and telecommunication. These sectors account for 30 percent of manufacturing input costs. At the time of the report, Japan's fuel prices were 30–40 percent higher than in the United States, transport costs 50 percent higher, and commercial rents 75 percent higher. It argued that serious deregulation could help deflate monopolistic prices.[18]

Within parts of the business community, deregulation is gaining supporters. When LDP Diet members allied to the liquor stores introduced a bill in 2001 to slow down and partially reverse deregulation of liquor sales, the Japan Franchise Association and the Japan Chain Stores Association gathered 1.5 million signatures and successfully preserved the reforms.

Such public debate is a welcome change from decision by fiat from a few bureaucrats and Diet members. Still, this change is only beginning. Many of the constituents who would benefit from deregulation are not well organized. As in the liquor case, potential competitors are far more potent than consumers, even industrial consumers. It was NTT's would-be competitors who pushed hardest on the interconnection fees, and new suppliers of electricity who acted in that arena.

The pace and power of deregulation depends, in large part, on the unity of the ministry in charge. Take METI. Some bureaus concerned with the economy as a whole are often quite progressive, while "vertical" bureaus supervising individual industries still see their proper role as mother hens. In 1996, years of hard work by a reformist METI official, Morihisa Naito, finally paid off when METI ended restrictions on the import of petroleum products.[19] Said one METI official in a private conversation:

> We were finally able to get the restrictions on petroleum imports lifted after ten long years of fighting because the Natural Resources Agency was part of METI and we could beat on them. But if the Resources Agency had been a separate ministry, we might still be fighting this battle.

Budget pressures are also important. The first big drive for deregulation and state enterprise reform came in the early 1980s, when voters refused to swallow a tax hike in order to bring down budget deficits. Hence the Nakasone administration shifted to spending cuts. It privatized several money-losing state enterprises, including Japan National Railway (JNR), Japan Airlines (JAL), Japan Tobacco, and Nippon Telephone and Telegraph. JNR alone lost 1 trillion yen a year, about 0.7 percent of GDP. Today, with deficits even larger, Prime Minister Koizumi has vowed to privatize or liquidate many state enterprises on the grounds that they drain the budget of 5 trillion yen ($40 billion) per year.

A final driver is international pressure and example. Many of the biggest steps—in finance, retail, airlines, and telecommunications—were triggered, or at least accelerated, due to international negotiations. Indeed, when the Diet passed a bill in 1989 relaxing entry and price regulations in trucking, a Japanese analyst called it epoch-making in that it occurred without any foreign pressure.[20] However, as we'll discuss in Chapter 22, foreign pressure succeeds only when there are powerful domestic forces pushing in the same direction.

The Dangers and Opportunities of Partial Reform

Sometimes half a loaf is better than none—but not in the case of deregulation.

All too often, Japan's halfhearted deregulation allows freer entry of new firms but, via informal methods, blocks the shakeout of the less efficient. The result is endemic overcapacity, and no one makes money. When Tokyo reformed the Large-Scale Retail Store Law in the early 1990s, big stores seized the newfound freedom to expand, convinced that they'd be bailed out if they overdid it. Despite poor sales, annual growth in floor space hit 6 percent during 1994–99, compared to only 2 percent in the regulated 1980s. That's one reason so many big retailers are failing today.

While some in Japan say the problem is deregulation per se, the real problem is the inevitable dislocations of a big transition, compounded by the fact that every forward step is taken kicking and screaming.

Japan cannot exist half regulated and half free. Usually whenever halfway regulatory reform has created stresses, the end result—albeit too far down the road—has been further deregulation.

Regulatory Reform Versus Deregulation

Some time ago, concerned policy makers decided that "regulatory reform" was a better term than "deregulation." The reason is that the right kind of regulations, such as financial supervision and competition policy, are needed even more in a deregulated environment. The OECD has stressed the same point:

> One notion of regulatory reform often heard in Japan is based in the link between deregulation and smaller government. . . . But too much focus on the size of government, rather than its role, can divert reform efforts. . . . Small governments can regulate as badly as big ones. . . . Radical and comprehensive deregulation is needed, but this by itself is insufficient because necessary market institutions are not yet in place.[21]

Competition Versus Monitoring

Telecom makes the case that what Japan needs is real competition, not better oversight over privatized monopolies.

When NTT was the only game in town for long-distance calls, Japanese customers had to pay 350 yen ($2.80) for a three-minute call within Japan. As deregulation gradually introduced new competitors—including foreign ones—the price dropped by 80 percent as of 1999 (Figure 18.1). Rates in Japan remained four times higher than in the United States, but more progress occurred as competition increased. By early 2002, Yahoo Japan said it would charge 7.5 cents for a three-minute long-distance call from anywhere to anywhere within Japan. Competition has induced similar drops in international phone rates and DSL service for the Internet. By contrast, in local calls, where NTT retains a share above 90 percent, there has been only a small reduction in prices from the rate of 10 yen (8 cents) per three minutes that has prevailed for decades.

Simply expanding the number of companies doesn't do the job. There must be free entry and exit so that incumbents fear extinction. It is a staple of economics that eight companies in an industry with no firm turnover will charge higher prices and be less efficient than eight firms in the same industry when firms regularly enter and exit.[22]

Progress So Far

Let's take a look at the record in some key sectors where there has been progress. (We won't discuss finance or retail, since these sectors are discussed in Chapters 3, 14, and 22.)[23]

State Enterprises

Koizumi is hardly the first prime minister vowing to reform FILP and the public corporations. Hashimoto did so earlier. Hashimoto ended the obligation of the postal savings system to turn all its money over to the MOF. As of fiscal 2000, if public corporations want to run budgets larger than the FILP allots, they have to issue their own bonds. That was supposed to subject projects to market discipline, but in practice investors usually treat these bonds as having a de facto government guarantee. Consequently, while the FILP budget for fiscal 2002 is down 22 percent, the total spending budget for the FILP entities was down only 13 percent. Still, a 13 percent decline is substantial.

Figure 18.1 **Competition Lowers Phone Rates**

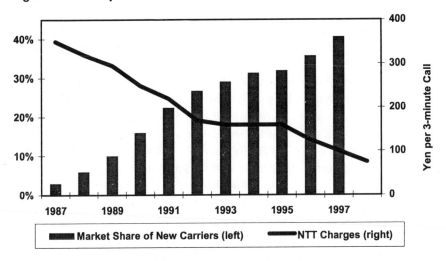

Source: OECD 1999b, p. 346–48.
Note: This is for a three-minute call from Tokyo to Osaka.

Despite a few valiant efforts, Koizumi's achievements as of early 2002 have been more show than substance. But it's still early in the game.

Repeatedly Koizumi has been forced to backtrack on bold promises. Koizumi originally called for releasing auto-related taxes totaling 6 trillion yen ($48 billion) from their current mandate that they be used only for road construction; he wanted to use some of the money for urban revitalization. The LDP stonewalled him. Originally he called for cutting the 5 trillion yen annual subsidy for state enterprises in half, then by 20 percent; he finally got an 11 percent cut in the fiscal 2002 budget. He called for liquidation or privatization of about one-third of 177 public and semipublic corporations, but what, if anything, he'll get is unclear. Koizumi apparently extracted a promise to abolish the Housing Loan Corporation, but what will actually happen remains to be seen. The precedents are not encouraging. Formally Koizumi succeeded in getting the Japan National Oil Company abolished, yet its operations will all be transferred to the Metal Mining Company, a public corporation under the jurisdiction of METI.[24]

Koizumi has also pushed through a stop to the government's 300 billion yen annual subsidy to the Japan Highway Corporation, but the road lobby is finding other means to build the roads it wants. As one anti-Koizumi

LDP-er said in December of 2001, "We're willing to give him the show if we get the substance."

In any case, privatization is not a panacea because the legacies of the past will stalk the future for decades to come. When the Japan National Railway was privatized in 1987, it left behind 23 trillion yen ($185 billion) in debts even after the sale of assets. By 1998, mismanagement by the JNR Settlement Corporation let the debt balloon to 38 trillion yen ($306 billion). The taxpayers will be paying off that debt for another fifty years. In 2002 Finance Minister Shiokawa has already said the taxpayers will have to take over much of the 3.8 trillion yen ($30 billion) debt of the Honsho-Shikoku Bridge Authority, and he said the same debt obligations may occur as other public corporations are privatized. If so, the newly privatized firm may look profitable, but only because it retained the assets while the taxpayer got the liabilities.[25]

Yet if Koizumi can at least succeed in reducing future parasitism, he will have accomplished something of importance.

Transport

As noted earlier, JAL, one of three Japanese airlines, was privatized in 1985. Traditionally, JAL monopolized international traffic, while ANA dominated at home. But in that year a U.S.–Japan agreement on international air travel required, in effect, that Japan have more than one international carrier. Since ANA was allowed into the international market, in return JAL had to be let into the domestic one.

Tokyo took this opportunity to deregulate domestically as well. Japan's airlines had to become more cost-competitive, because even Japanese customers were abandoning them on international flights. In 1986 Tokyo allowed three carriers to compete on routes with more than one million passengers a year, and two to compete on routes with between seven hundred thousand and a million passengers a year. Finally, after a series of phase-ins, the limit on the number of airlines serving any route was abolished in 1998.[26]

By 1997 ANA had 20 percent of the international market. In a mirror image, JAL's domestic share rose to 25 percent. The resulting price competition led to a 23 percent drop in ANA's revenue per passenger-mile from 1990 to 1999 and a one-third drop for JAL during the same period.[27]

In 1998 discounters Skymark and Air-Do were allowed to enter the market, but a counterattack by the main carriers has lowered their load factors below profitable levels. In fact, there are some suspicions that the three dominant carriers are cooperating with each other to resist cooperation both from the new airlines and from rail service.[28]

While entry of new firms is liberalized, it is not free. Permission from the Ministry of Transport is still required. Moreover, takeoff and landing slots—the key to reaching a profitable scale of operations—are limited, and they are allocated not by competitive bidding but by the ministry.

The net result was that, in the summer of 2002, Air-Do crash landed into bankruptcy and, as of this writing, is about to be absorbed by ANA. Around the same time, JAL absorbed the smaller Japan Air System. Thus, for now, the only remaining competitor to the two giants is Skymark.

Price regulation was gradually relaxed, and in 1999 it was abolished altogether. Discounting has increased to 27 percent below approved rates as of 1998. Some analysts predict a fall in ticket prices of 30–40 percent by 2005 or 2006. Whether that occurs, especially with the winnowing out of the challengers, will be a key test of airline deregulation.

JNR was privatized in 1987 and split into six private commuter firms (divided by region) and one freight company. Though the government remained the major shareholder, the newly privatized railways cut redundant staff in half, from four hundred thousand to less than two hundred thousand. Relieved of their debts, as we noted earlier, the combined group now earns a profit and pays dividends and taxes.

Entry and pricing was relaxed in trucking in 1990 and in the taxi business in 1994 and again in 2002. But relaxation is still not free pricing, as in the airlines. Still, new entrants in trucking have increased, prices have fallen, and productivity and profits are up. In the taxi arena, prices in Tokyo are twice those in New York, driving away customers. In 2000 taxis carried 25 percent fewer customers than a decade earlier. In January 2002 restrictions on new entrants and expansion of fleets were lifted. Price drops, which must still be approved, are expected.

Despite a high-tension showdown in port facilities between Japan and the United States, little appears to have changed. Japanese sources blame the problem on the heavy role of the *yakuza* (the Japanese mafia) in the ports. This makes the ports very expensive, causing Japan to lose out to other nations—for example, South Korea—when firms have a choice for regional trade.

Telecommunications

In an essay on deregulation, Sumner La Croix and James Mak argue that telecommunications deregulation, which began in 1985, was driven by fear of losing international competitiveness to firms from the United States, the United Kingdom, and other countries where deregulation had already proceeded, combined with a series of international negotiations.[29]

Up until 1985, NTT had a monopoly on domestic local and long-distance service, while KDD had the monopoly on the international side. At the end of 1984 the Diet decided to privatize NTT but *not* break it up. The Ministry in charge (MPHPT) did want to break it up in the interests of competition. This is the standard procedure in most strategic industries in Japan; there are few single European-style "national champions." However, NTT successfully used its clout with Diet members to resist. Liberalized entry, but not completely free entry, was allowed in long-distance and international service. In local service, NTT still has a 90 percent monopoly.

Under World Trade Organization (WTO) rules that came into force in February 1998, Japan was obliged to open its so-called Type I service to foreign firms, but it had done so earlier. Type I companies provide service using their own lines. As of 1999, 130 had entered the market, along with 4,500 Type II companies, i.e., firms that provide service using lines leased from Type I companies. These include satellite and wireless firms.

By 1997 new entrants had gained a 40 percent market share in long-distance calls and international calls. Additional pressure on phone rates came from callback services, whereby a Japanese caller can make international calls at U.S. rates by accessing a U.S. dial tone. By 1999 such services had gained 4 percent of the market. Japanese companies tried, and failed, to have such services banned—an important litmus test.

There has been less progress in local calls, where pricing has been somewhat liberalized but is not yet free. Still, when a new competitor, TTNet, reduced the rate for a three-minute local call from 10 yen to 9 yen—the first drop in a decade—it signed up 1.4 million subscribers in only six months. Then, at the end of 2001, Heisei Den Den introduced a charge of 7.5 cents for a three-minute local call. While this is down 25 percent from only a short while ago, prices remain far, far higher than in the United States, where residential consumers can pay a flat rate per call no matter how long the conversation.

One reason prices remain so high is that NTT has used its monopoly to charge high rates for interconnection fees needed by other service providers, a subject for U.S.–Japan negotiations (see Chapter 22).

The good news is that regulatory changes have allowed customers some alternatives to NTT's monopoly, and customers have seized on these opportunities.

Regulatory changes in cell phone service—initiated in 1994 under pressure of U.S. negotiators on behalf of Motorola—led to takeoff in this market (see Chapter 22). This raises the possibility that mobile calls will substitute for local calls through regular, fixed lines, thereby undercutting NTT's pricing power in local calls. Since 1997 the number of subscribers to NTT's local fixed-line service has started declining while mobile subscribers have continued soaring. On the other hand, NTT owns the dominant mobile provider, NTT DoCoMo, to the consternation of DoCoMo's own management.

DSL lines are proving to be a popular way of getting around the high local rates that can cause regular Internet service to cost up to $100 a month. In contrast to most countries, DSL service is cheaper than regular call-up service (see Chapter 16, p. 247).

If Japan really wants to create competition in local phone services, the first step is to break up NTT. There is no such plan on the drawing boards. In 2000 the JFTC issued an important report saying current measures do not provide enough competition, but it held back from recommending a breakup.[30]

Energy

Until 1990 the construction of new gas stations was restricted in order to avoid "excess competition." Until 1996 the import of petroleum products was restricted. Only refiners could import products; no one desiring to compete with the refiners could do so. Soon after the law changed, gasoline prices fell 20 percent just from the fear of imports even though the import share did not rise all that much. A few years later, Tokyo finally legalized self-service gas stations. Once again, the price benefits to consumers are substantial, with some self-service stations offering a price of 83 yen per liter, compared to 100 yen for full-service stations. Showa Shell says it will convert 10 to 20 percent of its five thousand stations to self-service by 2005.

Electricity is dominated by ten investor-owned regional monopolies regulated by METI as to entry, exit, rates, and expansion. With cost-plus rate setting, utilities have little incentive to cut costs or improve efficiency. In addition, high utility rates have financed disguised subsidies to well-connected interest groups like farmers and construction firms. Paul Scalise, global utilities analyst at Dresdner Kleinwort Wasserstein, calculates that the wholesale price of electricity in Japan, at $15 per kilowatt-hour (kwh) is twice as high as his estimate for the utilities' marginal cost of $7 per kwh. Only a fraction of this differential can be accounted for by network costs and so forth. When Scalise asked managers at Tokyo Electric Power (TEPCO) about this, they told him that most of the gap was the result of subsidies handed out to farmers, fishermen, construction firms, and other groups that TEPCO had to pay in order to prevent any political obstacle to the permits required to build their power plants.

The result is that not only consumers but also industrial users have traditionally suffered electric bills ranging up to twice as high as those in the rest of the OECD countries. In 1998, according to the International Energy Agency, Japanese households paid $.19 per kwh versus $.08 in the United States, $.16 in Germany and $.13 in France. Japanese industrial users paid $.13 per kwh versus $.04 in the United States, $.07 in Germany, and $.05 in France. That put Japanese manufacturers at a cost disadvantage in global markets. In response, in 1995 the Diet passed some reforms proposed by METI. It enabled a unified national wholesale market for electricity, together with liberalization of a utility's ability to set prices.

In 1998 independent power producers were permitted to supply electricity to some large corporate customers but not to households. The impact so far has been disappointing. As of the end of 2001, there were only six new entrants, with a tiny 0.4 percent of the market. One blockage is that the incumbent utilities charge high fees for the new firms to use their transmission lines, an analog to the interconnection fee NTT charges Internet service providers.

Back in 1997 METI instructed the utilities to lower their rates to German levels by 2001. But this has not occurred, in part due to insufficient competition. While German prices fell 30 percent in 2000, Japanese prices fell only 5 percent. In a note to investors, Paul Scalise commented, "We consider tariff [price] readjustments more a limited preemptive to potential new entrants, rather than a forced maneuver to match market movers."[31] One frustrated METI reformer complained, "Too bad we can't import electricity; that would lower prices here." The JFTC made the key point in a January 2001 report:

> Problems arise from the fact that incumbents enjoying the dominant market position exclusively hold network facilities that are crucial for market entry. In reality, mere deregulation does not make it easier for newcomers to enter the market. There are remarkable gaps in the competitive conditions between incumbents and newcomers. . . .
>
> Even after liberalization, dominant operators that are given the monopolistic position by sectoral laws exist in [the] public utilities sector. It is highly probable

that incumbents resort to anticompetitive activities. . . . [The] desirable situation is that no dominant operators exists in the market, in other words, [that] no regulation on dominant operators is needed.[32]

METI is now considering further steps, including a breakup whereby separate firms would handle production and transmission and trading of electricity. But the well-connected utilities are resisting mightily. Stay tuned.

──── 19 ────

Tax Reform

Don't Exacerbate Anorexia

Tokyo is now considering a host of tax changes. As it does, it needs to bear in mind not only the budget deficit but also economic anorexia. The great danger in this debate is that, in the name of reform a la Reagan-Thatcher, a number of changes would weaken consumer income and therefore consumer spending. This would be highly counterproductive.

Any discussion of tax changes is dominated by the question of who will pay to clean up the mess. Japan's huge deficits, the bad-debt problem, the public corporation mess, and population aging all dictate that taxes will eventually go up. Therefore, garbed in arguments about efficiency, incentives, and revenue enhancement is a political battle over who will get stuck with the bill. Unfortunately, the momentum doesn't bode well for a solution to Japan's problem. The measures most likely to pass are ones that will exacerbate anorexia without doing much about efficiency.

Current Distortions That Hurt Demand and Efficiency

Consumption Tax on Housing

With housing construction down 30 percent from its 1990 peak, tax breaks for housing would seem to be in order. Yet, in many ways, the tax code has added to the problem. For example, the 5 percent consumption tax is applied to a house at the point of purchase rather than being spread out. This adds a tremendous amount to the up-front costs. A 20 percent down payment turns into 25 percent when the consumption tax is thrown in. That prices many potential buyers out of the market. Simply stretching out the payment of the tax would be a simple yet helpful reform.

Moreover, mortgage interest payments are usually not tax-deductible (except for some temporary deductions put in as a stimulative measure in 1999).

One current proposal is an expansion of the size of gifts and inheritance that may be given tax free as long as the transfer of money is used to buy a house. At present, only the first 5 million yen ($40,000) of either a gift from a parent to a child or a bequest is tax free. When various deductions are considered, the amount can rise to about 18 million yen. One proposal is to raise this to 30 million yen ($240,000) as long as the money is used to buy a home. In the United States, the tax free level for gifts and inheritance is $600,000.

Real Estate and Land Taxes

Within an hour's commute from Tokyo center, almost half the land is either idle or nominal "farmland." What is behind this anomaly? One big reason is the tax code. Japan's real estate taxes and zoning regulations keep land artificially scarce and thus keep land and housing prices too high.

Due to zoning and "sunlight" regulations, the average height of buildings within the Tokyo metropolitan area is only 2.5 stories. Consequently, population density in Tokyo's twenty-three wards is *less* than in Manhattan or Paris.

Meanwhile, the real estate tax system creates perverse incentives. On the one hand, there is no tax penalty for leaving property useless. Property holding taxes on land are tiny. According to economist Richard Koo, when one looks at real market prices rather than misleading statutory rates and "assessed valuations," the property tax rate in central Tokyo can be as low as 0.06 percent (versus a statutory rate of 0.6 percent of the official land agency value). Some others say that, with prices dropping so fast, the effective tax rate is a bit higher, perhaps 0.4 percent. In either case, this compares to about 3 percent in New Jersey.[1] Farmland gains special tax breaks.

On the other hand, according to Koo's calculations, the maximum tax rate on selling land—when all the capital gains taxes, land transaction taxes, and assorted other taxes are included—adds up to a majority of the profits, sometimes reaching as high as 80 percent. So, what happens if some developer comes in, takes a risk, and earns a profit? If he loses, he loses. If he wins, the Ministry of Finance can take most of the profits.

While nonperforming real estate projects stand at the heart of Japan's banking crisis, these perverse taxes hinder resolution. Although some Koizumi advisers, such as Heizo Takenaka, would like to correct this great distortion, there was not even an effort to do so in the June 2002 package of tax reforms. That's because reform would hurt two powerful lobbies: farmers and current holders of real estate.

Interest, Dividends, Capital Gains

A failed stockholders' revolt at clothing-maker Tokyo Style has made famous the all-too-common syndrome of cash hoarding at Japanese companies (see Chapter 15, p. 239). What is less known is how the tax code reinforces such wastrel habits. The Japanese tax system gives incentives for interest income and capital gains at the expense of dividends. This is a mistake on both demand and efficiency grounds.

Currently the top rate on interest income is 20 percent. Long-term capital gains taxes are ordinarily 26 percent. However, in an effort to prop up stock prices, Tokyo eliminated the entire tax on capital gains on share sales up to 10 million yen ($80,000) on any shares bought after November 2001 and sold by 2005. The upshot is that both interest and capital gains are taxed at a far lower rate than ordinary income, whose top rate is now 37 percent (50 percent with local taxes included).

By contrast, dividend income is generally taxed as ordinary income for individuals—with partial credits for taxpayers with income below 10 million yen ($80,000) a year. From the corporate standpoint, interest expenses are deducted from income, reducing corporate taxes. But dividend expenses are not. When the double taxation (both corporate and individual payment) on dividends is added up, the top effective tax rate in Japan ends up being 71 percent, with the United States following at 68 percent.

Clearly, the tax system provides strong incentives for firms to borrow rather than issue stock, and for households to put their money into banks rather than the stock market. When householders do invest in stocks, they are induced to accept capital gains rather than to demand dividends. The OECD comments on how this stifles the shift of capital to new firms who could use it better:

> Since Japan, like many other OECD countries, taxes capital gains less heavily than dividends, corporations typically also have an incentive to retain their earnings. This tendency is reinforced by the mixed taxation of dividends, which encourages firms to limit their dividend payments to individual shareholders. This, in turn, could hamper the reallocation of funds from mature companies to their more innovative and fast growing counterparts, although it should be stressed that dividend payments between domestic corporations are tax exempted.[2]

These tax penalties for dividends also worsen anorexia. When dividends are paid, the money actually goes to consumers, who can then either spend it or invest in a better firm. Managerial empire builders don't get to hoard corporate cash flow.

Taxes can make a big difference in dividend payout rates. Take the United States. Until the 1980s, the dividend yield averaged 4.3 percent. But in the 1990s boom, it fell to only 1 to 2 percent. Why? As Jeremy Siegel, a Wharton School professor, points out, when the capital gains tax was lowered to half the tax rate on dividends, firms and investors shifted emphasis from dividends to capital gains. Whether or not this was advisable for the United States, it's very destructive for Japan. Yet current discussion in Tokyo unfortunately centers on further tax incentives for capital gains, not dividends.

Making Taxes More Regressive Hurts Consumer Demand

The biggest flaw in the current tax discussion is that it seems to move the entire tax system in a regressive direction—lightening taxes on companies and upper-income individuals while raising them on lower- and middle-income households. This is similar to the bias in medical reform (see Chapter 4), emphasizing fee hikes over efficiency from the providers.

True, Japan's actions are in line with international trends. However, whether or not such trends are appropriate for other developed countries, they are wrong for Japan. Japan's problems are different from those of other countries. The U.S. has too little saving, Japan has too much. There are two reasons more regressive taxation would hurt Japan:

- Japan is struggling to raise consumer demand. Yet such moves take away income from people with a higher propensity to consume, while giving more to those (richer individuals and companies) with higher savings rates.
- Japan has hitherto implemented its egalitarian ethic in ways that hinder economic growth. It should remove those economic distortions and pursue its egalitarian preferences through straightforward progressive taxes, which don't hamper growth. The more that taxes are flattened, the more people will try to achieve the same redistribution objective through more destructive means.

Japan is gradually switching away from income taxes, which are both countercyclical (i.e., they help dampen booms and busts) and progressive (i.e., they tax richer people and firms at a higher rate). Instead, it is switching to consumption and social security taxes, which hit the middle-income and poor people more heavily.

Already 38 percent of all national and local taxes in Japan are social security taxes, compared to an OECD average of 25 percent. In 1986, 73 percent of national taxes came from income taxes. By 1999, it was down to 57 percent, while the consumption tax provided 21 percent of revenue.

Tokyo wants to continue this trend. Back in 1998 Takenaka proposed a phased-in hike of the consumption tax to 14 percent. Officials currently talk of raising it to 11 percent by 2010 and eventually to 20 percent.

Meanwhile, the corporate tax rate has already been cut from 42 percent in 1989 to 30 percent by 1999. The top national marginal tax rate on individual income over 35 million yen ($282,000) has been repeatedly lowered from 65 percent to 50 percent and now stands at 37 percent. Takenaka proposed lowering it further to the 30 percent level now paid by corporations.

At the same time, Takenaka and the opposition Democrats (Minshuto) propose lowering the minimum income level at which people pay taxes. A salaried worker with a spouse and two children with annual income of less than 3.8 million yen ($30,000) is exempted from the income tax. According to tax expert Andrew DeWit, this amounted to about 18 percent of tax filers in 1997 (many of whom were still subject to local income taxes where the threshold was lower).[3] In the United States, the minimum threshold is about $20,000—two-thirds of the Japanese level—but when purchasing power parity currency rates are considered, the levels are comparable.

Takenaka argued for a further lowering of progressive taxes:

> The progressive system for inheritance and other taxes is pretty severe and it is a natural direction to make the taxation system more flat. . . . Are the people satisfied with the fact a fourth or third of salaried workers [who are categorized as under the tax threshold] are exempted from paying tax? Lowering the minimum taxable limit will be within the scope of discussions [of the Koizumi administration].[4]

These proposals are partly based on the misapprehension that Japan's tax system is already very progressive. That is true on paper, but not after one takes into account deductions, exemptions, and so forth. Hiromitsu Ishi, an academic economist who served as head of Japan's Tax Advisory Commission, wrote, "In terms of effective, not statutory tax rates, the income tax system in Japan is only mildly progressive and therefore has little effect on the relative distribution of income." An OECD study showed that in the mid-1990s the German budget (taxes and spending combined) reduced inequality by 35 percent and the American budget reduced inequality by 24 percent, but the Japanese budget did so by 22 percent.[5]

Japan's Ministry of Health, Labor, and Welfare has its own index measuring how much the tax system redistributes income, with a lower number meaning less redistribution. The index has steadily declined from 5.4 in 1981 to 2.9 by 1990 and 1.7 by 1996; surely it has gone even lower since then, given the imposition of the consumption tax and cuts in tax rates for the upper-income taxpayers.

Japan's tax and spending system is redistributionist. But it's not from rich to poor; it's from city to country, according to a study by Andrew DeWit and Sven Steinmo (see Chapter 20, p. 288).[6]

While Japan's problem of low productivity is now well understood, the roots of economic anorexia are not. When that misunderstanding is combined with the political clout of corporations, special interests, and upper-income voters, it's not surprising that discussion of tax reform is heading in a regressive direction.

——— 20 ———

Electoral Reform

Ending the One-Party State

The biggest obstacle to reform in Japan is its anachronistic one-party democracy (see Chapter 1, p. 7). Two requirements are needed to produce a political system genuinely responsive to the needs of the population:

- Genuine competition where parties (or coalitions) regularly alternate in power.
- A one-person-one-vote system where the vote of each city dweller counts as much as that of a farmer. Currently some rural districts get more than twice as much Diet representation as the most underrepresented city districts.

Proportional Representation System Divides Opposition

In 1994 Japan went through a major electoral reform advertised to reduce the influence of "money politics" and to usher in the era of competitive politics. It failed to do so.

The reform abolished the old multiseat-constituency Diet. In that system, three, four, or five members were elected from each district. Each voter had one vote, and the top vote getters won. The system forced the LDP to run members against each other. As political scientist Leonard Schoppa points out, these members could not compete based on ideology because they were from a single party with party discipline in Diet voting. Instead they had to compete by delivering pork to the district and using ample campaign funds to win the loyalty of its voters. That factor, combined with the fact that candidates could win with only 15–20 percent of the vote, boosted the power of the special interests and the local support organizations known as *koenkai*. Under this system, the opposition parties achieved better results if they contested fewer seats and therefore didn't divide their vote. The LDP ruled with less than majority support.

Under the new system, 300 members of the 480-seat Lower House of the Diet are elected in single-member-district (SMD), winner-take-all elections. The other 180 are elected in a party-based proportional representation (PR) system. The Lower House has the real power in Japan's Diet.

At the time, it was hoped by many that the new system would lead to a two-party (or two-coalition) system in which candidates needing 51 percent of the vote to win would have to appeal to broader constituencies on the basis of programs, policies, and ideas. It was hoped that the PR section would lead parties to campaign on the basis of ideas and programs, and that parties would alternate in power.

There was one big problem with such hopes. The only reform able to wend its way through the Diet in 1994 was a variation on the scheme that some Diet members within the LDP itself had come up with in 1990 as a device for keeping itself in power: the combination of SMD and PR. Indeed, referring to the compromise that Prime Minister Hosokawa worked out with LDP president Yohei Kono, the *Nihon Keizai Shimbun* editorialized:

> The Hosokawa-Kono agreement more or less ratifies a plan put forward years ago by the LDP that was designed to preserve the existing power structure while making a gesture to a public angry about political corruption.[1]

Traditionally, the LDP had favored a move to a complete SMD system, figuring that if pro-rural malapportionment were sustained, they could dominate the rural seats and some suburban seats, thus dominating the entire Diet. Many opposition parties, on the other hand, traditionally favored a pure PR system that would put the focus on parties rather than individual candidates. They figured the LDP's vaunted organizational powers and money would count for less. Second, each of the opposition parties could sustain its existence even with, say, 5 to 10 percent of the vote. In a winner-takes-all SMD system, small parties usually disappear.

Then, in 1990, a group of urban-oriented reformers—led by Tsutomo Hata, who would later briefly become a non-LDP prime minister after the LDP's 1993 split—came up with the plan for a combination of SMD and PR. The Hata group produced computer simulations showing that a move to a complete single-seat system could dethrone the LDP, because it would lead most of the LDP's opponents to coalesce into one big anti-LDP party. The Hata group apparently figured the combination of SMD and PR would keep the LDP in power but make it more urban-oriented.

The electoral reform that was passed by the reformist multiparty coalition in 1994 was basically a variation on the Hata scheme, hence the scathing *Nihon Keizai Shimbun* editorial. The scheme worked—for the LDP. Despite consistently getting less than 40 percent of the vote in single-seat districts, and even less in the PR tally, the LDP has been able to maintain power by allying with assorted small parties. In the June 2000 Lower House elections, the LDP's 41 percent share of the vote in the single-member districts gave it 60 percent of the SMD seats up for grabs (review Figure 1.2 in Chapter 1).[2]

Excess Rural Votes Keep LDP in Power

The LDP would get even fewer seats if it weren't for a malapportioned system that gives rural voters more power than urban ones.

Given its support among farmers, the LDP allowed rural areas to keep a large number of Diet members—even though they had lost population to areas that were more urban. In 1972 one rural district had five times as many Diet members per capita as some urban districts. If one divided early-1970s Japan into two zones of equal population, one more urban and one more rural, then the following situation obtained. Half the population lived in the more rural zone, but approximately 60 percent of the Diet members, 70 percent of LDP Diet members, and 80 percent of Tanaka-faction Diet members came from the relatively rural half of Japan.

In 1976 the Supreme Court ruled such malapportionment unconstitutional. Yet it never voided an election on those grounds. The Diet did some redistricting, but on the eve of the 1994 reform, in the most extreme gap, a single person's vote in a farm district was worth as much as 2.8 urban votes.

The 1994 reform made some headway on this malapportionment. While the PR system helped keep the opposition divided, it distributed seats quite equitably in terms of rural-urban ratios. While the SMD reapportionment was not as equitable, there was still substantial progress. After 1994, the maximum-minimum representation gap was reduced to 2.3. Actually, this understates the change because it looks only at the extreme cases. A better index shows that the distortion dropped substantially after 1994 (Figure 20.1).[3]

Nonetheless, even after the reform, the rural sectors still have disproportionate power. Political scientist Yusaku Horiuchi has divided the 300 single-member districts of the Lower House into two zones with 150 seats each, one urban and one relatively rural. Forty-five percent of the people live in

Figure 20.1 **1994 Reform Reduces Urban-Rural Distortion in Seats**

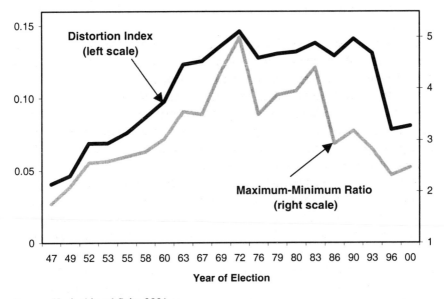

Year of Election

Source: Horiuchi and Saito 2001.

Note: "Maximum-minimum ratio" refers to ratio of voters per Diet member in the most extreme case. For example, a ratio of 5 in 1972 shows that the most densely populated urban district has five times the population of the most sparsely settled rural district, yet each elects one Diet member. The distortion index, formally called the Loosemore-Hanby index, measures the average deviation from perfect equality, and goes from 0 to 1. If all districts had the same population, the index would be 0. If one district had all the Diet members, it would be 1. Although the maximum-minimum index gives the appearance of more equality after 1972, the more inclusive Loosemore-Hanby index shows that there was little progress until the 1996 election, the first after the 1994 reform.

the rural zone, yet in the 1996 election they selected 50 percent of the SMD seats in the Lower House and 64 percent of the LDP seats. And there has been backtracking since then. After the 1994 reapportionment, 28 out of the 300 districts were thinly populated. By the year 2000, this had grown to 89, nearly 30 percent of all SMD seats. In early 2002, there was some rumbling about redrawing districts yet again to reverse the backsliding.[4]

The cities are the home of reform voters. In the June 2000 elections, the Minshuto swept the cities in the Lower House election, even defeating some sitting cabinet ministers. In Tokyo, for example, it won thirteen of the twenty-five seats at stake in Tokyo's single-member districts, leaving the LDP with only eight. The cities were also the launching pad for the grassroots revolt inside the LDP that put Koizumi in power.

There are reports that the LDP, trying to regain the cities, wants a return to the multiseat system in the cities in hopes that this will further divide the opposition.

Since malapportioned districting makes a big difference in elections, it makes a big difference in policy as well. Public works, subsidies, and other governmental largesse are disproportionately oriented to the rural districts to feed the LDP vote machine. In fiscal 1998, rural residents of Shimane prefecture received 3.6 times more public investment than urban residents in Kanagawa prefecture. And yet, according to the Japan Research Institute, public investment in Tokyo and Osaka stimulates the economy about 1.4 times more than investment in rural areas.[5]

A huge portion of the national budget is devoted to transfers to local governments. For example, in the fiscal 2002 national budget of 81 trillion yen, 17 trillion yen goes to debt service, 47 trillion goes to general expenditures, and the final 17 trillion yen is transferred to prefectural and local governments. In other words, aside from debt service, transfers to localities are one-third as much as national-level spending. And much of that national spending is skewed to the rural areas, according to political scientists Andrew DeWit and Sven Steinmo. They conclude that the fiscal system (taxes as well as spending) is highly redistributive, but not from income class to income class. Rather, it redistributes income from cities to the countryside.[6]

Yet when election results change, so does the flow of money. According to political scientists Yusaku Horiuchi and Jun Saito, when urban districts got more seats after 1994, they also started getting more money from the government.[7]

We believe that when cities get their fair share of Diet seats, they'll get not just more government money but more reformist policies as well. Elections matter. And, therefore, so do election rules.

Part Five

U.S.–Japan Relations
in This Crisis

——— 21 ———

The United States Is Not Japan

As the United States suffered a stock market plunge in 2000–2002, and then an outbreak of corporate scandals in 2002, the "resistance forces" in Japan seized upon these travails to provide grist for their anti-reform mill.

Aside from expressing some emotional satisfaction that an "arrogant, triumphalist" United States is getting "a well-deserved comeuppance," the resistance forces make two substantive arguments.

First, they argue, America is repeating the cycle of bubble and bust, deflation and malaise previously traced by Japan. Indeed, leading up to the recession of 2001, some in the United States also talked in the language of alarmism, from a book by a *Business Week* editor entitled *The Coming Internet Depression* to Paul Krugman's September 2001 essay "The Fear Economy."[1] The "resisters" in Japan say this proves that Japan's problems are merely one instance of a supposed "global crisis of capitalism." Consequently, no special institutional overhaul is needed in Japan. The same argument was made by Finance Ministry bigwig Eisuke Sakakibara in response to the Asian financial debacle of 1997–98.

Second, the resisters contend, structural reform is just a codeword for Americanization. However, the cure of "adopting the American" system would be even worse than Japan's disease. The electricity deregulation fiasco in California and the widespread corporate scandals clearly show that America is not the proper role model for Japan.

We would offer three responses:

1. America will not suffer anything close to Japan's "lost decade." On the contrary, its growth rate during the coming decade will most likely be 3 percent or more. The differences between the two countries are far more telling than the similarities.

2. Japan can reform without becoming a clone of America. Indeed, aside from a shameless level of executive greed not often exhibited in Japan, the real irony is that America's scandals stem from precisely the defect it shares

with Japan: insufficient checks and balances on corporate managers. Nothing in the misdeeds of some U.S. firms suggests that Japan would be better off with more inside directors, less shareholder power, and even less aggressive accounting than it has now.

3. There are clearly areas where the United States went overboard in its infatuation with the "magic of the marketplace." For example, in abolishing Glass-Steagall—the New Deal-era law that separated commercial and investment banking and that served as a model for Japan's Article 65, the United States clearly failed to put in place sufficient safeguards to prevent rampant conflicts of interest and other abuses. There were also insufficient safeguards for employees as America moved to the "defined benefit" plans known as 401Ks. There is no reason Japan cannot simultaneously institute reform and avoid such mistakes.

Bubble Troubles: Japan Versus the United States

All capitalist economies are prisoners of the boom-bust cycle. But there's a world of difference between the normal overheating of an investment boom and accompanying financial euphoria, such as the United States experienced, and the authentic bubble that Japan suffered.

Yes, parts of the U.S. stock market, particularly high tech, did become a bubble until it was popped in 2000. However, the overall economy remained healthy and resilient. That's one reason the recession of 2001 was the second mildest since World War II despite the terrorist attacks of September 11. By contrast, Japan's entire economy turned into a bubble.

No one factor alone could have caused Japan's bubble. It took the interrelated action of four separate distortions: outlandish stock prices, outlandish real estate prices, excessive bank lending tied to these asset prices, and excessive investment in physical capacity whose profitability required high asset prices. With the exception of technology sector stock prices, not a single one of these four distortions afflicted the United States. Let's look at them one by one.

Stock Prices

Many analysts made facile—and misleading—comparisons by superimposing the late-1990s rise in the Dow Jones index with the Nikkei 225 index in the 1980s. But such comparisons are useless without knowing what is happening with corporate profits. If a firm's profits double, then so can its stock price. Hence, the proper measure is the ratio of stock price to corporate earnings (the P/E ratio). During noninflationary periods in the United States—that is, except for the 1973–85 interlude, when oil prices were sky high—the P/E ratio for the Standard & Poor's 500 index has averaged about 17.

In Japan, the P/E ratio for the fifteen hundred companies in the first section of the Tokyo Stock Exchange rose from around 20 during 1975–83 to 35 in 1985 and eventually to a peak of more than 70. Many of the largest firms had PE ratios of 100. At one point, All Nippon Airways sold for 350 times earnings.

By contrast, the P/E ratio for America's S&P 500 index briefly rose to a peak of 36 in 1999 before falling back sharply. More important, talking about the S&P as a whole is like saying that, on average, a man and a horse have three legs. Just about all of the market's overvaluation can be attributed to action in technology stocks starting in early 1998 (Figure 21.1).

At the March 2000 peak, the tech sector of the S&P 500 reached a P/E ratio of 47. Among the one hundred largest stocks on the NASDAQ exchange, the P/E ratio hit an astounding 135 at its March peak. By contrast, the nontech stocks in the S&P 500 peaked out at 23 in 1999 and fell back to 17 as of April 2000.

The market did correct, but fears that this correction would decimate consumer spending proved to be alarmism. While the "wealth effect" did have some impact on consumer spending in the late 1990s, its impact was far less than historical trends would suggest. Perhaps consumers wisely judged that soaring stock prices were too excessive and short-lived to be relied upon. In any case, during the late 1990s, income and jobs proved a far better guide to consumer spending than stock prices. Not having spent excessively during the boom, consumers have far less need to retrench during the correction. Although consumer saving rates will likely increase, spending can still grow quite nicely as long as jobs and income remain on track.[2]

Land Prices

Had Japan's bubble been limited to the stock market, it would have left little lasting damage. But the bubble pervaded other assets as well—most notably land. In the 1980s, land prices in Japan's urban residential areas *quadrupled*. The land underneath the Emperor's palace in Tokyo was said to be worth more than the entire state of California. There has been nothing comparable in the United States. While there have been pockets of soaring prices, such as Silicon Valley and Manhattan, for the United States as a

Figure 21.1 **U.S. Stock Bubble Limited to Tech Sector**

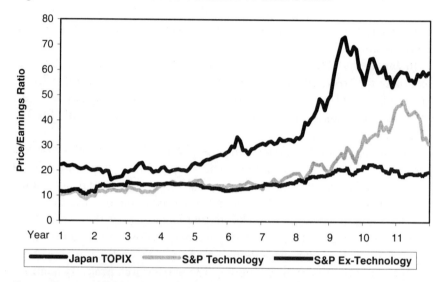

Source: Data provided by Yardeni.com and Dresdner Kleinwort Benson (Tokyo).

Note: The price-to-earnings ratio equals the stock price divided by profits in the previous four quarters. The chart compares U.S. stock prices in the 1990s with those of Japan in the 1980s. So, year 1 equals 1979 for Japan and 1990 for the United States; year 11 equals 1989 for Japan and 2000 for the United States.

whole, the average price for a new home rose only 50 percent over the entire past decade, about 4 percent a year.

Bank Debt

The critical ingredient that made Japan's asset bubble so debilitating is that it corroded bank balance sheets. Banks threw loans at borrowers whose ability to pay back required ever-higher stock and real estate prices (see Chapter 5).

The United States experienced a smaller version of this syndrome in the late 1980s, when many savings-and-loan institutions made real estate loans that depended on high land prices, which in turn depended on high oil prices.

U.S. banks learned their lesson. The viability of bank loans depends on the cash flow of business borrowers and the income of consumers—not the price of dot-com stocks or Manhattan condominiums. Those borrowers are in good shape. Corporate balance sheets are stronger than they've been in years. In early 2002, despite the recession, the net interest burden as a ratio to cash flow was lower than in the entire decade of the 1980s. While consumer debt rose to record levels, the ability to service that debt also rose as interest rates fell. Even with the recession cutting into income, consumer debt service as a portion of household income, 14 percent, was barely above the average of the past two decades.

Consequently, nonperforming loans (NPLs) at U.S. commercial banks were only 2.7 percent of all loans in early 2002, only half the 5 percent average of 1985–90 and the peak of 6.2 percent reached in 1991.

Excess Capital Investment

The final critical ingredient in Japan's bubble was excess investment in properties with little economic value—not just real estate, but also factories, stores, equipment, and so forth.

Once again we find few similarities in the United States. In 1999 real business investment in buildings—factories, offices, and stores—was only 6 percent higher than the level of ten years earlier. There was, of course, an investment boom in high-tech equipment. Real capital investment reached its highest rate in years: 14 percent of GDP compared to 9–10 percent during the 1980s. The difference is this: Traditionally, Japan has suffered from excess investment, whereas the United States has suffered from too little investment. The United States is in the process of curing its problem. America's investment boom was the conveyer belt for the information revolution.

The key test of whether investment is excessive or not is the productivity of that investment. Japan's bubble-era investment was associated with a sharp decline in the growth rate of Total Factor Productivity (TFP)—that is, the productivity of labor and capital combined (review Figure 2.5). By contrast, America's investment recovery was associated with a revival of TFP growth from 0.7 percent in 1975–95 to 1.4 percent during 1996–2000.[3]

To be sure, there was a lot of excess, waste, and outright fraud in the United States, as there has been during almost every boom for the past three hundred years. But consider this: In the early twentieth century, there were almost two hundred automobile companies. Almost all of them failed, of course, but the automobile as a technology remained. So it is with the Internet. It is yet another in the innumerable waves of technology that keep growth going.

The Bottom Line

We never accepted the so-called new economy paradigm. The Internet is no different from any of the previous waves of technology, from electricity to the automobile. Whatever problems may exist in the United States, the lift to productivity growth is real and lasting. We know it will last because the biggest boost to productivity has occurred not in the new-economy sectors that produce information technology, but in the old-economy sectors, such as banking, retail, and "rust belt" manufacturing that have revolutionized themselves by using IT. Growth of labor productivity in retail accelerated from 2 percent a year in 1987–95 to 6.3 percent during 1995–99.

The most reasonable estimates are that the United States can now grow 3 to 3.5 percent a year during the coming decade—down from the euphoric 4 percent rates of 1996–2000, but much higher than the 2.25 percent speed limit people spoke of a decade ago.

Corporate Malfeasance in the United States

In any country, managers perform most productively and honestly when they face the external discipline of fierce competition, shareholder power and strong regulatory supervision. The U.S. system of corporate governance presumes that directors, accountants, equity analysts, investment banks, accountants, and regulators are all independent of both management and each other. During the past decade, this independence was replaced by a rather incestuous relationship.

In Japan's system—rife with inside directors, cross-shareholdings among companies, keiretsu networks, and cozy oligopolies—the need for checks and balances is not sufficiently recognized even in theory (see Chapter 15).

Bouncing Back

All countries get into trouble from time to time. The ones with a responsive political economy resolve their problems much sooner.

Because Japan is still a one-party democracy, its leaders have not felt sufficient pressure to correct its systemic flaws. Unquestionably, President George W. Bush's initial responses to the corporate scandals were also too little, too late. Like the LDP, Bush has denied the systemic nature of the problem. Fortunately, the United States enjoys competitive politics and strong institutional investors. Fear of investor backlash and voter backlash is forcing a response in Washington, Wall Street, and boardrooms across the land.

The experience of other countries underscores the point. Consider South Korea. During the Asian catastrophe of 1997–98—when Korean GDP fell 7 percent—many observers compared it to Japan. In reality, it is recovering quite nicely, with projected GDP growth of 5–6 percent for the next few years. Information Technology industries have risen from 8 percent of GDP in 1996 to 14 percent in 2002. Korea seems to be successfully making the transition that Japan needed to make, but failed to do so, in the mid-1970s. Given all its similarities with Japan, two differences bear examination: Korea is far more globalized than Japan and has become even more so under Kim Dae Jung; and, Korea, unlike Japan, now has genuinely competitive party politics.

────22────

How the United States Can Help

An Economically Weak Japan Cannot Be a Strong Political Ally

It stands as a monument to bad timing. One month before Japan's bubble popped at the start of 1990, one of America's most brilliant economists wrote the following:

> An Asian economic bloc with Japan at its apex . . . is clearly in the making. This all raises the possibility that the majority of American people who now feel that Japan is a greater threat to the U.S. than the Soviet Union are right.[1]

When that economist, Lawrence Summers, became secretary of the U.S. Treasury, what kept him awake at night was not the mythical threat from a Japan that was supposedly too strong, but the all-too-real consequences of Japan being too weak. The point is not to single out Summers, but the contrary. The fact that someone as intelligent as Summers was temporarily taken in indicates the degree of hysteria then gripping the United States.

Today, the opposite mistake is being made. In much of Washington, Japan is simply off the radar screen. There are even some voices suggesting that the United States "let 'em stew in their own juices."[2] Such sentiments are shortsighted. Global stability is undermined by the ills emanating from a weak Japan.

The greatest damage is not seen bilaterally but in Asia. Japan's weakness was a major contributor to Asia's 1997–98 meltdown, which, in turn, provoked the scariest global financial crisis in decades. Japan's recession led to a cut in its own imports from Asia, while a weakened yen led to a steep drop in the export earnings of countries, such as South Korea, that compete directly with Japan. The final straw was that Japanese banks withdrew half of their loans to Asia from mid-1997 to the end of 1999, twice the 22 percent withdrawal by U.S. and European banks.[3] Japan's malaise certainly did not cause Asia's catastrophe, but it did make it significantly worse.

Japan's rejuvenation is critical to Asia's continued export-led industrialization. Until now, Japan has not provided much of a market (see Chapter 10, pp. 162–63). Since America's absorption capacity is limited, Asia's continued progress will be held back unless Japan imports more. As Indonesia's dicey transition emphasizes, Asia's economic health has clear security ramifications.

Beyond that, as long as Japan is economically stagnant and politically gridlocked, it will be focused more on its internal problems than on playing a role on the global stage. Yet to cope with new concerns in Asia—particularly the integration of a rising China—the United States needs an equal and politically engaged partner, not an unsinkable aircraft carrier and checkbook diplomacy.

Policy makers in the second Bush administration understand this. It was not the economists but security-minded officials such as national security adviser Condoleezza Rice and deputy secretary of state Richard Armitage who initially pushed most strongly on the issue of bank reform in Japan. They argued, rightly, that an economically weak Japan cannot be a strong political partner.

Bruce Stokes argued in a report for the Council on Foreign Relations that the United States has little stake in Japan's recovery unless that recovery entails greater openness to imports and foreign direct investment (FDI).[4] However, as we discussed in Chapter 9, Japan will find it very hard to institute reform without allowing more imports and FDI. Hence, even America's narrow commercial interests give reason to support reform.

The real question for American policy makers is not the criticality of Japanese revival but whether the United States can do anything about it. Can the United States influence the likelihood, pace, and shape of reform? Or must it simply wait as the drama unfolds on a purely Japanese stage?

Clearly, the success or failure of reform will be determined in Japan, not the United States. "The U.S. has no power to force the world's second largest economy to move in a direction it does not want to go," pointed out Bowman Cutter, the deputy director of the National Economic Council in the first Clinton administration.[5]

But, as we have argued in this book, reform is a direction in which Japan will increasingly want to go. In many cases where the forces of reform and resistance are stalemated, the United States can help tip the balance. "U.S. influence in Japan is like currency intervention," said a former officer at the U.S. embassy in Tokyo. "Large parts of the time, it is impotent. But at critical moments, it can help turn the tide."

An End to the Black-Box Paradigm

As a first step, Washington must recognize that its traditional operational paradigm toward Japan no longer works. American officials have often acted as if Japan were governed by a tight elite fairly unified in purpose. From this vantage point, Japan was a kind of black box. Carrots and sticks were used to influence Japan as a whole, but policy makers seldom felt the need to look at the conflicts of interest and ideas inside the box. Of course, on a tactical level, Washington regularly relied on individual politicians to act as "fixers" to break through bureaucratic logjams. But, on the strategic level, the monolithic paradigm usually held sway.

The black-box paradigm worked well enough during the era of single-party LDP dominance and a tight triangle between the LDP, the government bureaucracy, and big business. Those days are over.

This required change in mind-set is already beginning. In the so-called Armitage Commission Report, written shortly before the 2000 elections, Armitage wrote that, rather than promoting reform, the LDP "has focused primarily on hanging on to its dwindling power." But no credible opposition party has emerged, so the Japanese government is "stuck in neutral, incapable of more than muddling through." His willingness to speak so undiplomatically indicates that much of the U.S. elite no longer premises its policy on the assumption of permanent LDP rule.[6]

What Can the United States Do?

The first rule for the United States is "do no harm." All too often, policies based on the obsolete black box model have led to inadvertent support for the status quo.

In the early 1990s, the first Bush administration pressed Japan to increase public works spending by $500 billion over ten years. The intention was to stimulate Japan's domestic economy, elevate its imports, and thereby reduce its trade surplus. However, as reformist officials at the Ministry of Economy, Trade and Industry (METI) pointed out, this move "gave an allowance to the construction *zoku* (caucus)"—a bastion of corruption and antireformism.

Then, in 1993, when an anti-LDP reformist coalition government under Prime Minister Morihiro Hosokawa came to power, the Clinton administration hailed its emergence. Yet Washington's harsh tactics during the 1993–94 "framework" trade talks ended up pushing Hosokawa into a nationalistic-defensive alliance with the antireformists.

Admittedly, it is impossible to avoid all trade-offs between U.S. interest in reform and interest in other vital goals such as macroeconomic stimulus, trade issues, or security cooperation. But a better job can be done of taking such trade-offs into account (e.g., pushing fiscal stimulus through individual tax cuts rather than public works).

A third example came in the fall of 1998 during the political battle over how to solve Japan's banking crisis (see Chapter 5, p. 99). During that key window of opportunity, Washington chose to shore up Prime Minister Keizo Obuchi against the reformers! At a photo op during a summit, President Bill Clinton compared Obuchi's critics to the Republicans trying to impeach him. Treasury Secretary Summers's speeches focused on rushing money to the banks, while talk of conditionality became *pro forma*. When Obuchi bragged in the Diet of Clinton's support, the reformers were demoralized. Ichiro Ozawa, the leader of the Liberal Party, defected from the opposition coalition and allied his party with Obuchi. To be sure, the U.S. stance was only one factor, but it did help tip the balance—in the wrong direction.[7]

Once the money for the banks was passed, the U.S. Treasury again raised the issue of conditions, but as one Bank of Japan official put it, "The window of opportunity on further reform had closed."

In part the U.S. stance was driven by fear that political squabbles would delay injection of government money into the banks, a dangerous risk during the scary year of 1998. However, Treasury officials misjudged the situation, thinking the options came down to Obuchi's "money with no conditions" or the Democrats' original "no money under any conditions." They failed to appreciate how the Democrats' alliance with LDP reformers was moving it toward "money with conditions." More-nuanced memos sent from the U.S. embassy in Tokyo (where opinions were also divided) failed to register. A second factor was an internal debate in the U.S. government between a recovery-first-reform-later faction and a both-recovery-and-reform-now faction. The first group, which included Summers, argued that Japan was then too weak for radical reform. Finally, Washington feared that continued fighting could force new elections, and that the opposition was incapable of forming a government—at a time when speed was of the essence.

While Washington's motivations are understandable, it was a bad mistake in judgment caused by a mistake in perception. U.S. officials failed to see the significance of the banking debate for the politics of reform. Shoring up Obuchi was like shoring up Konstantin Chernyenko in the waning days of the Soviet Union.

Washington is in danger of making another mistake today. By adopting the view that the BOJ can cure deflation even in the absence of other measures, Washington risks unwittingly aiding those in Japan who want to use monetary stimulus as a substitute for reform. The Bush administration wants monetary ease as part of a trident that also includes dealing with the nonperforming loans and nonperforming borrowers. However, there is often a gap between what Washington thinks it is saying and what some people in Japan hear. Because the black-box viewpoint does not sufficiently factor in the institutions through which policies are implemented, it fails to see that disputes over seemingly technical monetary issues have far-reaching political-structural ramifications.[8]

There is yet another adverse consequence of the black-box paradigm. It leads Washington to oscillate between the stick of excessive stridence and the carrot of excessive conciliation. In 1997 and early 1998, Washington pressed Japan to apply fiscal stimulus and to inject public money into the banks. The advice was right, but Washington's tone came across as hectoring. When Obuchi threatened a nationalistic backlash, Washington reversed course. Alleged conciliation toward Japan turned into support for Obuchi.

For the most part, the second Bush administration has adopted the right basic stance, namely, that Japanese recovery is vital to the United States and there will be no recovery without reform. It has focused on exactly the right issues: the priority of dealing with the bad debt and bad borrowers. When various dodges have arisen out of Tokyo, such as yen depreciation, it has properly denounced them.[9]

Economic *Nai-Gaiatsu:* Seeking Allies

Beyond avoiding harm, the United States can make positive contributions to accelerate reform. It is not a question of personalities or parties, but policies and processes.

What the United States brings to the table is, ironically, its own desire for greater market access. Everett Ehrlich, former undersecretary of economic affairs, captured it best when he said: "We have too often thought of these [market opening] policies as unilateral concessions we demand of the Japanese. It is time to think of them instead as tonics for what ails Japan."[10]

Reformers in Japan have long sought *gaiatsu* (foreign pressure) to help them create changes that they were too weak to achieve on their own. During the 1999–2000 negotiations between Washington and the Ministry of Public Management, Home Affairs, Posts, and Telecommunications (MPHPT) regarding NTT's exorbitant fees for access to the Internet, one METI official said privately, "We hope the U.S. succeeds against NTT."

Imports and FDI are, in effect, veiled economic *gaiatsu*. It is unfortunate that economic *gaiatsu* is necessary, but it does seem unavoidable. As we discussed in the Compaq case (Chapter 10, p. 161), even a small entry by foreign players outside the cozy club can often trigger important changes in the way that powerful Japanese insiders operate.

U.S. political capital is limited. Hence picking and choosing battles is critical. Four conditions seem essential for success.

First of all, the most powerful leverage will occur where sectoral issues involving specific U.S. firms intersect with structural issues affecting the operation of the Japanese economic system. Without the urging of powerful U.S. constituents, mainly multinationals, Washington is unlikely to act. The most successful cases of sectoral-structural intersection have involved Toys R Us in reforming Japan's restrictions on the opening of large stores, the U.S. financial community in a series of financial agreements, and U.S. telecommunications firms such as AT&T in the dispute over Internet access fees.

Take the cell phone case. Today it seems that everyone in Japan walks around with a cell phone. It was not that way a few years back, when high prices suppressed demand. Motorola's pressure—via the U.S. government—to open the market created a revolution. Companies sold phones cheaply instead of leasing them at high rates. Phone call rates tumbled. In response, from 1994 to 1997, the number of cell phone subscribers increased from 500,000 to 24 million. Ironically, Motorola's own Japanese competitors—the very ones who had obstructed reform—were among the biggest beneficiaries. Seemingly, even when change would benefit Japanese players, achieving it often requires the participation of foreign outsiders who can provide the countervailing institutions lacking within Japan.

Second, action is most effective when the goals that the United States seeks for its own reasons coincide with the desires of major interest groups inside Japan. If only U.S. interests are at stake, with no corresponding interest group pressure in Japan, even the most ardent efforts often fail. The never-ending dispute over flat glass is a case in point. On the other hand, in many cases, Japanese business users of goods and services desire reforms that cut their costs. Leonard Schoppa's book *Bargaining with Japan* documents the criticality of "seeking allies."[11]

The term of art being used in Tokyo these days is *nai-gaiatsu*, that is, a combination of internal and external pressure (*naiatsu* and *gaiatsu*).

The poster child for *nai-gaiatsu* was reform of the Large-Scale Retail Store Law (*Daiten-ho*) in the early 1990s. What got the United States involved was the fact that Toys R Us had been legally blocked from opening a single store. But U.S. efforts worked because they coincided with mounting pressure from large Japanese retailers to lift the restrictions. METI, as usual, was divided. The Distribution Industry Division of METI's Industrial Policy Bureau, pushed by the large Japanese retailers, advocated modernization. METI even produced a document called "Vision for the Distribution Industry in the 1990s," which some U.S. experts say would have produced significant reforms had the policies it described been implemented. However, the Small and Medium Enterprise Agency within METI, a defender of the mom-and-pop retailers, succeeded in blocking the reforms. The METI minister at the time, Kabun Muto, was a mom-and-pop representative in the LDP who in 1999 created an antireform caucus in the Diet. In the end, it took a de facto U.S.-Japan alliance—a U.S. initiative that was given *sotto voce* support by Japanese discounters and part of METI, plus open editorial support from *Asahi* and *Nihon Keizai Shimbun*—to overcome firmly entrenched resistance. Once the *Daiten-ho* was reformed, Japan's big retailers took advantage of it. As we discussed in Chapter 3 (p. 53), this was important in slimming down the wholesale sector as well as reducing monopolistic prices.[12]

There was even a U.S. role in the chain of events leading to the "Big Bang" financial reforms (see Chapter 14). That's the conclusion of Robin Radin, who was managing director and general counsel of CS First Boston in Tokyo during the time of the negotiations, and who authored a "strategy book" used by Treasury officials. Radin, now a professor at Harvard Law School, makes the case that each increase in the presence of market forces made further market openings harder to resist. Back in 1984, the yen-dollar agreement between the United States and Japan reduced Japan's financial insulation from global markets, freed corporations from their dependence on Japanese banks by making it easier to raise funds outside Japan, and began the process of deregulating interest rates. Then the financial scandals of the early 1990s destroyed the credibility of the traditional regime and of the finance ministry itself. By the mid-1990s, argues Radin, the ministry had no choice but to respond in some way to the fact that the combined effect of these trends had rendered the traditional financial regime unsustainable. At the same time, reforms introduced in the little-noticed Administrative Procedure Act of 1993 provided the potential to curb the ministry's traditional arbitrary use of "administrative guidance" to protect financial cartels.

Taking advantage of these developments, a 1995 U.S.-Japan Financial Services Agreement "pushed the envelope" by introducing major changes in such areas as cross-border flows, introduction of new products, and asset management. Indeed, says Radin, it "established the policy platform for 'Big Bang' itself."[13]

In the 1999–2000 negotiations over the Internet access fee, the deputy U.S. trade representative, Richard Fisher, was careful to ally with Japanese interests rather than let the dispute be couched in terms of the United States versus Japan. Washington insisted that past agreements on "cost-based pricing" required that monopolist NTT lower its access fees by 40 percent over four years. NTT and the MPHPT said they would drop them only 22 percent in four years. Because of NTT's high local call rates and high access fees—the latter twenty times higher than those AT&T was charging in New York State at the time—someone in Japan wanting to use the Internet for 20 hours a month had to pay about $55 and someone using it 40 hours a month had to pay almost $100 per month. This compares to about $35 in Germany and $25 in the United States for 40 hours of usage. As a result, as of March 2002, only 44 percent of Japanese households were linked to the Internet, compared to 60 percent in the United States. Many Japanese business leaders, including some potential Internet competitors such as Sony and Toyota, criticized NTT. Taichi Sakaiya, then head of the Economic Planning Agency, publicly charged that NTT was hindering adoption of the Internet.

While the final agreement, reached in 2000, fell far short of U.S. goals due to NTT's political prowess, it led to a 20 percent cut in access fees during 2000 and helped set in motion further changes. That initial price drop enabled NTT rivals such as Japan Telecom and KDDI to enter the local phone call market with a price of 8.5 cents for three minutes and now other firms have lowered the price to 7.5 cents. While that price is still high by international standards, it was among the first cuts in the 10-cent rate that NTT had sustained for twenty-five years. In addition, the U.S.-Japan talks constituted part of the strong *nai-gaiatsu* pressure to limit NTT's ability to block new entrants for DSL service (see Chapter 16, p. 246). As we write this, the Telecommunications Council, an advisory council to the Ministry of Public Management, Home Affairs, Posts, and Telecommunications, is mulling an additional halving of access fees.[14]

Third, the most effective strategy is to set market forces in motion and let them do the heavy lifting. Government's powers are limited yet at times indispensable. Relatively small actions by government can loosen regulations and practices that suppress market forces.

Sometimes Japanese ministries have invited some foreign entry, hoping it will make Japanese players "leaner and meaner." The Ministry of Transport reportedly encouraged the alliance of United Airlines with All Nippon Airways as a way of taking Japan Airlines down a peg. Similar thinking in the Ministry of Finance helped increase the presence of foreign asset managers such as Fidelity. The ministries hope—and foreign skeptics expect— that the foreign presence will be big enough to stimulate domestic players, but not so big as to supplant them. However, the contrary will more often prove true: Once Pandora's box is opened sufficiently, it will be hard to control the outcome.

Fourth, reforms in the right areas can trigger systemic ripple effects throughout the economy. The more sectors of the economy that face competition, the harder it is to maintain moats elsewhere. As discussed in Chapter 13 (p. 194) the ripple effects on the system are likely to be larger in some sectors than others. Particularly critical are finance, retail, and telecommunications. Success requires picking and choosing the right battles.

Cynicism Is Not Realistic

When asked about the approach recommended here, some U.S. officials have objected that "seeking allies" has long been a standard arrow in the U.S. quiver. It is true that this posture has been tried from time to time, but so far it has not been raised to the level of a consistent strategic vision.

Another objection is that seeking allies has been tried in the past and has failed to elicit much Japanese support. However, past performance is not always a guide to future behavior. During the SII talks of the early 1990s Japan thought it was on top of the world; now it knows it's in trouble. It's hard to "seek allies" when there are few allies around. But the economic crisis is engendering new potential allies every day. Indeed, one former U.S. trade official contends that if Washington had maintained the cooperation with Japanese reformers that began in the SII talks, "Japanese deregulation and economic reform would be much further along than it is today."

To be sure, U.S. action must be guided by a realistic sense of what is and is not possible. Otherwise, the dashing of false hopes will lead to bitterness. U.S. influence is limited. The United States can aid Japanese reformers, but it cannot substitute for them.

Still, to the degree that the United States takes effective action, it can be of great help. A U.S. alliance with Japanese reformers can both increase the odds of reform's success and somewhat quicken the pace. Given the stakes, it's certainly worth the try.

Epilogue

23

The Phoenix Economy

Japan's economic fortunes have moved up and down so much in the past 150 years, it almost seems like a soap opera economy. Viewing Japan's current plight from the perspective of 2050, we have little doubt that the era from 1990 to 2010 will be seen as one of the country's major turning points, not the beginning of its demise.

Recall the image of Japan in 1854, when Commodore Matthew Perry's black ships first appeared off the coast. China was the great power in the region, Asia's Rome. Unimportant Japan was like something out of Europe's sixteenth century. Eighty-five percent of the people lived in rural towns and villages. It had none of the modern machinery, steel mills, steam engines, telegraphs, railroads, postal system, or newspapers already pervading the United States. Nor did it have modern business institutions such as banking and the public corporation. It had few natural resources aside from coal and silk.

However, it did have two remarkable assets. Its population was highly literate for a preindustrial country. Forty-three percent of boys and 10 percent of girls had some schooling in reading and arithmetic. There was a fairly lively trade in books in the upper circles of society. And a few years later, following the 1868 Meiji Restoration, Japan would be led by a brilliant elite of "thirty-somethings" determined to make it a rich, strong country.

The takeoff was explosive. By the 1940s, only seventy-five years after its emergence from medievalism, Japan produced a military powerful enough to seize almost all of Asia. Its planes and aircraft carriers were, for a while, almost able to fight the U.S. Navy to a standstill.

And then—desolation. In 1945, one-third of the country's housing and factories lay in ashes. Food was in such short supply—barely 1,000 calories per day—that riots broke out. The country's biggest trade problem was endless deficits. As late as 1957, even as knowledgeable an observer as Harvard professor (and later ambassador) Edwin Reischauer wrote that

Japan's "economic future [was] the darkest spot on the horizon." He worried Japan might never be able to export enough to pay for vital imports.[1]

In reality, Japan's economic miracle had recently begun, and by the 1970s Japan was an industrial superpower, with the second largest economy in the non-Communist world. In the 1980s Japan's economic prowess was as grossly overestimated as it had been underestimated a few decades earlier.

Then came the 1990s and the "lost decade."

As the first lost decade turns into the second, there is no quick relief in sight. Some observers suggest that Japan will never really revive. It will simply muddle through indefinitely, because Japan's political leaders believe that path will keep them in power. This book offers a more optimistic view of the future but also a more tumultuous path to that future. Certainly the evidence in Part Four offers no promise of an easy or early turnaround.

Yet we believe Japan will succeed. Only partly is this because the pain of inaction will ultimately surpass the pain of action. More fundamentally, Japan is a great nation currently trapped in obsolete institutions. Just talking to business people or academics or even bureaucrats in their forties or fifties fills one with hope. Japan abounds with bright, ambitious individuals who know what is wrong and who are capable of leading the new Japan. It does not have the feel of a failed state. What is missing is the program and institutional vehicle for all of these individuals to coalesce around. With time, that too will come.

Rather than a soap opera, Japan is a phoenix. Struck down, it rises, and rises yet again.

Today, even reform's greatest opponents feel obliged to mouth chants in its honor. Koizumi's entire appeal, and the way he came to power, was based on the population's yearning and hope for reform. If, as it is said, there is nothing so powerful as an idea whose time has come, then reform, while not yet come, is finally starting down the road.

—— Notes ——

Notes to Chapter 1

1. See McKinsey Global Institute 2000, "Executive Summary," p. 6.
2. Cabinet Office 2002c, p. 3.
3. From William Butler Yeats's "The Second Coming."
4. By the way, in the two decades since Thatcher arrived, per capita growth declined to 1.9 percent. But, since Italy and France were a bit lower than that, in the United Kingdom it felt like an improvement. See World Bank 2002 for growth rates.
5. Pempel 1998. There are some interesting differences between Pempel and myself on how this "regime shift" will play out. For a discussion, see Miura 1999.
6. Makin 2002; Fulford 2002; Posen 2001; Posen 2002.
7. Katz 1998a, pp. 180–86.
8. Calder 1988.
9. Katz 1998a, pp. 60–65, appendix D.
10. OECD 2000c, p. 95; OECD 1999b, p. 41.
11. Bayoumi and Collyns 2000, p. 144.
12. Terazawa 2001.
13. McKinsey Global Institute 2000, "Executive Summary," p. 4.
14. Weinstein 2001a, p. 45.
15. McKinsey Global Institute 2000, "Food Processing," p. 2.
16. Vlastos 1998.

Notes to Chapter 2

1. *Business Week* listed Eamonn Fingleton's *Blindside: Why Japan Is Still on Track to Overtake the U.S. by the Year 2000* as one of the "ten best business books of 1995" in its December 18, 1995, issue. Both *Foreign Affairs* and *Fortune* published excerpts.
2. Katz 1997.
3. Council on Economic and Fiscal Policy 2002. In the section entitled "Perspectives with Implementation of Structural Reform," the CEFP says that from 2004 onward, "Led by private demand, growth will be realized at a steady pace of at least 1.5 percent in real terms."
4. All of these comparisons are on the standard purchasing power parity (PPP) basis. PPP methods eliminate distortions caused by currency fluctuations. On a nominal currency basis, in 1996, with the yen at 108, Japan's nominal GDP per person was $35,000 compared to only $29,000 for the United States. However, such figures represent a "money illusion" rather than reality. Did Japan really become twice as wealthy between early 1990 and early 1995, a period in which the yen doubled in value but real GDP barely moved? Did Japan then abruptly become 60 percent poorer when the yen dropped back again? If your wages are twice mine but the prices you pay are three times higher, who has the higher living standard? To eliminate such "money illusions," economists adjust currencies to reach

a PPP comparison. PPP means that a basket of goods costs the same in the United States or Japan or Malaysia. That way one can judge how many hours of work it takes the average American or Japanese or Malaysian to buy a shirt or a car.

5. Bayoumi 2000a.

6. Note that in 1991, at the end of the bubble, Japan was actually operating 4 percent above capacity. So the swing in GDP caused by moving from above-capacity operation to below-capacity operation was 9 percent of GDP. However, any economy operating so far above capacity must eventually slow down. That is the nature of the business cycle. Hence in measuring the demand-side factors we are including only the 5 percent drop below capacity.

7. Ramaswamy 2000.

8. Bureau of Labor Statistics 2001.

9. Katz 1998a, p. 71.

10. Ibid., pp. 373–74.

11. Lincoln 2001a, pp. 60–75.

12. Bayoumi 2000a, p. 104. For a more detailed explanation of the economics of investment, TFP, and growth, see Appendix at http://www.mesharpe.com/katz.htm.

13. For example, even though the OECD pegged Japan's potential growth at 1.25 percent, it projected that Japan's actual growth would average 2 percent a year during 2000–05. The reasoning is this: Japan was then operating about 4 percent below full capacity. The OECD assumed it would take Japan until 2005 to get back to full capacity. Thus, growth in the next five years would average 2 percent in their view: 1.25 percent of potential growth plus 0.75 percent extra growth per year as Japan slowly got back to full capacity.

14. International Monetary Fund 2000b, p. 79; *Nihon Keizai Shimbun* 2000c.

15. Japan Economic Institute 2000a.

16. Organization for Economic Cooperation and Development 2000c, p. 95.

17. Organization for Economic Cooperation and Development 1999a, p. 41.

18. Memo provided to the author.

19. Japan Center for Economic Research, "Long-Term Forecast," various forecasts dated February 1998, January 1999, July 2000, and March 2001.

Notes to Chapter 3

1. This is a rough guesstimate. Machinery and metals account for about half of all manufacturing workers and for about 10 percent of the entire workforce. To capture pockets of efficiency within services, we make a stab at another 10 percent. For figures on relative TFP, see Katz 1998a, p. 30. For share of employment, see Cabinet Office 2001a, Table 5.2.

2. Council of Economic Advisers 2002, p. 52–61. McKinsey 2001.

3. McKinsey Global Institute 2000, "Residential Construction," p. 4.

4. For productivity figures, see Japan Productivity Center 2002; for output and employee figures, see Cabinet Office 2001a.

5. Weinstein 2001b.

6. Japan Productivity Center 2002 for 1990s figure. An earlier series from the center (no longer on the Web, and using the SNA 68 basis) is the source for the 4.7 percent growth rate during the 1980s.

7. There are major differences regarding textiles between the new SNA 93 data and the old SNA 68 series. In the old series, the sector labeled "textiles" had 1.1 million workers in 1990 and included apparel. In the new series, the sector labeled "textiles" had only 670,000 workers and did not include apparel. In the old, more inclusive series, textiles output per man-hour rose, whereas it fell in the new, less inclusive series. Apparently the brunt of the productivity growth was in apparel, not textiles per se. For more on this issue, see pp. 191–96 in Katz 1998a.

8. Statistics Bureau 2002b, Table 4.

9. For employee reduction, we are using the old SNA 63 series from Economic Planning Agency 2000, since it is more inclusive. See note 6. On capacity reduction, see *Nikkei Weekly* 2000a.

10. *Nikkei Weekly* 2000c.

11. Economic Planning Agency 2000, Table 4.012a, "Supply and Disposition of Commodities." These import penetration ratios differ from the ones we used to construct Figure 3.3, because in the figure we took imports as a percentage not of final demand but of total output, that is, final demand plus intermediate goods input. Once again we are using the old SNA series, partly because the data for the new series do not go back before 1990 and partly because, for textiles, the old series is more inclusive.

12. For output (measured by GDP in textiles), see Economic Planning Agency 2000. For number of firms, see Ministry of Economy, Trade and Industry 2002b, Table 7-6.

13. By contrast, food prices continued to rise another 12 percent during 1990–99 and began to fall only in 2000. Cabinet Office 2001b, Table 4.3, "GDP Deflators."

14. For the purpose of this comparison, we are using the broader SNA 68 data, which includes apparel in the textile category. The later, narrower SNA 93 data show an even larger discrepancy, with a 38 percent increase in GDP per worker during 1991–97 but a 10 percent decline in output per worker-hour during the same period.

15. See Figure 2.1 in Katz 1998a.

16. Sakakibara and Porter 2001.

17. Katz 1998a, Figure 2.5 and discussion on pp. 42–44.

18. Weinstein 2001a, pp. 39–43.

19. Porter, Takeuchi, and Sakakibara 2000.

20. Katz 1998a, pp. 42–44.

21. Porter 1990, pp. 414–415, 551, 555.

22. Porter, Takeuchi, and Sakakibara 2000, p. 29.

23. For Porter's most recent view, see ibid., p. 29. For our summary of his earlier view, see Katz 1998a, pp. 114, 126–27. For governmental support of the efficient exports, look throughout Chapter 6 of Katz 1998a. Additional data can be found in Elder 1998 and Anchordoguy 2002.

Robert Lawrence and David Weinstein (1999) argue that while imports aided TFP growth, exports did not. Hence export-oriented industrial policy could not have helped Japan. However, their methodology left out important considerations. Lawrence and Weinstein only examined whether exports improved TFP growth within a particular industry, say, textiles or steel. While they found that it did not, other studies have reached the opposite conclusion. More important, Lawrence and Weinstein did not test whether exports helped Japan move from low-TFP industries such as textiles to higher ones such as autos during the high-growth era. In fact, as productivity expert Dale Jorgenson showed, two-thirds of Japan's TFP growth during 1960–79 came exactly from that shift. Industrial policy and exports, in turn, accelerated that shift. See Katz 1998a, pp. 134–56.

24. Oyama 1999, pp. 3–4.

25. Ibid., Chart 6.

26. Ibid., p. 6.

27. Cabinet Office 2001b, Table 4.3, "GDP Deflators."

28. Oyama 1999, p. 6.

29. *Asia Wall Street Journal* 2001b, p. 4; 2001c, p. 1. Also, *Nihon Keizai Shimbun* 2001h.

30. *Nihon Keizai Shimbun* 2001g. Also, *Wall Street Journal* 2001b, 2001c.

31. Ministry of International Trade and Industry 1999a, p. 17. Among MNCs, 53 percent of their total exports go to their affiliates, while a third of their imports come from them.

32. Ministry of International Trade and Industry 1998.

Notes to Chapter 4

1. Bayoumi and Collyns 2000, pp. 25–27, 144.
2. Bank of Japan 2001a, "Deposits and Savings Rates (Banks) (2)." The BOJ site only covers instruments up to five years, but other sources indicated ten-year certificates of deposit were negligibly higher.
3. Depending on whether one uses SNA 68 or SNA 93, there is some discrepancy in the absolute numbers. In either case, the net loss of income to consumers was a huge 4–5 percent of national income.
4. *Nikkei Weekly* 2001e; Moody's Investors Service 2001.
5. *Nihon Keizai Shimbun* 2000i.
6. Ramaswamy 2000. See, in particular, the regression results on pp. 86–87.
7. Given a capital-to-output ratio of 2.4 in the business sector, net investment equal to 5 percent of GDP would expand capacity by 2 percent each year. Depreciation rates are based on the figures for "capital consumption" in Cabinet Office (2001b), Table 2.2, "National Income and Its Uses, Nonfinancial Corporations." We deflated these nominal figures to constant 1995 yen using the deflators for private business investment.
8. OECD 2000c, pp. 34–35.
9. Some of this information came in a note to the author from Michael Smitka, an economist who is expert on the auto industry. See also Smitka 1992; Japan Automobile Manufacturers Association 2002. For figures on operating rates and capacity reduction (or lack of it), see Ministry of Economy, Trade and Industry industrial production statistics available at: http://www.meti.go.jp/english/statistics/index.html.
10. On capacity, see Uriu 1996, pp. 225–30. For figures on operating rates and capacity reduction (or lack of it), see Ministry of Economy, Trade, and Industry 2002a. For evidence of higher steel prices at home than in the export market, see Tilton 1998 as well as Elder 1998, 2000.
11. Information on floor space is from Jesper Koll of Merrill Lynch (Japan) and *Nihon Keizai Shimbun* (2002c). On same-store sales, see "Preliminary Report on the Current Survey of Commerce" in Ministry of Economy, Trade and Industry 2002a.
12. OECD 1999a, pp. 11–12; Feldman 1999.
13. Unfortunately, the new SNA series that goes past 1998 doesn't cover the period before 1990 and is too different from the old series to make a proper adjustment. Anorexia did lessen with the recovery of 1999, but we cannot say by how much.
   The budget deficit figure of 11 percent, taken from the GDP tables, is much higher than the usual figure given by the general account of the national budget, because it includes all national and local government bodies.
14. According to a survey by *Nihon Keizai Shimbun* (2000h), during April–September of 2000, debts repaid by 1,200 of the top 1,600 corporations exceeded new borrowing or new equity issues to the tune of 3.9 trillion yen.
15. Household savings did increase sharply as a share of household *income* during the high-growth era. However, household income fell sharply as a share of GDP. These two forces neutralized each other; consequently, household savings as a share of GDP increased only a bit. See Figures 8.4 and 8.5 in Katz 1998a.
16. See ibid., pp. 198–200.
17. See the discussion of this on pp. 199–202 of ibid.
18. Ando 2000. Ando excludes land from the figures on both savings and net worth.
19. Ibid., pp. 4–5.
20. *Nikkei Weekly* 2000g.

Notes to Chapter 5

1. Bank of Japan 2002b.

2. The 26.5 trillion yen is the amount spent during 1998–2000. The figure comes from an internal MOF document provided to the author. Another 9.4 trillion yen was spent nationalizing failed banks such as LTCB and Nippon Credit, but 5 trillion of this was retrieved when private parties bought those banks from the government. Capital injections into solvent banks accounted for another 8.4 trillion. The rest, 13.7 trillion, was spent paying depositors of failed banks and buying up bad debt from solvent banks.

3. *Nihon Keizai Shimbun* 2001k. The IMF (2001a), pp. 106–8, believes the banks hold some 20–30 trillion yen ($160 billion to $240 billion) in unrecognized loan losses, enough to wipe out all the so-called Tier 1 capital at the regional banks and half the Tier 1 capital at the major banks. In 2001 the IMF asked Tokyo to let it come in and make an accurate assessment.

4. The required loan loss reserves for the unsecured portion of the loan are 2–5 percent for Class 2, 15 percent for Class 2a, 70 percent for Class 3, and 100 percent for Class 4.

5. Reed 2000. For interest rates on long-term deposits, see Bank of Japan 2001a. Some have described zero interest rates as a free "call option" on bad debts. The cost of keeping a bad loan on the books is negligible. Yet if somehow the firm recovers and the value of the loan increases, then the bank has gained a great reward at little cost.

6. Atkinson 2001a, 2001b.

7. The debt of the listed corporations amounts to 26 percent of all outstanding bank debt

8. Atkinson 2001b, p. 134.

9. IMF 2001a, p. 134.

10. Standard & Poor's 2000.

11. Mizuno 2001.

12. Dattel 1994.

13. Calder 1993, p. 213.

14. Japan Securities Research Institute 1988.

15. *Nihon Keizai Shimbun* 2000i. See also *Japan Weekly Monitor* 1999.

16. *Jiji Press* 1999; *Asahi Shimbun* 1999a.

17. *Asahi Shimbun* 1999b; *Washington Post* 1998.

18. Bergsten, Takatoshi, and Noland 2001, p. 72.

19. *Oriental Economist Report* 2000a; *Economist* 2001a; *Nihon Keizai Shimbun* (2001l).

20. *Economist* 2001b.

21. Private communication from Standard & Poor's.

22. In the spring of 2002 the spread between five-year bank debentures and risk-free government bonds widened sharply.

23. Hartcher 1998, pp. 130–31.

24. *Wall Street Journal* 2002a.

25. *Asia Wall Street Journal* 2001a, 2001b, 2001c.

26. Ibison 2002.

27. IMF 2001a, p. 132.

28. Cited in *Oriental Economist Report* 2001a.

29. Katz 2001b; *Oriental Economist Report* 2001a.

Notes to Chapter 6

1. Koo 2001. Koo does, however, insist that deregulation measures accompany fiscal stimulus, on the grounds that this would raise the rate of return on investment and thereby stimulate more investment.

2. Posen 1998, Chapter 5. Also see a debate between Posen and myself in Katz and Posen 1998. The three-year time limit on spending cuts was discussed in an August 1998 author interview with Posen.

3. The economic forecast was made in March 1999 and was cited in the press and confirmed to the author. The pronouncement that Japan had enough to recover was made at a March 1999 conference sponsored by the Center for Strategic and International Studies (CSIS) in Washington, DC.

4. E-mail reply to the author, December 27, 2001.

5. Bayoumi 2000b, pp. 25–27.

6. Kuttner and Posen 2001, pp. 40–42.

7. Some analysts prefer to look at "net debt," which reached 64 percent of GDP in 2002. By 2006 it will hit 84 percent of GDP, the highest in the OECD. In any case, many of the government assets used to calculate net debt are of dubious quality, such as loans and investments made by a myriad of state institutions. However one measures it, the debt burden is growing. See OECD 2001a, p. 36, and Asher and Dugger 2000, pp. 12–14.

8. Asher and Dugger 2000, pp. 1, 6. For an interview with Asher, see *Oriental Economist Report* 2001c. Posen 2002.

9. Moody's 2002.

Notes to Chapter 7

1. That is the title of a speech by Masaaki Shirakawa (2000), an adviser to BOJ governor Masaru Hayami. See a speech by BOJ deputy governor Yutaka Yamaguchi (1999) entitled "Monetary Policy and Structural Policy: A Japanese Perspective."

2. *Nihon Keizai Shimbun* 2002b.

3. Ueda 1999a.

4. Hubbard 2002b.

5. Krugman 2001a.

6. Ito 1999. Though Ito is no longer with the MOF, he continues to sound very much like it. In a Columbia University seminar in 2001, Ito went so far as to deny that a budget cut equal to 1 percent of GDP was contractionary, eliciting astonishment from economists in the audience. See *Oriental Economist Report* 2001f.

7. Ueda 1999b.

8. Hatakeyama 2001.

9. Cited in *Oriental Economist Report* 2001a.

10. Ibid.

11. If we use an eight-quarter lag, there is a 23 percent positive correlation between deflation in one quarter and the demand-supply gap eight quarters later. However, if we regress the output gap on lagged deflation and a trend variable, the deflation coefficient loses all significance.

12. Okamura communicated this in an e-mail to the author. Feldman 2002.

13. Morsink and Bayoumi 2000, p. 144.

14. Ueda 1999b.

15. Morsink and Bayoumi 2000, pp. 149–50.

16. Kuttner and Posen 2001, pp. 20, 24, 31.

17. Krugman 1998c, in which he refers to Krugman 1997 and 1998b.

18. Krugman 1998a. Whereas we attribute Japan's chronic investment-savings gap to a cartelized economy, Krugman points the finger at demographics. Given the decline in Japan's working-age population, he says, "[T]he country should save heavily to make provision for the future. . . . But investment opportunities in Japan are limited, so that businesses will not invest all those savings even at a zero interest rate. And as anyone who has read John Maynard Keynes can tell you, when desired savings consistently exceed willing investment, the result is a permanent recession. . . . What Japan needs to do is promise borrowers that there will be inflation in the future! If it can do that, then the effective 'real' interest rate on borrowing will be negative. . . . As a result they will be willing to spend more. . . . [I]nflation—or more precisely the promise of future inflation—is the medicine that will cure Japan's ills." For a critique by a BOJ economist, see Okina 1999.

19. Kregel 1999.

20. Nakagawa and Oshima 2000.

21. Krugman 1998d. All Krugman offers is a regression about interest rates *in the United States* and a self-described "leap of faith" (pp. 47–48) about how this might apply in Japan.

22. If we regress inflation on trend and GDP eight quarters earlier, the coefficient for trend is –0.00034 with a P-value of 2.71E-14. Lagged GDP has a coefficient of 0.39 with a P-value of 3.14E-12. In other words, each 1 percent *rise* in GDP is followed eight quarters later by a 0.39 percent *rise* in inflation. The adjusted R-squared is 76.7 percent. By contrast, if we reverse cause and effect by regressing GDP on trend and inflation eight quarters earlier, the coefficient for trend is –0.0007 with a P-value of 1.03E-21 and the coefficient for lagged inflation is *negative,* that is, –0.388 with a P-value of 2.92E-07. In other words, each 1 percent *rise* in inflation is followed eight quarters later by a 0.38 percent *decline* of GDP. This is the opposite of the prediction made by the inflation-targeting theorists. Calculation by author. See Appendix at http://www.mesharpe.com/katz.htm.

23. Krugman 1997.

24. Regressing inflation on trend, four-quarter lagged real GDP growth, four-quarter lagged import prices and eight-quarter lagged money supply (M2+CD) growth during 1977–90, produces the following results. The adjusted R-squared is 0.86. All independent variables are significant at a 1 percent level. The coefficient is 0.27 for GDP growth, 0.04 for import prices, and 0.18 for money supply growth. SNA 68 data. Author's calculation. See Appendix at http://www.mesharpe.com/katz.htm.

25. Regressing inflation on trend, eight-quarter lagged real GDP growth, four-quarter lagged import prices, and eight-quarter lagged money supply (M2+CD) growth during 1991–2000 produces the following results. The adjusted R-squared is 0.72. While GDP and import prices are significant at a 1 percent level, money supply is completely insignificant (99 percent P-value). The coefficient is 0.24 for GDP growth and 0.05 for import prices. SNA 68 data. Author's calculation.

Incidentally, during 1992–2001, using SNA 93 data, the correlation between changes in the monetary base and inflation or deflation a year later registers negative but is statistically insignificant. The correlation between changes in the money supply (M2+CDs) and inflation/deflation a year later is a weak 26 percent. See Appendix at http://www.mesharpe.com/katz.htm.

Notes to Chapter 8

1. Katz 1998a, pp. 197–98, 213–15.

2. Ibid., pp. 223–31.

Notes to Chapter 9

1. Katz 1998a, p. 257.
2. Bosworth 1998, p. 10.

Notes to Chapter 10

1. *Nihon Kezai Shimbun* 2001o.
2. *Nihon Kezai Shimbun* 2000j.
3. For more on this, see Norwell 2001a.
4. Milner 1988 on why exporters fight for free trade and Elder 1998 on why Japanese exporters, to this point, have rarely done so.
5. Economic Planning Agency 1996.
6. Katz 1998a, pp. 268–71.
7. Lincoln 1999, pp. 43–49. For further discussion of intra-industry trade, see pp. 251–53 of Katz 1998a.
8. The change in the price of oil can have a major, and illusory, effect on the apparent ratio of manufactured goods to total imports. For example, suppose Japan imports 100 yen worth of goods, of which 50 yen, that is half, is oil, and the other half is manufactures. Suppose the price of oil drops in half so that the oil import bill is now 25 yen. The result is that the total imports drop to 75 yen, and that oil imports now make up a third of all imports, whereas manufactured imports appear to have risen from half of all imports to two-thirds (50 out of 75 yen) even though the actual value of manufactured imports has not increased one yen.
9. For debates among economists on this, see Katz 1998a, pp. 263–67 and 300.
10. See Petri 1991 for a rigorous proof that distributors, not consumers, have been the traditional obstacle to more consumer good imports.
11. Similarly, manufactured imports doubled from 2 percent of GDP in the 1980s to 4 percent by the late 1990s. But with other countries making the same move, the ratio of Japan's import-dependence to that of the OECD as whole rose only slightly, from 30 percent in the early 1980s to 36 percent by 1997.
12. For an explanation of this, see Katz 1998a, pp. 48–50 and Appendix F.
13. MITI 1999a.
14. Katz 1998a, pp. 277–81.
15. Keizai Koho Center 2002, p. 107. This comparison is for 1999 when the yen rate was 114/$.

Notes to Chapter 11

1. Under Japan's Large-Scale Retail Store Law, small merchants had the legal power to delay or even de facto prohibit the creation of new large stores, domestic as well as foreign, on the grounds of excess competition. U.S.-Japan negotiations under the Structural Impediments Initiative (SII) during the first Bush administration changed the practice. This made it possible for Toys R Us to enter. For more on this, see Schoppa 1997, Chapter 6, and Grier 2001.
2. American Chamber of Commerce in Japan 2000a, p. 28. The 3 percent figure of foreign control of Japanese manufacturing exaggerates the foreign presence. A large portion of it is due to just two industries, petroleum refining and pharmaceuticals. Heavy FDI in petroleum is a legacy of the post–World War II military occupation of Japan. In many

industries, the foreign-controlled share is less than 1 percent and certainly far less than the foreign presence in the United States.

3. For more on cross-shareholding, see Chapter 15. See Vestal 1993, p. 53.

4. Booz, Allen, and Hamilton 1987, p. 22, reported that foreign firms in Japan found staffing difficulties even more inhibiting than "lack of market opportunities."

5. Alexander 2000b is the source for the $16 billion figure.

6. *Nikkei Weekly* 2001a.

7. Fields made this comment during a talk at a Columbia University symposium, March 23, 2001.

8. U.S. State Department 2001 summarizes the proceedings of a joint U.S.–Japan symposium on FDI held on April 2001 in New York City.

9. American Chamber of Commerce in Japan 2000b. See also Council on Foreign Relations 2000.

Notes to Chapter 12

1. *Nikkei Weekly* 2001g. See also Tett 2002.

2. Cited in *Oriental Economist Report* 2001g.

3. Cited in *Oriental Economist Report* 2001g.

4. August 2000 interview with author.

5. For further details, see Harner 2000, Chapter 6.

6. Two regulatory changes opened the door to foreign asset managers. Beginning in 1990, investment advisers such as Nomura Asset Management and Goldman Sachs were allowed to handle a certain amount of new money going into government pension funds. By 1998–99 all limits on the role of investment advisers had been lifted. In addition, between 1996 and January 1998, Tokyo gradually lifted the so-called 5-3-3-2 rule under which no less than 50 percent of pension funds had to be invested in guaranteed principal instruments such as government bonds, no more than 30 percent in domestic stocks, no more than 30 percent in foreign currency assets, and no more than 20 percent in real estate. The ostensible purpose of the 5-3-3-2 rule was safety, but it limited funds to low-risk, low-return investments. For more on this process, see Radin 1996 and 2000.

7. *Nihon Keizai Shimbun* 2000b.

8. *Nihon Keizai Shimbun* 2000a.

9. *Nihon Keizai Shimbun* 2001a.

10. For more on this, see Singer 2002.

11. In addition, with more and more foreign investors buying Japanese government bonds (JGBs) and more foreign firms issuing corporate bonds in Japan to take advantage of low rates (so-called samurai bonds), foreign financial firms are playing a larger role in these cross-border transactions.

12. Ibison 2002.

13. Harner 2000, p. 221.

14. Arnaud 2002.

15. Harner 2000, p. 80; *Nihon Keizai Shimbun* 2002d.

Notes to Chapter 14

1. The postal savings service had 371 trillion yen ($3 trillion) in deposits as of March 2001. Similarly, the *kanpo*—the postal life, casualty, and pension insurance business—had assets totaling about 210 trillion yen ($1.7 trillion) as of March 2000.

2. *Nikkei Weekly* 2001b.

3. Lincoln 2001b.

4. Tett 2002.

5. Taniguchi 2002.

6. During 1960–72, while consumer inflation averaged 5.8 percent, government-regulated interest rates ranged from 4 percent on three-month deposits to 5.5 percent on one-year deposits. In the first half of the 1970s a full 30 percent of the value of savings was wiped out by double-digit inflation. During the high-growth era, subsidized business investment drove high growth and therefore rising wages. What households lost as savers, they made up as wage earners. But, once the high-growth era ended, below-market interest rates fed anorexia.

7. Hartcher 1998, pp. 196–97; Schaede 2000, pp. 36–37; Vogel 1996, p. 180.

8. Hartcher 1998, pp. 161–67.

9. Weinberg 1996.

10. Kagami 2001; Statistics Bureau 2002f. The dividend payout rate has rebounded a bit in recent years, not because dividends are higher but because profits are lower.

11. Calder 1993, pp. 26–30. Kagami (2001) reports that, as late as 1935, the stock market provided 44 percent of all new financing for *zaibatsu* firms and 37 percent for non-*zaibatsu* ones.

12. Hanazaki and Horiuchi 2000.

13. Ishida 2001.

14. Patrick 2001, pp. 15–16.

15. Ibid., pp. 15–17.

16. Flath 2000, p. 275.

17. Some Japanese players tried to use internationalization as pressure for deregulation at home. In a prelude to the 1984 yen-dollar talks between the United States and Japan, Nomura Securities tried to enlist Washington's aid to get into the trust business—a preserve of the trust banks—via a joint venture with J.P. Morgan. The MOF did accede to Washington's request for foreign banks to get into the trust business, but only in alliance with Japanese trust banks, not Japanese securities houses. See Vogel 1996, p. 174 n.

18. In 1979 a few firms were allowed to issue unsecured bonds. In 1984 firms were allowed to issue equity-linked bonds (i.e., convertible and warrant bonds). In practice, only firms rated A or better have really been able to access the bond market. Moreover, these changes failed to free firms from dependence on the banks since most of these bonds involved some tie to a main bank. During the mid-1980s, 77 percent of all warrant bonds issued by Japanese firms in the Euromarket were guaranteed by banks. See Flath 2000, pp. 275–76; Miyajima 1998, pp. 49–53.

19. Akiysohi Horiuchi, as cited in Miyajima 1998, p. 57; also see p. 60.

20. See Vogel 1996, pp. 180–89, for an account of this struggle.

21. Ibid., p. 171; Schaede 2000, p. 184.

22. Before deregulation, brokers charged a fee of 1.1 percent for a trade of one million yen. Since deregulation, for face-to-face deals, the commission has dropped 10 percent, but commissions for telephone orders have dropped about 30 percent, and commissions for online orders are as much as 90 percent lower.

Notes to Chapter 15

1. *Nikkei Weekly* 2001c.

2. Ahmadjian 2001.

3. Kagami 2001. See Katz 1998a, pp. 79–80, for more on the way the 1930s and 1940s mobilization left long-lasting distortions.

4. Katz 1998a, pp. 76–77.

5. *Economist* 2001c.

6. While Canon may be a model for corporate strategy, it is hardly a role model for corporate governance. In a scoreboard created by Kathy Matsui, equity strategist at Goldman Sachs' Tokyo office, Canon came in only fiftieth among the top 362 firms. Moreover, Canon president Fujio Mitarai is a strong defender of the status quo on corporate governance issues, defending Shoei's management against the attempted takeover by MAC (see p. 237). Perhaps Canon's own performance shapes his perspective, but Canon enjoys an advantage that many of its brethren lack: 70 percent of its sales are made outside Japan. Global competition keeps its feet to the fire. See Matsui 2002, p. 27 and *Oriental Economist Report* 2002b, p. 10.

7. This is based on a briefing from Kenya Tachikawa of M&A Consulting.

8. That is, the number of new firms entering and old firms exiting divided by the total number of existing firms.

9. OECD 2001a, Chapter 7, "Productivity and Firm Dynamics."

10. The inordinate role played by firm turnover is remarkable even when one considers that firm turnover accounts for such a small share of GDP and employment turnover (only 8–10 percent).

11. For example, as of mid-2002, consolidated taxation would apply only to wholly owned subsidiaries, whereas consolidated accounting is much broader. Furthermore, the MOF planned to levy a 2 percent surcharge on firms choosing to use it.

12. Ishida 2001.

13. Koll 2001.

14. Interview with Porter in *Oriental Economist Report* 2001d.

15. *Nihon Kezai Shimbun* 2000e.

16. *Nikkei Weekly* 2001d.

17. Ostrom 1999. In the United States, among specialty retailers, five of the top ten in 1982 were replaced by 1994, with newcomers such as Circuit City and the Gap rising to the top.

18. Japan Fair Trade Commission 1999, p. 10.

19. Conversation with author.

20. See Katz 1998a, Chapter 6.

21. Sakakibara and Porter 2001

22. Sometimes industries with higher concentration show greater rivalry among the leaders. Where this is true, the export performance is enhanced, but it is the rivalry, not the size, that helps results.

23. For cross-shareholding trend, see Matsui 2002, p. 7.

24. Matsui 2002, p. 1.

25. See Upham 1998 for a dissection of the "nonlitigiousness" myth and an explanation of how it originated.

26. *Nihon Keizai Shimbun* 2002e.

27. *Nikkei Weekly* 2002b.

28. Mitchell 2002.

Notes to Chapter 16

1. Schaede 2000, p. 1.

2. OECD 1999b, p. 67.

3. Schaede 2000, p. 138.

4. JFTC 2002, p. 9. The 2001 total of 2,624 compares to 217 in 1997. In 1999 warnings had been issued to 429 liquor stores and 215 gasoline stations.

5. Japan Fair Trade Commission 2001, p. 14.

6. Nor does government tolerance of private anticompetitive action come under the purview of the WTO. For analysis and recommendations regarding the intersection of trade and competition issues, see International Competition Policy Advisory Committee 2000, Chapter 5.

7. *Nikkei Weekly* 2001f.

8. According to Schaede, these cases tend to be treated under Section 3 of the Anti-Monopoly Act, which governs "restraint of competition." However, fines are limited to a fixed percentage of the sales during the period of violation—6 percent for large firms. Even if a cartel raises prices 20 percent, the maximum fine is still 6 percent. There are no double or triple damages or punitive damages. So, even in the area of strictest enforcement, the disincentive to collude is minimal.

9. Schaede 2000, pp. 160–67. Beyond that, the JFTC chooses to deal with most unfair trade practices on an informal basis rather than launching a formal complaint.

10. Japan Fair Trade Commission 1999, p. 9; 2001, p. 3; private communication with Ulrike Schaede.

11. Schaede 2000, p. 170.

12. Japan Fair Trade Commission 1999, p. 13; 2001, p. 5.

13. Japan Fair Trade Commission 1999, pp. 2–7; 2001, p. 2; United States Trade Representative 2001, p. 221.

14. Japan Fair Trade Commission 1993, p. 15.

15. Japan Fair Trade Commission 1999, p. 14.

16. Schaede 2000, p. 110; United States Trade Representative 2001, p. 222.

Notes to Chapter 17

1. We used male employees for the comparison since the prevalence of part-time and temporary work among female employees skews those results.

2. Rebick 2001, p. 120.

3. See, for example, Pempel 1998, pp. 93–94.

4. Gordon 1998.

5. Genda and Rebick 2000, p. 89, report that, between 1991 and 1998, among large firms, the proportion of full-time male employees over the age of forty-five rose from 31 percent to 36 percent.

6. Rebick 2001, p. 90.

7. For details on 1990s downsizing, see Ahmadjian 2001.

8. This section summarizes Katz 2000.

9. OECD 1999a, pp. 58–59. Hamada 2002, p. 3. Robert Feldman had been an early advocate of this view and was cited in the OECD study. Similar analyses have appeared in publications by the International Monetary Fund and the Council on Foreign Relations. Feldman (2000) pointed out that if one looked at big corporations' recurring profits, 90 percent of the decline in ROA from 1985 to 1999 was due to the rise in the asset-to-sales ratio rather than a decline in profit margins (i.e., profit-to-sales ratios). We asked Feldman if this meant he was reconsidering his past emphasis on labor costs. He replied: "The reasons for the drop of ROA come from both the numerator [profits] and the denominator [assets]. All industries have suffered from excessive asset growth, which raises the denominator and thus lowers the ROA. Most industries have also suffered from wages outpacing productivity, so that profits did not rise as much as they should have. Thus, the numerator was suppressed, and the ROA held down. To put the entire burden on labor to solve the ROA problem would be unfair. To do so would take capital owners off the hook for bad oversight. To put all the burden on capital would be equally unfair, because depositors and life policy owners would take the hit for a malfunctioning labor market—which is not their fault."

10. Ministry of Finance 2001a. My thanks to Arthur Alexander for pointing out the change in the law. This does not necessarily imply agreement with the rest of my argument.

11. Value-added rather than sales is the proper measure because it eliminates all the double counting caused by payments to suppliers. GDP is a value-added concept.

12. In fact, there is a 78 percent positive correlation between the rate of wage growth and the profit share of value-added. If wages were the culprit, the correlation would have been negative.

13. ROA is really the combination of two factors: the ratio of profits to sales and the ratio of assets to assets. Dividing the first term by the second gives you ROA. Given the huge rise in the assets-to-sales figure, even a constant profits-to-sales figure means a decline in ROA. Assets-to-sales is the inverse of the sales-to-assets figure shown in Figure 15.1b.

14. McKinsey 2000, "Executive Summary," p. 6.

15. *Nihon Keizai Shimbun* 2002f and 2002g.

16. Statistics Bureau 2002e.

17. The average OECD country spends 2.7 percent of GDP on various labor market programs, from unemployment insurance to job retraining. Japan spends only 0.5 percent of GDP. The only other country to spend less than 1 percent of GDP on these programs is the United States, but the United States does spend 2.6 percent of GDP on income maintenance programs other than unemployment insurance, versus 0.9 percent for Japan. See DeWit and Steinmo 2002; Tanzi 2000.

Notes to Chapter 18

1. For a good collection of essays on the deregulation issue, see Gibney 1998.

2. Yayama 1998, pp. 97–102.

3. In part of Marunouchi, one of the prime business areas of central Tokyo, the ratio of floor space to the land plot can be no more than 1,000 percent.

4. DeWit and Steinmo 2002. The comparisons are for 1998.

5. McCormack 1996, p. 34.

6. Lincoln 2001a, pp. 175–76.

7. McCormack 2002, pp. 11, 18.

8. *Nikkei Weekly* 2001f.

9. McKinsey 2000, "Health Care," p. 17, Exhibit 20.

10. Ibid., p. 25, Exhibit 31. Since the prescription length for new drugs is shorter than for old ones, the patient has to come in more often, just to get a new prescription that, in the United States, would be done over the phone.

11. *Nikkei Weekly* 2001c.

12. McKinsey 2000, "Health Care," p. 26, Exhibit 32.

13. Leduc 2002.

14. McKinsey 2000. "Health Care," pp. 1, 8. For a contrary view, see Campbell 2002.

15. OECD 1999b, p. 43. EPA estimate cited in La Croix and Mak 2001, p. 236.

16. Quoted in *Nikkei Weekly* 2001e.

17. This is an assessment by METI officials themselves, according to Scalise 2002a, p. 5.

18. Government of Japan 1997.

19. See Katz 1998a, p. 31.

20. Cited in La Croix and Mak 2001, p. 222.

21. OECD 1999b, p. 18.

22. La Croix and Mak (2001, p. 232) make this point.

23. Unless otherwise noted, much of the data for the sections on transport, energy, and telecommunications come from La Croix and Mak 2001 and OECD 1999b.

24. Norwell 2001b.

25. *Oriental Economist Report* 2001e notes that as of March 2000, the interest-bearing debt of the remaining corporations totaled 115 trillion yen ($927 billion). This was supposedly more than offset by 197 trillion yen ($1.6 trillion) in assets. However, as with the JNR, Long-Term Credit Bank, and so many other cases, when settlement time comes, those assets may have the substance of cobwebs. The taxpayer will be stuck with the bill for decades of corrupt parasitism.

26. As of 1998, a single airline still had a monopoly on 75 percent of the routes in Japan. But the 25 percent on which there was competition included some of the most heavily traveled and lucrative routes.

27. Alexander 2000a.

28. Lincoln 2001a, p. 160. *Oriental Economist Report* 1999.

29. La Croix and Mak 2001, p. 223.

30. Japan Fair Trade Commission 2000.

31. For more on this issue, see Scalise 2002a and 2002b.

32. Japan Fair Trade Commission 2001b, pp. 1, 7–8.

Notes to Chapter 19

1. Koo 1998, pp. 172–73.

2. OECD 1999a, p. 153.

3. Ministry of Finance 2002e and private note from Andrew DeWit. Out of forty-five million tax filers in 1997, six million (13 percent) were below the threshold. Of another seven million taxpayers, three million didn't pay.

4. *Nikkei Weekly* 2002a.

5. Ishi and OECD, cited in DeWit and Steinmo 2002.

6. DeWit and Steinmo 2002.

Notes to Chapter 20

1. Cited in Johnson 1995, p. 212.

2. In an e-mail to the author, Len Schoppa wrote, "You are right that the PR segment has perpetuated division on the opposition side. Yet, Italy's system, which is very similar, has nevertheless created relatively unified *blocs* of parties competing for power. Some specific quirks of the Japanese system have played a particular role in preventing the system from producing *bloc* competition." See Cox and Schoppa 2002.

3. Horiuchi and Saito 2001.

4. E-mail communication from Horiuchi to the author; *Asahi Shimbun* 2000.

5. *Nikkei Weekly* 2001g.

6. DeWit and Steinmo 2002.

7. Horiuchi and Saito 2001.

Notes to Chapter 21

1. Mandel 2000. Krugman (2001b) wrote: "There is a distinct resemblance between what happened to Japan a decade ago and what was happening to the United States economy just a few weeks ago."

2. Katz 2002b.

3. Bureau of Labor Statistics 2002.

Notes to Chapter 22

1. The quote is from Summers 1989. Despite the sentiments in this article, during the first Clinton term (1993–96) Summers was a force for moderation regarding trade policy toward Japan.

2. When asked about U.S. efforts to prod Japan on reform, Edward Lincoln, a Brookings Institution economist and former special economic aide at the U.S. embassy in Tokyo, told *USA Today* in its March 3, 2000, edition, "Why should it be our business to make the Japanese more efficient?. . . I would say maybe it's time to just shut up and let the Japanese stew in their own juices."

3. Japanese withdrawal continued through at least 1999, when loans fell by 24 percent, compared to a mild 3 percent withdrawal by other banks. See Bank for International Settlements 2001.

4. Bruce Stokes made this argument during a panel discussion with the author. See also Stokes 2000.

5. Interview with author, 1994.

6. Cited in Ennis 2000. See also an interview with Richard Armitage in *The Oriental Economist Report*, April 2000, p. 3.

7. For more on Clinton's support of Obuchi against the reformers, see Katz 1998b.

8. See interview with Glenn Hubbard, chairman of Bush's Council of Economic Advisers, in Hubbard 2002a.

9. Katz 2002a.

10. See Erhlich's preface in Okubo 1996.

11. Schoppa 1997.

12. Schoppa 1997, Chapter 6. The split continues to this day.

13. Radin 1994, 1996, 2000.

14. Ministry of Public Management, Home Affairs, Posts and Telecommunications 2002. See Fisher 2000 and *Oriental Economist Report* 2000c on the outcome of the talks. See also *Nihon Keizai Shimbun* 2002f for more recent developments.

Note to Chapter 23

1. Reischauer 1957, pp. 316–17.

—Bibliography—

Ahmadjian, Christina. 2001. "Convergence and Continuity in Corporate Governance Reform in Japan." Speech at Columbia University, March 23.

Ahmadjian, Christina, and Patricia Robinson. 2001. *Safety in Numbers: Downsizing and the Deinstitutionalization of Permanent Employment in Japan.* Unpublished manuscript. October 2001.

Alexander, Arthur. 2000a. "Japan's Aviation Industry: Deregulation Advances on Broad Front." In *Japan Economic Institute Report*, Part A. May 26. At http://www.jei.org/Archive/JEIR00/0021A.pdf.

———. 2000b. "Prospects for the Japanese Economy: Looking Beyond the Next Quarter." In Japan Economic Institute Report. August 25. Part A, pg. 11. At http://www.jei.org/Archive/JEIR00/0033A.pdf.

American Chamber of Commerce in Japan. 2000a. *Making Trade Talks Work.* Tokyo: American Chamber of Commerce in Japan.

———. 2000b. "Improve the Tax System to Respond to the Internationalization of Business." September 29.

Anchordoguy, Marie. 2002. "U.S.-Japan Relations and Japan's Industrial Policy Toward Its Electronics Sector." Paper presented at the Conference "Japan and the U.S. Reconsidered" sponsored by the Economic Strategy Institute, Washington, D.C., January 2002.

Ando, Albert. 2000. "On the Japanese Economy and Japanese National Accounts." National Bureau of Economic Research report. At http://www.nber.org.

Armitage, Richard. 2000. Interview in *Oriental Economist Report,* April 2000, p. 3.

Arnaud, Regis. 2002. "Kansai Financial Firm Shows the Way." *Oriental Economist Report,* February 2002.

Asahi Shimbun. 1999a. "MOF Failed to Act on Illegal Loans." May 24.

———. 1999b. "Disgraced Banking 'Fox' Put in Charge of the Chicken Coop." June 1.

———. 2000. "Lower House Redistricting Must Ensure Vote Equality." August 16.

Asher, David, and Robert Dugger. 2000. *Could Japan's Financial Mount Fuji Blow Its Top?* MIT-Japan Project Working Paper 00-01 Cambridge: Massachusetts Institute of Technology. At http://web.mit.edu/mit-japan/Products/wp00-01.html May 2000.

Asia Wall Street Journal. 2001a. "Authorities Tell Shinsei to Ease Up." September 26.

———. 2001b. "Japanese Agency Orders Shinsei to Raise Lending." October 5.

———. 2001c. "Japanese Official Says His Criticism of Bank Wasn't Politically Motivated." November 8.

Atkinson, David. 2001a. *Totally Rethinking Japanese Asset Quality.* Goldman Sachs (Tokyo). July 18.

———. 2001b. *Japanese Bank Asset Quality.* Goldman Sachs (Tokyo). October 31.

Bank for International Settlements. 2001. *Consolidated International Banking Statistics,* assorted issues. At http://www.bis.org/publ/index.htm.

Bank of Japan. 2001a. "Deposits and Savings Rates (Banks)." At http://www.boj.or.jp/en/siryo/siryo_f.htm.

———. 2001b. "Flow of Funds." At http://www.boj.or.jp/en/siryo/siryo_f.htm.

————. 2002a. "Banking Accounts of Domestically Licensed Banks." At http://www.boj.or
.jp/en/siryo/siryo_f.htm.

————. 2002b. "Loans and Discounts Outstanding of Banking Accounts of Domestically
Licensed Banks by Interest Rate." At http://www.boj.or.jp/en/siryo/siryo_f.htm.

————. 2002c. "The Bond Market (Secondary Market)." At http://www.boj.or.jp/en/siryo/
siryo_f.htm.

————. 2002d. "Long-Term Data Series." At http://www.boj.or.jp/en/siryo/siryo_f.htm.

————. 2002e. "*Nikkei* Stock Average." At http://www2.boj.or.jp/en/dlong/etc/data/
ehstock.txt.

————. 2002f. "Principal Accounts of Foreign Banks." At http://www.boj.or.jp/en/siryo/
siryo_f.htm.

Bayoumi, Tamim. 2000a. "Where Are We Going? The Output Gap and Potential Growth."
In Tamim Bayoumi and Charles Collyns, eds., *Post-Bubble Blues: How Japan Responded
to the Asset Price Collapse*. Washington, D.C.: International Monetary Fund.

————. 2000b. "The Morning After: Explaining the Slowdown in Japanese Growth." In
Tamim Bayoumi and Charles Collyns, eds., *Post-Bubble Blues: How Japan Responded
to the Asset Price Collapse*. Washington, D.C.: International Monetary Fund.

Bayoumi, Tamim, and Charles Collyns, eds. 2000. *Post-Bubble Blues: How Japan Responded to the Asset Price Collapse*. Washington, D.C.: International Monetary Fund.

Bergsten, Fred, Takatoshi Ito, and Marcus Noland. 2001. *No More Bashing: Building a
New Japan-United States Economic Relationship*. Washington, D.C.: Institute for International Economics.

Booz, Allen and Hamilton. 1987. *Direct Foreign Investment in Japan: The Challenge for
Foreign Firms*. Tokyo: American Chamber of Commerce in Japan and the Council of the
European Business Community.

Bosworth, Barry. 1998. "The Asian Financial Crisis: What Happened and What We Can
Learn from It." *Brookings Review,* vol. 3 (summer), pp. 7–10.

Bureau of Labor Statistics. 2001. "Multifactor Productivity Trends, 1999." At http://
stats.bls.gov/news.release/prod3.nr0.htm.

————. 2002. "Multifactor Productivity Trends, 1999." At http://stats.bls.gov/news.release/
prod3.nr0.htm.

Cabinet Office. 2000. *System of National Accounts (SNA) Data on CD-ROM. Tokyo, Japan.*

————. 2001a. *System of National Accounts (SNA) Data on CD-ROM.* Tokyo, Japan

————. 2001b. "National Accounts Data for 1990–2000." At http://www.esri.cao.go.jp/en/
sna/h12-kaku/12kaku-snamenu-e.html.

————. 2001c. *Recent Economic Results from Regulation Reform.* At http://www5.cao.go.jp/
keizai3/2001/0629seisakukoka7-s.pdf.

————. 2002a. Web site. At http://www.cao.go.jp/index-e.html.

————. 2002b. National Accounts data. At http://www.esri.cao.go.jp/en/sna/menu.html.

————. 2002c. *A Changing Japan.* January 2002. At http://www5.cao.go.jp/shimon/2002/
0125pamphlet-e/menu.html.

Calder, Kent. 1988. *Crisis and Compensation: Public Policy and Political Stability in Japan*. Princeton: Princeton University Press.

————. 1993. *Strategic Capitalism: Private Business and Public Purpose in Japanese
Industrial Finance*. Princeton: Princeton University Press.

Campbell, John. 2002. "Health Care: International Comparison." NBR: U.S.–Japan Discussion Forum. At http://lists.nbr.org/japanforum/. June 6, 2002.

Carlile, Lonny, and Mark Tilton, eds. 1998. *Is Japan Really Changing Its Ways? Regulatory Reform and the Japanese Economy*. Washington, D.C.: Brookings Institution Press.

Census Bureau. 2002. "Foreign Trade Statistics." At http://www.census.gov/foreign-trade/
www/.

Cerulli Associates. 2000. Presentation at Japan Society of New York, September 10.

Council of Economic Advisers. 2001. *Economic Report of the President, 2001.* Washington, D.C.: U.S. Government Printing Office. At http://w3.access.gpo.gov/usbudget/fy2002/pdf/2001_erp.pdf.

———. 2002. *Economic Report of the President, 2002.* Washington, DC: U.S Government Printing Office.

Council on Economic and Fiscal Policy. 2002. *Structural Reform and Medium-Term Economic and Fiscal Perspectives.* January 25. At http://www5.cao.go.jp/shimon/2002/0125pamphlet-e/menu.html.

Council on Foreign Relations. 1999. *Report on Revised National Accounts on the Basis of 1990* (CD-ROM version). Tokyo: Economic Planning Agency.

———. 2000a. *Future Directions for U.S. Economic Policy Toward Japan.* Report of the Independent Task Force on Japan. New York: Council on Foreign Relations.

———. 2000b. *Report on Revised National Accounts on the Basis of 1990* (CD-ROM version). Tokyo: Economic Planning Agency.

Cox, Karen, and Leonard Schoppa. 2002. "Interaction Effects in Mixed-Member Electoral Systems: Theory and Evidence from Germany, Japan, and Italy." *Comparative Political Studies,* forthcoming.

Dattel, Eugene. 1994. *The Sun That Never Rose: The Inside Story of Japan's Failed Attempt at Global Financial Dominance.* Chicago: Probus.

Denison, Edward, and William Chung. 1976. "Economic Growth and Its Sources." In Hugh Patrick and Henry Rosovksy, eds., *Asia's New Giant.* Washington, D.C.: Brookings Institution.

DeWit, Andrew, and Sven Steinmo. 2002. "The Political Economy of Taxes and Redistribution in Japan." *Social Science Japan Journal* 5, no. 2.

Economic Planning Agency (EPA), Government of Japan. 1996. *Economic Survey of Japan, 1995–96: Reforms Usher in New Perspectives.* Tokyo: Economic Planning Agency.

———. 1999. System of National Accounts (SNA) Data on CD-ROM.

Economist. 2001a. "Fiddling While Marunouchi Burns." January 27.

———. 2001b. "Distress." March 1.

———. 2001c. "Lay-offs with No Sign of Revival." August 30.

Elder, Mark. 1998. "Why Buy High? The Political Economy of Protection for Intermediate Goods Industries in Japan." Prepared for delivery at the annual meeting of the American Political Science Association, Boston. September 3–6.

———. 2000. "Globalization and the Political Economy of Trade Protection in Japan in the 1990s: Steel vs. Autos." Prepared for delivery at the Midwest Political Science Association, Chicago. April 27–30.

Ennis, Peter. 2000. "US Foreign Policy Elite Ponders Future Ties with Tokyo." *Oriental Economist Report,* November 2000, p. 1.

Federal Reserve Board. 2002a. "Foreign Exchange Rates." At http://www.federalreserve.gov/releases/H10/hist.

———. 2002b. "Charge-off and Delinquency Rates at Commercial Banks." At http://www.federalreserve.gov/releases/ChargeOff.

Feldman, Robert. 1996. *The Golden Goose and the Silver Fox: Productivity, Aging and Japan's Economic Future.* Tokyo: Salomon Brothers.

———. 1998. "Japan: The Posen Program, Warts and All." *Global Economic Forum,* September 26. At http://www.msdw.com/gef.

———. 1999. "The Heart of the Matter." *Global Economic Forum,* August 27. At http://www.msdw.com/gef.

———. 2000. "ROA Whodunit" and "How Much More Restructuring?" *Global Economic Forum,* May 31, August 31, and September 4. At http://www.msdw.com/gef.

———. 2002. "Joe Friday and the CPI." *Global Economic Forum,* January 14. At http://www.msdw.com/gef.

Financial Services Agency. 2001. "The Status of Risk Management Loans of All Banks in Japan." At http://www.fsa.go.jp/news/newse.html.

————. 2002. "The Status of Risk Management Loans of All Banks in Japan." At http://www.fsa.go.jp/news/newse.html. (Only on the Japanese-language site.)

Fingleton, Eamonn. 1995. *Blindside: Why Japan Is Still on Track to Overtake the U.S. by the Year 2000.* Boston: Houghton Mifflin.

Fiorillo, James. 2001. "Just Giving the Business Away." Tokyo: ING Barings.

Fisher, Richard. 2000. Interview in *Oriental Economist Report,* June 2000, pp. 6–7.

Flath, David. 2000. *The Japanese Economy.* Oxford: Oxford University Press.

Fulford, Benjamin. 2002. "The Panic Spreads." *Forbes,* February 18.

Genda, Yuji, and Marcus Rebick. 2000. "Japanese Labour in the 1990s: Stability and Stagnation." *Oxford Review of Economic Policy* 16, no. 2.

Gibney, Frank, ed. 1998. *Unlocking the Bureaucrat's Kingdom: Deregulation and the Japanese Economy.* Washington, D.C.: Brookings Institution.

Gordon, Andrew. 1998. "The Invention of Japanese-Style Labor Management." In Stephen Vlastos, ed., *Mirror of Modernity: Invented Traditions of Modern Japan.* Berkeley: University of California Press.

Government of Japan. 1997. *The Program for Economic Structure Reform* (English summary). Tokyo: Government of Japan.

Grier, Jean. 2001. "Japan's Regulation of Large Retail Stores: Political Demands Versus Economic Interests." *Journal of International Economic Law* 22, no. 1.

Hamada, Koichi. 2002. "Can We See the Light Through the Tunnel?" Paper prepared for the Philip Trezise Memorial Symposium on the Japanese Economy. The Brookings Institution, Washington, DC. April 8–9. At http://www.brook.edu/dybdocroot/fp/proects/trezise/hamada_2002.pdf.

Hanazaki, Masaharu, and Akiyoshi Horiuchi. 2000. "Is Japan's Financial System Efficient?" *Oxford Review of Economic Policy* 16, no. 2.

Harner, Stephen. 2000. *Japan's Financial Revolution: How American Firms Are Profiting.* Armonk, N.Y.: M.E. Sharpe.

Hartcher, Peter. 1998. *The Ministry: How Japan's Most Powerful Institution Endangers World Markets.* Boston: Harvard Business School Press.

Hatakeyama, Noboru. 2001. Op-ed article in *Mainichi Shimbun,* January 28.

Hatzichronoglou, Thomas. 1999. *The Globalisation of Industry in the OECD Countries.* Paris: OECD. At http://www.oecd.org//dsti/sti/prod/sti_wp.htm.

Horiuchi, Yusaka, and Jun Saito. 2001. *Electoral Reform and the Distribution of Public Expenditures: Evidence from Japan.* Paper presented at the annual meeting of the American Political Science Association, San Francisco, CA. July 19.

Hubbard, Glenn. 2002a. Interview in *Oriental Economist Report,* January 2002, pp. 8–9.

————. 2002b. " Impediments to Growth in Japan." Speech given at Conference on Structural Impediments to Growth in Japan in Tokyo Japan. March 19.

Ibison, David. 2002. "It's a Banking Business, But Not As the Japanese Know It." *Financial Times,* August 5, p. 12.

International Competition Policy Advisory Committee. 2000. *Final Report.* Washington, D.C.: U.S. Justice Department Antitrust Division.

International Monetary Fund. 1998. "Japan's Economic Crisis and Policy Options." In *World Economic Outlook,* May. At http://www.imf.org/external/pubs/ft/weo/weo0598/index.htm.

————. 1999. "Divergences in Growth Performance Among the United States, Europe, and Japan: Long-Run Trends or Cyclical Differences?" In *World Economic Outlook.* October. At http://www.imf.org/external/pubs/ft/weo/1999/02/index.htm.

————. 2000a. *World Economic Outlook.* May. At http://www.imf.org/external/pubs/ft/weo/2000/01/index.htm.

———. 2000b. "Divergences in Growth Performance Among the United States, Europe, and Japan: Long-Run Trends of Cyclical Differences?" In *World Economic Outlook.*

———. 2001a. "Annex 1: Ongoing Weaknesses in Japan's Corporate and Financial Sectors." *International Capital Markets.* August. At http://www.imf.org/external/pubs/ft/icm/2001/01/eng/index.htm.

———. 2001b. *World Economic Outlook.* December. At http://www.imf.org/external/pubs/ft/weo/2001/03/index.htm.

———. 2002. *World Economic Outlook.* April. At http://www.imf.org/external/pubs/ft/weo/2002/01/index.htm.

Ishida, Mamoru. 2001. "Corporate Governance in Japan-Theory, Practice and the Future." Paper presented at Proceedings of ICM 2001, Xi'an, China, May.

Ito, Takatoshi. 1999. Op-ed article in *London Financial Times,* October 19.

Japan Automobile Manufacturers Association. 2002. Statistics. At http://www.japanauto.com/statistics.

Japan Bank for International Cooperation. 2001. *JBIC Survey: The Outlook for Foreign Direct Investment.* Tokyo, Japan.

Japan Center for Economic Research. *Long-term Forecast*, various issues, 1998, 2000, and 2001. At http://www.jcer.or.jp/eng/index.html.

———. 1998. "Japan's Balance Sheet in 2025—Long-term Economic Projection." At http://www.jcer.or.jp/eng/index.html.

Japan Economic Institute. 2000a. "Long-Term Prospects for Japan in a Comparative Economic and Political Context." Interview with Charles Wolf of RAND Corporation. *JEI Report* 26A, July 7.

———. 2000b. August 25.

Japan Fair Trade Commission. 1993. "Executive Summary." In *A Fact Finding Survey of Industrial Sector Transactions in Regard to the Flow of Flat Glass.* Tokyo: Japan Fair Trade Commission.

———. 1999. *Annual Report on Competition Policy, January–December 1999.* At http://www.jftc.go.jp/e-page/report/annual/CLP99HP.pdf.

———. 2000. *Competition Policy in the Telecommunications Sector.* June 12. At http://www.jftc.go.jp/e-page/report/survey/2000/tuusin.html.

———. 2001a. *Promotion of Regulatory Reform and the FTC's Position on Competition Policy.* At http://www.jftc.go.jp/e-page/report/survey/2001/20010330RR.pdf.

———. 2001b. *Deregulation and Competition Policy in Public Utilities Sector.* At http://www.jftc.go.jp/e-page/report/survey/2001/20010110deregulation.pdf.

———. 2002. *Recent Activities of the Fair Trade Commission.* June. At http://www.ftc.go.jp/e-page/Recent/0206recent.pdf.

Japan Productivity Center for Socio-Economic Development. 2002. *Indexes of Labour Productivity by Industry.* At http://www.stat.go.jp/english/1431–03.htm.

Japan Securities Research Institute. 1998. *Report on Japan's Stock Price Level.* Tokyo: Japan Securities Research Institute.

Japan Weekly Monitor. 1999. "MOF Norms Led LTCB to Dress Up Balance-Sheet Figures." May 17.

Jiji Press. 1999. "Miyazawa Admits MOF's Responsibility for Funds Lost on NCB." July 26.

Johnson, Chalmers. 1995. *Japan: Who Governs?* New York: Norton.

Kanno, Masaaki. 2002. "Japan Averts Crisis for Now." In *Global Data Watch.* J.P. Morgan (Tokyo), January 11.

Kagami, Shigeo. 2001. "Reforming Corporate Governance in Japan." Heidrick & Struggles International, April 17.

Katz, Richard. 1997. "Japan's Self-Defeating Trade Policy: Mainframe Economics in a PC World." *Washington Quarterly.* March. Washington: Center for Strategic and International Studies.

————. 1998a. *Japan: The System That Soured—The Rise and Fall of the Japanese Economic Miracle.* Armonk, N.Y.: M.E. Sharpe.

————. 1998b. "Japan's Slow Road to Reform." *Christian Science Monitor,* September 29.

————. 1999. "FSA—Factionalized Supervisory Agency." *International Economy Magazine,* May–June.

————. 2000. "Japan's Declining ROA: Excessive Wages or Excess Assets?" Paper presented at the Japan Economic Seminar, Columbia University, New York City. November 18.

————. 2001a. Review of *Why Did Japan Stumble. Journal of Japanese Studies* 27, no. 1.

————. 2001b. "Reading Yanagisawa's Mind." *Oriental Economist Report,* August, p. 7.

————. 2002a. "Washington Not Seeking Weaker Yen." *Oriental Economist Report,* January, p. 7.

————. 2002b. "Limited Damage." *Oriental Economist Report,* August, p. 3.

Katz, Richard, and Adam Posen. 1998. Debate on Japan's fiscal policy in *International Economy Magazine,* November–December.

Keizai Koho Center. 2002. *Japan 2002: An International Comparison.* At http://www.kkc.or.jp/english/activities/publications/aic2002.pdf.

Kobayashi, Keiichiro. 2001. "Miyakodayori 14: Debt Disorganization—Part 2: Policies and Scenarios." Research Institute of Economy, Trade and Industry (RIETI), Tokyo, March 19.

Koll, Jesper. 2001. "Japan's Restructuring Alive and Well." Merrill Lynch (Tokyo), September 6.

Koo, Richard. 1998. "The Land Factor: An Economic Disaster." In Frank Gibney, ed., *Unlocking the Bureaucrat's Kingdom: Deregulation and the Japanese Economy.* Washington, D.C.: Brookings Institution.

————. 2001. "The Japanese Economy in Balance Sheet Recession." *Business Economics,* April.

Kregel, J.A. 1999. "Krugman on the Liquidity Trap: Why Inflation Won't Bring Recovery In Japan." Manuscript.

Krugman, Paul. 1997. "What's Wrong With Japan?" Op-ed article in *Nihon Keizai Shimbun.* At http://web.mit.edu/krugman/www/nikkei.html.

————. 1998a. "Setting Sun—Japan: What Went Wrong?" June 1998. At http://web.mit.edu/krugman/www/jpage.html.

————. 1998b. "Japan's Trap." May 1998. At http://web.mit.edu/krugman/www/jpage.html.

————. 1998c. "Further Notes on Japan's Liquidity Trap." June 1998. At http://web.mit.edu/krugman/www/jpage.html.

————. 1998d. "It's Baaack! Japan's Slump and the Return of the Liquidity Trap." *Brookings Papers on Economic Activity,* no. 2. At http://web.mit.edu/krugman/www/jpage.html.

————. 2001a. "Purging the Rottenness." *New York Times,* April 25.

————. 2001b. "The Fear Economy." *New York Times,* September 30.

Kuttner, Kenneth, and Adam Posen. 2001. "The Great Recession: Lessons for Macroeconomic Policy from Japan." *Brookings Papers on Economic Activity,* no. 2 (October 18, 2001, version).

La Croix, Sumner, and James Mak. 2001. "Regulatory Reform in Japan: The Road Ahead." In Magnus Blomstrom, Byron Gangnes, and Sumner La Croix, eds., *Japan's New Economy: Continuity and Change in the Twenty-First Century.* Oxford: Oxford University Press.

Lawrence, Robert, and David Weinstein. 1999. "Trade and Growth: Import-Led or Export-Led? Evidence from Japan and Korea." National Bureau of Economic Research Working Paper 7264.

Leduc, Benoit. 2002. "Health Care: Prescription Drugs." NBR: U.S.–Japan Discussion Forum. At http://lists.nbr.org/japanforum. May 7, 2002.

Lincoln, Edward. 1999. *Troubled Times: U.S.–Japan Trade Relations in the 1990s*. Washington, D.C.: Brookings Institution.
———. 2001a. *Arthritic Japan: The Slow Pace of Economic Reform*. Washington, D.C.: Brookings Institution.
———. 2001b. "Time to End Postal Savings." *Sentaku*, June 2.
Makin, John. 2002. "Japan in Depression." *Economic Outlook* (American Enterprise Institute), January.
Mandel, Michael. 2000. *The Coming Internet Depression: Why the High-Tech Boom Will Go Bust, Why the Crash Will Be Worse than You Think, and How to Prosper Afterwards*. New York: Basic Books.
Matsui, Kathy. 2002. *Corporate Governance: A Quiet Revolution?* Goldman Sachs, Tokyo. July 5.
McCormack, Gavan. 1996. *The Emptiness of Japanese Affluence*. Armonk, N.Y.: M.E. Sharpe.
———. 2002. "Breaking the Iron Triangle." *New Left Review*, January–February.
McKinsey Global Institute. 1992. *Service Sector Productivity*. Washington, D.C.: McKinsey Global Institute.
———. 1993. *Manufacturing Productivity*. Washington, D.C.: McKinsey Global Institute.
———. 1996. *Capital Productivity*. Washington, D.C.: McKinsey Global Institute.
———. 2000. *Why the Japanese Economy Is Not Growing: Micro Barriers to Productivity Growth*. At http://mgi.mckinsey.com/mgi/japanese.asp.
———. 2001. *U.S. Productivity, 1995–2001*. At http://www.mckinsey.com/knowledge/mgi/reports/productivity.asp.
Milner, Helen. 1988. *Resisting Protectionism: Global Industries and the Politics of International Trade*. Princeton: Princeton University Press.
Ministry of Economy, Trade and Industry (METI). 2002a. "Statistics." At http://www.meti.go.jp/english/statistics/index.html
———. 2002b. "Census of Manufactures." At http://www.stat.go.jp/english/1431–07.htm.
———. 2002c. "Quarterly Survey of Japanese Business Activities, April–June 2000." At http://www.meti.go.jp/english/statistics/index.html.
Ministry of Finance. 2001a. "Financial Statements Statistics of Corporations by Industry." http://www.mof.go.jp/english/ssc/historical.htm.
———. 2001b. *Highlights of the Budget for Fiscal Year 2002*. At http://www.mof.go.jp/english/budget/e011221.pdf.
———. 2002a. "Foreign Exchange Reserves." At http://www.mof.go.jp/english/e1c006.htm.
———. 2002b. "Balance of Payments." At http://www.mof.go.jp/e1c004.htm.
———. 2002c. "Trade Statistics." At http://www.mof.go.jp/english/1c015f1e.htm.
———. 2002d. "Foreign Direct Investment." At http://www.mof.go.jp/english/e1c008.htm.
———. 2002e. "Japanese Tax System" (1999 edition). At http://www.mof.go.jp/english/zei/report2/zc001a.htm.
Ministry of Health, Labor, and Welfare (MHLW). 1999. *White Paper on Labour*. At http://www.mhlw.go.jp/english/wp/wp-l/index.html.
———. 2002a. "Consumer Price Index." At http://www.stat.go.jp/english/data/cpi/1581.htm.
———. 2002b. "Monthly Labour Survey." At http://www.mhlw.go.jp/english/database/db-l/index.html.
———. 2002c. "Foreign Exchange Reserves." At http://www.mof.go.jp/english/e1c006.htm
———. 2002d. "Persons Who Changed Jobs." At http://jin.jcic.or.jp/stat/stats/09LAB71.html.
Ministry of International Trade and Industry (MITI). 1998. "Highlights of the 27th Survey of Overseas Business Activities of Japanese Companies." At http://www.miti.go.jp/english/statistics/index.html.
———. 1999a. "Summary of the 1999 Survey of Overseas Business Activities." At http://www.miti.go.jp/english/statistics/index.html.

————. 1999b. "Quarterly Survey of Japanese Business Activities, Statistics." At http://www.miti.go.jp/english/statistics/index.html.

————. 2000. "Quarterly Survey of Japanese Business Activities, April–June 2000." At http://www.meti.go.jp/english/statistics/index.html.

Ministry of Public Management, Home Affairs, Posts and Telecommunications. 2002. "Information and Communications in Japan. White Paper 2002." At http://www.johotsusintokei.soumu.go.jp/whitepaper/eng/WP2002/2002-whitepaper.pdf.

Mitchell, Arthur. 2002. "A Proxy Fight in Tokyo." *Asia Wall Street Journal.* June 4.

Miura, Mari. 1999. "Japan in Hard Times: The SSJ Forum Debate on the Japanese Political Economy." *Social Science Japan Newsletter,* December. At http://web.iss.u-tokyo.ac.jp/newslet/SSJ17/SSJ17.pdf.

Miyajima, Hideaki. 1998. "The Impact of Deregulation on Corporate Governance and Finance." In Lonny Carlile and Mark Tilton, eds., *Is Japan Really Changing Its Ways? Regulatory Reform and the Japanese Economy.* Washington, D.C.: Brookings Institution Press.

Mizuho Securities. 2002. "Japanese Stock Market-Review of Investor Activities." At http://www.mizuho-sc.com/english/ebond/equity/trends.html.

Mizuno, Atsushi. 2001. "Fixed Income Morning Memo," Deutsche Bank Group, March 27.

Moody's Investors Service. 2001. *Japanese Life Insurance: 2001 Industry Outlook.*

————. 2002. "Japan: A Rating Agency Perspective 2002." Speech by Vincent Truglia at a conference sponsored by Nomura Securities in Kyoto, Japan. April 11.

Morgan Stanley. 2000. *Global Economic Forum,* December 11. At http://www.msdw.com/gef.

Morishima, Michio. 2000. "Why Do I Expect Japan to Collapse." In Craig Freedman, ed., *Why Did Japan Stumble? Causes and Cures.* Cheltenham, UK: Edward Elgar.

Morsink, James, and Tamim Bayoumi. 2000. "Monetary Policy Transmission in Japan." In Tamim Bayoumi and Charles Collyns, eds., *Post-Bubble Blues: How Japan Responded to Asset Price Collapse.* Washington, D.C.: International Monetary Fund.

Nakagawa, Shinobu, and Kazuo Oshima. 2000. "Does a Decrease in the Real Interest Rate Actually Stimulate Personal Consumption?" Working Paper series. At http://www.boj.or.jp/en/ronbun/ronbun_f.htm.

Nihon Keizai Shimbun. 2000a. "Foreign Firms Struggle to Win Individual Assets." July 3.

————. 2000b. "Report Says LTCB Had Only Itself to Blame." August 21.

————. 2000c. "BOJ Pegs Potential Econ Growth at Measly 1 Percent." October 28.

————. 2000d. "Investment Funds Still Lack Public Trust." November 27.

————. 2000e. "Market Share Yet to Show Effect of Restructuring." July 14.

————. 2000f. "Analysis: Industries Divided over Call for Import Restrictions." November 8.

————. 2000g. "Spending on Elderly Welfare Programs to Quadruple by Fiscal Year 2025." October 8.

————. 2000h. "Debt Payback Exceeds Borrowing at 70 percent of Listed Firms." December 17.

————. 2000i. "Report Says LTCB Had Only Itself to Blame." August 21.

————. 2000j. "Industries Divided over Call for Import Restrictions." November 8.

————. 2001a. "Goldman Sachs Tops List of M&A Advisers." January 4.

————. 2001b. "Insurance Sector Gains Foreign Flavor." March 5.

————. 2001c. "Japanese Firms Appointing More Outside Directors." July 16.

————. 2001d. "Foreign Investors Lay Claim to Big Chunk of Local Stocks." July 2.

————. 2001e. "Policyholdings Fall 2.1 percent at Life Insurers." June 9.

————. 2001f. "FTC Guideline Says Refusal of Power Supply Illegal." November 16.

————. 2001g. "Toshiba to Shift All Domestic TV Production to China." March 18.

————. 2001h. "Automakers Boost Overseas Output 8.8 percent in 2000." March 27.

————. 2001i. "Pension Bills Give Firms New Options." July 2.

————. 2001j. "Record 177 Employee Pension Plans Trim Benefits." June 8.

————. 2001k. "Banks Miss Impending Corporate Failures in Loan Assessments." June 26.

————. 2001l. "Bad Debt Problem Keeps Getting Worse." February 5.

————. 2001m. "Credit Guarantee Bodies Repay 1 Trillion Yen in Failed Firms' Debt." April 28.

————. 2001n. "29 Trillion Yen in Loan Guarantees Extended by Govt Program: METI." April 20.

————. 2001o. "Economic Reform Should Focus on Free Trade." May 7.

————. 2001p. "Nikko Salomon Lead-Manages Most Stock Offerings in FY 2000." May 9.

————. 2002a. "Takenaka to Mull Cutting Top Income Tax Rate." January 20.

————. 2002b. "Troubled Banks Should Receive Public Funds: Takenaka." February 23.

————. 2002c. "Supermarkets Reduce Floor Space, Outlets Amid Deflation." June 27.

————. 2002d. "Foreign Life Insurers' Japan Market Share Tops 10% in FY 01." July 27.

————. 2002e. "Tokyo Style Investors Took Long-Term View." July 17.

————. 2002f. "Telecom Council Proposes Halving NTT Interconnection Fee." August 1.

————. 2002g. "Govt Mulls Trimming Job Insurance Benefits for Elderly." June 9.

————. 2002h. "Total Unemployment Insurance Benefits May Fall 30%: METI." June 11.

Nikkei Weekly. 2000a. "Manufacturers Rushing to Slash Excess Capacity." June 12.

————. 2000b. " Textile Manufacturers to Seek Protection from Chinese Imports." December 25.

————. 2000c. "Unlikely Trendsetter Uniqlo Forces Retail Giants to Adapt." April 24.

————. 2001a. "Foreigners Breathe Life into Japan Inc." January 15.

————. 2001b. "State-Run Lenders Lock up Loan Markets." October 1.

————. 2001c. "No Method to Medical Cost Madness." November 5.

————. 2001d. "Time Is Ripe for Spinoffs in True Sense." October 15.

————. 2001e. "Past Performance Dogs Deregulation Efforts." September 17.

————. 2001f. "Family Ties Fatten Public Corporations." August 6.

————. 2001g. "Foreign Brokers Upset at Stricter Inspections." September 24.

————. 2000h. "City Dwellers Want LDP to Pay Up." June 4.

————. 2002a. "Industry Exodus to China Heightens Domestic Fears." January 14.

————. 2002b. "Institutions Threaten Corporate Governance." July 22.

Norwell, Julie. 2001a. "Civil Trade War: Trade Becomes a Domestic Issue in Japan." *Oriental Economist Report*, July, p. 13.

————. 2001b. "Koizumi Struggles to Deliver on Reform Promises." *Oriental Economist Report*, December, p. 7.

Okina, Kunio. 1999. "Monetary Policy Under Zero Inflation—A Response to Criticisms and Questions Regarding Monetary Policy." In "Research Papers Released by Institute for Monetary and Economic Studies." At http://www.boj.or.jp/en/ronbun/ronbun_f.htm.

Okubo, Sumiye. 1996. *Prospects for Growth in Japan in the 21st Century*. Washington, D.C.: Department of Commerce.

Organization for Economic Cooperation and Development. 1996. "Employment Adjustment, Workers and Unemployment." In *Employment Outlook*. Paris: OECD.

————. 1997. "Is Job Insecurity on the Increase in OECD Countries?" In *Employment Outlook*. Paris: OECD.

————. 1999a. *Economic Survey of Japan*. Paris: OECD.

————. 1999b. *Regulatory Reform in Japan 1999*. Paris: OECD.

————. 2000a. *OECD Economic Outlook*. May. Paris: OECD.

————. 2000b. *OECD Economic Outlook*. December. Paris: OECD.

————. 2000c. *Economic Survey of Japan*. Paris: OECD.

————. 2000d. *Recent Trends in FDI*. Paris: OECD.

————. 2001a. *OECD Economic Outlook*. June. Paris: OECD.

———. 2001b. *Economic Survey of Japan.* December. Paris: OECD.

Oriental Economist Report. 1999. "Big Three Airlines Gang Up on the New Boy." February, p. 8.

———. 2000a. "Falling Contractors." August, p. 13.

———. 2000b. "Behind Japan's Declining ROA." July, pp. 7–8.

———. 2000c. "Telecom Deal: A Big Deal." August, p. 16.

———. 2001a. "The Anesthesia Option." March, pp. 9–11.

———. 2001b. "Forecasting Reality." July, p. 9

———. 2001c. "Interview with David Asher." July, p. 10.

———. 2001d. "Interview with Michael Porter." May, p. 11.

———. 2001e. "Liquidate or Privatize: Semi-public Companies Need Reform." August, p. 11.

———. 2001f. "Say It Ain't So." December, p. 14.

———. 2001g. "Shooting the Messenger." October, p. 14.

———. 2002a. "Conspiracy Theories." April, p. 14.

———. 2002b. "Diamond in the Rough." August, p. 10.

Ostrom, Douglas. 1999. *The Search for New Corporate Superstars: Japanese Firm Mobility in the 1990s.* Japan Economic Institute Report no. 12A. March 26.

Oyama, Tsuyoshi. 1999. "Stagnation and Structural Adjustments of Nonmanufacturing Industries During the 1990s." Tokyo: Bank of Japan. At http://www.boj.or.jp/en/ronbun/ronbun_f.htm.

Patrick, Hugh. 2001. "From Cozy Regulation to Competitive Markets: The Regime Shift of Japan's Financial System." Columbia University Center on Japanese Economy and Business Working Paper no. 186. At http://www.gsb.columbia.edu/japan/pdf/wp186.pdf.

Pempel, T.J. 1998. *Regime Shift: Comparative Dynamics of the Japanese Political Economy.* Ithaca, N.Y.: Cornell University Press.

Petri, Peter. 1991. "Market Structure, Comparative Advantage, and Japanese Trade Under the Strong Yen." In Paul Krugman, ed., *Trade with Japan: Has the Door Opened Wider?* Chicago: University of Chicago Press.

Porter, Michael. 1990. *The Competitive Advantage of Nations.* New York: Free Press.

Porter, Michael, Hirotaka Takeuchi, and Mariko Sakakibara. 2000. *Can Japan Compete?* New York: Perseus Press.

Posen, Adam. 1998. *Restoring Japan's Economic Growth.* Washington, D.C.: Institute for International Economics.

———. 2001. "Japan 2001—Decisive Action or Financial Panic." IIE Policy Brief Number 01-4. March. At http://www.iie.com/policybriefs/news01-4.htm.

———. 2002. "The Looming Japanese Crisis." IIE Policy Brief Number PB02-5. May. At http://www.iie.com/policybriefs/news02-5.pdf.

Radin, Robin. 1994. "Negotiating Principles for Opening Japan's Financial Markets." Tokyo: CS First Boston.

———. 1996. "The Regulation and Deregulation of Japan's Financial System." Harvard lecture, May 2.

———. 2000. "Japan's Big Bang: Historical Context and Future Prospects." Harvard lecture, March 10.

Ramaswamy, Ramana. 2000. "Explaining the Slump in Japanese Business Investment." In Tamim Bayoumi and Charles Collyns, eds., *Post-Bubble Blues: How Japan Responded to Asset Price Collapse.* Washington, D.C.: International Monetary Fund.

Rebick, Marcus. 2001. "Japanese Labor Markets: Can We Expect Significant Change?" In Magnus Blomstrom, Byron Gangnes, and Sumner La Croix, ed., *Japan's New Economy: Continuity and Change in the Twenty-First Century.* Oxford: Oxford University Press.

Reed, John. 2000. Speech at the New York Japan Society, May 2.

Reischauer, Edwin. 1957. *The United States and Japan.* New York: Viking Press.

Sakakibara, Mariko, and Michael Porter. 2001. "Competing at Home to Win Abroad: Evidence from Japanese Industry." *Review of Economics and Statistics* 83, no. 2, pp. 310–22.

Scalise, Paul. 2002a. *Electricity Deregulation in Japan.* Tokyo: Dresdner Kleinwort Wasserstein.

———. 2002b. *The Powers That Be.* Tokyo: Dresdner Kleinwort Wasserstein.

Schaede, Ulrike. 2000. *Cooperative Capitalism: Self-Regulation, Trade Associations, and the Antimonopoly Law in Japan.* Oxford: Oxford University Press.

Schoppa, Leonard. 1997. *Bargaining with Japan: What American Pressure Can and Cannot Do.* New York: Columbia University Press.

———. 2000. Unpublished memo analyzing June 2000 Lower House elections.

Shirakawa, Masaaki. 2000. "Monetary Policy Cannot Substitute for Structural Policy," January 29. At http://www.boj.or.jp/en/ronbun/kwp00e01.htm.

Siegel, Jeremy. 2002. "The Dividend Deficit." *Wall Street Journal,* February 13.

Singer, Jason. 2002. "Foreign Banks Encroach on Nomura's Slot as Japan's Most Powerful Investment Bank." *Wall Street Journal,* January 8.

Smitka, Michael. 1992. "Decline of the Japanese Automotive Industry: Domestic and International Implications." Working Paper no. 65, Center of Japanese Economy and Business, Graduate School of Business, Columbia University, September.

Standard & Poor's. 2000. "Bank of Japan's Inevitable Interest Rate Hike May Pose Short-Term Pressure, Longer-Term Benefits." August 10.

Statistics Bureau. 2002a. At http://www.stat.go.jp/english/1-1.htm.

———. 2002b. *Labor Force Survey.* At http://www.stat.go.jp/english/data/roudou/154.htm.

———. 2002c. *Imports by Commodity* and *Imports by Country.* At http://www.stat.go.jp/english/1431-12.htm.

———. 2002d. *Social Security.* At http://www.stat.go.jp/english/data/nenkan/1431-18.htm.

———. 2002e. *Unemployment Insurance.* At http://www.stat.go.jp/english/data/geppou/index.htm#p.

———. 2002f. *Profit and Loss and Disposition of Profit.* Table 5-11b at http://www.stat.go.jp/english/data/nenkan/1431-05.htm.

Stokes, Bruce. 2000. *A New Beginning: Recasting the U.S.–Japan Economic Relationship.* Washington, D.C.: Council on Foreign Relations.

Summers, Lawrence. 1989. "The Ishihara-Morita Brouhaha." *International Economy,* December.

Summers, Robert, and Alan Heston. 1995. *Penn World Tables, Mark 5.6a.* Diskette version from National Bureau of Economic Research in Cambridge, Mass.

Taniguchi, Tomohiko. 2002. "Japan Financial Services Agency: A Bully and a Manipulator." March 11, 2002.

Tanzi, Vito. 2000. *Globalization and the Future of Social Protection.* International Monetary Fund Working Paper WP/00/12.

Terazawa, Tatsuo. 2001. "Monetary Policy: A Drug Or Anesthesia?" *Miyakoyadori 10.* Research Institute for Economy, Trade and Industry. February 20.

Tett, Gillian. 2002. "Short-tempered in Tokyo." *Financial Times.* March 5.

Tilton, Mark. 1998. "Japan's Steel Cartel and the 1998 Steel Export Surge." Washington, D.C.: Japan Information Access Project. At http://www.nmjc.org/NMJC-HTML/jiap/Tilton/TiltonFinalPaper.html

Toyo Keizai. 2000. "Who Can Judge NTT?" July 22, pp. 84–88.

Ueda, Kazuo. 1999a. "Why the BOJ Held the Line." *Wall Street Journal,* September 22, p. 10.

———. 1999b. "Japan's Experience with Zero Interest Rates." *Journal of Money, Credit and Banking,* November 1.

United States Trade Representative. 2001. *Foreign Trade Barriers*. At http://www.ustr.gov/html/2001_japan.pdf.

Upham, Frank. 1998. "Weak Legal Consciousness as an Invented Tradition." In Stephen Vlastos, ed., *Mirror of Modernity: Invented Traditions of Modern Japan*. Berkeley: University of California. 1998.

U.S. State Department. 2001. "Japan's Changing FDI and Corporate Environment." At http://www.state.gov/p/eap/rls/index.cfm?docid=4049.

Uriu, Robert. 1996. *Troubled Industries: Confronting Economic Change in Japan*. Ithaca, N.Y.: Cornell University Press.

van Ark, Bart. 1995. "Manufacturing Prices, Productivity and Labor Costs in Economies." *Monthly Labor Review,* July, pp. 56–73.

van Ark, Bart, and Dirk Pilat. 1993. "Productivity Levels in Germany, Japan, and the United States: Differences and Causes." *Brookings Papers on Economic Activity: Microeconomics* 2. Washington, D.C.: Brookings Institution.

Vestal, James. 1993. *Planning for Change: Industrial Policy and Japanese Economic Development: 1945–90*. New York: Oxford University Press.

Vlastos, Stephen, ed. 1998. *Mirror of Modernity: Invented Traditions of Modern Japan*. Berkeley: University of California.

Vogel, Steven. 1996. *Freer Markets, More Rules: Regulatory Reform in Advanced Industrial Countries*. Ithaca, N.Y.: Cornell University Press.

Wall Street Journal. 2001a. "Japan's Bailout Plan Puts New Twist on Previously Unsuccessful Tactics." March 5.

———. 2001b. "Japan Must Finish Stalled Reforms, Many Say, or Risk Losing Its Might." March 16.

———. 2001c. "Japan's Aiwa Plans to Halve Work Force, Close 8 Plants." March 27.

———. 2002. "Japan Construction Reform May Lack Perceived Force." March 6.

Washington Post. 1998. "Japanese Punish Finance Officials; Employees Were Wined, Dined by Firms." April 28.

Weinberg, Neil. 1996. "Shortchanged Investors." *Forbes,* July 15, p. 54.

Weinstein, David. 2001a. "Historical, Structural and Macroeconomic Perspectives on the Japanese Economic Crisis." In Magnus Blomstrom, Byron Gangnes and Sumner La Croix, eds., *Japan's New Economy: Continuity and Change in the Twenty-First Century*. Oxford: Oxford University Press.

———. 2001b. Unpublished Excel spreadsheet on total factor productivity in the U.S. and Japan provided to the author.

World Bank. 2000. *World Development Indicators* (CD-ROM). Washington, D.C.: World Bank.

———. 2002. *World Development Indicators*. Washington, D.C.: World Bank..

Yamaguchi, Yutaka. 1999. "Monetary Policy and Structural Policy: A Japanese Perspective." At http://www.boj.or.jp/en/press/koen044.htm.

Yayama, Taro. 1998. "Who Has Obstructed Reform?" In Frank Gibney, ed., *Unlocking the Bureaucrat's Kingdom: Deregulation and the Japanese Economy*. Washington, D.C.: Brookings Institution.

Index

Open market operations, 126
Organization for Economic Cooperation
    and Development (OECD), 18, 37,
    241, 248, 254, 266, 269, 276,
    280–282
Ostrom, Douglas, 233
Overseas production, 56
Oyama, Tsuyoshi, 52
Ozawa, Ichiro, 100, 116, 301

Paradox of thrift, 70
Patrick, Hugh, 209
Pempel, T. J., 10
Pension benefits, 251
  pension and social security crisis,
    79–80
Pension Fund Association (PFA),
    238–239
Pension funds, 176, 182–184, 202–203,
    229, 238
Perry, Matthew, 311
Personal consumption, 60–61
Personnel costs, 252–254
Phillips curve, 122
Plaza Accords (1985), 19, 45, 78, 136
Policy effect, 105
Political economy, 3–4, 194, 296–297
Porter, Michael, 46–49, 219, 230, 234
Porter Prize, 218
Posen, Adam, 13, 108–110, 114, 128
Postal savings system, 198, 270
Predatory pricing, 243
Price controls, 261
Price deregulation, 215–216
Price factor, 51
Price fixing, 244
Price-keeping operations, 66, 121, 182,
    198–199
Private demand, 59–60, 70
Private investment, 78
Privatization, 272
Productivity, 17, 20–21, 283
Productivity growth, 3, 51
Profits, 51, 255
"Program for Economic Structure
    Reform," 267
Proportional representation, 284–286

Protectionism, 16
Public corporations, 262–264
Public debt, 59, 110–114
  debt-to-GDP ratio, 110–111, 114
Purchasing power, 4

Quantitative easing, 117–119, 128–129

Radin, Robin, 304–305
RAND Corporation, 37
Real estate taxes, 279
Rebick, Marcus, 248
Recession (1997-1998), 50, 70–71, 99,
    106
Reed, John, 86, 101
Regulated/protected sectors, 47, 49, 261
Regulatory reform
  dangers/opportunities of partial reform,
    269
  deregulation vs., 269
  drivers for, 267–269
  opposition to, 266–267
  potential gains from, 266
Reischauer, Edwin, 311
Research Institute on Economy, Trade,
    and Industry (RIETI), 100
Restructuring, 230; see also Corporate
    reform
  backward sectors and, 41–43
Retail sector, 68, 195
Return on assets (ROA), 254–257
Rice, Condoleezza, 299
Ripplewood Investment Group, 97, 165,
    173, 186–189
Romer, Paul, 20
Roosevelt, Franklin D., 129
Ross, Wilbur, 189
Rural votes, 286–288

Sachs, Jeffrey, 151
Saito, Jun, 287–288
Sakaiya, Taichi, 305
Sakakibara, Eisuke, 291
Sakakibara, Mariko, 46–48, 234
Sakura Bank, 94
Sanyo, 92, 95
Savings rates, 65, 73, 77–78

Richard Katz is Senior Editor of *The Oriental Economist Report,* a monthly newsletter about Japan (www.orientaleconomist.com), and is also a special correspondent in New York for *Shukan Toyo Keizai,* a leading Japanese business weekly.

His 1998 book, *Japan: The System That Soured—The Rise and Fall of the Japanese Economic System* (M.E. Sharpe), accurately predicted Japan's current economic travails. It received favorable reviews by the *Wall Street Journal, Business Week, Far Eastern Economic Review,* and the *Japan Times,* among others, and is regularly used in university classrooms. The Japanese version, *Kusariyuku Nihon To Iu System* (Toyo Keizai Shimposa) was very well received by some of the leading press in Japan, including *Nihon Keizai Shimbun* and *Asahi Shimbun.*

Mr. Katz's views on Japan are regularly cited in the world's press and his op-ed articles have appeared in such publications as the *New York Times, London Financial Times* and the *Asian Wall Street Journal.* He authored the article on Japan's economy for the Microsoft Encarta Encyclopedia.

In 1998, he testified in Congress on Japan's role in the Asian economic crisis. In 2000, he served on the Task Force on Japan of the New York Council on Foreign Relations.

For several years, he doubled as a Visiting Lecturer in Economics at the State University of New York (SUNY) at Stony Brook.

Mr. Katz earned his M.A. in Economics from New York University (NYU) in 1996.